THE MOUNTAINS OF SERBIA

THE MOUNTAINS OF SERBIA

Travels through Inland Yugoslavia

ANNE KINDERSLEY

JOHN MURRAY

Printed in Great Britain by
Richard Clay (The Chaucer Press), Ltd.,
Bungay, Suffolk
0 7195 3300 7

In memory of
HUGO DYSON

A Reminiscence of the Uprising

Serbia is a great mystery:
The day doesn't know what the night contrives,
Nor the night, what the dawn gives birth to:
The bush doesn't know what the next bush dreams,
Nor the bird, what goes on
Among the boughs.

The lizard doesn't know what crawls under the stones,
Nor does the maize stem foresee
What's being planned in the next field.
Every hour everything changes.
There's not one corner nor one leaf which isn't
A mystery of its own.

Who knows, too, what it hides within itself,
That innocent bright drop of dew?
Those busy cries of peasants
Which from hill to hill are heard –
Perhaps they're hatching a plot?

Who will ever know in that land
What the young girl
Hides in her bosom,
What grievous secret
The child bears in his hand?
Not to mention the old women, bent with age,
Making their way towards some goal or other.

In that land the winds, too,
And the scents and the streams and the rivers,
And the church bells
Carry the secret news;
At the first bend of the road
Where the wood begins,
Who knows what you may meet?

In that land the enemy
Mayn't trust in the hare's track,
Nor in the print of the oxen's hooves.
There are perhaps secret resolutions
In the reapers' songs
And the strokes of the woodcutter's axe
And the hidden lullaby from the cradle.

From Desanka Maksimović, *Spomen na Ustanak*

CONTENTS

Foreword xv

First and Second Impressions 1

I THE OLD SERBIA

Historical Background 13

1 Studenica and the Ibar Valley 18

2 St Sava's Cave: the Hermit Raphael 33

3 Žiča: Archbishop and Abbess 39

4 Through the Sandžak 48

5 Saints' Day at Sopoćani 60

6 The Mountains of Golija 71

7 The Patriarchate of Peć 82

8 The Road to Dečani 92

9 Prizren: the Emperor's Town 101

10 Gipsies at Gračanica 110

11 From Novo Brdo to Kossovo Field 120

12 Morava: Prince Lazar and Princess Milica 130

13 The Court of Despot Stephen at Manasija 144

14 Down the Danube 155

15 Among the Vlachs 168

II THE NEW SERBIA

Historical Background 183

16 The Frankish Hills and the Hungarian Plain 190

17 Soldiers, Patriarchs and Traders 199

18 Šumadija: the Wooded Land 213

19 Slava at Cikote 227

20 The Changing Fortunes of Belgrade 233

21 Life in the Serbian Capital 242

Appendices

I *Further places to visit* 257

II *Serbian Heroic Poetry* 262

III *Serbian Dynasties* 266

Notes 269

Further Reading 272

Glossary 275

Index 279

ILLUSTRATIONS

(*Numbers 2, 8, 11–13, 38 are by Richard Kindersley; numbers 27–31 are by the Author*)

1 The hermit Raphael on a visit to Žiča. *facing* 14

2 Studenica: the tiny King's Church, the refectory and belfry, the Church of the Mother of God. 15

3 Studenica: detail from east window, Church of the Mother of God. 15

4 Mileševa: the Virgin of the Annunciation. *Veronica Lieven* 30

5 Sopoćani: a group of Apostles from the Dormition. *Veronica Lieven* 30

6 Near Mileševa: a village mosque at Hisardžik, with the ruined Byzantine fortress above. *Foto-Putnik, Belgrade* 31

7 Žiča monastery. *Foto-Putnik* 31

8 Sopoćani seen from the hills above. 46

9 Sopoćani: procession round the church on St Cosmas' and St Damian's Day. *Melanie Anderson* 46

10 Golija valley. *Žika Milutinović* 47

11 The White Church of Karan. 62

12 Tombstone of a soldier in the churchyard at Karan. 62

13 St Peter's, Novi Pazar. 62

14 In the foothills of Golija: ploughing near Ivanjica. *'Review', Belgrade* 63

15 Kossovo buffaloes take refuge from the heat. *Mladen Grčević (for 'Review')* 63

16 The east end of Dečani church. *Foto-Putnik* 94

17 The 16th-century icon of Stephen of Dečani painted by the monk Longin. *T. Dabac* 95

18 Church of the Mother of God, Peć: Archbishop Danilo II offers his Patriarchate to his patron, the Prophet Daniel. *Sreten Petković* 95

19 Old Serbian women walk along a Peć street. *Ethnographical Museum*, *Belgrade* 110

20 Gračanica: the prophet Elijah fed by a raven. *Sreten Petković* 110

21 The Ottoman Sultan, Bajazeth I. *Bodleian Library*, *Oxford* 111

22 Gračanica: a gipsy woman with her child. *Melanie Anderson* 111

23 Gračanica: the northern side seen from Bora's yard. *Melanie Anderson* 111

24 Novo Brdo: the castle on the summit, with the cathedral walls below. (*Nikola Majdak for*) '*Dunav-Film*', *Belgrade* 142

25 Manasija: a 15th-century monastery fortified against Turkish invaders. *Foto-Putnik* 142

26 A hermitage built into the crags of Gornjak. *Foto-Putnik* 143

27 A Vlach house under the Roman walls of Gamzigrad. 143

28 Vlach girls at Negotin Fair. 158

29 At the fair: the owner of a covered wagon with her oxen. 158

30 Viktorina with her sheep at the summer pastures. 159

31 Whitsunday at Duboka: procession with offerings for the dead. 159

32 The dramatic profile of Golubac castle on the Danube. *Foto-Putnik* 190

33 The Iron Gates of the Danube at Djerdap. *Foto-Putnik* 190

34 Sremski Karlovci: the chapel which commemorates the Peace of Carlowitz. *Foto-Putnik* 191

35 Sunflowers: the great Pannonian plain. *Miodrag Djordjević (for 'Review')* 191

36 The graceful 17th-century church of New Hopovo. *Vojvodina: Institute for Protection of Cultural Monuments* 206

37 In the Fruška Gora: the sloping vineyards of Velika Remeta. *Vojrodina: Institute for Protection of Cultural Monuments* 206

38 Stana's brothers roasting lambs for the *slava*. 207

39 Šumadija: a countryman appraises a girl from the town. *Dragan Jevtić* 207

40 Novi Sad: the porch of the Almaška Church. *George Tabaković* 222

41 The Stanišić family of Belgrade in mid-19th-century city costume. *Katerina Ivanović (National Museum, Belgrade)* 223

42 Serbian soldiers in the First World War. *Miodrag Petrović (Military Museum, Belgrade)* 223

43 Portrait of Karageorge, leader of the 1st Serbian Uprising. *Attributed to V. L. Borokovski (Historical Museum, Belgrade)* 238

44 Belgrade in 1849. *Milivoj Nenadović (City Museum, Belgrade)* 238

45 Autumn in Šumadija: Ostrvica hill. *Miodrag Djordjević (for 'Review')* 239

MAPS (*By K. C. Jordan*)

Serbia *between* 6–7

Plan of Belgrade 246–7

FOREWORD

We had a house in Belgrade from 1964 to 1967, when my husband was on the staff of the British Embassy there. We enjoyed two lives during those years: the closed circle of a small international community, for the most part irrelevant to our surroundings, and an ever-deepening contact with Yugoslavs we met in the capital and on our travels. The idea of writing this book evolved gradually and through several pieces of good fortune. I had hoped to learn just enough Serbo-Croat for everyday use, but the late Oton Grozdić, an inspiring language teacher, persuaded me to study it further. Asim Peco and Živojin Stanojčić patiently carried on his work and I gained from them a lasting interest in their literature. To speak and read Serbo-Croat, however badly, was like breaking down an insuperable barrier. I was encouraged to travel by the British Ambassador of that time, Duncan Wilson – himself an authority on South Slav history – and by his wife. Lastly, among our friends in Belgrade were writers and art historians whose enthusiasm for their country fed my own.

We travelled all over Yugoslavia, through Slovenia, Croatia, Bosnia-Hercegovina, Montenegro and Macedonia. Each of her six Republics has kept its identity, and after two years, I came to recognize that Serbia, in which we lived, had traditions of her own. The past still lived on in the present, and could be traced in the countryside most accessible from Belgrade. Talking to people I experienced a return to essentials: they valued the transience of life and ritualized it. But 'everything's changing (*sve se menja*)' as old men said to us, and Westernization is gradually flattening out their own inheritance. I could only record what we saw while it lasted.

The frontiers of Serbia fluctuated continually during the Middle Ages and again during the 19th and 20th centuries. I have kept to the present-day Republic of Serbia, with its two autonomous regions of Kossovo and Vojvodina. The history of the Serbs makes this a single if complex whole, and for this reason I have treated the country more or less chronologically. It was odd to find an older world existing within a Marxist state; I have felt justified in limiting myself to this living past, as Tito's Yugoslavia is well-documented.

This portrait of Serbia includes an introduction to the medieval Byzantine monasteries, and to the landscape and life around them. Under the Turks, and especially in the 18th and 19th centuries the principal monuments are the memoirs of men who wrote, or if illiterate, dictated their life histories. I have included journeys to some lesser-known regions: the southern hills where we walked are virtually unrecorded country and we felt the lack of any suitable reading to guide us. We could not find much in print that explained the unfamiliar attitudes which puzzled us in our own household and in the villages; we were perpetually questioning other Yugoslavs for an answer, and that takes time which not everybody may have on shorter visits. I have tried to sketch some of the basic shocks and pleasures that Serbian life has to offer. They are never-ending: perhaps that is the reason why I find myself returning again and again to Vuk Karadžić's 'small Slav nation living among the mountains of the south'.

While the responsibility for opinions expressed in the book remains my own, I owe a great debt to many people in England and Yugoslavia. It is impossible to name them all, but they include: the Staff of the Slavonic Reading Room, Bodleian Library, Oxford; the Director and Staff of the Gallery and Library of Matica Srpska, Novi Sad; the Institute for Protection of Cultural Monuments in Belgrade, Kraljevo, Petrovaradin and Priština; the Museums at Negotin and Zaječar; and in Belgrade, the Serbian Academy of Sciences, the Botanic Garden, the Natural History Museum, the Ethnographical Museum, the Military Museum and the Fresco Gallery of the National Museum.

Sreten Petković and Anne Pennington have given most generous assistance throughout, the first on the history of art, the second on problems of translation. Further help has come from: Phyllis Auty, John Campbell, Dimitrije Djordjević, Radu Flora, Muriel Heppell, Elizabeth Hill, Rachel Hood, Božidar Kovačević, Veselin Kostić, Peter Levi, Veronica Lieven, Dušanka Lukać, Mother Mary, Elisabeth Montefiore, Dimitri Obolensky, Milorad Pavić, Kosta Pavlović, Margita Ristić, Hugh Seton-Watson, Gavro Škrivanić, Dimitrije Stefanović, Mary Sutton, Rajko Veselinović, David Winfield and Ivo Zdravković.

I much appreciated the hospitality given in Belgrade by Rosemary and Terence Garvey, Ivanka and Vladimir Kovačević, Nada and Ljubomir Prodanović, Mary and Denison Russinow, Kirsty and Michael Tait.

I remember with gratitude my mother-in-law, whose legacy enabled me to continue travelling. Lastly, my husband, Richard Kindersley, through his own knowledge and understanding of Yugoslavia, and through his constant encouragement, has provided support beyond all measure.

My acknowledgements are due to Cecil Anrep and to Denis Wright for permission to use unpublished material on pp. 65 and 180 respectively, to *History To-Day*, which printed part of Chapter 11 as an article, and to Desanka Maksimović and Vasko Popa for use of poems in copyright. *The Memoirs of Prota Matija Nenadović* are quoted on p. 219 with the consent of the Oxford University Press.

Finally, I would like to thank Hebe Jerrold for making the index and Kenneth Jordan for skilfully compressing so much material into his two maps.

A.K.
1975

NOTE ON PRONUNCIATION

Serbo-Croat words may at first sight look daunting to pronounce, but if these guidelines are followed, the reader should soon feel at ease with proper names.

c = *ts* in *cats*
č = *ch* in *church*
ć = sound between *c* in *church* and *t* in *tune*
dj, *dž* = *j* in *jug*
g = *g* in *get*
j = *y* in *yes*
lj = *lli* in *million*
nj = *ni* in *minion*
r = always rolled; between consonants it becomes a vowel: *ur* in Scottish *burn*
s = *s* in *sad*
š = *sh* in *shin*
ž = *s* in *pleasure*

a as in *far*
e as in *bed*
i as in *give*
o as in *for*
u as in *push*

Adapted from W. A. Morison, *The Revolt of the Serbs against the Turks* (1942).

FIRST AND SECOND IMPRESSIONS

A raw yellow mist was seeping in from the river as the train drew into Belgrade Station. I could see Richard, fur-hatted, waiting on the platform and beside him, a big white-moustached porter who was unmistakably a Slav. It was early morning and I had spent two days and nights on the train, in part of an antiquated double suite built for the old Orient Express. It had a closet where the massive wash-basin was set in mahogany, and over my bed there was a plush-lined hollow to hang a fob-watch. '*C'est fait pour les grands pachas, ça*,' said the sleeping-car attendant; but the days of travelling in such style were past, and the suite had been divided between myself, with a ticket sent by the Foreign Office, and a disconsolate Scottish engineer going out to build the new steel works at Skopje.

Following the porter and his trolley, we bumped against a crowd of peasants, who were pushing their way onto trains or sitting on bundles or fast asleep on benches, as if the station were one of many encampments on some endless journey. I did not know it but I was looking at a living map of inland Yugoslavia, of the different races who had swirled about the Balkan peninsula, masses swept north and east by the invading Turk or famine, and some shifted south by the Austrians and Hungarians. A few months later, and the crowd would not have seemed so confusing. I remember, because I hated seeing it, that a woman was holding a live goose upside-down by its legs. She was one of a group of shabby, grotesque figures, tightly shawled against the winter, with their ballerina skirts sticking out over a dozen petticoats – later on, I could have picked them out as Slovaks who had come straight from their villages in the great Pannonian plain, where the Habsburgs had settled their ancestors to guard the Danube frontier. Now they were bringing poultry, eggs, cream and vegetables from their muddy, rich lands to market in Belgrade. The stocky men I noticed, their brown frieze jackets scribbled over with black braid, and their leather sandals turned up into peaks at the toe, were Serbs from the hilly country to the south of the city. They carried yokes from which hung pails of soft cheese, and swung through the station as if it were a farmyard. I thought their wives drab-looking in their factory-made cardigans and pleated skirts. Then there were tall, ruddy-faced men in white skullcaps and dark jackets with a wide square flap of collar like an English seaman's. They turned out to be Albanians, Moslems from Peć or Priština, who made for Belgrade, a long way north of home, because it was a market for labour as well as for produce – where they could heave coal or chop wood and send back money for their families or to purchase a wife. The married men came alone, for their wives stayed at home in strict Islamic seclusion; if by chance one came to Belgrade, she might be locked up in her husband's room all day while he was out working. There were young gipsy women from the same region, in town on their own; and I could recognize them at first glance, for they looked like gipsies anywhere, with brown faces and black plaits of hair. They seemed confident and exotic in their draped trousers and bead-decked scarves. They laughed a lot, though they were so poor and thin, as they dandled their babies and offered wooden spoons for sale. I had never seen such a crowd, complete with drunkards whose journey had been sustained by too many swigs of homemade plum brandy; schoolboy-faced soldiers loaded down with knapsack and rifle, very orderly in their red-starred caps and long blue greatcoats; and dark-suited townsmen holding briefcases who looked insignificant there. The station was more a fair than a terminus: milling with figures, it seemed a Balkan Derby Day.

The earliest impressions of a new place are like a bunch of threads: the ends are hidden in someone's hand and one does not know which are long and which are short, which are to be thrown away and which lead somewhere. Looking back, the people I first saw at the station were to form the longest thread.

The station now has platform tickets and is far less picturesque; this arrival was in 1964. It was my first experience of Belgrade, though I had been to Yugoslavia before in 1959, on a brief journey through Montenegro and Macedonia; it had been beautiful and exciting beyond words and the unexpected had lain round every corner. I wondered where it had got to, as the Belgrade winter of 1964 blew itself out in dry winds and sleety blizzards. We tried to escape from the town but our car tyres were sucked down into the slippery mud of unmetalled country roads. I found nothing to do but to look out of the hotel window at the seedy, gilded spire of the Cathedral Church, and to count the cockroaches that scuttled across the bathroom floor after midnight as fast as Cinderella making for home.

Then spring arrived with a rush. In the woods, greenish hellebores and bright blue scillas came up as soon as the snow had melted. Even the marshes were spiked with yellow flags and cupped water-lilies grew under them. I was shown Pasque flowers, paeonies and iris in a sandy place, Deliblatska Peščara, north of the town. Orchards flowered, and at night fires flickered under apple-trees against a late frost. With the first warmth of the sun, peacocks spread their brocaded tails on the wall of Ravanica monastery, and a man ploughing rested his horse in the shadow and blanketed it against a chill from the sweat. I began to see how the people on the station, or some of them, lived. Everyone came out of their houses: the women to go to the cemetery and take food to the graves of the newly-dead, old men to idle by the roadside and to spin their tales to strangers. They might walk to the nearest fair, the best way to find company, or to a Church feast. Till lately most villages had held a pre-Lenten carnival, with women dressed up as men who chased other women through the streets and frightened them with kisses. Easter was the greatest festival of all.

Summer came quickly too, a time of great heat: to quote Laza Lazarević, 'It seemed . . . exactly as if the whole of nature drooped, swooned, hung out its tongue, then gasped for breath.' City people went on holiday to watering-places in the hills, or to the coast. Every small town by a river showed the same scene; boys splashing and swimming, trying to keep cool. In the valleys one could stop by roadside springs and drink pure water that rinsed dust from the mouth. The monastery feasts continued: St John Baptist in July, the Dormition of the Virgin in August. Christ's Thorn had blossomed and now grew seed-pods like spinning-tops. Pumpkins swelled up, planted between the maize-stems, and wheat turned gold. In the middle of one field an old Ford stood, edged with corn-cockles, a spray for the crops in its rusty boot.

With autumn, the harvest poured in: maize, wheat, barley, rye, oats and buckwheat – a giant's granary. Fruit was abundant: dark plums and Hamburg grapes, peaches, apricots, apples, watermelons and mulberries. The peasants gathered sunflowers, poppies and tobacco, and built red and green peppers into shining pyramids. Sugar beet was loaded onto lorries and driven off to factories. The harvest spilled into churches: a bunch of sticky grapes, or a corn dolly shaped like a cottage, hung on the iconostasis. The ground-floor room in one monastery was covered with drying beans and peppers; apple, pear and quince were laid in front of an icon. Farmers distilled plum-brandy in a Heath-Robinson arrangement of tin pipes and cylinders and cauldrons. Townspeople thought of buying a vineyard at this season, and started slow bargaining as they tasted grapes on a slope near the the Danube. At the wine-festivals the crowd linked arms to dance in a ring, or sang at their tables. It was the time for weddings. On the road, a horse-drawn cart, painted and garlanded, carried a Serbian bride and groom and their guests, umbrellas up against the last warm bout of sunshine. Gipsies got married, to wander along in vague swarming procession. Everyone made merry and went about while they could. The last cattle-markets were held before winter closed in.

Soon the weather turned hard. Frost catkins hung from the trees, and the landscape lost its high colouring: black branches rose out of glittering snow fields. Only the evening sky burnt red and clear as crab-apple jam. People stayed in their houses, keeping alive, coming out when they had to sell or buy food in the town, or to go to a feast-day. Iron-rimmed cartwheels splashed through the mud or bumped over frozen ruts. St Nicholas' Day and Christmas marked the end of the year.

The calendar had a very real meaning and the seasons their own strong rhythm, for the Danube climate, with its bitter winters and dust-choked summers, was far sharper than ours, and the land had to be worked as fast as possible. The overriding impression was of an ordered world, medieval in its pattern. Lady Day, Lammastide, Michaelmas and Candlemas are half-forgotten in England. In Serbia the country year is still plotted by the Feasts of the Orthodox Church, which have become interwoven with farmers' needs and pagan custom. At Epiphany (Theophany) the cross was thrown in an icy river, and men went to fetch it out: Dionysus still lived. On Whitsunday, young people plighted their troth; on St George's Day, flocks were moved to summer pasture. Even in Belgrade, a country pulse beat oddly on: at Christmas and on other feast-days we saw men carrying sucking-pigs wrapped in plastic bags, to roast on spits in their garden plots. At Easter they carried lambs.

I found I was making a journey into the past, but a journey of discovery, not of nostalgia. I was continually reminded of the Middle Ages. Because I still could not manage the language, I failed to make much contact with people, so it was like turning the pages of a Book of Hours, and meeting, not the saints and lords and ladies who live in the foreground of each illuminated page, but those tiny insect-like figures from the small-scale landscape beyond, and seeing them through a magnifying-glass. I had once peered closely at a medieval French miniature of the Flight into Egypt: painted into the background were two peasants toiling uphill. I saw them again in Serbia: it was late winter and they were coming back from market, their faces shut and unsmiling, resisting, with all their energy, the harsh cold. The same artist had drawn a wide river behind the Virgin, St Joseph, her Baby and the donkey: on its shore a man sat fishing with a long pole, a basket beside him. In early spring, as I looked down from a high bridge at the flooded iron-grey Sava, he was on the bank, unloading shining fish from a water-filled box in his punt until he had filled a bulging sack which he dragged after him to a shanty across the puddled ground. Then he came back for two heavy punt-poles. He looked very old and utterly intent on his task, as if he must work on until the moment of death.

The third group of figures that the French painting showed were even tinier, and at first I thought they were dancing. When I looked closer, I saw that it was a dance of death: Herod's soldiers snatching babies from their mothers and killing them, the Massacre of the Innocents. Soldiers like them live on in the memory of Serbian peasants. It is only twenty-five years since people barred their doors at night, and children shivered with terror in case the pro-Nazi terrorists from Croatia, the *Ustaše*, should come to burn and torture and kill. Before that, in the Balkan Wars of 1912–18 it was the same. An old woman of seventy, in her reminiscences, describes a scene similar to that in the Book of Hours, where her mother hid a grown-up daughter, daughter-in-law and sons in the loft. Three drunken Bulgarian soldiers burst in: 'Knives glittered on their rifles'. She and her two little sisters, all under ten, stood by their mother, 'like corpses newly-buried'.

> When [the soldiers] had rummaged and searched and found nothing, they came to my mother and asked her with the voices of wild beasts: 'Tell us, you Serbian bitch, where are your daughter and daughter-in-law?' My mother said to them in a trembling voice: 'My lads, my daughter's got married, but I haven't married off my son because I put him to school and sent him to the front. My husband too is at the front, but my younger son has gone with a friend to the mill, and I have no other family except these three children and myself.'
>
> At that, one Bulgarian soldier began to belabour my poor mother with the butt-end of his rifle, and a second struck her two or three blows. Then blood gushed from her nose and mouth. A . . . soldier said to her:

'Say where your daughter and daughter-in-law are, because your neighbours have told us that in the big house over the hill, a beautiful maiden and a young bride are to be found. Either take us to them, or we'll kill you and your three little daughters tonight.'

He attacked her again and she fell half-fainting to the floor, begging them to spare her for her children's sake. Another soldier restrained his comrades, and she was saved; others were less lucky.

Before the Bulgarians, it had been the Turks; before them, back into furthest time, barbarian invaders. For the Serbs, outside their houses cold, famine, war and death have always lain in wait.

As we went more into the country and began to talk to people, some of these medieval figures drew closer. They now resembled Chaucer's pilgrims: I met the nun who spoke heavily-accented French, the monk who enjoyed the pleasures of country life, and the poor parson who faithfully tramped about his far-flung parish on foot and visited everyone in need. (He later went off to a monastery on Mount Athos.) In any one of the villages he served, you could look into the fenced yard of a dirty cottage and see the widow who owned Chanticleer in the *Nun's Priest's Tale*, with her pigs wallowing about, the cock with his hens, and a few cows and sheep looked after by a child in a field nearby. Even her food was the same: bacon, coarse bread, eggs and milk. A man in one church talked just as Chaucer's Pardoner had done when showing the 'pigges bones' which did duty for saintly tibias. The Serb opened his reliquary chest for us, vowing that inside there were 'bits of all the saints painted on the lid: St Mary Magdalene, St John the Baptist, Mary the Mother of God. . . .' And like the Pardoner, he extracted money for a peep at the relics.

Of course these first impressions of people were stereotypes, drawn from chance memories of books and paintings, and as with all stereotypes, they soon cracked into pieces, though there was an element of truth in them.

Serbia remains a place where you have to scratch the surface to discover the meaning of things. There are other parts of Yugoslavia – Slovenia, for instance – where the *genius loci* is more open to view: elaborate costumes and baroque buildings, rushing torrents and walls of rock. In Serbia I was looking at a landscape familiar to Blake:

> For double the vision my Eyes do see,
> And a double vision is always with me

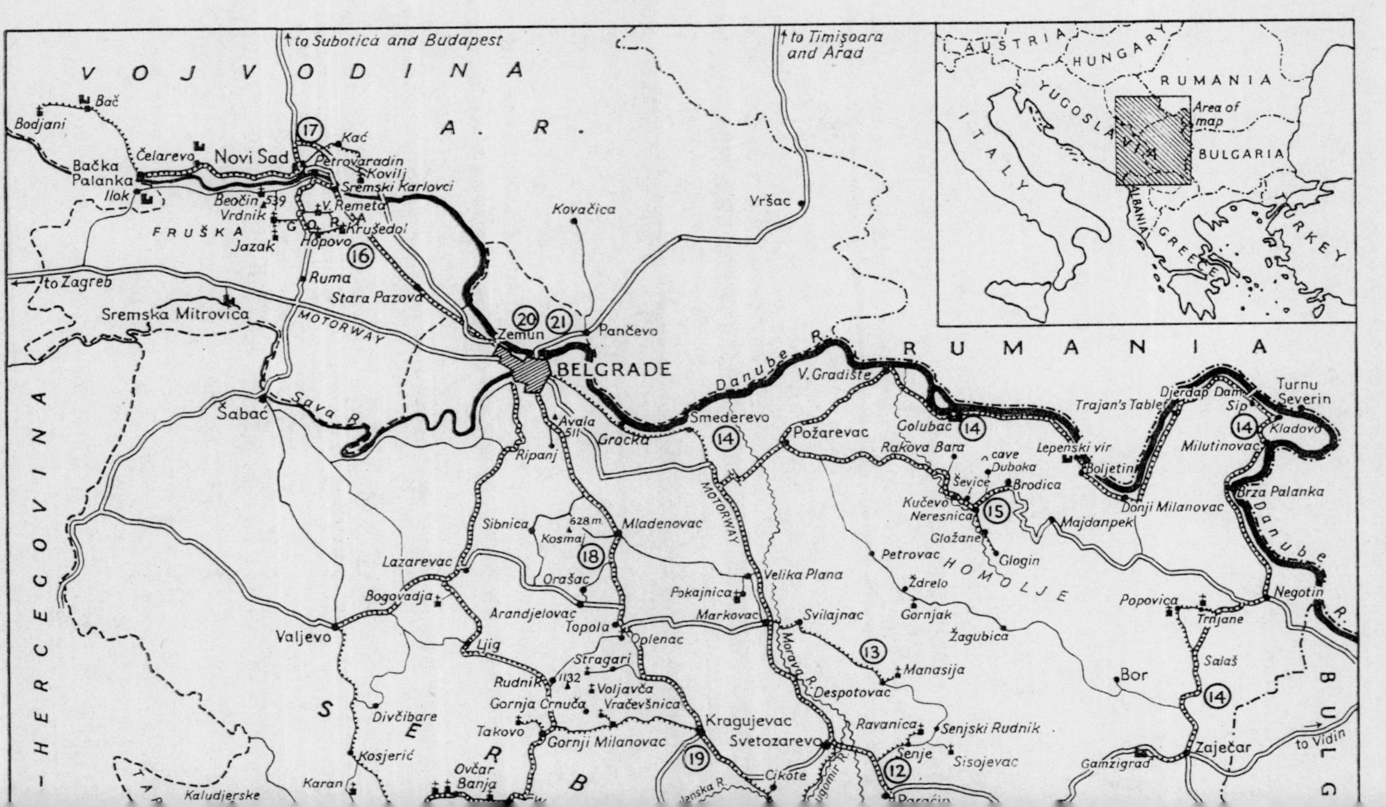

to Subotica and Budapest
to Timişoara and Arad
VOJVODINA A.R.
AUSTRIA
HUNGARY
RUMANIA
YUGOSLAVIA
ITALY
BULGARIA
ALBANIA
GREECE
TURKEY
Area of map
Bač
Bodjani
Bačka Palanka
Čelarevo
Novi Sad
Kać
Petrovaradin
Kovilj
Sremski Karlovci
Ilok
Beočin
539
Vrdnik
V. Remeta
FRUŠKA GORA
Krušedol
Jazak
Hopovo
Ruma
Stara Pazova
to Zagreb
Sremska Mitrovica
MOTORWAY
Zemun
Pančevo
Kovačica
Vršac
BELGRADE
Šabac
Sava R.
Avala 511
Ripanj
Grocka
Smederevo
Danube R.
V. Gradište
Požarevac
RUMANIA
Golubac
Rakova Bara
cave
Duboka
Ševice
Brodica
Kučevo
Neresnica
Gložane
Glogin
Lepenski vir
Boljetin
Trajan's Table
Djerdap Dam
Sip
Turnu Severin
Kladovo
Milutinovac
Donji Milanovac
Majdanpek
Brza Palanka
Negotin
HERCEGOVINA
Sibnica
628 m.
Kosmaj
Mladenovac
Lazarevac
Orašac
Bogovadja
Arandjelovac
Topola
Oplenac
Valjevo
Ljig
Stragari
Rudnik
1132
Voljavča
Gornja Crnuča
Vračevšnica
Divčibare
Takovo
Gornji Milanovac
Kosjerić
Karan
Ovčar Banja
Kaludjerske
SERB
Pokajnica
Velika Plana
Markovac
Svilajnac
Morava R.
Despotovac
Manasija
Kragujevac
Svetozarevo
Cikote
Ravanica
Senje
Senjski Rudnik
Sisojevac
Paraćin
Petrovac
Ždrelo
Gornjak
Žagubica
HOMOLJE
Bor
Popovica
Trnjane
Salaš
Zaječar
Gamzigrad
to Vidin
BULG
12
13
14
15
16
17
18
19
20
21

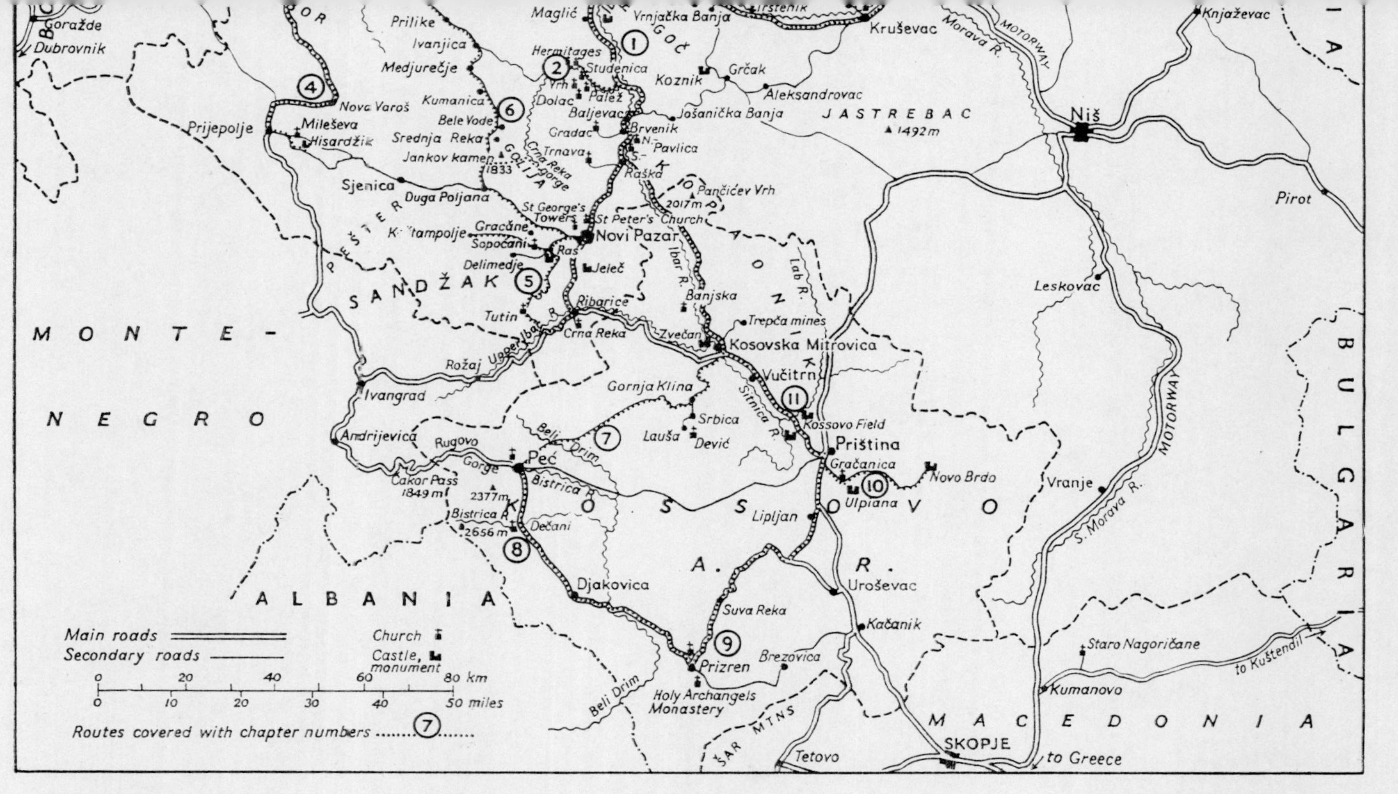
MONTE-NEGRO
ALBANIA
BULGARIA
MACEDONIA
KOSOVO
SANDŽAK
JASTREBAC
▲1492m
GOLIJA
Goražde
Dubrovnik
Prilike
Ivanjica
Medjurečje
Maglić
Vrnjačka Banja
Kruševac
Knjaževac
Morava R.
MOTORWAY
Niš
Pirot
Leskovac
Vranje
S. Morava R.
Kumanovo
Staro Nagoričane
to Kuštendil
to Greece
SKOPJE
Tetovo
ŠAR MTNS
Hermitages
Studenica
Vrh
Dolac
Palež
Baljevac
Brvenik
Gradac
Trnava
Pavlica
Raška
Crna Reka gorge
Koznik
Grčak
Aleksandrovac
Jošanička Banja
Nova Varoš
Kumanica
Bele Vode
Srednja Reka
Jankov kamen
1833
Mileševa
Hisardžik
Prijepolje
Sjenica
Duga Poljana
St George's Towers
St Peter's Church
Pančićev Vrh
2017m
Gracăne
Sopoćani
Ras
Novi Pazar
Delimedje
Jeleč
Ibar R.
Lab R.
Banjska
Trepča mines
Ribarice
Tutin
Crna Reka
Upper Ibar R.
Zvečan
Kosovska Mitrovica
Vučitrn
Rožaj
Ivangrad
Andrijevica
Gornja Klina
Srbica
Lauša
Dević
Sitnica R.
Kossovo Field
Priština
Gračanica
Ulpiana
Novo Brdo
Beli Drim
Rugovo
Gorge
Peć
Čakor Pass
1849m
2377m
Bistrica R.
Bistrica
2656m
Dečani
Lipljan
Uroševac
Kačanik
Djakovica
Suva Reka
Prizren
Brezovica
Holy Archangels Monastery
Beli Drim
Main roads
Secondary roads
Church
Castle, monument
0 20 40 60 80 km
0 10 20 30 40 50 miles
Routes covered with chapter numbers .... 7 ....

It is a country where you go out to see the sights, and end by seeing history.

This exciting taste of the past in the present never quite dulled. It was very varied. I have already tried to suggest the sense of an ordered medieval world. Then there was the novelty of being in oriental surroundings. To turn a corner in Belgrade was to find myself half-way East: to come upon a fretted 16th-century mosque, or a courtyard in which buttons, baskets, engraved silver were made and sold from tumble-down kiosks, and cafés where Turkish coffee, *baklava* and *halva* could be had. Time mattered less than in Western Europe: a certain indolence prevailed.

Most important of all was the taste of Byzantium, of its spirituality and grandeur. I first experienced this on Easter Sunday, when someone took us to a small monastery. Everything had gone wrong. Our acquaintance had assured us that the Liturgy would begin at ten in the morning (it had begun at two and finished at nine) and that the road to the monastery was excellent (it was a quagmire and we had to be dug out by a monk who had once worked in a garage). The place was pretty enough: a cluster of low buildings set among orchards and vineyards above the Danube, but the church was a white-washed 19th-century structure. We could only expect a disappointing day.

We were wrong. It turned out enchanting. The Abbess came to meet us, and an elderly priest, and a gipsy woman from the neighbouring village. 'I am an Orthodox gipsy,' she said, flashing silver teeth at us, 'not one of your pagans.' The Abbess made us welcome at a table in the garden, by the south wall of the church, and the sun shone through us all. Two other priests appeared, one of them newly-ordained, and the old priest praised his virtues until the young man turned scarlet-faced, and looked at his boots. A smiling nun brought coffee and *slatko* (fruit preserved in syrup) and stayed to chat. White goats were tethered on the green hillside above us; near them was a grove of quince-trees in flower. 'You must come again in the autumn,' said the Abbess, 'and I will give you a sapling quince for your garden in Belgrade. It should bear fruit quickly, before you have to leave Yugoslavia for good.' She took us into the church. The old priest came too. Inside, it was very dingy: religious oleographs hung on the wall, the candles appeared to be made of brown fudge, and an oil-lamp of scarlet glass burnt with a lurid flame. The air smelt heavily of spices.

A group of peasants arrived: old woman, young woman, old man and baby. The old man whispered something to the priest; they wanted the baby christened. We were told to stay. The service began: a lock of the baby's hair was cut and the mother spat three times on the ground to drive away the Devil from her child's soul. Meanwhile the stone floor sweated damply beneath my feet, and I started to shiver. The Abbess noticed, and a nun was sent for two chairs and a rug. Usually Orthodox worshippers stand, but we were made to sit at the back of the church, our feet on the rug. There were holes in it and the chairs were rickety, yet suddenly I realized they had a kind of glory. We were being honoured by the nuns as guests to any monastery had been honoured throughout centuries. It was of no importance that the chairs were falling to pieces or that moths had got at the rug: they were symbolic of thrones carved from ivory, of silken floor-coverings set before Constantine and Helena, or of any of the 'Orthodox kings and queens, faithful princes and princesses' who are remembered in prayers for the dead by the Eastern Church. These lands had once been part of the Byzantine Empire on its northernmost verge, and the Imperial tradition remained. Even some of the words we were using came from the Greek: we called the Abbess, *igumanija* (ἡγεμών), and her refectory, like our Belgrade dining-room, *trpezarija* (τράπεζα). If a monk was mentioned, he was a *kaludjer* (καλόγερο) a 'good old man'. Our leave-taking, some hours later, after a tremendous lunch, was again full of ceremony, for we sat once more round a table in the garden and drank their wine while priests and nuns sang us an ancient farewell chant as if it were the most natural thing in the world.

There, as in Greece, it was simple people in small places who recalled Byzantium most clearly. They bridged the gap between the Middle Ages and the present more easily than I could. In another of these tiny monasteries – Gornjak, in Eastern Serbia – a monk showed me a hermitage cut in the steep rocks of the gorge.

'Who lived here?' I asked.

'Oh, one Gregory from Sinai.'

I supposed the hermit to be recently dead. It was not until some time afterwards that by chance I read about the 14th-century monks on Mount Athos, the hesychasts, who had preached a new mysticism, their goal a vision of the Divine Light, to be achieved in solitude and silence. They had endured much opposition, and their leader, Gregory of Sinai, had fled with them first to Bulgaria. Legends being only half-true, it was one of his followers, a Greek, Gregory the Younger, who had gone some years later to Gornjak: one of a group who had spread out through Eastern Serbia. Others were to reach Russia and to build up an enduring tradition there of the holy man, the *starets*.

Because Byzantium had survived in the villages, mostly by means of uneducated priests, its traditions were twisted together inextricably with local magic and superstition that the ancient Slavs must have brought down from the north or have found already there in the Balkans. In this country oak-trees as well as Orthodox saints are sacred, and the dead are sent on their way with wheat-grains as well as with prayers. 'We Slavs created the vampire,' said a Marxist friend; and went on, after a few spine-chilling ghost stories, 'Of course, none of this conflicts with materialism in any way.'

Society had once been patriarchal here, and kinship remained vitally important. We knew a painter, a married man, who had lost both his parents, and another acquaintance commented that nothing could be more terrible in life than that. His wife did not count: the values were those of the old ballads: 'It's hard for him who's without his own kindred anywhere in the world.'* Edith Durham had noted, early this century, that the word 'friend' always implied someone connected by marriage or kinship ties (*kumstvo*).

With this set pattern of relationships, everyone knew where they were. A total hospitality, unfamiliar to us, was normal. If we were guests, we could do no wrong. In England, you can qualify a guest: he may be difficult or easy, and you may limit your welcome accordingly. To South Slavs this would be inexplicable. Total hospitality means total tolerance, generosity and endeavour on the part of the host, and we had to adapt ourselves to practise it in return.

Age was another absolute. In the family, the young respected the old. We saw the outward signs: a girl kissing the hand of a wrinkled woman, the old men at a village wedding seated in the best place and supplied with the strongest drink. I wondered whether they kept their status because, up to the present, anyone old is bound to have lived a hard if not tragic life, and this has been true for centuries. The old were the survivors, and their survival gave them dignity. At the same time, they knew their place, and would yield the central role to those younger and stronger than they were. Even in sophisticated families the grandmother stayed well in the background: she kept house and looked after the grandchildren, while her daughter or daughter-in-law went out to work. We would see her for a moment or not at all. She

* 'Teško svuda svome bez svojega.'

might criticize the younger women but she accepted that her life was limited to the family and to friends of her own age. In return, her children would support her at home through illness to death, whatever the difficulties.

Personal honour was also a question of kinship and could not be side-stepped. A country girl worked for us and turned out to be dishonest: after she had left, her brother-in-law came to call and offered to pay for the damage done; she was, he said, 'a shame on her family, a shame on Serbia, a shame on England'.

The villages had originally been groups of families, very democratically organized. No one thought himself better or worse than another. In the 1930s, it had been possible to go and talk to Ministers in Belgrade cafés. Recently the Abbess of a 15th-century monastery in need of repair had written to 'Tito and Jovanka' just as she would have written to the King and Queen in earlier days – and had got help.

There was much to admire in all this. A pattern of living had stayed whole, though it was rough at the edges. I missed the subtlety of taste and manners that prevails in the West. Every time I went back to England I welcomed the *douceur de vivre* based on centuries of peace, yet I was homesick for Yugoslavia. The minor graces might be missing there, except in Dalmatia and Zagreb and sometimes in Belgrade; instead there was a grand style which depended on vanished splendours and miseries. I had been wrenched round to face eastwards and northwards, towards the churches and palaces of Byzantium, the bazaars of Istanbul and the vastness of Russia. It was bewildering to be launched on so much strangeness: in order to make any sense of it, I had to learn the outline of the past.

PART ONE

The Old Serbia

HISTORICAL BACKGROUND

The Serbs appear comparatively late on the scene of conquest, retreat and migration recorded all over the Balkans since prehistoric times. The earlier inhabitants of this region were known as Illyrians, and the Romans under Trajan invaded and settled their lands along the Danube. The Eastern Emperor Justinian took over fortresses that the Romans had built, and he and his successors in Byzantium tried to hold off fierce barbarian raids from the north. Only in the 7th century A.D. did the Avars and Slavs finally surge across the Balkans, and a few years later came the Croats and Serbs – Slav or Caucasian by origin – who were quickly assimilated by the first wave of Slavs. The Croats fanned out westwards, while the Serbs penetrated south of the Danube and dotted the forest with their meagre settlements. The Illyrians fled before the newcomers, probably into what is now Albania. The Serbs pushed on southwards to the mountains, and for two hundred years lived as hunters and shepherds in the austere ranges watered by the Piva, Tara and Ibar rivers, a region now partly in Montenegro, partly in Serbia. Slowly the Serbs began to organize themselves under their own princes, and in the late 9th century, when Cyril and Methodius were making their first missionary journeys among the Slavs, Serbian envoys accepted Christianity and political vassalage direct from Byzantium.

Byzantium

The full effect of both acts was greatly delayed, as the Serbs' life remained unstable. Their country was always to be a battleground, and at that time it was the powerful Bulgarians who ravaged their lands. A new era began for them in 1014, when the Byzantines defeated the Bulgarian Emperor Samuel and established their own supremacy in the Balkans. The Byzantine Emperor Basil II celebrated this victory by a solemn thanksgiving in the Parthenon, then the Church of the Mother of God.

The Serbs formed two princedoms: Zeta (later Montenegro) and Raška (later Serbia).* They did not consider vassalage to be a passive existence, and

* The Serbs were to suffer a prolonged Turkish occupation of their lands, while the Montenegrins, apart from a short time in the 17th century, stayed strongly independent. As a result, the Montenegrins, with a few exceptions, remained on their own territory and the Serbs emigrated in large numbers to other South Slav lands and to Hungary; Serbian minorities are to be found all over present-day Yugoslavia.

in Raška the leader Stephen Nemanja began to try out his strength. He joined with Venice to fight Byzantium in 1171, but was routed by the Emperor Manuel Comnenus. After Manuel's death, Nemanja made alliances with Hungary and with the German Emperor Frederick Barbarossa who wanted a free passage for Crusaders through Serbia. He also gained a great deal of territory and a Byzantine princess for daughter-in-law. In 1190 came Nemanja's triumph: Byzantium recognized Serbia as an autonomous state.

The Nemanjid State

In the early 13th century, the astute rulers of the new state welcomed Western influence. Stephen Nemanja had been baptized into the Church of Rome, and his second son, Stephen the First-Crowned, was so-called because of his crown received from Papal envoys. Soon afterwards, Nemanja's third son, the remarkable statesman-monk later canonized as St Sava, secured the independence of the Serbian Church from the Orthodox Patriarch at Nicaea. This wavering between East and West is a recurring theme in Serbian history. On this occasion it ended in a decision for Byzantium, which could offer the Serbs their own national Church; Rome could not. From then on, medieval Serbia was linked to the West by trade and by some Roman bishoprics on the coast, but it drew mainly on the Byzantine inheritance in law, government, religion and culture. In common with other states within the Byzantine commonwealth, the stronger it became, the more it needed the resources of the Imperial civilization.

The Serbs wanted a Christian theocracy, political stability and new lands. They escaped the destructive Mongol invasions of the 13th century and this helped them to achieve their aims. The Nemanjid dynasty produced two remarkable rulers: Milutin (1282–1321) and Dušan (1331–55), who brought about the full flowering of the medieval Serbian state. The rule of law started with Milutin, and Dušan gave the Serbs their first legal Code, the *Zakonik* of 1349. This is based mostly on Byzantine, partly on customary law. It reveals most vividly the social conditions of Dušan's day. Serfs existed, but the rights of a 'poor spinning woman' were protected. Foreign merchants travelled freely through the land. Vlach shepherds herded their flocks up to mountain pastures. Priests had to be restrained from practising sorcery, nobles from fighting each other. Every aspect of feudal life is covered, and the general impression is of a monarch, sometimes traditionally harsh, sometimes unexpectedly merciful, and always adaptable to the needs of his time.

Under the strong rule of the Nemanjids, natural resources were developed and Serbia grew wealthy. In the lowlands, well-tilled fields yielded wheat

1 The hermit Raphael on a visit to Žiča

2 Studenica: (*l.* to *r.*) the tiny King's Church, the refectory and the belfry, the Church of the Mother of God

3 Studenica: detail from east window, Church of the Mother of God

and flax famous throughout Europe; in the forests, hunters continued to trap marten and ermine for their much-prized skins. Most significant of all, economically, was the exploitation of mines which had been neglected since the Roman occupation. Saxons, Ragusans and Italians were brought in to work them. Serbia leased three gold mines to Ragusa and received 30,000 ducats in return. In the 13th century, the first silver coins were minted. The Serbian Court had once shocked a Byzantine envoy by its simplicity: he had deplored marrying princesses into a family where one daughter-in-law, dressed in homespun, sat spinning at her wheel. Now Theodore Metochites, who visited Serbia in Milutin's reign, could give a more satisfactory report of appropriate luxury, and as a result, a marriage was arranged between the Imperial princess Simonida and the Serbian king. Dušan continued to live regally: he ate off a silver plate and his mother's ring was made by the finest craftsmen in Byzantium.*

In Serbia, as in Byzantium, temporal and religious sovereignty were combined in the person of the ruler. The Nemanjids, inspired by St Sava in his lifetime, founded monasteries whose Abbots became royal advisers, for the links between Church and State in medieval Serbia were particularly close. The kings could also show their *philanthropia*, their love of man, just as the Byzantine Emperors had done, by manifesting it in great works of art scattered throughout their lands, and they were discerning patrons. Serbian Diets were convened to choose the most beautiful sites: the meadows of Dečani or the mountains of Sopoćani. Architects came from the Adriatic coast, and built some church exteriors in the Romanesque style. For the interiors, the finest fresco-painters were summoned from Byzantium or Salonica, and here the times favoured the Serbs. After the sack of Byzantium by the Crusaders in 1204 there was less to be done in the capital and artists went further afield to Russia and the Balkans, where they probably taught their craft to native monks. Painting and literature were closely linked. Serbian monasticism enjoyed the rich legacy of a Slavonic language and liturgy that derived from the work of Cyril and Methodius, and St Sava had introduced Byzantine Church books. With these as models, Serbian monks wrote saints' lives and chronicles and hymns, the best of which can delight the modern reader by their vitality and poetic strength. The monk-painters, whether Greek or Serb, transferred stories of saintly Nemanjid kings to the frescoes on the church-walls. The greatest foundation of all was outside Serbia: the monastery of Hilandar on Mount Athos, where Stephen Nemanja, who had earlier been re-baptized into the Eastern Church, died an Orthodox monk, and which became a famous centre of learning. Hilandar is a small

* Both are to be seen in the National Museum at Belgrade.

community today, but you can meet Greeks in Chalkidhiki who owe their first schooling to the monks there.

Temporal conquest was never far from the minds of the later Nemanjids. Dušan extended the Serbian lands, already enlarged under Milutin, until they stretched from the Neretva to the Gulf of Corinth, from the Iron Gates of the Danube to the Thracian coast. Epirus, Albania, Thessaly and Macedonia came within his frontiers. He used mercenaries from all over the known world: Greeks, Latins, Tartars and Spaniards fought in his armies and were paid with his own gold or with loans from prosperous monasteries. Dušan himself was as great a leader in war as in peace. He profited from the decline of Byzantium under Ottoman pressure. He had himself crowned 'Emperor of the Serbs and Greeks (*Romaioi*)'. He thought of taking Constantinople, only to die of a fever on the way there, in 1355. Whether he hoped to save Byzantium from the Turks, or whether to gain the Byzantine Empire for himself, remains a mystery.

After his death the Nemanjid state, which had lasted for nearly 200 years, began to dwindle. The feudal lords squabbled over Dušan's successors; lands were divided, and in 1371 a nobleman, Prince Lazar, ruled over a much smaller Serbia. The Ottoman Turks were now so strong that their conquest of the Balkan peninsula seemed inevitable. Macedonia fell to them in 1371, after the battle of the Marica; Serbia, according to tradition, succumbed after her defeat at Kossovo in 1389 when Prince Lazar was killed along with the Ottoman Sultan Murad I.

Kossovo

Kossovo is the most important date for the Serbs in the whole of their history: the actual battle, together with the half-legendary poems it inspired, remains the symbol of Serbian national identity. If the Nemanjid Empire has been proof to the Serbs that they were once a civilized state and could be so again, then Kossovo has been proof that they were warrior heroes. The second piece of knowledge was the more necessary to them when under Turkish domination, because it gave them hope that they could fight again and win their freedom. The Kossovo myth took its final shape in epic verse which fed the mind and spirit of the Serbs for centuries.* Prince Lazar, who sacrificed himself in battle for his people, became the greatest hero of the popular imagination, and not Tsar Dušan, the lawgiver and conqueror.

Though Serbia became nominally a vassal state, the Turkish conquest of her lands was a gradual process. Owing to the temporary defeat of the Ottomans by Tamerlane in 1402, Lazar's son, Stephen Lazarević, was able to

* See Appendix II.

revive Serbia as a Byzantine Despotate which lasted until the taking of Smederevo in 1459, six years after the fall of Byzantium itself.

The Turkish occupation caused much of Serbia's medieval past to vanish for ever. It is the surviving monasteries and churches which tell her story most eloquently.

I
STUDENICA AND THE IBAR VALLEY

Arrival by night – the Abbot – a highland gorge – a sepulchre for princes and a Court chapel – the Lenten fast – monastery life

In the darkness, a voice out of heaven cried 'Bata', and Bata standing beside me at the foot of an impenetrable wall called back 'Goca'. As if a spell had been broken, the wall dissolved: unseen doors creaked open, and from the pale space of courtyard within came a slight girl in trousers. Goca held a heavy key in her hand. 'The monks are asleep,' she said, 'but they left everything ready.' I forgot I was tired and cold, and we crept up wooden stairs to the guest-rooms. Goca and I were sharing the Bishop's suite. We each had an oriental rug as bedspread and on the wall hung machine-tapestries of Balmoral stags and eagles. We talked till we dozed off. Goca was a librarian from Belgrade; she had come here to Studenica to sort out some of their manuscripts. Tactful, efficient and friendly, she was one of the wandering scholars who people the interior of Yugoslavia. Bata, an art historian, was another. We had become friends after he and Richard had met by chance in Greece, on the quayside at Mount Athos. They had trudged companionably across the Holy Mountain together to the Serbian monastery at Hilandar, where Richard, under Bata's wing, had found himself, like me, in episcopal quarters. Bata looks a boy with a good-humoured face, and it is a mild shock to find he has an impressive knowledge of medieval frescoes in Yugoslavia. As a student he walked over the hills uncovering churches lost in undergrowth or hidden by boulders. When he goes travelling he keeps to one habit acquired on his youthful explorations: wherever he is, at midday he changes into a clean shirt as if he were a 19th-century Englishman putting on his dinner-jacket in the jungle.

On this occasion, we had crossed the uplands of South Serbia and the Sandžak by Land-Rover, as he wanted to see for himself some remote churches which were in need of State funds for their restoration. An architect and a conservation official had joined us, and after the hard work done each day, we had spent the evenings sociably in a *kafana*. The journey had provided many pleasures. I had seen churches hidden behind cement-works, in mountain pastures, in a cave, that I should never have found on my own.* We had risen at dawn and watched the sun light up Byzantine wall-paintings, and as night fell we listened to a muezzin calling under the crescent moon. With Studenica, the first great medieval monastery to be built in Serbia, I was near the end of my wanderings. Bata would leave me there and go back to Belgrade, and so would Goca, while I stayed on for a few days with the monks and found my own way home.

Bata and Goca stand for the present; the monks for the past. A close bond existed between them, based on their common interest in the monastery. For the monks, the monastery was their life, for Bata and Goca, the centre of their studies. Both parties recognized an inheritance to be cherished. Next morning, the Abbot and Bata drank their plum brandy together as men who had confidence in each other. The daily bus was leaving. I said farewell to the scholars and settled in with the monks.

The Abbot of Studenica has a very fine presence. His features have a kind of transparency about them: his brown skin is taut, his black eyes serene above the depersonalizing monkish beard. He is like a prince of the Church: his monastery has taken first place among all the other monasteries of Serbia for 700 years, and he finds it normal that the Archbishop of Canterbury should come and preach there as he did in 1966, and just as normal to go out and chop wood for hours with the younger monks and hired workmen. He has a habit of pushing his tall black cylinder hat off his brow when he talks, completely relaxed. Now, as we looked across the monastery courtyard, he said, 'Imagine what it was like for our people under the Turks. They weren't allowed to ride their horses or to dress properly† but they came down from the hills and found – this.' He gestured towards the Church of the Mother of God, only a few yards distant from us, a Romanesque church of shining marble which towered out of the greensward and daisies. Within are royal tombs: Stephen Nemanja's, founder of the Serbian medieval dynasty, and his son's, Stephen the First-Crowned. Nemanja had built the church with the help of two other sons: St Sava and King Vukan of Zeta at the turn of the 12th and 13th centuries.

The Abbot went away to his farms, and I thought how the sight of the church must have awakened for the oppressed peasants a memory of

* See Appendix I, pp. 257–58.

† The Serbs were forbidden to wear green as the Turks did.

lost glory which echoes in their poems, where a queen has a gold ring set with stones so brilliant they could make a dark room blaze with light. In Turkish times the monasteries had seemed, as Vuk Karadžić wrote, 'signs which bear witness that once upon a time the Serbs had Emperors and Kings'.

Round the main church are others added by different rulers: two still stand,* and the foundations of more are now being excavated. An 18th-century engraving shows nine little churches bobbing like pinnaces around a big sailing-ship. The courtyard wall today encloses plenty of rooms for the monks and their guests, a restored medieval dining-hall, a gate-tower. Beehives and fruit-trees stand inside the enclosure, just as they do in the engraving. In front of the monastery is a churned-up piece of ground, mud in winter, corrugated dust in summer, with a solitary house to whose wall a few whinnying ponies are always tethered – a trading-post for the hill-villages. This level plot of land lies high; below it, fields slope down to the Studenica river: above it rise mountains and forests.

The Studenica is a tributary of the Ibar which slashes a deep gorge roughly from south to north through the centre of the Serbian mountains. It is guarded by castles, and more castles are dotted about the wild country which rises east of the Ibar and finally drops down into the main Morava valley. This was the other direction from which invasion – by Bulgars or Cumans – was likely to come. The Ibar was the geographical axis of medieval Serbia. About half-way down the main valley, and a little to the west of it, was the first capital, Ras, now hidden underground, on an ancient trade route from the Adriatic to Byzantium. To the north, near the junction of the Ibar with the Western Morava, stands the red-painted church, Žiča, which celebrates the foundation of an independent Serbian Church. The monasteries, put up by different kings and one queen as their mausoleums, lie in more hidden places, up in the mountains to the west. Studenica is meant to be remote. A 19th-century gazetteer makes it ten hours' march from the nearest town and when Stephen Nemanja first saw it and chose it as his tomb, 800 years ago, it was a desert place, a hunting-ground for wild beasts.

*

* The smaller and earlier of these, St Nicholas, dates from the first half of the 13th century. The surviving frescoes are freely and strongly painted, especially the head of St John Baptist on the pilaster to the north. The rustic wooden Deisis is 17th-century work and probably came from another church as it is two Apostles short. For the King's Church, see below, pp. 25–28.

As the Abbot left me that morning and I went into the church, it seemed overwhelmingly a tomb. First came the outer wall of the west front, massive blocks of hard, honey-coloured stone* that emphasize the small size and tender body of any living being. Then I passed through a marble doorway set in a high arcade of stone, and felt at once colder, smaller, beneath a great height of whitened vault. I was in the outer narthex, a majestic ante-room with two small side-chapels: the southern one full of family portraits of the dynasty and some frescoes, scratched and faint, of Stephen Nemanja's relics being brought from Mount Athos, a serial story based on St Sava's Life of his father. King Radoslav, who had all this built and painted in 1233, was Nemanja's grandson, and cherished his cult in death.

Ahead there rose a marvellously beautiful cliff of greyish marble, once the original west front of the church, and at the centre of this cliff is a small wooden door set in a cluster of slender pillars which seem to make it recede further away across the marble pavement. This entrance to the mausoleum within is guarded at ground-level and pillar-top by griffins and lions leaping from the wall. The patroness of the Church, the Mother of God, watches over it from a sculptured tympanum, as she holds the Christ-Child on her knee, and angels in turn guard her. It was her icon that Stephen Nemanja asked to have held before his eyes as he lay dying.

The west wall is the more dazzling by contrast with the church's rough outer shell of stone. The tympanum and the door itself are framed in wide bands of sculptured birds and beasts, caught and wreathed in leaves and flowers and fruit: dragon, eagle, basilisk, acanthus, vine – the familiar and the fantastic are all there in brilliant white marble, while the inner face of the doorway is lined with small but monumental figures of Christ and the Apostles. The grey wall soars up to take the vault, once the roof, which it seems to support on shallow curves of blind arcading based on corbels: animal or human heads. West and East meet in this decoration: one figure recalls Chartres, others, Byzantine ivory miniatures. It is a reminder that Stephen Nemanja came from the Adriatic coast as a Roman Catholic, and that Stephen the First-Crowned had first a Byzantine, then a Venetian wife. The whole of this splendour is part of the entrance to a tomb, and through the door, the themes of death begin. The inner narthex is clearly lit, and on the south wall is the tiny figure of Nemanja's wife, dressed as a nun, kneeling before the Mother of God. She was

* Though once they may have been plastered over and painted red like Žiča.

buried here, though her tomb, and that of her son Vukan and others of her family, have gone.* The light also falls on other reminders of death: the Last Judgement and the Passion of Christ, frescoes done in the late 16th century.

You can see Pilate washing his hands Turkish fashion, with water being poured onto them from a ewer and caught in a basin underneath, just in the way the Meteora monks washed Robert Curzon's hands in the last century, and the Peć nuns mine, in this: very cooling in hot weather, like putting one's hands under a waterfall. Nearby, down below, is the Last Supper, with the Apostles very friendly round a marbled table. At the centre, Judas is painted in profile so that he cannot put the evil eye on you. He is an ugly creature, and his way of leaning to the left apishly copies the gentle movement of St John the Evangelist towards Christ. The bitter herbs of the Jewish Passover lie about the table. Up at the top of this wall, there is the Last Judgement beginning: two angels rolling up the scroll of Heaven, an Omega of ribbon: on the east wall, Christ sits in judgement above a vertical river of fire, and an archangel separates good men from bad. Under this is another little door. If you step through it you arrive in the main part of the church, light, high and open, with plenty of windows. In the southwest corner lies Stephen Nemanja, home after a long journey. St Sava was at Hilandar to record his father's last words on his death-bed: 'My child, do me this favour, put on me the habit which is to be my shroud, and prepare me thoroughly in a holy manner to lie in my grave. And strew rushes on the earth, and place me on them. And place a stone under my head, so that I may lie here until the Lord come to take me hence.' Soon he died, and St Sava flung himself down on the body, weeping long and bitterly. First he buried his father at Hilandar, where a miraculous vine grew out of his tomb. Then the Holy Mountain became a very unsafe spot for royal bones after the Crusaders took Byzantium in 1204, so St Sava brought his father's remains back to his own kingdom as he had wished. Another son, Stephen the First-Crowned, has described their arrival at Studenica by night, the funeral chants sung over the holy relics, and the swinging of perfumed censers as the procession moved towards the grave prepared by Nemanja for himself.

The tomb is a plain box of stone and Nemanja painted on the wall above it looks a humble, hesitant person as he is led towards Christ by his sponsors, St Sava and the Mother of God, not like the ruler whom

* In 1974, her tombstone was found during excavations in the courtyard.

the Byzantine Emperor Manuel I Comnenus had painted on his palace-wall: 'a man, only not of such a stature as nature gives to men, but grown very tall and with a splendid air'. But then Manuel, who had defeated Nemanja in 1171 and had him led as a rebel through the streets of the capital, may have wanted to show off his conquered adversary, whereas at Studenica, Nemanja is a simple monk who happened to be a prince. He is also a spicy kind of saint; an old peasant told me, 'His body gives off such a sweet smell, like violets, you notice it as soon as you enter the church.' It seemed proper that someone had put a bunch of marjoram on his tomb, and that the 16th-century painters had faithfully restored, high above him, a fresco of the three women bringing spices to the Tomb of Christ: a lovely scene, with its steep rocks and waving grasses, skilfully fitted into the angle of a wall, and a symbol that the church founder, Nemanja, had also brought a gift to Christ, and hoped for his mercy.

By contrast, Stephen the First-Crowned lies more splendidly than his father, in a 19th-century Viennese casket worked in silver, which a Karageorge princess had made for him. It is in front of the iconostasis, on the right, and beyond, in the altar-space, are noble figures of Church Fathers. King Stephen is very popular locally, and the casket was covered with offerings: a hank of wool, sprigs of basil, a pair of baby gloves bound with scarlet thread and a garish tea-cloth embroidered with the words: 'A present from Jasmina Djurković.' Under the tomb I noticed a packet of lump sugar. What lay above was a gift for the monastery; what lay below gained healing power and was taken home for the sick. The shrill-voiced old nun who cooked for the monks had implored me, as a barren woman, to crawl under this tomb; and the baby-gloves were probably someone else's plea for fertility. The saint's bones must always have exercised a powerful charm, for no Nemanjid relics travelled further or more frequently than his under the Turks, and he even has a spare tomb in the Studenica treasury. Perhaps the Serbs were afraid his remains would be burnt like St Sava's, for they hid them in remote monasteries up and down the country and only took them home in 1839 when Serbia was free. As late as the First World War, the relics were off again, that time to the Montenegrin mountains. Now Stephen the First-Crowned lies again in the monastery he helped to complete, and the monks ask for his prayers in intercession.

If you turn slowly back to leave the church, you are met by the grandest image of death, the Crucifixion of 1209, which has survived, comparatively undamaged, in its original beauty. 'The King of Glory' is written on the short cross-piece of wood at the top of the Cross. This inscription, and the placing of the subject on the west wall, where one would expect to find the Dormition of the Virgin, must have been the deliberate choice of St Sava. The figure of Christ stands out from a deep blue ground patterned with small angels and with golden stars. His agony is expressed in the closed eyes and tense mouth, the weary pose of his head, in the long thin, apparently boneless arms which barely support his creased ribs and sagging stomach.* His suffering is reflected in the faces of the mourners: the Virgin Mary's face is all heavy sad lines, while her hands gesture acceptance and grief. St John the Evangelist bows his head on his hand, and the Captain of the Guard, Longinus (later promoted saint by the Church), very gaily-clothed, looks puzzled, as if things have gone beyond his understanding. The prettiest figure, the woman on the far left, had her face touched up in the 16th century, and has lost the mournful dignity of her three companions. The treatment of death, in this fresco, is formalized as well as humane. The blood which falls from Christ's hands and feet does so symmetrically, his hair is ringletted, and his body is gracefully draped in a white and gold cloth. On the right a busy angel leads away one woman, a symbol for the synagogue; on the left, another angel propels a second woman towards Christ, and she, the Church, catches in a bowl the blood that comes from his wounded body. The richness of the painting never overcomes the austerity of its theme; St Sava had been in contact with Imperial craftsmen at Byzantium and Nicaea. The smaller scenes above the Crucifixion – the Raising of Lazarus and the Entry into Jerusalem – also illustrate the power and glory of Christ: they are 16th-century restorations of 13th-century paintings, and again their placing must have been intentional.

The great church at Studenica is a tomb, but one which lets in the light. There are mausoleums which are dark and hopeless in their finality, but St Sava's aim here was to show the majesty of death, the humility of kings before it, and Christ's Crucifixion as a prelude to further life. Leading out of the cupola is a tiny north chapel, where once the choir was put to sing. In this clear frescoed space must have

* The figure of the dead Christ, especially the treatment of his head, has similarities to Western art, especially to a slightly later crucifix by Giunta Pisano at Santa Maria degli Angeli, Assisi. See D. Talbot-Rice, *Byzantine Painting, the Last Phase* (London, 1968), pp. 46 and 69.

sounded the service written by St Sava to the eternal memory of his father – Stephen the ruler, Simeon the monk – who lies there:

> Thy great and most honourable monastery cries out in praise,
> Having thee for inhabitant and for builder
> And for lover of thy fatherland, O wise one,
> And hymning thee in song without ceasing:
> We beseech thee, Simeon, wise in the wisdom of God,
> Pray zealously for thy flock,
> That it may reap the fruit of thy endeavours,
> And that thy flock may be preserved in safety.

I came out of the church by the south door, and sat on the steps, in the sun, level with the carved cat's head at the bottom of one pilaster. I fancied this cat, which has twisted stone whiskers. It is worth walking round the outside of the church, as the altar-window is a treat in stonework, too. Father Simeon came along to lock up the church; the building is far too precious to be left open; some treasures had recently been filched and they were thinking of getting a dog. Father Simeon is not at all like the Abbot, for his appearance belies his character. He looks sly and wears a shabby velvet cap. His beard is wispy, his eyes two shiny prunes, and if he can, he will make a joke as soon as he sees you. He is a melancholy jester like Jaques: a sad, cultivated person at heart. He takes visitors round the churches, and is a very good guide. He has listened to the art historians who come and settle for weeks to swoop and peer at the frescoes from scaffolding. He never tells you things by rote, but gives you saints' legends at his ease. He works under hard conditions. The churches are unheated and, despite his thick cloak, he was shivering in April after an hour or two spent with tourists. We made a quick dash to the monastery office, where an old iron stove turned the air stuffy with heat. There we drank Turkish coffee, the coffee-tray lying among seed catalogues, a jar of honey, a typewriter and the church register, which a younger priest in gumboots, Father Sava, had just brought in and was entering up.

Then we went out again into the courtyard for Father Simeon to unlock the King's Church, which is small, whitewashed and built to a cross-in-square plan by King Milutin in 1314. An Imperial envoy had commented favourably on the way this Serbian monarch lived, and one can see why. He had a proper sense of his own royalty. Here is a Court church, and its frescoes are of a kind commissioned by the

Palaeologue family themselves. The king and his Byzantine queen Simonida are painted in full regalia. They are not humble suppliants like Stephen Nemanja and his queen in the other church, but take their places triumphantly alongside Christ and St Anne at the foot of the south wall, equal in size with them. Milutin, as donor, holds a model of the church in his hands; Simonida, a sceptre. They are dressed in Byzantine fashion. Archbishop Danilo II, a friend of Simonida's, has described her setting off on a journey looking just like this, 'clothed in royal raiment and golden girdles, with pearls and precious stones, the Imperial purple'.

The painting in the church reflects the spirit of late Byzantine humanism: rational, joyful, intent on an ideal beauty. A new tenderness has crept into the style, in the enchanting serial story of the Life of the Virgin, [1] emphasized because of the church's dedication to her parents Joachim and Anne. In the scene of her birth, on the south wall, they embrace under their haloes.

'Look,' said Father Simeon, 'that baby's being bathed, and bathed right, the woman's testing the hot water with the *back* of her hand.' It was true, and the baby in question was the newly-born Virgin Mary. He pointed higher up in the same scene: 'They liked to be precise, in those days. What's on that tray?' I could see the midwife carrying it towards St Anne who lay in a big bed. 'Surgical instruments, everything that's necessary for childbirth.' Only a figure of Destiny, fanning the baby in her cradle, suggests anything supernatural. The colouring is rich: very dark blues, a brownish red, pale greens and yellows and grey and warm mauve, a little white. The frescoes tell a story, and tell it with great economy, in the scenes which flow in horizontal procession along the middle of the south and north walls and in the Double Communion level with them in the apse. People are walking round the walls, pausing to enact scenes from a sacred drama. To the north Mary enters the Temple: 'She danced with her feet and all the house of Israel loved her.' A file of graceful women follow her and her parents, painted tall and important, bring up the rear. Here the colours are harmonious and restrained – pink, dark blue, pale gold and grey. In the Double Communion, the stillness of the central figures of Christ contrasts with the movement of the Apostles towards him. Earlier, as in the mosaics of St Sophia at Kiev, that movement was hieratic. Here it has broken up into naturalism. Some Apostles hurry along, eager in devotion, others turn back to look for a companion who has got left behind, but the narrative depends on a few telling gestures of hand and head, and the design remains disciplined.

Some of the traditional Twelve Great Feasts,* each in their separate frames above the Virgin's Life, have a new dynamism. They are strongly triangular compositions, perhaps influenced by the shape of the vaulting over them. On the right of the window of the south wall is the Baptism of Christ (19 January) which replaces the Western Epiphany. Here it is painted with extraordinary vigour: St John on the bank bends towards Christ in mid-river, and Jordan, a muscled antique godling, springs away to fetch another pitcher of water. The Transfiguration (19 August) is on the west wall. There the central figure of Christ has a strong movement, stressed by the jagged diagonal lines of his draperies and of the rock under his feet. He seems about to leave for Heaven, 'his raiment white as the light' in St Matthew's words, while the other figures are anchored to the earth: Moses and Elijah stand four-square on flat rocks and the three distraught Apostles below, Peter, James and John, crouch or lie heavily on terra firma. It is followed by the Entry into Jerusalem (Palm Sunday). On the north wall are the two most significant scenes. In the Crucifixion, quite different from that in the big church, the figure of Christ is applied to the lines of the Cross; the angels weep above him, the outstretched pleading arms of the Virgin Mary do duty for the feelings of the mourning women grouped behind her. It is a painting that states one fact: that suffering exists. Then comes the Harrowing of Hell which in the Eastern Church symbolizes the Resurrection. Christ stands on the fallen gates of Hell, which are crossed beneath his feet, and with a strong movement he hauls up the patriarchal figure of Adam and a heavily-draped Eve. The end of his cloak flies up behind him like a single wing driven by the wind. Crowds of prophets and saints dressed as kings hold out their hands to him. It illustrates some stanzas used in the Orthodox service on Holy Saturday, when the voice of Hell cries out:

> He came to me and destroyed my power;
> He shattered the gates of brass;
> The souls that I used to hold has this God raised.[2]

* The Feasts start at the east end, on the triumphal arch which encloses the apse. The Annunciation (7 April), extremely faded, is painted north and south of the iconostasis. Level with it, on the south wall, follows the Nativity (for Christmas Day, 7 January) but for the Presentation in the Temple (15 February) the painter has doubled back under the Annunciation, probably because the space was just right for two groups of figures. Pentecost is missing and the Ascension almost invisible in the apse.

Just as the Crucifixion recalls Good Friday, so does the Harrowing of Hell reflect Easter.

Another Feast, the Dormition of the Virgin (28 August), is in its customary place on the west wall. It is a massive composition, usually crammed with buildings and people, but here the central part is lost, though angels with tapers and a crowd of sorrowing Apostles can be plainly seen. The story is different from the Western Assumption, and derives from a jumble of traditions of how, when the Virgin was dying at home in St John's house in Jerusalem, the Twelve Apostles, busy preaching the Gospel all over the world, sailed back on clouds to see her. Thomas was late but the others got there in time. She commended her spirit to Christ and he came down and took her soul up to Heaven in his arms: this is the swaddled 'baby' so often seen in the frescoes. When Thomas hurried in from India three days afterwards, the tomb was opened at his request; it was empty. So much for the legend. In church decoration the subject emphasizes the Resurrection of the Virgin, and the worshipper had only to turn east to the curve of the apse to discover her, perpetually interceding for humanity.*

The unknown artist or artists of the King's Church shared the same narrative style as Michael and Eutychius, who painted fine churches for Milutin and other patrons in Serbia and Macedonia. The wall-painting here is distinguished by its tension and rhythmical unity: the strong vertical line of the kings and saints down below, the ribbon-like movement of the Virgin's Life banding the walls above them, and over them again, the upward pull of the Great Feasts.

The King's Church at Studenica is a perfect royal chapel built by a king confident in his role and his faith. It is the statement of a conquering dynasty: Milutin erected a magnificent mausoleum for himself at Banjska (now ruined, and his body gone to Sofia), and added smaller churches like grace-notes to monasteries and cities alike.

The stories told on the walls would be easy to follow for anyone, educated or not, who went regularly to church services. The next morning, as I stood at the Saturday Liturgy among a congregation of peasants and chanting monks crowded together under the cupola, I realized that this was a church to look at in two ways, in time or beyond

* The Serbs, like the Russian Orthodox, keep to the Old (Julian) Calendar, while the Greeks, except for the monks of Mount Athos, use the New (Gregorian) Calendar as in the West. The dates given in the text are from the New Calendar, to help anyone who wants to go to a monastery feast-day.

it – as a 14th-century treasure or as an Orthodox church where decoration fuses with worship.

An Orthodox church is an eternal image of the whole world. The saints and kings of earth cover the lower walls; they are familiar neighbours for the churchgoer. Higher up is the Holy Land, in the Virgin's Life and the Great Feasts and in the Double Communion. Heaven is symbolized by the Mother of God in the apse and above all, in the cupola, by the solemn Christ Pantocrator* surrounded by the Heavenly Liturgy of angels carrying instruments of the Passion, while the four Evangelists sit writing on the pendentives below. The Visible and Invisible Church all worship together and no barrier exists between the living and the dead.

These narratives of the saints, of Christ and his Mother are not the Bible-in-pictures: they are for the believer, like icons, images of great religious power. As the Church Calendar passes by, Otto Demus thought, the framed Feasts each come to the front for veneration, and then step back for another twelvemonth. They, and the other subjects, have for their sources the Bible, the Apocrypha, the sermons of the early Fathers and the services themselves. The congregation can see portrayed on the wall the words chanted by priest or deacon. There is a profound relationship between late Byzantine art and the celebration of the Liturgy.

To be present at this service in any Byzantine church is to be aware of a meaning in religious art that is foreign to the West and which at first is difficult to absorb because the themes and treatment seem stylized. When they begin to be familiar, these subjects grow in depth, their richness of expression reveals itself, and more surprisingly, their variety. The artists of this time held a paradox within themselves: they worked from set formulae but the details of their execution were often intensely personal. How much is due to inspired choice within tradition, how much to patron, how much to painter, is open to question, but the result can be deeply moving.

It was Lent. I went to church, if I woke up in time. The morning prayers began at five, and the Liturgy, which was celebrated on Saturdays and Sundays, followed at seven. The Lenten services were long, especially *B'denie* or Vigil, which consists of several offices rolled into one; it lasted for three hours, after the day's work was over, but before the evening meal. Like so many Orthodox services it had a

* Missing in the King's Church.

pleasing casualness, being held in the dining-room, where lectern, lamp and icon stood in one corner. I also shared the monks' meals. The Orthodox fast is very strict; 'the Lenten season', wrote the monk Dositej in 1783, 'when reign the bean and her sister the lentil, when peas and cabbage govern the earth'. They were in the fifth week when I was there, and it lasts for seven. Not only do they forgo meat, but also fish (except on Palm Sunday and the Feast of the Annunciation), eggs and milk products. Oil is used only on Sundays. This meant we had spinach boiled with young nettles, beans, potato soup, pickled cabbage, stewed fruit, wholemeal bread and herb tea every day, with a banquet of stuffed paprikas and nut cakes after church on Sunday. There was always coffee, *rakija* (two kinds, strong and not so strong) and a pinkish wine which tasted like retsina. The food was well prepared by Mother Evgenija, the nun who favoured fertility rites. It was certainly nourishing and did not pall if you ate it for three or four days as I did, but for the monks it must have been a long ordeal, and Father Simeon hurried to bring out the cut-glass decanter of *rakija* each evening.

Despite the hours spent at worship, and frequent forays to pay the accounts or to do monastery business in the nearest town, the Abbot was wide awake after supper. In the morning, as he went to catch the bus, he had seen a comet with a tail that streamed across the sky: 'The peasants say this means war, but really, there's no interruption in the wars nowadays, Israel and the Arabs, Vietnam, they go on all the time. . . .' His turn of mind is historical, and he likes to reflect on the characters of Eden or Aneurin Bevan or Churchill – here Father Simeon, who was reading *The Second World War*, joined in. They wanted to know the causes of violence in Northern Ireland. Then the Abbot talked about the spiritual life of the Serbian monk: of how he regretted there was no great mystical or devotional tradition for them to draw on. It was a pity that Serbia had severed itself from Greek influence in the 19th century. They had needed to send monks to Greece or Russia to enrich their interior life. He added that St Sava, the founder of his own monastery, had very well understood the Serbian mentality: everywhere else monks had to take a vow of absolute poverty, but St Sava gave Serbian monks pocket-money, because he knew it was easier for 'our people'.

The religious life must always be hard to understand for an outsider, all the more so if one comes from the Western Church to visit the Eastern. At Studenica the educated monks were open-minded, but

4 Mileševa: the Virgin of the Annunciation

5 Sopoćani: a group of Apostles from the Dormition, which dominates the west wall of the nave

6 Near Mileševa: a village mosque at Hisardžik, with the ruined Byzantine fortress above

7 Žiča monastery: most of the buildings are painted dark red in imitation of monasteries on Mt Athos

this was rare. The Serbian Orthodox monasteries are marked by a devout simplicity, and at times this simplicity makes for problems. Usually the novices come from pious local families who are honoured to have a child accepted at a famous monastery. In England, girls and boys used to be sent up to work at the great house; in Serbia, God is Lord of the Manor. Monks and nuns are hard-working but often of low intelligence and unable to absorb whatever basic schooling State and Church have offered them. Nuns especially can be bigots. Once I failed to cross myself in Orthodox fashion, and a nun ranted at me that I was a heretic of heretics. Book-learning is generally opposed. A young nun studying English gave up under pressure from the older sisters: 'It won't make you pray any better.' This is nothing new: in the 18th century the monk Dositej ran away because his Latin lessons were stopped. The Abbot of Studenica was right. The Serbian Church has always been isolated. The Ottomans, the mountains and a certain native obstinacy have made it so. In its closed medieval universe, the subjects most talked about were miracles and farming. It was a world within the other world of contemporary Yugoslavia, and to come out of it was to stride across the centuries with seven-league boots on.

Despite occasional ructions, I remember the monasteries as safe strongholds of peace. Going up the long valleys to Kalenić or Studenica was like making a pilgrimage to the end of the world, while Sretenje was perched on a crag half-way to heaven and inhabited by nuns as ethereal as angels. So it should be. Earth and Paradise are brought close together in Orthodox worship, and the monasteries serve as a tangible invitation to faith.

At Studenica, as elsewhere, the monastery provided a focus for the whole district.* Father Sava, the young monk in gumboots, acted as parish priest, and the conversation at the evening meal among the five or six monks present was often about who was ill, who had died, in the neighbouring villages. Father Sava had a motorcycle bought out of farm profits, and with this he could cover a lot of ground in one day. Because it was Lent, many people wanted their houses blessed and sprinkled with holy water before Easter. He would come back having been to forty houses. The villages consisted of scattered hill farms and it had taken him from dawn till dusk, 1500 ft up and down rough tracks.

* Even its buildings are still copied. In 1970, the stonemason at Studenica, Belisarius, put up for himself a new house which has eleven cell-like rooms and a dining-hall to hold thirty 'for feast-days'.

This was one side of the monastery life: the blessings, the funerals in the mud, an old woman struggling down the hillside to take Communion on Sunday, and the people who were given shelter within the monastery: a weakly young man, and an old widower, Branko, who worked in the fields. Years before, when we had come briefly to Studenica, we had seen an idiot boy being baited at a church feast in the courtyard by local youths until a monk drove them away; a moment so uncannily reminiscent of *Boris Godunov* that Richard and I had looked at each other without a word. The monks at Studenica, like many country people in Serbia, seemed to be carrying out the Corporal Works of Mercy described in their Prayer Book: 'To feed the hungry . . . To harbour the homeless. To visit the sick . . . To bury the dead.'

The care given to the needy in Serbian monasteries was given to everyone. If I left to go on a long car journey alone, I would be asked by Father Simeon to send a postcard announcing my safe arrival. This protective concern is limited to children in the ordinary world; but the monastic mind assumes each person to be a child of God.

2

ST SAVA'S CAVE: THE HERMIT RAPHAEL

An elderly guide – journey to the hermitages – return to Studenica – the gateway grave

Of the ten monks at Studenica, not all lived in the monastery. Once, in a Belgrade drawing-room, someone had told me of seeing three anchorites, in black habits and cowls which almost hid their faces, swinging into the King's Church for the Liturgy, and afterwards hurrying away up the hillside. 'They live in holes or caves in the mountains,' he said; 'old men. They must be misanthropes.' No one else knew anything about them, it seemed, except an elderly friend born nearby; he gave one hermit's name as Raphael and said he had lived up there a long time and was, well, shrewd.

My time flowed by, rhythmically and quickly. I asked the Abbot if Raphael would resent a woman visiting him? 'No, not a bit, he likes company.' The old man named Branko was sent for as a guide. He was upset to be visiting the holy man in his working clothes, but the Abbot gave him no time to change into his Sunday best.

A rough road, edged by lime-kilns, led up the valley. It had been raining hard; Branko wore sandals and grumbled as he picked his way through the mud. We passed a farm; the owner called out warmly: 'Uncle Branko! Where have you been all this long time?' We took *rakija* with him; my presence was explained. At the next farm, a mile on, the same thing happened, and the next, and the next. . . . Branko, now more cheerful, told me he was a childless widower; at his wife's death ten years before, he had had no family to go to, so he moved up from the small town to work and live at Studenica. Branko was a casualty from the kinship network; he had exchanged one pattern of life for another. He was not well-off, nor was he lonely; he got his daily bread from the monks and his self-respect from his neighbours, with whom his age was a passport to friendship.

The sun came out. Below us wheatfields sprouted, thinly green and translucent, and slopes of dark tilth made ready for maize-planting went down to the rocky bed of the river, now in spate. On the hills ahead, a marble quarry cut a clean square out of the forests. Crossing a bridge, we came to the monks' flourmill, set over a raging torrent, with a mill-race to one side. Further on, a track turned off to the right into an Alpine side-valley, where cows swished their tails and mumbled mouthfuls of flowery turf. At the head of the valley a Turkish house appeared, its upper storey projecting over bright blue wooden pillars. The lower hermitage, said Branko, taking a zigzag path through the woods, thick with primroses and violets. He struck up an old song about St Sava, and his quarrels with his father about becoming a monk. I sang back 'Tom Bowling', '. . . about a soul who went to heaven'. Bowling did, after all, go aloft. 'Just like the radio,' said Branko. 'Now some of your Liturgy.' I gave him the Magnificat; we were going steeply uphill and it came in breathy gusts of sound. Branko told me he had a *gusle* at home, he would play it to me later. He spoke some of the songs; he plainly could not chant them without the accompaniment he was used to.

Below the house we found Fathers Kasijan and Teoktist collecting wood. They told us to call in on the way back from Raphael, for they were as busy as bees. The woodshed was already half-full of logs stacked up for winter, some fruit-trees had been newly grafted, the twigs tightly bound in branches split like clothes-pegs. Behind the house the path went on up through the woods. It was mid-morning and the sun beat down hotly through bare branches just nubbed with green. The Swiss touches in the landscape went on: the path was so well-kept, and nailed to treetrunks were rustic poker-work signs in Cyrillic: 'To the upper hermitage of St Sava.' Suddenly we emerged onto the other face of the mountain, a cliff of white marble dropping sheer into the Studenica valley below. A path wide enough for a horse had been notched into it, and a great many flowers had settled in the pockets of scree: silvery aromatics, yellow primulas with hairy leaves, sedums and saxifrages. Round the next corner, the cliff curved inwards to form a natural amphitheatre whose walls rose 900 ft above the river. On the far side, level with us, a bulging plastered beehive, four storeys high, was slapped against the rock – Raphael's dwelling. I could see a long wooden pier, built up from a narrow ledge below on columns of hewn rock mortared together. This led round the rock-face as far as the hermitage. A new gate and bell-tower barred the path. Branko pulled the rope, and a bell clanged out across the abyss and echoed back to us. A flock of birds flew up from the depths, but nothing else happened. We went through the gate. Chunks of marble were piled at the side of the path. We reached a small chapel at the entrance to the pier. Branko holloaed at the beehive. A window was thrown open and a voice shouted back. Then Raphael appeared at the door of his house, a tall old monk with a matted white beard and a greenish-black cassock. He came closer. Everything about him was slightly askew – his hat, the set of his eyes – and this gave him a jolly, untidy look.

'You were a long time coming,' said Branko grumpily.

'Welcome, welcome! Of course I was a long time, I was on the top floor, putting something to rights, had to come all the way down. Who've you brought with you?'

'An Englishwoman. Have you any thread? I want to mend my coat.' He clutched the lapels to his neck. 'I would have put on a better one if I'd known I was coming to see you, Father.'

'Well, there's needle and thread inside.'

He led us further along the pier, through a wooden-roofed dining-room which he had built over it. The structure jutted out over the precipice, and you could sit and gaze through the glass windows at a startling view: the white cliff to which a few saplings clung curved out to right and left, but in the centre there was only air for a long way, until the eye met the mountains which rose south of the river. Farms stood on their lower slopes: at night the hermit must have been able to watch the lights, far away beneath him.

'It's the finest dining-room in Serbia,' I said to Raphael.

'I'll tell them that at the monastery, next time I go down.' He smiled, and his smile was slightly askew as well.

We entered the house through a door set sideways in the rock. Raphael first went to live there thirty years ago, and was rising seventy. It was an empty ruin when he came. The hermitage is shaped like a boat, being built against concave rock, and Raphael has made a landing and a room on each floor, with stout wooden ladders for a staircase, so it is very much like being on board ship, and Raphael is as handy as any sailor; his carpenter's saws hung on the wall. He is a good mason, and the blocks of marble on the path were for his tomb, which he is hacking out of the rock just beyond the front door. He built the pier; earlier, a very long ladder had been the only access to the hermitage. Inside on the landing, he had hollowed a small cellar out of the rock. The Abbess at Ljubostinja, sixty miles away, told me he had taken her wine, five kilograms of it, saying: 'I won't pay you, but I'll pray for you and your nuns, all the year.' Sure enough, a large wicker-covered demijohn was just visible. Everything was in beautiful order. In the ground-floor kitchen, pots and pans hung neatly on the wall; a rack held cups and glasses covered with a cloth. On the first floor was his original dining-room, on the second floor a spare room – 'It's not quite finished yet' (like most spare rooms?) – and on the third floor his own living quarters, warmed by an old iron stove with a flue that led through the roof – or rather, the top of the convex outer wall. The room was more or less wallpapered in icons. Branko and I sat on Raphael's wooden bed which had a straw palliasse. The hermit made coffee for us, putting the brass *džezva* inside the stove to boil. 'Please, can I have that needle?' asked Branko. Raphael found it and some cotton in a pile of his belongings. Branko started sewing himself into his jacket. Raphael gave us very good coffee. He was from Šumadija, and spoke a beautiful clear Serbian. I asked him why he had become a hermit. He had been a monk further south, he said, when he grew dissatisfied with the world:

'In my youth women had long sleeves and long skirts, and look at them now, some of them have skirts shorter than thine, Anna, and sleeves above the elbow. And then, brother quarrels with brother. You've done well not to have any children: no one can count on having a good son any longer. That earthquake at Banja Luka now, it was the judgement of God: He was warning them. In the old days, people worked hard to go to Heaven. They don't any longer.'

His world was full of medieval horrors and marvels: a child had just been born to a girl aged twelve – he had read it in the papers. Raphael was not so much cut off from the outer world as insulated from it. He knew the local bus timetables by heart, and which part of the muddy road we had followed would be tarmacked over by the next year. He certainly saw people from the villages, as many come to the chapel for its *slava* on St George's Day, and the sick make pilgrimages there. They put money on the place where St Sava's ribs are supposed to have dented the rock as he slept, and drink the delicious water from his 'Barrel', a spring caught in a cistern below the house. They make a vow to give something to the hermitage if they recover. Raphael also showed us fifteen litres of corn oil, which someone had brought him. It is an ancient privilege, confirmed even by Turkish decrees, for these anchorites to receive wine and oil in exchange for their prayers. Raphael was a holy man living in a sacred place, and he knew his dues. When we left him, he asked me to post him half a kilo of good incense from England, and I did.

Legends of St Sava have grown up naturally in these surroundings. He meets the Devil on a mountain path, and outwits him in growing onions (the only vegetable that will flourish there today). When a snake tries to kill a sleeping shepherd girl, he turns it to stone. Possibly St Sava did spend some time here, for the chapel of St George dates from the 12th century, and St Sava came to Studenica from Mount Athos with its anchorite tradition. The hermitage is certainly medieval, and has been in use since, though Raphael liked to deny this. In 1813, when the Turks set fire to Studenica, a monk named Sofronius fled to the cave, taking with him many precious manuscripts. When, in fear of his life, he had to move on, he burnt all this treasure to ashes, not wishing it to fall into heathen hands.

A refuge from one's enemies or the world, this place, with its white cliffs and circling birds and gulfs of air, peopled only by Raphael and his companions; the black squirrel whom I saw frisking along the crags, and a green lizard enamelled onto stone in the sun.

Branko was starving. We hurried down hill to Father Kasijan. Over lunch, Branko begged him for *rakija*.

'You shouldn't have any till evening,' the monk said reprovingly.

'I'm worn out. I can't walk home without it,' said Branko piteously.

'All right, then.' Out came the bottle, and Branko began to revive. Father Kasijan apologized for the bread, which was burnt and a bit doughy in the middle: 'You see, I went out, and Father Teoktist is young, he doesn't quite understand the oven yet. If I'd been at home, this would never have happened.' Father Teoktist steered clear of us, and went on chopping wood outside. Father Kasijan is a compulsive talker, a hermit of merely three years' standing. He likes to commune with the birds and the beasts; now that morning he'd seen a bird sitting on a heap of wood; it had wonderful eyes and an air of great wisdom. He is strongly anti-Catholic: why did they have to invent Purgatory when there is nothing in Holy Scripture to prove it? Rather zenophobic, too: St Sava freed the Church from 'those Greeks'.

We left Father Kasijan, Branko carrying a sack of apples the Abbot had ordered. He lagged behind, then insisted on stopping to see a farmer who gave him more *rakija*. He put on speed: 'You and I make good company,' he said, 'very good company.' Soon the apples bothered him. He saw another house: 'Let's stop again.' I took the apples and walked on. Branko, after all, looked frail. I lost sight of him, but as I reached the monastery, he panted up level with me. Appearances were preserved for Father Simeon and the Abbot talking on the steps.

'Branko's tired out,' I murmured.

'Branko travels well,' the Abbot replied.

The last glimpse of the monastery is of the eastern gateway. As I drove away next morning, I could see the two tombstones beside it, the graves not of royalty but of ordinary people from the neighbourhood. One belongs to a mechanic who died in 1899: the inscription is crammed tight onto a narrow slab of stone:

At Studenica here
In his five-and-
twentieth year
Here he lies
entombed, forlorn
in the place where
he was born.
He his mother's
arms forsook
for into his young
head he took
the notion that
away he'd fly
and life in the wide
world would try
everywhere things
worked out well
he gained friends
Then, change befell
He grew ill and
medicine sought
But his span of
life was short
Much do grieve
his family
Djunisija, God
pardon thee.

3

ŽIČA: ARCHBISHOP AND ABBESS

The castle of Maglić – nuns on the farm – a Sunday service – the Bishop's palace – the life of St Sava – frescoes of heaven and earth

The road out of Studenica passes a sawmill smelling of pinewood and goes down to the Ibar gorge, where I turned north, trying vainly to spot Lawrence Durrell's figtree, which he mentions in a children's story about this region.* There *are* figtrees here, the botanists say: Dubrovnik merchants, who used the sheltered valley for a trade route, introduced them. As a consolation, great bushes of yellow broom, tipped with red, flamed out from the grey rock. The road twisted to reveal a fortress which towered over the river from a grassy hilltop, nicked by a defensive ditch. The lame ferryman was in his hut. He hauled me across the river in a punt, by using an overhead line, while the water sucked and swirled below. He stopped at his home on the opposite bank: a farm with one vivid green field. The path up to the castle led through purple hellebores and wild lilac in bud. Inside the thick walls, it was windless: scented violets grew everywhere. Straight ahead were low walls, the remains of an audience chamber with steps going down to a crypt beneath. On the left are the ruins of St George's Church; a pillared niche shows a trace of scarlet paint from a vanished fresco.

Maglić is very ancient, possibly Roman in origin. Its greatest days were in the 14th century, when Archbishop Danilo II of Žiča, the friend of King Milutin and Queen Simonida, rebuilt it. He made himself a fortified palace there, put up the church and cells for the monks. Maglić is spacious, as an archbishop's palace should be. Though it has little decoration, it must have had certain comforts: charcoal braziers for heating the rooms of Danilo and his monks, wax candles to light them. But Maglić is mainly a stronghold. Danilo knew something of the dangers of war, for as Abbot of Hilandar in 1307 he had been the hero of its terrible siege by the Catalan Company,

* *White Eagles over Serbia.*

Byzantine mercenaries turned pirate. One of his pupils has left a description. In the famine, men tore at the grass with their teeth. The Holy Mountain was sacked and 'mountains and caves, hills and valleys, and every road were full of dead bodies, naked and unburied, presenting a fearful and moving spectacle to the onlooker'. Danilo's own weakness and hunger made him feel 'as if he were in the body of a stranger' but he escaped to Skopje with some of the monastery treasure for King Milutin. He sent men out by boat who bought and fetched back wheat and hired mercenaries from abroad to fight 'those thrice-accursed heretics'. In the end he beat them off, and sent his king as spoils of war the commander's armour worked in gold. This done, Danilo went off to be a hermit, like St Sava, until Milutin summoned him back to Serbia as Archbishop.

Probably because of Danilo's military experience, Maglić is different from other fortified monasteries in Serbia, such as the Holy Archangels near Prizren and Manasija off the Morava valley, which strike one as monastic buildings protected from marauders by their tightly-drawn girdle of walls and towers. Maglić by contrast is made for siege-warfare, a place from which you could throw powdered chalk into the enemy's eyes, or grab at his machines with long hooks and cables.

The castle spreads along the flattened top of a ridge 300 ft above the river. It is surrounded on three sides by water: the Ibar isolates it, west and north; a tributary stream, passing through a steep ravine, protected it from attack in the south. Its most vulnerable point is to the east, where the natural ridge continues. On that side the rock was excavated to make a deep moat. The donjon rises sheer above this; three strong towers face slightly southwest towards the valley, and there are four other towers set at intervals in the high wall of the keep, facing southeast or northwest. It is very solidly built, and stands in a strategic position as it commands the road that has been a major military route. It was used by Serbian insurgents in 1815, when a few of them fell on 1500 Turks marching northwards. The Germans in the Second World War built a blockhouse under it, whose battlements oddly imitate those of the castle above. By then, a railway line had also to be protected. Fortunately the people in the village of Maglić, who live among their plum-orchards on the hill across the road, helped to preserve the castle. They restored it in the early years of this century. All too many castles in Serbia have been pulled to bits by peasants who built their new houses out of the stones.

* * *

The Ibar, further down, turns sluggish as the gorge flattens towards the valley of the Western Morava. As I drove north from Maglić, I could see the red cupolas of Žiča rising on the far bank, and a road that circles round by Kraljevo bridge brought me there. I called on the Abbess, Mother Justina, and after the ritual coffee and jam, she showed me round. Because she is a dedicated farmer herself, she does not hide her concern for every corner of the property. The church and monastery are so windswept that she had planted firtrees for shelter: 'They've grown well; d'you remember, when you last came here (in 1959) how bare the ground looked?' She is small, rosy-faced and neat, with a friendly reserve that makes her all the more likeable, a woman with resources of her own to draw on. Although she appears so young, she has been Abbess for ten years. She uses her authority unobtrusively. As she told nuns to weed strawberries, and workmen to open up turf for a flowerbed, she reminded me of the headman's wife, in the old Serbian *zadruge*, who would dole out daily tasks to daughters, daughters-in-law, cousins and nieces.

In Orthodox religious life, farming and worship coexist. Some monks like Father Sava at Studenica may go out to the parishes, but most nuns are peasant women who learn to read just enough to follow the services; teachers and nurses are rare. The nuns are bidden to work – that means to hoe and plant and sometimes even to plough – and to pray. At one level, they live rather as their own families do. With both monks and nuns, I was conscious of being on a farm: one of the pleasantest things in the monasteries is the mixture of trimness and untidiness in the right places: snowy bed-linen and spotless floors within, while outside, hens run squawking away and pigs sun themselves undisturbed in the dust.

Mother Justina took me down below the monastery to the river lands where she grows wheat and maize in rotation. The path ran through orchards of peach and apple in swelling bud. She shook her head: 'That fencing is not what it should be.' In the early 14th century, Archbishop Danilo II, farmer as well as soldier, had planted these same fields with 'the plenteous fruit of each tree which nourishes man'. Destruction by war and replanting has alternated ever since. Žiča was so accessible that it was often plundered. If Studenica ranks first, then Žiča must have ranked richest, in the days when Stephen the First-Crowned set it up by charter with a gift of fifty-odd villages, eight mountains and more than 200 shepherd families, Maglić being thrown in, and some land as far away as Lake Skadar, on the present

Albanian frontier. Nowadays Žiča, like Studenica, has just sixty hectares of land – thirty arable and thirty woodland – because it is a 'first-class historical monument'.

We had reached a farmyard, close by the river. On the whole, livestock in monasteries get better care than those on the average peasant holding, and here, in the late afternoon, a nun was feeding plump white chickens. Two sheds held tethered cows of different breeds: one Swiss, a Friesian heifer and some less distinguished beasts.

'Native, you could call them,' said Mother Justina; 'I try to improve the herd, little by little, each year. How much does a milking-machine cost if you buy it in England? I would so like to have one: it would make work much easier for my sisters. Do the cows remain calm when it's in use?'

A couple of horses were next door to the cows, and in an old barn stood a barouche, in excellent order. We saw goats and kids, sheep and lambs, all thriving under cover in the cold April weather. Two fierce snarling dogs, one yellow, one black, were tied up close in the yard, and set free at night to keep guard. Although they had food and a kind of shelter, they did not share in the general good treatment, perhaps because they were non-productive.

We went onto the stewpond, of which the Abbess is proud just as a medieval abbess in England might have been. She had brought some bread with her, to make the fish rise, and we walked along a rickety pier to drop crumbs into the water. Some of the bread lodged in clumps of reed. A solitary carp came up for a nibble. The rest stayed down, unwisely waiting for the warm summer sun, when the nuns hold carp-feasts under the willow-trees.

Back through the monastery again, and to the graveyard, set on a knoll across the road. Monks lay there, their bodies brought home to Žiča from Studenica or Hilandar – and a few nuns. Before the Second World War, Žiča had been a men's community, but the Germans killed the monks, and after the war, as elsewhere, nuns came to replace them. I saw no memorial to the massacre, only a renewal of peace: the beehives ranged in a sheltered corner, and a pyramid of long shiny acorns for sheep-fodder beside them.

Two nuns were making candles in a little house, workmen's quarters. One showed me the oblong metal frame with thread tied across it at intervals – like a squared-off harp – which she was dipping and dipping into melted beeswax, till the coated thread thickened into slim brown columns, to be cut off when cold and sold to church-goers. Then the

Abbess pushed open a door in the further wall and there was a plum-tree, its white petals touching a wooden table and bench beneath, vineyards and woods beyond. Below us were green watermeadows flecked with sheep, and to the north, the dark hills of Šumadija. We rested a little and talked again about her management problems. She had no tractor or car, only a cart and the two horses I had seen, for getting into Kraljevo to buy whitewash. With their own fruit, vegetables, grain and flourmills, the community are more or less self-supporting. This is a pattern common to most monasteries. During the winter the nuns use knitting-machines, and are paid to make up garments for local women. (Serbia, like England, is cardigan-country.) A few nuns are too old to work but a novice or two come each year from the district, and 'we are very careful about whom we take'. One friend saw a group of these making their religious profession at Žiča, and described the Abbess' entry into the church: she wore a vast pleated cloak, under which four novices sheltered – an act full of ancient symbolism.

It was getting late, and the next day was Sunday. 'You are fortunate,' said Mother Justina, 'our Bishop is back from the Synod at Belgrade. A great many people will come to church tomorrow.' I went off and found myself a bed at Vrnjačka Banja, an agreeable spa nearby.

Outside the monastery gateway on Sunday the wind blew bitterly cold, and a man was cleaning his car there, oblivious of the weather and of the chanting that sounded from within. Žiča has been much restored. Its exterior is no longer beautiful, but it remains impressive. A high wall encloses all the buildings, most of them reddish; as you go in, on the left is the Bishop's palace, a pseudo-Byzantine block of harsh carmine brick, built post-war and a source of local admiration, and in the very centre of the enclosure stands St Sava's church of the Holy Saviour, with its towers and cupolas, painted a deep red in imitation of the churches on Mount Athos.

Deep within the church, down a tunnel of arches, was a round star-cluster of light, and as I went closer, it separated out into the dotted points of altar-candles. Smoking incense veiled the scene behind the open doors of the iconostasis, where priestly figures moved in shadow: the white-bearded Bishop, two priests and a deacon with him. Their brocaded vestments shone silkily out of the darkness, and when at times a jewelled crown was placed on the Bishop's head, the stones in it blazed out, caught by candle rays. Nuns were singing resonantly behind a red velvet curtain in the south transept, from which they moved to and fro: they had changed from being aproned familiar figures to remote participants in the service. Once the Abbess and another nun, with tall black hats on top of their veils, led forward a very young sister with a towel draped over her shoulders, while the Bishop was washing his hands after the Liturgy. Her head was bowed, and she stood passive as a beast of burden until the towel was taken from her. In the congregation, where men and women stood apart from each other, the smell of soap downed even the incense.

Afterwards the Bishop waited in front of his palace and the nuns filed up to kiss his hand. Mother Justina and I had coffee with Bishop Vasilije in his parlour, a formal occasion, rather like taking coffee with an Old Testament prophet, his beard was so white, his air so venerable, his voice so deep. He went off by car to Kraljevo, and the Abbess showed me his house: lemon-trees in the hall, peacock-feathers in the bedrooms, on the landing an oleograph with black devils grinning out of Hell, and an old map of Palestine. She unlocked the Library, where Serbian saints' lives stood next to the works of John Dos Passos and Saul Bellow in English. Monastery libraries contain a strange medley; in another, I found the score of *Madame Butterfly*. The guest-wing had furniture given by a single family: a complete bourgeois interior, with faded cretonnes, Chinese ivories and a plate from the 1851 Exhibition. It had an empty orderliness: the furniture stood at right-angles to the walls, the muslin curtains were starched but the portraits hung crazily crooked. 'Only his Grace's visitors sleep here,' said the Abbess respectfully, and closed the door.

It was St Sava who made Žiča a bishop's seat. He began to build the monastery in 1208 – his royal brother Stephen was its founder – when he was living at Studenica, and it was a part of his grand design to establish Serbia in Europe with a church and kingdom of her own. After the Crusaders had occupied Constantinople in 1204, the Byzantine Emperor retired to Nicaea, and it was there in 1219 at the court of Theodore Lascaris that the ecumenical Patriarch consecrated St Sava archbishop, and sent him home again with a present of mules and purple saddles to go with them.

St Sava became a lawgiver who drew up Codes for Church and State. He held Councils of Bishops at Žiča, though their proceedings now make dusty reading. St Sava built churches on field and plain and hill. Most important of all, he ensured the Nemanjid succession, first by reconciling his brothers Stephen and Vukan, and, after Stephen's death, by crowning a nephew, Radoslav – whom he did not much love – at Žiča. As an old man he grew weary of his duties, handed over his see to a former pupil and set off as a simple pilgrim to the Holy Land. His last known letter, to the Abbot of Studenica, was sent from Jerusalem, which he was happy to have reached. He ends:

> . . . if God gives me a little strength, I will go to Alexandria, to the Patriarchate, to show reverence to St Mark. And thence I shall go to Mount Sinai, and when I return, if I am alive and God permits, I shall be with you by the Spring.

But he died on the way home, while on a visit to the Bulgarian Tsar, and it was only his body that returned to Serbia, by royal request, and became an object of veneration at the monastery of Mileševa. Today churches as far apart as Seattle and Birmingham and Perth in Australia are named after St Sava of Serbia.

Now that the congregation had gone, I could look closely at the church, which had first been painted according to St Sava's instructions. What is left is a fine bare church, its cupola sparsely patch-worked with frescoes.* There is very little painting left from St Sava's time, because the monastery was sacked by the Bulgarians about 1290. But a great deal was restored by an active Archbishop some ten years later, and the painters were careful to keep to the monumental spirit of the earlier work. While it is tragic that so little remains of the original frescoes, Yugoslav art historians have scrupulously reconstructed their arrangement from hints and signs, and with their help enough can be made out to imagine St Sava's church. His plan was highly individual. In Serbian medieval churches, the founders have almost always left the mark of their own personality. St Sava after 1219 wanted an Archbishop's church, didactic and monastic in feeling: the bishops who are left round the altar stand grave and simple. On the southeast wall St Cyril wears the same kind of cap, pulled right down on his forehead, as Father Simeon does at Studenica. It is odd, this procession of Bishops where the Double Communion should be: St Sava had them moved skywards from their usual position on the wall, and put a whole portrait gallery of more bishops in painted frames below. In the south

* It is not easy to wander about in this church as the nuns have railed off the space under the cupola to keep their choir-stalls private. If you can find a copy of the book *Žiča*, by Milan Kašanin and others, it is a revelation to look at the detailed photographs there.

transept are some fine figures of the Apostles. Peter's hand is raised in the precise, three-fingered blessing of the Orthodox; Luke is neatly tonsured. Round the nave are the saints: hermits and wonder-workers, doctors of the Church and holy warriors – bearing witness, and gesturing with finely-shaped hands. On the south wall is a reminder of the Crucifixion: the Virgin with the Christ-Child has an angel to her left who carries the instruments of the Passion. On her right is a huge, magnificent figure of St Nicholas. On the west wall, low down, is the Christ-Child in medallion, between two angels royally dressed (an early motif in Byzantine art, rarely found in this later period) where the curve of the angels' arms echoes the curving circle above. Up on the west wall, the Dormition of the Virgin is a 14th-century restoration: perhaps because of this, it is less freely painted than the same subject in the King's Church; the body of St Paul, at the foot of the Virgin's bier, is bent into a right-angle. Yet the head of Christ, and the pose in which he holds the little winged Psyche which does duty for the Virgin's soul, are beautiful in the extreme. The colouring is warm: browns and reds and golds interspersed with dark blue and white. A later earthquake has cleft the whole composition vertically like the crack of doom.

In the side-chapels, the patron saints of the two royal brothers were portrayed: St Stephen Martyr to the south, St Sava of Jerusalem to the north. If you pass from the nave into the south chapel, there is a painting of St Stephen Martyr's sarcophagus being taken to the Emperor Constantine at Byzantium on the south wall. The scene to the right, where the relics leave Jerusalem, upheld by four worthies of the church, has a strong rhythm based on the repetitive movement of the braced heads and hands and bodies which support the coffin. The colouring is clear and subtle: blue, gold, white, mostly. Going out of the church, you find the exo-narthex, once a council chamber, whitewashed, the architecture altered. Probably the original church had two storeys above the exo-narthex, which along with the tower formed the Bishop's residence. On the first floor of the tower, a chapel survives from the mid-13th century, with some frescoes, notably of Constantine and Helena, done in provincial style and commissioned by King Radoslav, who was also responsible for the vanished frescoes in the exo-narthex. The architecture of Žiča belongs to a theocracy when a bishop could live 'above the church' (as the Patriarchs had done long ago in Constantinople) and when he and his brother the king both expected to use the narthex of the church for their Councils.

8 Sopoćani: seen from the hills above

9 Sopoćani: nuns, priests, Bishop and congregation in procession round the church on St Cosmas' and St Damian's Day

10 Golija valley: half forest, half open downland, with a *koliba* in the foreground

Some of the most interesting paintings that are left are to be found as you come out under the tower into the porch. Like so much else at Žiča, they have to do with the medieval Serbian Church. The present paintings date from the time of King Milutin. I faced outwards and saw on the west tympanum a firm reminder to churchmen of their duties. There are Christ and his disciples: Christ's left hand grasps, pincer-like, the head of a stocky small boy with large feet – an illustration of St Matthew: 'Except ye be converted, and become as little children, ye shall not enter the kingdom of heaven.' I looked back towards the church and on the inner surface of the arch, to the north, a gigantic St Peter holds the Church of God above his head, like Atlas with a globe, and to the south, St Paul raises high the book of Christian doctrine. An edifying story of the Forty Martyrs of Sebaste, who suffered freezing to death for their faith, is painted on the south and north walls, and the original charter of the monastery is written out under it. So far, all these subjects are ecclesiastical, but the east wall goes on to stress the unity of Church and State. On either side of the doorway are the founders of Žiča, Radoslav left, Stephen the First-Crowned, right.* Above them the Virgin is enthroned with Christ; the three kings, the angels and the shepherds are clear enough, but one peers to decipher the other figures. Here the Orthodox Liturgy will help, and an ancient hymn written for Christmas Eve:

> All that hath breath praises Thee . . .
> What shall we offer Thee, O Christ . . . ? The angels offer Thee a hymn; the heavens a star; the Magi, gifts; the shepherds, their wonder; the earth, its cave; the wilderness, the manger; and we offer Thee, a Virgin Mother.[1]

The two graceful, swaying women beneath the Virgin's medallion are Earth and Wilderness bearing gifts. Below, Milutin and his courtiers join in this hymn of thanksgiving, as do his archbishop and his clerics, the men with high hats and trailing ribbons on the left. The whole porch is like a solemn joyous dance, in which St Peter and St Paul, Earth and Wilderness, the martyrs, the angels, Milutin and his people take part. It is a fitting entrance to St Sava's church. His foundations each speak in their own language. The Virgin's Church at Studenica says: 'Here lie dead kings in hope of the Resurrection' and Žiča: 'Behold the power of the Church on earth.'

* Those in search of curiosities should look at the donors' portraits in the modern church dedicated to St Sava: (Nicholas II of Russia, ermine-caped, who sent the painters), and in the chapel over the main gateway (three stout brothers in their best suits, merchants from Kraljevo).

4

THROUGH THE SANDŽAK

Mileševa and St Sava's Tomb – the Minaret of Hisardžik – Jerena's castle – a Moslem wedding procession – Novi Pazar – buying a carpet – St George's Towers

The monastery where St Sava's own body was enshrined, Mileševa, on the borders of Bosnia and the Sandžak, lies beside an ancient trade route from Dubrovnik to Byzantium. Merchants and ambassadors, secret agents and antiquarians passed this way, and reading their memoirs is like turning over the pages of a visitor's book with frank comments in English, Italian, Turkish and Russian. Richard, a French friend, Anne Lissac, and myself followed in their tracks.

Mileševa is cupped in a wooded valley, just where the old road begins to climb into the mountains. The whole enclosure looked inviting as we drove up. The whitewashed church was tinkered with in the last century. Buildings press close to it: a red-tiled Turkish house, the belfry with its ribbed grey roof and the low monastery block. When we arrived, village people were drawing water at the well. The nuns' garden felt very sheltered. Monastery gardens in Serbia grow the plants of Elizabethan England: at Easter you stand among quince-trees in flower with crown imperials at your feet. Now it was a warm summer evening and the air was scented with a profusion of Madonna lilies and round pink roses.

A long table and benches stood ready for allcomers. Most people walk to church from so far away that they must eat before they go home again. We joined the group who were drinking coffee in front of the monastery doorway. An old white-bearded priest, a peasant and a nun sat there. The priest was from Čačak, a provincial town. When he heard we came from Belgrade, he gave us a long homily on the sinfulness of life in the capital, while the peasant, thoroughly drunk, his nose as red as a poppy, said nothing, only nodded his head regularly like a metronome in agreement with the priest's words. The three of us relaxed happily; it was, said Anne, because we'd stepped back a hundred years in a moment. Then came difficulties. Sister Anna displayed a sour caution towards foreigners – the Abbess was away, our letter hadn't arrived – but when she heard we had brought our own food, her reserve lifted and she said we could stay the night. Mileševa is no longer rich, and the fear of giving inadequate hospitality lurks there as in other places. The soil is poor, and the neighbourhood is strongly Moslem, all of which means fewer gifts in money and kind from the people. I could see a minaret slicing the sky in a dip between two hills. Then the light faded and we went to bed.

We slept well between stiff clean sheets. In the morning we talked French, as Anne, whose English is perfect, cannot stand foreign languages on an empty stomach. But she had to, for when we carried our provisions into the kitchen, the nun who cooked us breakfast was a Serbian chatterbox:

'Last year, I went on a pilgrimage to Jerusalem, and saw the new hotel the Americans have built there. It was lovely, too; I ask myself if I'm not spoilt now, after seeing that kind of thing.'

She came from Sarajevo and talked about Ivo Andrić's novels. She took us round the church and was knowledgeable about the frescoes, though she did not stay long as she had to go back to her work. It was a mystery how she had ended up as cook at Mileševa, but a pleasure too as her cooking was very good indeed.

A monk called Naum was also staying at Mileševa. I found him sitting in the nave, surrounded by sardine-tins full of paint, while he copied a scene off the walls for the Fresco Gallery in Belgrade. The sardine-tins were full of his own mixtures, which he preferred to modern paints as being nearer the original colours. When a young man he had learnt how to make them from old Russian monks at the icon-painting school. They had taught him to use plants and even different kinds of earth, the strongest *rakija* to set the gold used for haloes and the tooth of a wild boar for smoothing things over. An ordinary pig's tooth would serve as well, he had found.*

* The techniques of Byzantine fresco-painting are different from those of icon-painting. Icons are usually painted in tempera on a base of size and whitening, a process known to ancient Egyptian and Minoan art. The fresco-painters learnt most from the Romans' skill in lime technology. They used a base of lime mixed with straw and had to work quickly before the lime dried out, so plaster joins can often be traced along the 'frames' of scenes. For colours, they used ochre, haematite, terre-verte, chalk, carbon and cobalt. Their preliminary drawings consisted of incised lines in the plaster. Sometimes, as at Mileševa, a wax or oil-based medium was used for faces. The Athonite monk Dionysos of Fourna wrote a delightful and traditional *Painter's Guide*, probably in the 16th century. It is translated by A. M. Didron, in *Manuel d'Iconographie Chrétienne* (Paris, 1845).

Mileševa became St Sava's tomb partly by chance. King Vladislav, the second son of Stephen the First-Crowned, had it built and painted as his own mausoleum, and St Sava encouraged him, about 1234, to endow Mileševa with such munificence that it ranked second in the land; Studenica being first. After St Sava's death in Bulgaria, Vladislav had his remains brought to Mileševa, the bodily presence of the saint being a great prop to the Nemanjid dynasty. A pupil of Sava's wrote a service for the occasion:

> . . . King Vladislav
> as did once the prophet David
> leapt high before the sacred shrine,
> dancing and making merry,
> filled with joy and gladness
> to see his uncle
> come back to his own home.

Vladislav was to be forgotten soon after his death; Mileševa became famous as the shrine of St Sava for centuries to come.

Posterity is unfair, as usual, because the enduring loveliness of the church is due to Vladislav's plan for his own sepulchre. His tomb was placed under his portrait on the south wall of the nave: a young worried-looking king presented by the Mother of God to Christ. All round him were and are frescoes of great splendour. The architect he used probably came from the Adriatic coast, as there is a Romanesque feeling about the high walls and the cupola tacked on top, but one of the nave painters seems to have been from Byzantium and to have had a deep understanding of classical Greek art.*

We looked closely at two examples – one neglected, one well-known: the figure of St Stephen Martyr on the eastern side of the southwest pilaster, and, not far from him, on the south wall just above Vladislav, the Angel of the Empty Tomb. St Stephen is twice the size of the saints who flank him: he is godlike, massive and still. His features have little expression: they are reminiscent of finely sculptured stone. He stands out from a background which imitates gold mosaic, his draped robes, claret and blue-green, are simple, his deacon's towels a strip of jewelled gold stuff. He is at once Byzantine prince and Greek divinity. This is even more true of the Angel, with his rich colours (the fresco was fortunately protected by 16th-century overpainting) and perfect symmetry of feature. The Byzantine canons of beauty are so strictly

* Other painters at Mileševa were Slavs, for abbreviated instructions to them survive on the walls.

observed that this angel could very well illustrate Anna Comnena's description of Constantine Ducas, then her betrothed: 'He was blond, with a skin as white as milk, his cheeks suffused with red like some dazzling rose that has just left its calyx. His eyes were not light-coloured, but hawk-like, shining beneath the brows, like a precious stone set in a golden ring,' and he was 'seemingly endowed with a heavenly beauty not of this world'.[1] This angel has a grave cold gaze, a sure left arm which points to the tomb, a wide wing which overshadows the two shrinking women. His size and purity and power are awesome, and he hails from Mount Olympus rather than from the Christian heaven. In the nave at Mileševa, it is impossible to stop short at the courtly glory of Byzantium: we were drawn back into the oldest source of their art.

Not all the nave painting shares this magnificent conservatism. Mileševa is of its time: it belongs to an age of transition and is full of contrasts. Beneath the classical angel the little crumpled tired-out soldiers by the tomb, with their zigzag legs, are quite a different matter: in the realism of their painting they seem the distant forebears of Piero della Francesca's soldiers in the Resurrection at Borgo San Sepolcro. High on the south vault under the cupola, the Deposition from the Cross has elements of old and new. In its intensity of emotion the painting harks back to the Macedonian art of half a century earlier, but it has a new softness and fluidity of movement.* The gentleness of the women caressing the dead Christ is balanced by the matter-of-fact Nicodemus who is removing the nail from Christ's feet with a pair of pincers: he might be any craftsman performing a task intently and to the best of his ability. The gentleness is there again in the enchanting Virgin of the Annunciation of the south side of the altar-space: she is large-eyed and diffident, but her throne is Byzantine.

In the old narthex, one forgets the Greeks and Italians and remembers the Serbs – especially Serbian monasticism. St Sava's body once lay under his likeness on the east wall. To the north he is surrounded by remarkable portraits of Nemanjid kings, to the west, by saints. All the figures are emaciated, holy, ascetic, against an austere blue ground. Royalty here is devout and plain-living and knows nothing of the courtly glories shown in the nave. The life of monks and anchorites is extolled, perhaps on St Sava's advice. St Onofrius, a hermit, looks just as a medieval writer said he did:

* At Siena a small Deposition, No. 12 in the Pinacoteca, is very close in detail to this scene at Mileševa.

> . . . and I caught sight of a man far off . . . most fearful in form . . . all covered with thick hairs like a beast, and white as snow, for he was grizzled with age. And the hairs of his head and of his beard reached even to the ground and they covered his body like a garment. And he was girt at the hips with leaves from the plants of the wilderness.

The exo-narthex is different again. It is low and dark: a monumental charnel-house, as it is covered with frescoes of the Last Judgement. Christ sits in Glory with the angelic host on the east wall, pitiless angels drive lost souls to Hell on the south and the details are taken one after another from a famous Homily of St Ephraim the Syrian.

Time has turned Mileševa into a treasury of rich fragments; it can never have been all of a piece like some earlier or later churches, so sudden are the changes of technique and feeling from one part of the church to another – even from one wall to the next.

In a way these contrasts stress the church's own peculiar unity. All the frescoes were painted in Vladislav's lifetime, and Svetozar Radojčić sees in them a kind of royal biography: the pomp of Vladislav's accession to the throne, in the nave; the development of a deeper, more spiritual life in the narthex; and the gloom of the king's downfall in 1243 – when the third brother, Uroš, took the throne – in the apocalyptic exo-narthex. Once again, as at Žiča, the personality of the founder imposes itself on the traditional framework. Despite the stature of his saintly uncle, Vladislav has left his own monument.

The later records of Mileševa are packed with detail. Two medieval rulers of Bosnia were crowned there. Ivan the Terrible sent gifts to the monastery. Monks went to Venice in the 16th century, learnt printing and returned home to establish an important Cyrillic printing-press. They also bound, illuminated and copied books – all this in fear of Turkish oppression, and one monk finished his manuscript on 18 May 1508, 'in harsh times, under the rule of the wicked Emperor Bajazeth, who breaks the law, blasphemes the Holy Trinity and is insufferable to Christians'.

Travellers from Western Europe noted a curiosity: the bones of St Sava had become sacred to Jews and Moslems in the neighbourhood, who came to kiss the hand of the wonder-working saint. By putting gold and silver into his tomb, they gave more alms to the monastery than the Christians did. Henry Cavendish, Bess of Hardwick's son, went by way of Mileševa to Constantinople and his servant Fox wrote: 'Yt may be thought that thys patryarck was a great taker when he was alyve that takes so much being dead.'[2] Soon after, in 1595, the Turkish authorities got to hear that their fellow Moslems 'believed in St Sava and were crossing themselves' and that St Sava had revenged himself on the Turks by causing their defeat in Hungary. They removed St Sava's body and burnt it on Vračar hill at Belgrade. The Serbs relate that amid tempest and hail of fantastic violence, the saint's body rose above the pyre and hovered in the sky like a little cloud.*

Some years ago archaeologists uncovered at Prizren the remains of the medieval Serbian Emperor Dušan. He was reburied in Belgrade, at the Patriarch's wish, not in the Cathedral church by the river but at St Mark's on Vračar. In the late 17th century, when monastery after monastery went up in flames, Mileševa suffered the same fate, and her monks joined the great migrations northwards. Most of them went to Szentendre, the Serbian settlement north of Budapest started by wealthy merchants. Mileševa was rediscovered by 19th-century travellers. In 1857 the Russian Consul at Sarajevo, Alexander Hilferding, visited the monastery and found it a ruin. Only ten years later, still under the Turks, restoration work began. In 1881 the young archaeologist Arthur Evans, then a Balkan correspondent for the *Manchester Guardian*, told his readers,

> 'for blended force and grace, nothing that I have seen of Giotto's excels the Angel of the Resurrection on the walls of the royal Servian foundation of Mileševa.'[3]

The Turks finally left the Sandžak in 1913.

While Richard went fishing in the stream below the monastery, Anne and I decided to investigate the minaret that we had seen in the distance; it was now cool enough to think of walking. We strolled along in the shade for an hour or more, grateful to find ourselves in a mossy lane with trees leaning over it, and not on the other side of the valley where the old road to Byzantium wound dustily through puffs of pink sumach bushes.

The minaret turned out to belong to a mosque shaped like a house, and all round it were smaller houses: the village of Hisardžik. A man welcomed us: 'Please come in. I have a good house, there's no dirt anywhere!' He gestured towards a cottage and we followed him. He spoke the truth, it was clean and very tidy. His wife's entire wardrobe of

* Levitation counts, even today. An Englishwoman recently returned from Jerusalem was taken to a Serbian village. 'Tell me, lady,' she was asked, 'does the tomb of Christ still hover in the air?' 'No, not any more.' The response was vigorous: 'And to think that I gave that young beggar alms, the other day, so that he could journey to see such a miracle! Lord, Lord, he can't have gone further than the inn at Rudnik!'

four *dimije* hung on hooks on the wall. Perhaps it is easier to have things in order when you own fewer possessions, or perhaps untidiness breaks in when you start leading a more hurried urban life; at any rate, I seldom saw a peasant house where anything was out of place, though standards of cleanliness varied. Slovenliness seemed to increase with tourism: a Yugoslav friend once protested at her none-too-clean sheets in a hotel, only to be told, 'But a colonel – an educated man – slept in them last night. . . .'

At Hisardžik, a baby of four months lay in a cradle carved from a single piece of wood. A young woman rocked it gently, while her husband explained that she was his second wife, his first had died at thirty-five. He made the girl fetch a large framed photograph of her predecessor to show us: she displayed it quite impassively as if she were used to doing so. The man seemed content. He worked some hours away at Čačak, and only came home once a week by bus. The house was solidly built. At first sight they did not seem too badly off – only, the baby looked very small for four months, and when the husband had asked his wife to give us yoghourt, there had been none in the house. Nor were there many sheep or cows to be seen in the fields. The *muezzin* opened up the mosque for us: it was as usual full of pretty kelims. He had inherited the post from his father, who now lay under a handsome gravestone outside, a change from the tipsy stone rods topped with a crumbling carved turban which mark Moslem burial-places throughout the countryside. We read the inscription on another tomb: again, a young woman. I asked the *muezzin* about the ruined castle which I could see on a crag above. He called it Jerena's castle (*Jereningrad*). 'A rich woman didn't know what to do with her money, so she had that fortress put up.' We were always hearing variations on this story, which has its origin in the building of the 15th-century fortress at Smederevo on the Danube. At Hisardžik the castle had in fact been the property of the Bosnian king Tvrtko and had effectively commanded the main road. The Turks only captured it in 1465. Nearly a century later, the Venetian envoy Ser Catharin Zen had climbed up from the monastery to visit the garrison. One of the Turkish guards was a Venetian prisoner who had presumably been converted to Islam. They were much moved to recognize each other in that place: 'Mi conosce et io lui.'

Back at Mileševa Richard had not caught any fish. Sister Anna called out to us: 'There you are! Come quickly if you want to see a Moslem wedding!' On the road beyond the monastery gate, a procession had halted. Everyone had a horse. One rider sat playing his accordion, while another sang to it. A third carried a striped flag as a wedding banner, and a girl held an open blue umbrella over her head as a sun shade. 'We're off to fetch the bride from Prijepolje,' said the standard-bearer; 'we should get back to the village with her tonight.' His horse shied a bit and they set off again for the town, singing and playing, while the banner hung twisted on its pole for lack of a breeze.

* * *

To reach Novi Pazar from Mileševa you must follow a southerly variant of the old road to Byzantium for a hundred kilometres over the mountains, across the high pasture lands of Sjenica and down past the bryony-wreathed houses of Duga Poljana. I was only later to have a glimpse of how the shepherds of the Sandžak lived, at Koštampolje above Sopoćani.

Novi Pazar is an oriental town with some modern buildings. It was a flourishing medieval city under the Turks: another halting-place between Italy and the Levant. The road from Dubrovnik was joined by another road from Sarajevo to the west of the town. To the east, the roads forked: one branch led to Byzantium through the Ibar valley and then over the Kopaonik massif to Niš; the other led further south over mountains to Kossovo, Skopje and Salonica. In time, the north–south route through the Morava valley from Belgrade to Niš was considered to be safer for travellers, and in the 18th century Novi Pazar fell into decline. Sarajevo became the market for the Sandžak. After the Congress of Berlin in 1878, this region was given to Turkey, garrisoned by the Austrians who closed the Bosnian frontier, and the Sandžak was for a while virtually sealed in. So it has remained a rather backward place. The Austrians had wanted to build a Sarajevo–Niš (or Skopje) railway as part of their *Drang nach Osten*, but could never get permission to do so.

The big Turkish *han* or resthouse, a reminder of Novi Pazar's former importance, stands at the junction of the Dubrovnik–Salonica roads. Travellers have varied in their recommendations of *hans*. Miss Irby and Miss Muir Mackenzie, in the last century, had their own tent pitched comfortably on the floor; Gabriel Louis-Jaray, in this, called them 'méchantes auberges ou l'on trouve principalement de la vermine'.[4] When my eyes got used to the twilight inside, I found the place had become a storeroom, piled with bags of cement, a vast shadowy raftered space, two storeys high and supported by wooden pillars. Here, formerly, the horses were tethered all night while their masters warmed themselves at a central fire or slept in the open first-floor gallery at the street end of the building. As late as 1912 Gaston Gravier saw caravans of men and heavily-laden horses crossing the Sandžak in convoy and making for the markets of Salonica as they had done since the days of antiquity: they took out cheese, butter, pitch and oats and brought back corn, flour, salt and tobacco. The men went armed with guns for the most part; cartridge-belts were slung about them. They were a highly organized community, with a *kalaušče* or leader who gave them orders and did any bargaining necessary. The number of days allotted to the journey was exactly calculated: each watering-place and halt for the night was well known. In summer they slept out of doors, but in the winter men and animals alike were swallowed up into the *han*. Nowadays the long-distance loads go by lorry or rail, but the cavalcade that comes in to market at Prizren, Peć or Novi Pazar is picturesque enough.

I reached Novi Pazar alone, as Richard and Anne had to return to work in Belgrade, but Celia Williams, then studying at Belgrade and a pearl among travellers, came to meet me there. It helps that she is a good linguist, and better still, she is at home with everyone and they recognize it instantly. Our guide was a Montenegrin who had lived there for some years.

'How do the Orthodox and Moslems agree?' I asked apprehensively.

'Not too badly, I would say,' he smiled. 'My wife's family are Moslem, of this town, but – you understand – she is educated: we met as students in Belgrade.'

He took us to the Altum-Alem mosque, which is a finer building outside than in. It has good rugs of a village kind: nowadays, the best kelims are in the mosques, as at Hisardžik. Above one window was a naïve painting of a watermelon with a knife stuck in it, apparently ready for the believer to help himself to the delights of Paradise. The *hodža* of the mosque was a terrible bore. He had a flat-boned Slav face with a Turkish nose set in the middle of it. Smirking, he kept on telling us things we knew already: that Mohammed had 200 names or how the Koran was translated into English and Serbo-Croat. We kept on hoping that he would say at least one unfamiliar thing, but he never did. Pomposity wrapped him round as firmly as did the bands of speckless white material wound round his cap to form a turban for Friday. We managed to get up in the women's gallery without him.

'They didn't have such a bad time of it as you might think,' the Montenegrin whispered. 'When the unmarried girls sat here, they used to peer through the lattice-work and quiz the young men they fancied, and the young men couldn't look back: it must have been maddening for them.' Outside in the garden, the trestles for the dead and the table on which they were laid out and washed stood white and scrubbed, waiting for the next comer.

We thought that Novi Pazar might be a good place to buy a carpet, and asked advice from our guide. He took us to see his aunt by marriage, who, like many people in the town and in the countryside around, wove several kelims each year. Her whitewashed Turkish house with its upper storey lurching forward, stood behind a high wall with a small door. In the Moslem tradition, house and garden were invisible from the street. We went to sit with the whole family in the first-floor room. Their name meant 'sons of Black Ahmed'.* The room was oblong and we were arranged on its edge. We sat on the *minderluk* – a bench which lined the walls of the three-sided window-embrasure and extended back into the room. As it is a sitting and talking place and in the old days meant for sleeping on as well, it is always softened by a profusion of rugs and cushions and woollen coverings. Even so, it is sometimes a trifle narrow by Western standards and we had to be careful not to slide off it.

We set about things slowly on both sides. First we drank rose-petal cordial and discussed how it was made. You must at all costs have scented rose-petals, said the older women, and they must be dried and turned patiently in the summer sunlight – this sounded back to all antiquity, to Persian flower-gardens and the song of nightingales – and then, one of them continued, you needed citric acid, but that could always be obtained from the local supermarket. We admired their carpet, a fine old kelim which covered most of the floor. It had a hole in it, dating, they told us, from the war, when a bomb fragment had fallen on the house. The ceiling above had been skilfully mended with pale, smooth planks of beech. Next we were offered juniper-cordial: it was so bitter that even the equable Celia protested *sotto voce*.

'Have you noticed our pictures?' the head of the family asked. 'One is Mecca and one is Medina: the Holy Places of the Prophet.' They

* Probably they were descendants of the famous rebel Black Ahmed, who, while chief of the garrison at Novi Pazar, took control of the whole region. He 'beat and pardoned anyone he liked' until in 1843 the Bosnian Vizier sent to have him killed: his body was said to have been riddled by forty-two bullets.

were the brightly-coloured oleographs which are sold in Skopje market along with more flamboyant ones of Moslem fairies and monsters. 'Mecca' had a black-draped coffin-tomb in the centre, but 'Medina' was unmistakably the Taj Mahal. We murmured interest, while an art-nouveau lady, neglected, coolly gazed down on us from another wall.

Our hostess brought in Turkish coffee and poured it from the brass *džezva* into tiny cups. Several kelims were displayed. They were very well made, in the geometric patterns characteristic of this region and of Pirot, but the colours, as so often, were harsh: crudely-dyed emerald, vermilion and royal blue outlined in black and white. In the corner of the room, over a chest, was a pretty, shabby rug with a formal pattern: the old Turkish *kruške* (pears) on a soft red ground. But for that the family would not take even the modest price we offered. The mother said: 'It is old, I am ashamed. I made it such a long time ago. . . .' Finally she allowed me to buy it for a song and in Belgrade it was identified as a hundred-year-old heirloom. A new carpet, like a new house, is a desirable thing in a poor country, while antique-collecting remains a fad of more prosperous nations.

At the eastern entrance to the town stands St Peter's Church (*Petrova Crkva*) which is a very ancient place. Legend – and historical fact – hover over St Peter's. Its records as a church go back to the 10th century, and in the 12th, by tradition, Stephen Nemanja used it as a Parliament house. According to medieval chroniclers a good many important decisions were taken there, including the condemnation of the Bogomils for heresy. St Peter's reminds one that Novi Pazar grew out of Ras, the first capital of the Nemanjid state.

It is a dark, impressive little church with a two-storeyed nave. The few remaining frescoes have been smudged and blurred by time and the Turks, who used this church as a powder-magazine and St George's Towers as a barracks; but the saints have a distinguished look. The southern chapel was full of broken tombs and bits of sculptured stone. In this detritus of history one object stood out: the head of some medieval personage carved in shallow relief, who with his round eyes and pointed beard bore a bizarre resemblance to the Janssen bust of Shakespeare at Stratford.

St Peter's is plumped down on a dusty knoll – blue with chicory flowers in summer – once the burial-mound of an Illyrian king whose golden ornaments and Greek vases have gone to Belgrade. The church sits just above the Raška valley, where herds of water-buffalo, prized for their thin nourishing milk, lumber about the meadows, and water-mills whirr softly along the banks – all signs of Moslem cultivation.

High on the steep bare ridge above, Stephen Nemanja put a fortified monastery, St George's Towers (*Djurdjevi Stupovi*). He built it in 1171, when he wanted to flaunt his victories, and it still dominates the landscape as he meant it to do. It is worth going up there.* Of the church a single noble arch remains – the western vault of the cupola – and through it, north and south and east and west, you look down on the mountain-ranges which Nemanja and his descendants held, and in whose dark folds they built their palaces and castles. Above the western face of the arch gallops a stormwashed figure of St George. His cloak is stretched along the air; he urges on a pale green horse as huge and strong as himself.

The painters and architects co-operated more closely than usual, and you can just see a prophet – above St Mark on the northwest pendentive – standing in the graceful niche designed for him.†

A chapel was carved out of an entrance-tower to the monastery by King Dragutin, a hundred years later, to celebrate an agreement made with his brother Milutin – who broke it; they're painted together on the west wall. Little else is left on the hilltop. Here was the abbot's throne, say the experts, pointing to a dent in a stone bench; over there, in a shallow pit, the monks kept their wheat. . . . But it is the giant warrior saint, and the mountains quite subdued, which stay in the mind: this is a place to stand and call yourself conqueror.

* If you leave Novi Pazar by the upper town, and pass between a petrol-pump on the left and a modern church with a belfry on the right, you will find a new road going uphill to the left over open ground.

† In the National Museum at Belgrade are two frescoes which belong to the semicircular spaces under the cupola: Pentecost (west) and the Raising of Lazarus with the Entry into Jerusalem (north). Soon it may be possible to see all these frescoes *in situ*, for the Serbian authorities are faithfully restoring the church. Already the two massive towers to the west which gave the church its name are going up again. Eventually the open arch with its view will be blocked, as it originally was, by exterior walls. Then the frescoes can be preserved or reinstalled. Though the architect responsible is a perfectionist who matches stone to honey-coloured stone, the place will certainly be less evocative – but Yugoslavs do not believe in the pleasures of ruins.

5

SAINTS' DAY AT SOPOĆANI

The worshippers – women in a trance – fair and feast – Church of the Holy Trinity – a talkative painter – the flocks of Koštampolje

Ras itself is now mostly underground, but is about to be thoroughly excavated. Its name today is Pazarište, and it lies seven kilometres northwest of Novi Pazar, where the road forks left to Tutin and right to another Nemanjid foundation, Sopoćani. Ras had a castle on the overgrown hill between the two roads, and a settlement, probably of merchants, on the flat land across the river. Once a medieval paved road linked Ras to Sopoćani: now, because of a hydro-electric scheme, it is tarmac.

I planned to stay several nights at Sopoćani, where there is a rest-house. Richard and I had already visited this most ravishing of Serbian monasteries on the First of May (Labour Day) when all the neighbourhood had roistered in the dining-room and we had gone short on food and sleep. This time I had come back in July for a Church feast-day, the Holy Wonder-Workers, St Cosmas and St Damian (*Sveti Vračevi*).

As we drove up the valley in the twilight the air grew sharp. We were nearly 3000 ft high and the Raška had become a mountain stream full of trout. We left the car at the resthouse and walked up to the monastery through spiky plants which had rooted deep among the rocks: mulleins, teazles and acanthus-leaved thistles, they lined the way like the long candle-torches raised by the angels in one of the Sopoćani frescoes. Through the dark plants the church on the hill shone out, a great lantern full of light. When we went into the courtyard that, too, flickered alive: there were fireflies everywhere in the grass.

The nunnery buildings in one corner were deserted: everyone had gone to church. The evening service was being sung by four priests. The peasants had crowded in, and an old monk, usually tended by the nuns, sat nodding and muttering in a corner. There was a general feeling of expectancy: it was the eve of a feast-day; much more was to come in the morning.

Early, by 8 o'clock, the church was a tight press of people. The nuns were there, the number of priests had grown to ten, and Bishop Paul had arrived from Priština. He was, we were told, a very saintly man, a monk come from the Holy Mountain (Athos).

The monastery was founded by Uroš I, that younger brother of Vladislav who seized the throne from him. 'Golden-winged eagles' – Theodosius had called the two of them; a later chronicler, less complimentary, recalled Uroš' grating voice. Uroš made his mausoleum at Sopoćani. Like Vladislav at Mileševa, he was neglected for one greater than himself – Stephen the First-Crowned's bones lay here for a while. Now, even while the liturgy was being sung, women had come to the tomb under Uroš' portrait, to seek a cure for their illnesses as they had done for centuries. Offerings of wool were piled in creamy mounds like curds on Uroš' tomb. Some had been carefully washed and fluffed like cloud, some was dank and oily fleece. The women seemed in a trance: one lay draped across the slightly domed top of the tomb, pressing down the wool, but another had crept under the pall at the 'head' end, and did not budge until moved away by a nun to make room for a peasant girl with a child. Later in the day, I saw a woman press her forehead and palms of her hands against the tomb, and stay quite still as if gathering virtue from it, for a long time.*

After the service ended and hundreds of people had streamed out to follow the priests and their banners round the church in procession, there was a lull. 'If only we could find the local schoolmaster,' I said confidently to Celia, 'he'd tell us what's happening.' At this, he appeared like a jack-in-the-box, and turned out to have only one interest: getting work in Germany. We retreated into the church. Celia was tolerant: 'How *were* you to know?' Soon peasants began to come back into the church for one thing and another while the merriment and dancing began outside in the courtyard. In front of the iconostasis a priest blessed and gave *žito* (presumably for a dead relation) to an old man and woman who carried it into the outer narthex and gave it to other elderly people, their friends and neighbours. A younger woman tried to take a spastic girl about ten years old to kiss a holy icon, but her legs and arms flailed so that her mother could not direct her steps in the right direction towards the icon table. One old woman prayed loudly: 'Lord have mercy on me! Lord have mercy on me!' A tired priest came muttering through a side-chapel and afraid that I'd go in

* This ancient practice, F. W. Hasluck thought, was based on the idea that the beneficial influence of a sacred place works more powerfully on someone asleep or in a dream.

there (it was behind the iconostasis and therefore not for women) dumped a lectern across the entrance as a barrier, meanwhile snapping at me: 'Only for priests!' A monk near the entrance of the church dipped a branch of sweet basil in holy water and sprinkled it on the people who bowed before him. One baggy-breeched peasant, forage-cap in hand, stood tall, white-headed and handsome at his prayers: his eyes were fixed on the fresco of Christ appearing to the Women in the Garden. We found out afterwards that he was a great traveller to feasts and market-days, for we were to meet him again on Easter Monday at another gathering in Western Serbia. The whole church was full of people going their own ways as worshippers.

The service and the fair are all one; as a priest said: 'There are two sides to man's life, the material and the spiritual – the first, house, car, clothes and so on; the second, singing, dancing, joyfulness and merriment.' Life is uncertain, and each celebration is of the eternal moment.

Outside in the big courtyard the fair got under way. A dwarfish gipsy with a blue handkerchief tied round his head against the burning midday light beat on his drum. His two companions played loudly on clarinet and accordion. There were two rival bands, and two round dances (*kolo*) in progress. Fairs like these are a great marriage-mart for the Orthodox in the neighbourhood. A man may ask a girl to dance, take her home and after a while, if all goes well, marry her. The simplest and cheapest way is a runaway marriage in which the girl is abducted from her home. Among the Moslems, there are still many forced marriages and at Novi Pazar we were told of young men carrying off their true loves on motorcycles, away from angry parents.

In the shady parts of the courtyard, cooled by trees or by the outer wall, families sat and feasted. Food is very important in Serbian life. It is a sign of prestige, and a village family often displays its prosperity – or runs into debt – by the funeral feasts taken to eat in the graveyard, Saturday by Saturday, for a year after a close relation's death.* It is a sign of festival: in a country which has always been ravaged by war and famine you must banquet while you can; no one knows what the next day will bring. . . . It is a sign of hospitality: the stranger's plate is

* 'The peasants, in quaint and bizarre garb, did not look out of place at the barbaric festival; but strange beyond words was the sight of a lady in a fashionable pink costume who, attended by a maid carrying a basket, approached a marble tombstone on which, under glass, was the photograph of a gentleman in a frock-coat. She lighted the tapers and censer, and the maid and she spread a clean serviette on the grave, and laid on it a dinner-roll, a plate of cherries, and a bottle of white wine, merely nibbling a cherry or two as a symbol.' Edith Durham at Niš, from *Some Tribal Origins, Laws, and Customs of the Balkans* (1928).

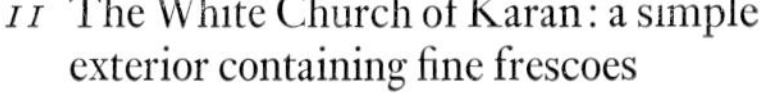

11 The White Church of Karan: a simple exterior containing fine frescoes

12 This tombstone of a soldier from the First World War stands in the churchyard at Karan

13 St Peter's, Novi Pazar, built on top of an Illyrian burial-ground

14 In the foothills of Golija; ploughing near Ivanjica

15 Kossovo buffaloes take refuge from the heat

always piled high; food is forced on the guest as if to fatten him for slaughter – heavy, delicious, indigestible food, course after course – but it is to do him honour. No one has ever thought of such a thing as a balanced meal in Serbia: there has not been a long enough period of peace or civilization to evolve such refinements. At a country festival like this, the food is appropriate. The Sandžak peasants brought no mere picnics to Sopoćani. Each family spread their food on a long cloth on the ground. Garlic sausages, hot with paprika, lay strewn about, and a milder kind of smoked pork, tightly bound with thin cord to compress it as it dried. These were sliced thin, and nibbled with strong *rakija*, at the beginning of the meal. Plates of cold roast sucking-pig flanked piles of sweet green peppers, chopped with onion, cucumber and tomato to make a salad. Big loaves which weighed four pounds or more each were sawn into chunks, for 'no Serb can ask a blessing on a table without bread', and his consumption of it must be six times that of an Englishman. *Kajmak*, virtually salted Devonshire cream, was spooned out of enamelled dishes. One bowl held a rich yoghourt made of sheeps' milk. A jar of sour cucumbers from the winter preserves stood by as a relish. The women served the men, and only ate after they had finished. No dish was cleared away, so that anyone could go on eating as long as he liked. The wine was in big wicker-covered demijohns, easy to carry across country, beside which a litre bottle would have looked like a miser's offering.

By the afternoon, about twenty men, replete, had gathered under one tree. They were all of them middle-aged to old and squatted in two long rows facing each other, with one man at the head. They stayed there talking for several hours, and I could not hear what they were saying to each other. They looked like the village headmen seen by Vuk Karadžić at a similar fair 150 years back: they had come to 'hold a council'.

In the early evening, just three of them were left. The pedlars were beginning to pack up their wares and the clicking and popping of the shooting-range had stopped: the owners were dismantling their stall. Only the gipsy's drum continued to beat and dust from the dancers' feet rose to cloud the air round the church. People saddled their horses and rode off. They shouted a monotonous *guslar* chant as they jogged along: it went in short strophes – a pause, a verse, a pause – the sound came loud and wordless across the valley and faded as they reached the hills. By 9 o'clock the nuns were sweeping the church clean as a whistle, helped by an old man who slowly scraped away candle-grease. Celia made me give a lift to the accordion-player: 'Poor man! He looks so tired. . . .' Delighted by his luck, and by her youth and prettiness, he made rapid proposals to her. He was a wandering gipsy from the Pešter uplands, and he earned a living by playing at weddings and fairs.

The feast-day was over: it had been a gathering such as Dobrica Ćosić shows villagers dreaming of, when besieged in a church by the Nazis:

> And at the fair, there will be many tents all round this church, all kinds of musicians, fiddlers and trumpeters from all the district will play there. And imagine, we will all drink beer out of big glasses.[1]

In the quiet of the next day, I went back to look at the church. Uroš had wanted a cathedral. After his death, his successors respected his wish by building on in the early 14th century the necessary open exonarthex and belfry. Roofless now, it makes a pleasant place to sit, especially as the Parable of the Rich Man and his Barns, painted on the west wall, shows so many medieval people in a state of extreme exertion.

Uroš probably built the church between 1245 and 1260, and the frescoes within were done later between 1263 and 1268. Just inside the main door, the paintings of the inner narthex spell out very clearly the founder's aims. The subjects are either theological: those considered suitable to a Bishop's church – for example, the very complicated story of Joseph on the west wall – or else they deal with Uroš' own family. The narthex makes one sense the solidity of the Nemanjid theocracy, and how much already lay behind them. The number of royal subjects suitable for glorification had increased with time: writers and painters both used them. Here, on the east wall, the Council of Stephen Nemanja has been added to the seven Ecumenical Councils, for the first time in Serbian painting, though Stephen the First-Crowned had already touched on this theme in his biography of his father. The death of Uroš' mother, Queen Anna Dandolo, is on the north wall. It is arranged like the Dormition of the Virgin: son and grandsons, daughter and daughter-in-law, courtiers and an archbishop, replace Apostles and angels, while Christ and his Mother stand on the left to receive the queen. Uroš' own wife was Helen of Anjou – she is the faded figure who kneels to kiss her mother-in-law's hand here. When she came to die, her death was sanctified too, this time by the chronicler-bishop, Danilo II. He describes her son praying to her as to the Virgin Mary:

> Blessed art thou, O mother my lady . . . blessed art thou, for armed with the sign of the cross, thou hast torn asunder the devil's snares . . . blessed

art thou, O lady my mother, and again I say blessed, for I, a sinner, wait in hope to receive, through thy prayers, pardon for my sins on the dread and fearful day when all men shall be weighed in the balance.

The narthex shows what Uroš was about, making a cathedral to house his family tombs, but the narrative, documentary quality of the painting in no way suggests what is to come in the nave. At Ohrid the Church of St Sophia is all underwater blues and greens, and much of Sopoćani has these colours too, but more in the background. What predominates here is the wonderful flush of pinks deepening to claret, so that even in the cold morning light the church has a sunset warmth. On the curve of the apse, bits of gold leaf, chipped and faded, lit then dulled again. No one quite knows the date of Sopoćani nor whose were the several different hands that painted the noble scenes on the nave walls. They may show the influence of the Palaeologue renaissance at Nicaea, and probably Byzantine Court painters were sent at Uroš' request. One of them in particular, who painted the lower zones in the nave and apse, gave the whole of this part of the church its monumental unity and balance, and no historical reasons can quite explain the quality of his painting. It is timeless, serene in its harmony:

> The single figures, stately, majestic, & really drawn & modelled, combining antique grandeur with Quattrocento Florentine light & shade. We were reminded of Cavallini, of Giotto, of Duccio, and of the Villa dei Misteri at Pompeii.*

The different scenes, perfectly placed, answer each other across the spaces of nave or apse or cupola. The idea of linked scenes (usually one from the Old, one from the New Testament) on either side of the nave, goes back to the 5th century, but the paintings at Sopoćani are not merely arranged in pairs, they respond to each other, antiphonally – and often the response becomes an affirmation of faith. So in the apse to the north Christ, framed by a simple pedimented doorway, appears to the Apostles; opposite, to the south, he reappears, against the same architecture, to convince Doubting Thomas. Above his appearance to the Apostles, is the angel with the women at the Empty Tomb, and opposite, the answer to their queries, Christ manifests himself to the same women.

I went over to look at this fresco, the same one at which the tall peasant of the day before had gazed so movingly. The two women crouch heavy, hunched and earthbound while the figure of Christ soars free a little above the ground. They clasp his feet in their hands (as

* Thus Bernard Berenson, in a letter to his wife. MS dated Novi Pazar, 25 July 1936.

in St Matthew's Gospel) and the woman on the right (Mary Magdalene?) has a Giotto-like face, strong in profile, intent on the tangible yet marvellous vision before her which she can barely believe in: her mouth is pulled down with grief and her eyes question the face and hands of Christ turned towards her in blessing.

In the nave the pattern continues, with the Crucifixion on the south wall looking across to the triumphant Harrowing of Hell on the north. In the Crucifixion you can still see the lovely angular figures of the Mother of God and St John the Evangelist backed by saints, and the dramatically-posed soldiers opposite: the Cross has disappeared. The Harrowing of Hell is faded but of great beauty, especially the central figure of Christ pulling up Adam into Heaven, with Eve stretching out her hands beseechingly to be helped up next. Here, Good defeats Evil in the Resurrection. Below the bending Christ is a diagonally set mass of broken doors – the Gates of Hell – shifted presumably by the angels who are so busy chaining up devils below. Their feathery wings are light against the heavy door-panels. David Talbot-Rice noted that at Sopoćani the appearances of Christ after death inspired the finest frescoes of all.

These paintings have all suffered damage. The Turks turned the church into a granary: wheat-grains rubbed against the frescoes and lodged in the cracks. The Germans stabled their horses there, leaving it knee-deep in mire. At times Sopoćani stood roofless, open to all weathers. Yet so far, in Vasko Popa's words:

> Time has gnawed at it
> And broken its teeth.[2]

Nowhere is this more evident than in the grandeur, miraculously untouched, of the scene on the west wall. It is very large and very surely handled. The Dormition of the Virgin is by now a familiar subject, and here once more is the solemn Christ standing above his Mother's bier. He appears to hold in his arms a baby wrapped in swaddling clothes, but it is really the soul of the Virgin Mary that is so bundled up. An archangel helps him gather it into Heaven. One distinction of the fresco lies in the grouping of the figures: in the left foreground some of the Apostles stand close together. Two lean towards each other in sorrow, but St Peter, nearest the Virgin's bier, rests his head on his hand as he watches her, alone. The other group of apostles on her right are further from each other. Two bow low over the foot of her bier, St John turns away and weeps. Their grief is silent, but high up on a balcony to the left a group of women, tearing their hair and wringing their hands, give an accent of violence. The centre of the wall – the space between Christ and the bier – is filled with a crowd of serenely sad-faced angels, holding tall candle-torches, whose vertical lines carry one's eyes upwards to the Christ in Glory. To the left and right of the angels, the pillars of two classical buildings echo more substantially the candle-holders. The balance and rhythm of the whole, the gravity of its mourning, are unforgettable. As for the light, the monk Domentijan wrote in the 13th century a description which would serve for this and other frescoes at Sopoćani:

> This is no light which rises in the East and sets in the West, which ends in time, which disperses with the coming of night and which we see in common with the animals . . . already we may see this light with the peerless angels.

It is difficult to leave this church. Celia had gone out earlier to rest, and in the end I came and sat in the roofless outer narthex. Sister Zora, who was one of the ten nuns left at Sopoćani, saw me with a notebook and said: 'I could have written a thick, thick diary about what's happened here, but there's no time. . . .' She was twenty-nine, and had been there since she was fourteen. Her home was at Gračane on the hill above, but her mother died young and she was left to a stepmother's care. When she was first in the monastery she worked too hard in the fields and was very ill with hernia. Now her duties were in the kitchen, or else she showed visitors round. She took me up to have coffee with her under the beech-tree at the monastery gate. We sat and dawdled pleasantly. A sturdy girl, swinging a thick fair plait, came towards us. She wore baggy *dimije* and knitted as she walked. Sister Zora petted and made much of her; an Albanian, she had run in and out of the monastery since she was a child. Suddenly a big man, with tousled dark hair and a white overall, strode out of the church and flung himself down on the turf, stretched out his arms like a cross, then lay still. I thought he was going to sleep, but words burst out of him in a shout: a jingle which made the nun laugh with her bubbling convent laughter. He sat up, threw back his head and joined in. Then he repeated cheerfully:

> 'If grass you eat
> And grass you lie on
> And you're clad in grass,
> Then your heart's of iron!'

He lay down flat again, cruciform, white on green. Sister Zora began to laugh again and so did he, lying in the sunlight while she and I watched from the shade, man, grass, church and shimmering hills beyond.

The stranger was Milovan, an 'academic painter' from Belgrade who was copying frescoes to go in an exhibition abroad (I remembered now that I had been surprised to see a thermos and a sandwich-box beside an icon in the church). He showed us where the verses came from: they were painted on the wall of the narthex, beside an ascetic saint clothed in grass: St Paul of the Thebaid. Then he took us to what I had long wanted to see: the faint scratched signature of the Patriarch Arsenius, just visible on the frame of a doorway. This was the Patriarch who in the late 17th century had led one of the largest migrations to the lands north of the Danube, to save his people from the Turks.

In the evening at the resthouse, Milovan told us more of what he had seen and heard as he worked in churches up and down the country. Near the altar at Dečani, he said, some medieval painter had slipped in two tiny nude figures, probably for the fun of it: 'They're so small that you can't really tell which is male and which is female, but they're very well-drawn, all the same. . . .' He had met two kinds of gipsies in Serbia: the wilder ones are called 'Russian gipsies'. They always have good horses and 'they ride through a village like a storm'. There are bogeyman stories about them, of the kind that used once to be told in England: they steal babies and blind them, then train them to beg. . . . Milovan loved the monasteries: 'They are the title-deeds of our inheritance,' he said roundly. Someone set him off by quoting a poem, and he quoted back lines about a ruined church which was a *meta vetrovima* – a target to the winds – and for the rest of the evening the enthusiasm of two Serbs for their own history and poetry filled the room we were in.

The next day we decided to go a little further into the curious isolated hill-country of the Sandžak. Gaston Gravier described it well:

> . . . tout restait arrêté, figé, cristallisé. On a l'étonnement de retrouver là, dans toute sa fraîcheur – chose unique peut-être en Europe, l'Albanie mise à part – une civilisation d'un caractère médiéval, ou même plus ancien encore, car, à certains égards, il semble bien qu'il y ait en recul.[3]

We took a rough road which led southwest to Koštampolje, the eastern edge of the Pešter plateau, famous for its pasture-land. At first we climbed through outcrops of rock and there was not a house in sight: it seemed unlikely that any animal could graze the land around. After two miles or so we came out onto wide plains which rose to more stony hills north and south. We were on a shelf of land only a few hundred feet higher than Sopoćani, and in another world. The colours were subdued, monochrome under a pale sky. Cattle and sheep dotted the grassland: Pešter sheep, elegant with their swept-back horns, have always been known for their fine wool in the markets of Salonica and Istanbul. Little arbours on four poles, roofed with dry brown leaves, had been built here and there to shield them from the heat, and animals now huddled in their shade. Otherwise, only squares of oatfield broke the monotony of the plain, and in the distance were summer dwellings – encampments of grey wigwams against the sky. Close to, they turned out to be wattle-and-daub houses, some with steep thatched roofs, placed in twos and threes. The people who lived in them were Moslems: women walked across the fields in bright red ballooning trousers, their headscarves and blouses of pure white. Often one carried a baby on her arm and a water-pail on her head. The flocks were guarded by turbanned men. We stopped at one group of huts and talked for a while to a woman weaving a carpet on a frame in the open air. She brought out stools and a sheepskin, and gave us lumps of sugar for *slatko* and a glass of water instead of coffee: for even the poorest will bid a stranger welcome: perhaps far back in their minds it is a propitiation against danger. Her cow and some twenty sheep grazed under her care on the family's summer pasture, while she did the cooking for herself and four children in a round earth-roofed hut with a hole in the roof: her only bought possessions seemed to be an iron cooking-stove and some pots and pans. The family slept in another hut, dark and orderly, where she had a bed and the children had piles of blankets of her own weaving. In the winter they lived in a house about a mile away: they moved here on St George's Day and stayed until the reaping was finished. I found her dialect hard to understand, but Celia made it out with her usual ease.

'What date is that? August?'

'I don't know. Maybe – maybe not. When we have finished the work.' The names of the months meant little to her, but the neighbour's daughter, who had come to listen, said that it was always August when they went back to their homes. She was twelve, and at school in Novi Pazar.

'My husband's in Belgrade,' the woman went on. 'He's young, he's gone away – and look at me, I'm old.' Her cheeks were two well-wrinkled apples, not a tooth remained in her mouth, and her plaits of hair swung down dull and lustreless under a scarf. Her husband was due back in a few days. There were already four children under six. The baby lay in a big wooden cradle covered with a ragged cloth, his head pocked with greenish sores. A little girl had burnt her arm on the stove, but it was healing nicely: 'I put fat on it and then, forgive me for saying so, lady, I soaked a cloth in urine* and tied it over the wound.'

The neighbour's daughter said that the new elementary school at the village would be fine: 'It has lavatories, parquet flooring, everything you can think of.' Her voice brought us back to the present.

This part of the Sandžak is full of strange legends and customs. During *Sveti Vračevi* we had wandered to the source of the Raška, close to the monastery. It gushes down a steep cliff in a place where a cave goes deep into the mountain. Below, the spring flows into a big pool. People came there in crowds to wash in the healing water: it is supposed to come from Delimedje on the other side of the mountain, and the story goes that a ram thrown in there reappeared in the Raška (I have heard the same tale at another river-source in Hercegovina). Women had tied threads of wool to the bushes, in the hope that they would leave their illness behind with this token offering of their garments, and thereby of themselves. In sympathetic magic a person's clothing can be used for good or evil purposes. They chose a sacred place to do this: the cult of springs of water must be very ancient among Indo-European peoples.

There are other beliefs connected with the country nearby. Somewhere to the north, near the Ljudska river, lurked a dragon who demanded an annual sacrifice of maidens until St George came and killed it. Even after the last war, a ceremony persisted from pagan times: at Whitsuntide young men and girls from Sopoćani went up to a lake above the village to bathe naked and to plight their troth. It may still go on, as no one cares for strangers, whether Yugoslav or foreign, to know much about these things.

* Urine is sterile, and folk-medicine is not to be despised.

6

THE MOUNTAINS OF GOLIJA

The dancing bear – Arilje church – the forester's wife – supper with the botanists – the chief of police – fishing in Studenica gorge

Serbia is not all ancient monuments. North of Sopoćani and west of Studenica lies the remote and beautiful Stari Vlach* country. It is quite different from the Sandžak. The people are Orthodox, of mixed blood, the descendants of ancient Illyrians fleeing the Celts, medieval shepherds from Albania seeking their fortune in prosperous Serbia, and 19th-century Kutzovlachs from Northern Greece escaping the notorious Ali Pasha of Jannina. They are all now assimilated with the Serbs they found there. You can reach the western part of this region, Golija, from the road between Novi Pazar and Mileševa – or, as I did, from Belgrade.

'Better watch out for bears,' said people in the capital when they heard I was to drive some botanists to Golija in June. On this journey we met only a dancing bear, led by a gipsy, tame as the bear in the Belgrade zoo who must watch its own shadow on the 15th of February to see if it will be winter or spring.† The dancing bear was about because it was the eve of Veteran's Day and the whole of Serbia seemed to be celebrating the holiday. At Požega, schoolboys stuck like flies to a wedding-procession in the main street: they were hoping for handfuls of small change, their due from the *kum*, here the marriage witness, and if he forgot, they would yell at him: '*Kum*, may your pockets burn!' Further on, at a country inn, almost all the men were drunk and singing (different) songs in unison to an accordion; then the music took them and they formed an uncertain circle for dancing. One peasant in a forage cap was a great virtuoso, but the others were shufflers, including one who could not bear to leave his bottle of plum brandy behind,

* 'Old shepherd'.

† If the sun shines and it sees its own shadow, winter will go on, but if it is dull and the shadow invisible, spring will come.

but danced holding it; the movement slowly churned the liquor into a fine white froth. A peasant girl came round selling red cherries from a big basket. The music stopped, then started up again as someone paid for another round of it: dancers do this in turn as drinkers do in England.

We drove on past Arilje, a small Royal church which people are eager to show you because it proves their medieval ancestors had nice table manners: one fresco shows saints eating their dinner with knives and forks, another, a Despot whose lace-edged handkerchief dangles from his hand.* Up the valley, fields of early-ripening wheat made bronze lakes which lapped the foot of the hills. Only after Ivanjica, a town that is half apple orchard, do the sombre forests of spruce begin. They are just brushed with colour: a scarlet-berried elder high on a cliff, or by the road dark pink lychnis with silver leaves. The scarce houses looked silvery, too, from their wooden-tiled roofs built steep as witches' hats for the snow to slide off them. Thirty kilometres from Ivanjica, on the hill's shoulder, was a clearing in the forest, and from it you could see across to Jankov Kamen ('Janko's Stone'), a domed mountain ridge covered with woods and alpine meadows, the highest point. In the clearing called Bele Vode two modern houses had been built: one house was the inn, the other belonged to the Forestry Service and there we were to stay a night or two.

The forester's wife came to watch while I unpacked: she asked: 'Are all those things yours? *All* of them? *Yours?*' She was probably amazed not at the quantity – which was small – but at the idea of personal possession, for in the country most things are held in common, and the surprised traveller may find his hairbrush or picnic-bag being used in good faith by someone living in the same house. Foreigners are treated with such princely courtesy that they often steer clear of this annoyance.

We had to forage for our supper. There were four of us: Professor Blečić was elderly, with a rich deep voice, still a prodigious walker, knowledgeable, considerate and cautious. Dr Tatić was a round-faced giant, discursive, reliable, and an excellent botanist. Then there was Atanasević, a thin young geographer, who had come to help the botanists complete their vegetation map of the area. He was the quietest of the three, listening to the talk and suddenly throwing in a sharp remark of his own. Dr Tatić was the quartermaster of the party. Half a mile away he found peasant houses where he bought cream-cheese

* See Appendix I, p. 258.

and fresh milk; put together with bread, bacon and whisky from our own stores, this made a good rough meal.

I found it difficult to sleep. The air at this height was piercingly cold, and moonlight streamed into the room. I woke with a jump to flute music and a counterpoint of rifle shots. The light was like day: I thought I must be dreaming, only the dream changed to the sound of men's voices and horses clip-clopping away. In the morning they said a wedding-party had gone by, an elopement as the bride was being carried off without her father's permission: it was cheaper to do it that way.

We ate a hearty lunch at breakfast, for the people at the inn had just killed a sheep, and we decided to go on to Jankov Kamen. In the forests the towering trunks of spruce and beech stood as firm as stone pillars. Springs gushed out of the limestone beside the rough road, and nearby the huge leaves and tall flower-stems of monk's rhubarb grew in jungle-like luxuriance. Peacock butterflies were sailing about in all their splendour, but as soon as they settled on a plant they closed up and looked quite drab. Once again the forest gave way to meadowland. It was June and the flowers were different on all sides. In a damp hollow grew sheaves of the honey-scented globe-flower, with frail yellow petals, and in the long field-grass were red catchflies, tiny bladder gentians, orchis and the prized black vanilla orchid caught in a cloud of white silene.

At the top of the next ridge we reached the line where, until 1913, the Serbian–Turkish border lay. Old wooden stakes mark it from east to west across the ridge; they were put there in 1878, after the Congress of Berlin, and today it is still the frontier of the Sandžak. You can see a long way from here. Immediately below the ridge some steep hills push up out of the lower land: the steepest is called Koznik ('Little Goat') and another, the Careva Glava ('Emperor's Head') may well have got its name from the medieval kings who had their capital, Ras, close to it. Although it is not very high country – Jankov Kamen is about 1800 metres above sea-level – it gives an overwhelming sense of space to see these vistas: southwest to Montenegro, northeast to the hills above the Morava valley.

The south side of Golija is more open: the forests of the north face become meadows sprinkled with spruce trees, some quite tiny, all over the green turf: further down are oaks. The whole landscape is seamed with paths as an old man's face is criss-crossed with wrinkles, but where they lead to is a mystery: there are few villages. Perhaps they are shepherds' paths from pasture to pasture, or from one distant market to another; the paths are a reminder of the armies and migrations and caravans which have wandered across these hills in the past. Certainly people still walk long distances without thinking much of it, like the woman we met that morning who had come on foot from Novi Pazar, a good thirty kilometres away, 'to see a man about some wood', or a young man encountered later on, visiting Golija for the shepherd girls.

Back at Bele Vode that evening, the four of us talked late. The others told their family histories which were a microcosm of Yugoslavia. Professor Blečić had come straight from Montenegro to Belgrade, and his most detailed work had been a book on the flora of his native mountains. He went back to his birthplace yearly, to the finest fishing in the noblest gorges that any man could imagine. Dr Tatić also came of Montenegrin stock, from a known clan, but sometime in the distant past an ancestor of his had killed a Turk found trying to ravish a woman of the family. The whole *zadruga* fled east over the hills and as far as the side-valleys of the Morava, a district which many Montenegrins had already chosen before them. They had to change their name for fear of reprisals. Tatić's parents lived on in the same vineyards where their ancestors had settled, and he usually returned home for the grape-harvest. Atanasević was a Serb, from the southwest originally – 'a hill near Valjevo is covered with us' – though later a group had gone north across the Danube into Austrian territory and had stopped at Pančevo, not far from Belgrade; there Atanasević had been born and continued to live, commuting by motorcycle to Belgrade, sometimes with a keg of limeflower honey on the pillion for his friends.

The next day, we began to meet people. First the clerk from the Co-operative came to call, a trim young man who was fattening a pig on the ground floor of his house: his job was to keep accounts of the planting of seed-potatoes in fields 1400 metres high. He had typed out a letter and wanted me to translate it into English: it was to a Dutchman called Henk whom he had met at a railway station, and who had promised to send him a tape-recorder. The Professor and Atanasević went off mapping by themselves. Then I walked with Tatić to the next village to see Nikola, the supervisor of the potato fields, and we hunted for Colorado beetles; fortunately there were none. Nikola took us to his *koliba* – the wooden house where shepherd families move for summer pasture. He spread a rug on the grass and his eldest son sat and talked with us. The cottage lay high up among fields planted with buckwheat.

In front, Nikola's wife had arranged her pots of geraniums – behind, sheep were penned in the shade at the edge of the forest. The winter village could be seen across the valley: steep grey roofs again with an occasional new red one, set low on green slopes covered with plum-trees. Far above it were forests, cut by those zigzag paths across the hills.

Nikola and his wife brought brandy and sausage, fried eggs, white cheese, tomatoes, chopped onions and warm bread, then a bowl of milk with the cream still on it. After this welcome – to them a snack for strangers, to me a feast – we turned homewards.

About half a mile from Bele Vode, the forester, very agitated, came running to meet us, and took Tatić aside. As they talked, they both glanced towards me. I thought that Richard, in Belgrade, must be ill or dead and they were afraid to tell me.

It was less catastrophic. The local busybody had seen my car, with a foreigner's number-plate, and had reported me to the police on suspicion of being an Italian timber-merchant without a licence. The forester, who thought he would lose his job for harbouring me, had panicked. Tatić and I decided to drive to Ivanjica to clear up the matter. It was a burning hot afternoon and the Chief of Police had gone bathing in the river. Two boys went unwillingly to fetch him from the farther shore; to show their disdain they paddled slowly across on their backs, and puffed smoke rings as they went. In time, the Chief of Police, a man of great charm, appeared in his bathing-trunks. He examined my passport with damp, expert fingers, murmuring: 'Dear lady, you really shouldn't have bothered . . . we're sending the right forms up on the bus tomorrow.' We shook hands formally, and he slipped back into the water. We went back to the forester's and pacified him and were joined there by the Professor and by Atanasević who had walked thirty kilometres.

The last day on Golija we spent all four together: the others were mapping the distribution of oak and beech for their survey. For this, we went a short way back along the road to Ivanjica and turned off at a swampy place which had once been a lake and had shrunk into a pond. It was the traditional gathering-place for a *sabor* in late July, but now it was deserted except for three black-and-white squirrels who went scampering into a spruce tree, and an eagle owl sitting silent on a branch. We struck up above the lake through woods where ants had built great pyramids of pine-needles. The path widened into a green ride, then opened onto a bluff of steep meadow, so thick with flowers that it had turned into a tapestry of wild sweet william, big white daisies, purple field gentian fringed within like passion-flowers, and a small yellow broom whose sharp stems made it deadly to animals. For human beings the field was a heavenly sight, all the more so for what lay beyond it: the gentle valley of the Moravica, with its cottages and oak-woods, and further off to the northwest, the square-topped fortress rock of Mučanj, where Tito's rival Mihailović had held out during the war. On the southern horizon the mountain wall of Montenegro cut off the rest of the world. After Atanasević had finished his map, a geologist suddenly turned up; within a few minutes we were discussing the high rate of divorce in Belgrade, and its possible causes.

We drove home to Belgrade the next day, which was a holiday twice over, being Ivandan (John the Baptist's Day) for those who believe in saints, and the Day of Liberation as well. In the gorge west of Čačak, where there are a number of small monasteries,* the road swarmed with monks and nuns: old men with long white hair and beard streaming in the wind, their black robes hanging dusty at the hem, and nuns carrying baskets full of food: the crown of each nun's head was round as a melon under her tight veil. A raft crammed with peasants and religious was poled slowly across to the far bank of the river. 'If your husband had been with us,' said Atanasević from the back of the car, 'we would be *tutoie*-ing him by now.'

I did go back to Golija with Richard a month later. The flowery meadow above the lake had been cut and smelt of hay, and barrels of wild raspberries stood cooling under the roadside springs – pigs rubbed against them and licked up the juice that seeped like blood into the puddles. We went this time mainly to fish, and drove straight up to see Jovan, the foreman at the potato warehouse near Jankov Kamen, who had promised that his brother would act as guide to the unknown waters of the Upper Studenica.

Jovan was there when we drove up. He stood, a grey-clad monolith, on the edge of the hill, and only stirred into movement at our approach: 'I've been looking out for you all the month; you said you were coming.' For a moment it seemed to both of us that he had waited there the whole time, towering above the earth, while mist and rain encompassed him and he scanned the horizon for the coming of strangers. We arranged to fish the next day, Wednesday, but Jovan wanted to

* See Appendix I, pp. 258–59.

make sure whether it was the 10th or 11th too, and even consulted a calendar to check. Dates for him were evidently a sign of prestige, of the world of accounts and factories, a sign that he no longer thought like the woman at Koštampolje in terms of saints' days and harvest, but belonged to modern times.

In the afternoon we tried to revisit Nikola. As there was no one at his house we walked on to the next village and came first to the churchyard with its tiny chapel. An offering of green wool and two lumps of sugar had been placed before the icon; outside, the tombs were decorated with possessions and ornaments: scarves, wreathes and flags for the women, and, saddest of all, above a child's gravestone hung his miniature watering-can. In this part of the country, as in the neighbouring Sandžak, the graveyards are maps of pagan custom. At Kumanica, above Ivanjica, we had seen the tomb of an unmarried girl: a wooden cross, on which were arranged her spindle, some unspun wool, her comb, fork, plate, bunch of sewing-thread, cloths – already grown ragged from the weather – stamped with a black cross; macabre reminders of a life cut short.

The tombs in these villages are made of stone and shaped like dress-boxes standing on end. Designs of leaves and grapes and birds twirl up the narrow sides: they are village Byzantine, crudely drawn and painted over in brown, white, blue, green, yellow and pink, but recognizable as the same motifs you find on the iconostasis at Nerezi in Macedonia, or on Maximian's ivory throne at Ravenna. Much earlier than that, the ancient Greeks in the Balkans used the same vine-pattern on their tombs.

We went on down into the woods by the river to fish. There was a noise of men scything hay – swishing, pausing, shouting across the hillside. The hill-country is always full of faint sounds: children who guard the flocks cry to each other from opposite sides of the valley, and their voices are high like birds; once we heard a boy playing his flute.

We reached the potato warehouse by seven the next morning. Jovan and his gap-toothed brother Miroslav were waiting for us there: it was extremely cold. Miroslav had a primitive, very long fishing-rod made from a branch. First we took the Land-Rover over fearful mud and bumps, then walked along forest paths, while an eagle kept us company in the sky. We came out by a lonely *koliba*, with no one about. Then we set off on a steep descent towards the gorge, down, down over meadows that looked like parkland, with scattered trees that grew high on the greensward. The slope was endless, the whole landscape so fresh and seemingly well-cared for that it would have been no surprise to see a Palladian house set somewhere in the valley. Instead we came upon the river, which flowed through a gorge some five miles long. The Studenica is fine even in its lower reaches by the monastery but here, quite close to its source, it carves its way out of a wild fastness of plants, trees and rocks, and makes a sanctuary for man and beast of a kind that must be rare in Europe.

At the opening of the ravine there was still a path and a weasel ran across it, then paused, quite fearless, to look back at us. It had a round, inquiring face, creamy-coloured, brown-tipped coat, and a long furry tail, and it was carrying a bundle in its mouth. After a moment it went quickly off on its own business again. Miroslav called it *nevestica*, the little bride, and said it lived in the ground. Further up the river, with a saddled horse standing by, were watermills. Water was channelled into wooden troughs above them and hurtled in a small race below the building. Inside one mill, in almost complete darkness, a man was putting things in order to grind some flour. He was the only person we saw in the gorge.

The path now came and went. We clambered over dead treetrunks, mossy and rotten with age, which had fallen across the riverbed, jumped onto stony beaches, or waded through the water as we crossed and recrossed it. The glen was steep and sheltered, which made everything grow to a great size: dark-blue monkshood stood taller than a man, with its roots almost in the water. This was the same plant whose poison had been used in the early Middle Ages by the soldiers of Zeta and Raška to tip their arrow-heads. Once Richard tripped and fell and stayed where he was, for he found himself lying on a bed of bilberries, with raspberry canes and wild redcurrants pushing through them, so that he had a whole feast at arm's length. . . . He and Miroslav fished in a pool under a waterfall and pulled out trout which flashed silver in the light. We had with us a hunting-dog, and he chased joyfully up and down the steep sides of the gorge looking for hares or ran ahead of us and doubled back: he must have covered three times as much ground as we did but showed no sign of tiredness. We came to a clearing in the trees. In the green turf were marks: the foundations of a house and paths leading to it. Later we left the river and walked up through the forest.

'We couldn't have done this before the war,' said Miroslav; 'there were bandits in these woods, and they only came out to steal our livestock or take our money; I remember them when I was a child and guarding the sheep.'

'Who were they?'

'Oh, comitadji, Turks and such-like, they built themselves hideouts in these woods.'

Above the forests were more pastures where sheep grazed and a woman lay asleep, cradled in the trodden-down groove of the path. She might have recited the charm against sleeplessness:

> . . . The wind blows over high mountains, wide meadows, great waters, barley full of ears, frail hemp, rooted maize, plump fruits and grape-laden vineyards; the wind blows over foxes, wolves, hares, bears, harts, does, sheep, goats, horses, oxen, cocks, pigeons, tits, quails, cuckoos, partridges, magpies, crows, jackdaws, nightingales, sparrow-hawks. . . . The wind blows over all and everything, until it blows a heaven-sent dream. . . .

We tried to step over her, but she woke with a start, rubbed her eyes, and then took us to drink milk at her *koliba*. We entered through a small door set high in the wall. Chickens cackled and ran about in the first room which had an open fire on a central hearth and a hole in the roof for the smoke. Like everyone else she was salting down food for the winter, and pans of *kajmak* and milk had been put on shelves all round. As at Koštampolje, very little had been bought, though this house was far more solidly built. In the inner room, the rough table and benches were all homemade, the blankets homespun; one bed was made of wood with thongs lashed across it. A metal stove heated the room and here a pipe led to the roof. An amorphous pile of cloths and garments had been pushed onto the corner shelf above the bed, and a square basket nailed up to take all other belongings. Children's shoes lay scattered on the floor: they run barefoot in summer and a few years ago, country girls in Belgrade found it pinching torture to wear shoes in the house. The inner room had small square windows, one glassed in with a single fixed pane, the other left open to the air: a wide shaft of sunlight poured in and caught the dust whirling.

We parted from Jovan and Miroslav at the warehouse on Jankov Kamen. Jovan promised to send us a barrel of *kajmak* to Belgrade. It never came, but his brother, when sent a fishing-reel, wrote back a letter signed 'Thy fisherman, Miroslav.'

We fished again in the late afternoon below the woodcutters' settlement at Golijska Reka. Half-wild horses, grey, roan and dappled, grazed up by the road: a foal trailed after them. The stream looked tiny but was full of small trout moving about the clear pools. A jeep drew up and some men tumbled out: 'You say you've caught some trout, show us a sample, then.' They drove on, leaving behind them an old man of eighty, Čika Nikola, who had been President of the local fishing Society at Ivanjica for over thirty years, and was anxious to know who had been our guide on the Studenica:

'Miroslav, that's all right, he's paid his dues. You needn't pay anything – we let foreigners and our own tourists in free – it's these local people who're the trouble. . . .' He grumbled about the men who had brought him up in the jeep: 'Stopped in every inn, they did, and drank I don't know how many brandies. They must have downed twenty or thirty by now. I shan't catch any trout, it's too late in the day. The young men nowadays, the way they behave. . . .'

He had worked as book-keeper in a French-owned antimony mine before the war, and now lived in Ivanjica. We took him back to Bele Vode to wait for his companions. They arrived, drunker than ever, before supper. We sat with Čika Nikola, by then silent with exhaustion, and a road surveyor – a Wild-West character in a broad straw hat and a black waistcoat swinging loose. He pressed Serbian salad on us in ever-increasing quantities from a common dish, and poured out *rakija* to cries of 'our Serbian whisky'. Sober, he might have been quite good company, but drunk he was not, and we sidled off to bed as soon as was decent.

The road surveyor lodged in the town, but for the men who lived on Golija there was little else to do except soak in the *kafana*. Every evening the same two peasants came in to drink themselves stupid on thin beer, with shouts of 'Plus, plus' as they emptied their glasses. One of them got more and more wooden-faced, until he looked like a zombie and hung over people's shoulders to watch them play cards. The next morning he was a human being again, as he poured petrol into a car and chatted to passers-by.

Life in these highlands has never been an idyll. We saw the pastures as an earthly paradise in summer, but they only support a simple life: the land is not rich. The region has always been a labour reserve: and people who leave do not come back again except on short visits. The peasants learn from relatives that a different life is to be enjoyed elsewhere, and the first faint stirrings of unease, the impact of industrialism, can be discerned on Golija. The Co-operative clerk, baby-faced and unhappy after four years among the potatoes, wanted to emigrate, but had no special skills or languages. Miroslav the fisherman asked Richard if he owned a factory in England. A little girl in the house where I bought milk said: 'My father wants you to buy me an English sewing-machine. He's taken me away from school so that I can sit at home and sew.' Education and communications have begun to change things: for one child who is kept at home (illegally), two will go to school in the town if relations there can give bed and board. Foreign countries are names to conjure with: a dream of prosperity to the young, far-distant lands to the old. An elderly man enquired: 'D'you have a frontier between America and England?'

The Serbian mountain regions are, all the same, among the few unspoilt areas of Europe. We stayed longer on Golija than elsewhere, but we found that even where hotels had tarnished the edge of these wild places we could take paths over the hills for thirty miles or more. Each range had a different character. At Jastrebac the beechwoods in spring were the freshest, clearest green, and pine and larch smelt sweet in the sun. On Divčibare the earth formed a damp cushion of pink heather and grape hyacinths and white daphne – a natural rock-garden among silver birches. Goč had strange dry juniper hills. The Tara gorges opened onto fields of orchis, and Zlatibor was most flowery of all: a thin skin of earth, stretched over grey rock, grew long meadow grass in June and blossomed red and white and purple.

The paths were used by local people who stopped to talk to us. They were interested in us and, as on Golija, the mention of England brought a variety of responses. Veterans of the Salonica front knew about the Englishwoman (Flora Sands) who had fought there and how she could haul a cannon uphill that seven strong Serbs could not manage. Once we walked into a mountain village and the *kafana* owner gave us free brandy because the last Englishman he had seen was Colonel Bailey – dropped in by parachute during the Second World War – who had bought a mare with gold concealed in his belt.

We listened to their proverbs which we could not match, and which often seemed to reflect their traditions: 'Without company, no bravery'; 'Without health, no wealth'; 'Without pains, no brains'. Two 19th-century travellers here, Miss Irby and Miss Muir Mackenzie, chose a German saying for their epigraph: *Hinter den Bergen sind auch Leute*. They were right. The mountain landscapes are often dazzling, but it is 'the people behind the mountains', with their conservative ways of thought and oddly imaginative speech, who have stayed longest in my memory.

7

THE PATRIARCHATE OF PEĆ

Old Metohija – the markets of Peć – the Patriarchate – dancers from Montenegro – Albanians and Serbs

The ancient town of Peć turns two faces to the traveller and one is that of a frontier post. It is backed by the mountain wall of Montenegro, which seems to seal it in from the west. Not so: the wall is cracked open by a pass, and for centuries it has linked merchants and craftsmen and armies with the coast at Kotor.* A few miles to the south is Albania, and every evening the Corso is noisy with men from all over the place.

Being a border-town Peć is rich in markets. I managed to get there on Friday, which is market-day, and with me came Elizabeth Balsom who had been a student in Belgrade. Where I look for churches, she looks for politics: we were both kept busy on this particular journey. Peć set us talking about the markets of Yugoslavia, of how they make a fantasia upon a single theme: regional custom. We had both been in Ljubljana: there the peasants sell hanging carnations for wooden balconies. In Zagreb they bring crochetted mats to grace city tables; in Belgrade, peppers and tomatoes for winter preserves. In Sarajevo Moslem women buy white kerchiefs printed with strawberries – something like the one Othello gave Desdemona; in Priština the cobblers make rough leather sandals, soled with old motor tyres, for plainsmen – Richard's are still in use.

We found the main market in the centre of the town. It is shaped like an octopus, the body being the open space of the stock market, where men squat patiently all day beside their single kid or lamb or donkey up for sale. The tentacles which draw in the buyer are winding streets with booths selling filigree jewellery, gaudy slippers and men's clothes. The tailors are busy running up suits for local Albanians: they are made of white frieze and have swirls of black braid sewn onto the tight-sleeved jackets and hipster trousers – a wide cummerbund holds things together, and a short-sleeved overjacket, with a sailor's collar that hooks up into a hood, covers the lot. It is a dandy's costume, swaggering

* Over this pass, the Čakor, the Serbian army made an epic retreat in 1915 to Corfu.

and virile – for a highland dandy who must protect himself against wind and rain.

In another corner we saw oblong cushions of sacking stuffed with straw furniture for the same Albanians. The cushions are covered and placed all round the walls of the room, on the floor: they are very comfortable if you can sit cross-legged and not tuck your legs sideways under you like a Westerner. Between two houses a plank bridge crosses a stinking trickle of water and brings you to another open space where carpets are sold. Peć is a carpet town where women dip their newly-woven rugs in the river, and street ditches run red with scarlet dye. The colours of the rugs are crude and the wool harsh, but some have vigorous red-and-black designs of double-headed Albanian eagles – hard to distinguish from Habsburg or Serbian birds. The best rugs are still the old ones, hung out on washing-lines or used as cart-coverings.

Another market at Peć takes place a mile out of town towards Dečani. It is a flea-market, unpromising at first sight, a long dusty lane strewn with old clothes mouldering into rags. Further down is a field, whose fences are hung with women's costumes: we were to see Christian women on the road wearing them, but this was like dressing a doll: we could work out the construction, layer upon layer: embroidered dress, aprons, sashes, socks, shoes and the scarves which, draped and twisted, would become high wimples. One stall was specially for brides: much tinsel and satin there. Women hawked old Turkish quilts and cushions, and we had to fight off a middleman, Suleiman the Genie, who buys such things with great panache and expense for a Belgrade Museum and for stray foreigners.

The markets sketch out a pattern of Christian and Moslem life, but the second face of Peć is surprising: it is a cathedral town. Two kilometres from the centre, towards the pass, lies the Patriarchate.

Peć was for a long time the centre of the Serbian Church, and this area, now part of the Kossovo region, was called *Metohija*: 'church lands'. In 1253 Archbishop Arsenius I, rightly sensing danger from Bulgarians and Cumans, moved his episcopal seat from Žiča to Peć: the single church there had belonged to Žiča since the time of Stephen the First-Crowned.

The tombs to be found at Peć are those of archbishops and a patriarch because, unlike the other monasteries, it is an ecclesiastical rather than a royal foundation. Court and Church were closely linked: St Sava was not the only royal relative to become an archbishop nor the only high cleric to act as a statesman; and Serbian kings gave their monasteries more property and privileges than was common in other countries under Byzantine influence.

The Patriarchate huddles under the mountains. It is a complex of three churches attached along a spine-like narthex, with a small chapel to the south. The churches are a world apart from the clear chiselled marble of Studenica or Dečani. Their rough stone walls blur and merge to make one building: a corner has been rounded off, or a door sunk in a wall as patrons and builders have succeeded each other. If you start in the very centre, in Arsenius' Church of the Holy Apostles, it is like walking into a cave lit from a hole in the roof – the windowed cupola. While it is the oldest church in Peć, built in the first half of the 13th century on an existing foundation – it feels far more ancient than it is, a very secret place. St Sava, who probably planned the church, and Arsenius I, who commissioned the frescoes, are thought to have based their designs on the Church of Sion in Jerusalem which St Sava had seen – by tradition the site of the 'upper room' where the Last Supper and Pentecost had taken place, and so the 'mother of churches'. The new church at Peć was to be the hallowed mother church of Serbia in its turn.

So the new church had to be painted full of visions, some of them in the same order as in the church of Sion: under the cupola, on arched surfaces, are to be found the Descent of the Holy Ghost, the Mission of the Apostles and the Doubting of Thomas; under them, the Last Supper. All good imitations add something of their own and the founders of Peć added their own visionary painting, the most beautiful in the church, in the cupola itself. There is the Ascension: Christ Pantocrator in a mandorla upheld by peaceful angels, separated by green trees, below him amazed Apostles, dramatic in their gesticulation and awe, and among them the tranquil, statuesque figure of Christ's mother, her arms held 'wider than the skies', her features painted with extraordinary realism as if from a strong peasant face.

In the late 13th century, after Arsenius' death, – he was buried in the church as he intended – a whole series of new paintings were added in the west part of the church, the 'old' narthex, with quite a different aim. The subject is Christ's Passion, but it is like watching a theatre. On the south wall, in the top zone, a soapy Judas paws Christ to give his treacherous kiss. On the north wall, the cock crows above a jittery St Peter who denies his master. These emphasize the drama of the Gospel stories as, in the Western Church, a mystery play with human actors might have done. Radojčić quotes St Basil: the church is a theatre for angels and men.

We left by the west door. Two solemn portraits, over life-size, faced us – the Mother of God and St Nicholas. Though painted on the wall, they are virtually icons. It is a lovely church, the Holy Apostles, smallish, mysterious, full of surprises, a rich and various place, the kernel of a marvellous bumpy fruit, the Patriarchate itself.

As so often, the next age thought little of it. The Serbian archbishop Nicodim 'improved' Peć by adding on a church to the north, during the years 1321–4. The frescoes were painted about 1340. He dedicated the church to St Demetrius. Nicodim – and Danilo II and Joanikije after him – concentrated on the needs of the church and its liturgy. The church is stricter than the Holy Apostles, it is concerned with edifying the faithful: the martyrdom and miracles of the patron saint and the Councils of the Church do that.

St Demetrius might well have been a South Slav saint but turned into a Greek one. He was martyred at Sirmium (now Sremska Mitrovica near Belgrade) in the 5th century. His bones were taken to Salonica, which quickly became the centre of his cult, and from this time contradictory legends about him abound: the most popular made him a warrior saint. The frescoes here illustrate another version: they show his steadfastness in upholding the Christian faith and seem to be based on a pious Byzantine hagiographer of the 10th century, Simeon Metaphrastes. On the north wall you can read four incidents from left to right like a strip cartoon. St Demetrius, a secret Christian who had risen to be proconsul under the godless Emperor Maximian, is arrested and brought before his master on charges of preaching the Gospel. The saint blesses Nestor, a young Christian, to whom he promises a martyr's crown if he will kill Lyaeus, the Emperor's favourite gladiator. Nestor kills Lyaeus in the presence of Maximian (and is then killed himself at the Emperor's orders – this is not shown). Lastly, the imprisoned St Demetrius is stabbed to death by soldiers. On the south wall, you will find St Demetrius' funeral and his defence of Salonica. These frescoes date from 1340 but were gone over again in the 17th century.

On the west vault, it is possible to pick out the Council which Stephen Nemanja summoned to deal with Bogomil heretics. Stephen is dressed as a monk with a black cowl and a white beard. St Sava's Council is also there, and two ecumenical Councils. The Church had grown more powerful, and these paintings are strongly didactic: this is how the Church is governed and the bishops want the congregation to know it. Yes, a strict church, we thought, only softness keeps breaking in: with the frilly, graceful angels in the apse or with the Nativity of Christ being framed in flowers and grasses and fruit trees. Nicodim employed two master-painters with their assistants, and they shared out the work so thoroughly, Byzantine fashion, that one, John, painted most of the righthand section of the Communion of the Apostles, and the other, whose name is unknown, did the left. Their styles are quite different: an odd arrangement.

Nicodim died young, and it was left to Danilo II, his successor and the heroic Abbot of Hilandar, to build the third church, that of the Mother of God, about 1330. Danilo II was the greatest church-builder among Serbian ecclesiastics; his royal master Milutin built even more. Possibly Danilo and Nicodim had planned the complex of Peć to imitate another Athos monastery, Vatopedi, closely connected with the Nemanjids, for the arrangement and dedication of the churches is the same. Most art historians, with the exception of Radojčić, are inclined to pass over this church, though the scenes from the Life of the Virgin, and the saints up in the apse and down on the other walls are fine. As you enter, on the left, is a turbanned warrior saint in oriental dress. He has a white tunic with black embroidery, golden selvedge and scarlet sleeves: he looks like a Moghul painting and he is St Jacob the Persian, a great favourite in Byzantium. Just in front of him is Danilo's tomb.

As a whole, this church reminded us of an illustrated book. The paintings are like miniatures grown large: minutely detailed, carefully shaped to the wall-space they occupy, the Nativity and its paired composition, the Harrowing of Hell, might almost be capital letters from an illuminated manuscript, they are so tall, brilliant and clear. The church reflects Danilo's personality: it was he who built the tower outside the church as a writing-school for Slav monks, and then brought in monks from Athos to teach them Greek. If it is not too fanciful, this church is bookish, where Nicodim's preaches a sermon. Danilo has two portraits of himself, one above his tomb, with St Nicholas at his side – and St Nicholas is celebrated again in a small chapel just outside, where the 17th-century frescoes include his restoration of sight to King Stephen of Dečani. The second portrait of Danilo shows him as donor, with the prophet Daniel leading him to the Virgin. As usual, he carries her a model of his church, and the arcades of his new narthex can be clearly seen.

Danilo's narthex marks the new standing of Peć. Arsenius had thought it would be a temporary episcopal seat but by Danilo's time it had become permanent and later in the 14th century it was raised to a Patriarchate. Danilo originally built a ceremonial entrance to the churches with soaring arcades. It united the whole complex along the western façade. Danilo had painted on the eastern wall a genealogical tree of the Nemanjid dynasty. He also ordered another portrait of himself as donor. Figures of the Mother of God and of Christ and of the archangel Michael have survived – more than that, we do not know. There is plenty to see, but it was done later.

At the end of the 14th century the Turks overran the Balkans and the medieval Serbian churches were left to decay. But in the mid-16th century a peculiarity of Ottoman rule caused the patriarchate of Peć to flourish again.

The Sultans avoided the creation of a Turkish ruling class for fear of being overthrown, and they recruited military and civil officials from among their subject peoples. Their levy of boys for the Corps of Janissaries is familiar, less so their custom of appointing young foreigners as administrators. Many were Slavs: one, Mehmed Pasha Sokolović (to give him his Ottoman title) had been destined for the Church by a relative, then Abbot of Mileševa. Sokolović rose to be Grand Vizier and in 1557, as Second Vizier, appointed his brother Macarius to be Serbian Patriarch: the office had been in abeyance under the Turks. Macarius' vast Patriarchate included Budapest and Skopje, and he had ambitions to become leader of the Orthodox Church in the Balkans.

He wanted to foster national pride, and the place where he began was the Peć narthex. He blocked up the ruined arcades built by Danilo II and ordered the whole wall-surface to be covered with paintings. He insisted on the strength of the Serbian Church and no less than thirteen archbishops and patriarchs of Peć decorate the north and east walls of his narthex. Among the saints, St George the New, a goldsmith who was martyred at Sofia in 1515, is promoted to encourage resistance to the Turks. He wears a hat like a beehive and holds an Orthodox cross. Macarius also planned a liturgical revival, and he gave his congregation at Peć a rich diet of feasts and fasts and Biblical stories as they came into church. The narthex today strikes one as very varied. Macarius was fortunate in the craftsmen he employed. Their leader was a certain Andrew, and under him they painted elegantly, in rich colours. The portrait of St Luke, bearded and tonsured with a jewelled Gospel-book, or by contrast, the scene of Christ in Glory at the Last Judgement, show their range.*

When they had finished at Peć, Macarius sent them on to do over the narthexes of Studenica and Gračanica. Peć started an artistic Renaissance within the Serbian Church: village chiefs, Serbs serving with the Turks, well-to-do artisans saw it and gave money for their own churches to be painted. It is still possible to find extremely remote churches where these craftsmen went – such as Dević in Kossovo or Crna Reka in the Sandžak.† Macarius also encouraged literature: many books were copied – liturgical texts, Kings' Lives, the Code of the Emperor Dušan. The rule of the Patriarch Macarius – for he ruled like a vassal prince with considerable powers – is a proof that in any Dark Age there are periods of light. The rule of law still held – it was only later, as the Empire grew decadent, that the Ottoman Porte lost control and the Imperial provinces endured disorder and savagery. Peć in the late 16th century is an oasis in the Balkans under Turkish domination, and the buildings of the Patriarchate provide a visual interpretation of Church history over three centuries.

Peć can still show the face of a cathedral town. On Palm Sunday the Patriarchate is crowded with local people and Montenegrins. A choir of middle-aged ladies in good coats and skirts were singing a dull 19th-century version of the Liturgy under their choirmaster. 'How did you like it?' he said afterwards. 'We've only been going a year; it'll be better when you come next time.' The ladies took us off to a large lunch with the nuns, who were often their sisters: it was the first time that I had found a monastery recruiting from townspeople: Peć is a churchy place and for a moment the choir-chatter sounded like tea at the Deanery. Then the Balkans flowed back.

A feast brought out the old and infirm who live in the monastery. Their presence is taken for granted and the nuns care for them with total compassion. In a ground-floor room the Abbess' mother held court. A nun herself, she was bed-ridden. Her legs, crossed under her on the blanket, had withered into sticks of bone. She looked like a *memento mori* but could just turn her black-veiled head towards us; she was cackling with curiosity: 'I heard you were here; you came yesterday, didn't you, from England, from England.' Even more

* St George the New is in the second zone, east wall, St Luke on the northern pillar in the centre of the narthex, and the Last Judgement in the western part of the vault.

† See Appendix I, pp. 258–59.

grotesque was the way poor Simka, who had had a fearful stroke, had been put into her best clothes for the occasion. Half-dumb and gibbering with fright, she went stumbling about in soft Turkish trousers and embroidered waistcoat, her silver necklaces tinkling. No one could manage to soothe her.

Through the windows, in the courtyard between the monastery buildings and the church, hundreds of young people were by now dancing in the open air. People will dance the *kolo* for hours, even all night long, perhaps because it is so monotonous. A circle of them link arms – behind each others' shoulders, in a V-pattern – and then the steps are simple: three paces to the right, an extra tap with the foot and everyone is off to the left again; three paces, tap, and back to the right. So they never shift much but dance on and on in the same patch of dust. At Peć they had been given small wreaths of willow in the church and had let them fall to the ground: now the twigs were being crushed to powder by remorseless trampling. There was room for style: some dancers crossed their feet in arabesques, others lifted their heels high like prancing horses. A stale, hot smell lingered in the enclosed courtyard. Elizabeth went away to get some tea, for which she frequently has a craving. The nuns run a mill and I retreated there. It was cool and I listened to the millstream which is channelled close to the churches. The friendly Sister Juliana, who was in charge, came to check the millstones grinding wheat and maize for the monastery. I stayed to watch her tip golden flour into a wooden chest; then, refreshed, went out again.

Looking across the river from the Patriarchate, I could see a steep green hillside, and on it were bushes like yellow mist caught in the grass: forsythia – the only place outside China where it grows wild as far as I know. I had been up there to look at the buttery brown-veined flowers and shiny oval leaves. A young Albanian had shown me the way and now as I was trying to puzzle out the two worlds of Peć – the cathedral town and the trading-post – I remembered what he had said. His parents had come over the frontier during the war; he had been born in Yugoslavia. He was a practising Moslem and went to the mosque every Friday. He felt deeply Albanian, though he had sensed the close comradeship of Slav soldiers during his military service: 'When one of our company was killed in an accident, we were all in it together, you see.' In or out of the army, he liked the Montenegrins best: 'We know where we are with them: they have the same tradition of keeping their word, they have tribes, an idea of honour . . .'

This part of Yugoslavia, immediately north of the Albanian border, is a debatable land. The Turks brought crafts and some customs, a system of taxes, a way of cooking, to this corner of the Balkans. Most important of all, they brought the Islamic religion, though some Albanians remain Roman Catholic, due to Franciscan influence in the past, and the Serbs are Orthodox. Superficially, the towns and the people look oriental, but the Turks never kept as firm a hold here as they did in Bosnia, where they converted the Slav landowners to Islam. At times the Serbs dominated, through their Church, or the Albanians, through tribal force. To each race it is still their own territory. Their history is one of continual conflict with each other and of occasional alliance against the Turk, their common oppressor. When they fought each other it was for possession of rich lands which produced wine and wheat: treasure to mountaineers like the Albanians, a heritage to the Serbs. In an old poem the Albanian highwayman Musa Kesedžija meets the Serbian prince Marko:

Pass, Marko, don't pick a quarrel,
Or dismount and we'll drink some wine;
But yield to you – that I will not,
Though a queen did give you birth
In a pavilion on soft cushions,
And swaddled you in purest silk,
Bound you with golden cords
And fed you on honey and sugar.
Though a stern Albanian woman gave me birth
Among the sheep, on a cold flagstone,
And swaddled me in a black cape,
Bound me with bramble-stems
And fed me on oatmeal porridge,
Yet she besought me often
Never to make way for any man!

The Albanians are proud, austere tribesmen with a great deal of panache, extremely honest on the whole; but when they are not they are like Musa and like the men Brailsford met on his travels early this century: robbers on a grand scale, never petty pilferers. They are a fighting people who have much in common, as my acquaintance had pointed out, with the Montenegrins. They share many South Slav customs – which have survived longest in Montenegro – about marriage and mourning; they venerate the same saints (here Islam and Christianity blur) and shudder at vampires together. But the Albanians are not Slavs. They are probably descended from the original inhabitants of the mountains below the Danube, the Illyrians, whom the first Slavs drove southwards. In their own minds, Serbs and Albanians are bitterly separate. Anyone English who lives in Wales will sense in time the ancient memories of oppression there. Here, both races have these feelings drawn from the recent past. Travellers in the 19th and early 20th centuries continually report Serbs murdering Albanians and Albanians, Serbs. Other countries were always ready to meddle in the affairs of Albania itself which in the last hundred years came under Turkish, Italian, Yugoslav, Soviet and now Chinese influence. None of this has made for stability. At present, Serbs quote the Albanian birthrate, which is very high, and are discomfited to find themselves a minority in 'their' land, while the Albanians within Yugoslavia display a growing pride in their own language and history. Along the road from Peć to Dečani are high grey farmhouses – Albanian *kule* (towers) – fortified against all comers. They have tiny windows for guns set high in the thick walls, and they typify this borderland where each man has had to fend for himself and his kindred.

8

THE ROAD TO DEČANI

Return from market – the Church of the Ascension – a painted hymn – King Stephen's jewels – an icon and a poet – Father Justin in the treasury

I would rather walk than drive along the road to Dečani, especially when it has been market-day at Peć and people are going back to their villages. We slowed down and watched the procession passing by. The carts were crammed with people dressed in the clothes we had seen for sale. The Christian Albanian women had peaked medieval hats secured by a folded wimple that passed under the chin and was knotted up high: the ends hung down over one shoulder. These women had a pale under-dress, a short yellow or red-pleated apron or bustle at the back, and a long red apron in front. The Moslem women have simple white scarves; it is their men who are the peacocks, in braided splendour. Sheep travelled in a wicker coracle in the back of many carts. Donkeys and calves sometimes stood behind the driver. Each cart was drawn by two horses with red and blue beaded harness. Shaggy white dogs followed most families: they are the Šar mountain breed, much prized by shepherds and fierce as wolves when guarding their own territory.

In the distance were folded hills, brown with sweet chestnut and black pine against the purity of snow mountains beyond. Close to Dečani the hills were of orange earth and grey rock. Dečani village, on the main road, is a dull nothing, but a smaller road turns off to the right and follows a mountain river tumbling over stones. We were slowed up by girls herding silky goats. Then came the monastery: above it is a gorge and we could see fantastic crags with trees sticking out horizontally: another place where hermits lived, but empty now. An Albanian Catholic priest, a small man wearing a dark suit with a dog-collar, came out of the gateway, followed by two burly parishioners in round felt caps; they got into his Fiat Topolino and drove off.

They and we belonged to the present – but of all the monasteries this one has changed least since it was built. A monk offered us water from their famous spring. We looked around the same piece of riverland as did king Stephen of Dečani on his first visit here, according to his 15th-century biographer Abbot Camblak:

> [Stephen] commanded stonemasons to come swiftly: the best craftsmen from the coast were to be appointed as builders. Once he had pitched his tents he stayed there, delighting in such a beautiful abode, for it was set very high and cleared of all kinds of trees, the region being very branchy and very fertile, at once level and grassy. On every side flow sweet waters, and great springs gush out and the place is fed by a clear river – whose water, before tasting gives a glow to the face, and afterwards gives a sweet sensation as it runs through the body, so that none can satisfy their longing for this water. High mountains and their steep slopes enclose Dečani on the western side, and thence comes the purity of the air. On the eastern side stretches a great meadow, watered by the same river. Such a place is honourable and worthy for the building of a monastery.

Stephen had chosen the place for his own tomb. He began to build the church in 1327 and his son Dušan completed the frescoes in 1350. We could see some of the raw materials lying about from which the church was made: blocks of purple stone flecked with white are heaped by the quarry up the road. Sweet chestnuts – the wood used by carpenters for the church – grow within the monastery bounds, and probably, though we did not put it to the test, the greasy mess of chalk and gravel at the river's edge would make as good mortar as it did for the original builders. The Abbot goes on:

> Outside, it is most wondrously constructed of dressed marble, red and white together. One block is matched to another most beautifully and with great craftsmanship to make the surface of the whole church look like one stone.

The stripes of marble and stone have weathered to soft purple and gold. Like the Virgin's church at Studenica, which it resembles externally, Dečani was built by a Westernized architect. In this case, his name is known: Fra Vito of Kotor – a Franciscan from the coast. The main outline of his church is sober and sharp, the arcading restrained. Then the Friar and his craftsmen burst out into exuberant detail familiar to anyone who has haunted medieval churches in Western Europe. Centaurs blow trumpets above the west door, dragons with foxy heads droop downwards like a fur stole over the central window of the south wall. At the east end, below the arcading to the right, is a grotesque head with puffed cheeks and rolling tongue; the window there has a basilisk in the tympanum – something like a cock with a serpent's body – and a mermaid with two tails doing the splits in the frieze on the lefthand side.

Behind the basilisks and the mermaid we found the vegetable garden planted out just as it was in the 18th century – there is an engraving to check by – plots of earth edged with box and two yews trimmed into dark curved pyramids.

The monks' lives gave the same feeling of continuity. We were looked after by Father Justin, a cheerful self-educated man in his mid-thirties. He took pity on Elizabeth and myself – it was very cold there in early spring under the mountains – and had us up to the kitchen to get warm by the fire. He made it clear they led a very gentlemanly life and didn't work much in the woods and fields: they paid men to be woodcutters and to look after the cattle and pigs and hens, because 'a priest is a priest, and our Abbot is an up-to-date man. Now at ——, the monks work much harder, their Abbot's a stickler for tradition, you see, and they don't eat meat as we do. . . .' Something echoed:

> The reule of seint Maure or of seint Beneit,
> By cause that it was old and somdel streit
> This ilke Monk leet olde thynges pace,
> And heeld after the newe world the space.
> . . . .
> What sholde he studie and make hymselven wood,
> Upon a book in cloystre alwey to poure,
> Or swynken with his handes, and laboure,
> As Austyn bit? How shal the world be served?
> Lat Austyn have his swynk to hym reserved!
> . . . .
> His bootes souple, his hors in greet estaat.
> Now certainly he was a fair prelate;
> He was nat pale as a forpyned goost.
> A fat swan loved he best of any roost.

Father Justin and his Abbot did not hunt as Chaucer's monk did, nor wear such fine clothes, but they had quite a lot in common. We only saw the Abbot once in the distance: he was huge, 'a manly man', and, we were told, a very good shot. His predecessor, the Russian Theodosius, refused to let the Germans bring their guns into his courtyard, and when a German officer levelled a pistol at him, the Abbot asked if they could fight it out with their bare hands. He won the struggle

16 The east end of Dečani church

18 Archbishop Danilo II offers his Patriarchate to his patron, the Prophet Daniel: a 14th-century fresco in the Church of the Mother of God, Peć

17 The 16th-century icon of Stephen of Dečani painted by the

which followed and the Germans never tried to bring arms within the monastery again.

Seeing us revive, Father Justin got out his keys and let us into the church. Elizabeth and I were dazzled as our eyes met yard upon yard of unfaded fresco, on the vaults, on the walls, on the pillars, everywhere. Elizabeth liked it best of all the churches she had seen. I said how could she: it was an encyclopedia, all right for art historians.

We had both jumped to conclusions. Dečani does have a powerful attraction: the whole church glows as it must have done originally. Almost every scene is clear and brilliant, and very little damaged – so it is a relief not to have to peer at legs and arms and fragments of haloes set in crumbling plaster. For all that, it hovers on the edge of decadence. Much of the painting is mechanical, and its elaborate plan weakens the spiritual meaning which lies behind Eastern church art, and merely serves to show off the vast repertoire of subjects that can be treated within a sacred building. Only I had been too quick: the vast *mappa mundi* on the walls does contain a pattern.

We had gone in at the west door, into the narthex. There the archangels Michael and Gabriel stand waiting on either side with a stern welcome. Gabriel, light and ethereal, has barely finished writing out his message on a scroll, and his slender fingers are curved round the pen: 'I stand, the scribe of this holy place, and lead into the temple the pure in heart, and drive the unclean away.' Michael holds his completed message in his hand. He wears armour and a scarlet cloak. His sword is raised, and he threatens to use it on any of the wicked who try to get past him. They are telling you what the church is for: use by the faithful. This is brought home by other guardian figures: further on, the Mother of God and Christ are holding a conversation on either side of the nave door. (It is more usual to find them in the apse.) Her scroll reads:

> 'Receive the prayer of thy mother, O master, lover of man.'
> 'What are you asking, O mother?'
> 'Forgiveness for the sinful ones who have angered thee.'
> 'They do not repent.'
> 'Save them and give, for thy sake.'

An open Gospel records his conclusion: 'I am the light of the world: he that followeth me, shall not walk in darkness.'

Beyond them is the climax of worship, first the cupola, where the majestic face of the Pantocrator floats in golden space – the still centre of awe. There and below, the monumental painting is some of the finest and earliest in the church. Then, further eastwards, in the apse, is the Mother of God again. The painting of her head and hands is finicky, but she stretches her arms wide in prayer to include the whole world, and the two archangels reappear to flank her, this time in stiff, glittering robes. It is with the idea of human inadequacy and divine intercession that Dečani begins.

It continues with a codification of church art. A theologian may have planned it: perhaps Archbishop Danilo II from Peć or the first Abbot of Dečani. We went back to where we came in and looked at the narthex. It is covered with little paintings which illustrate the saints' days for a whole year, in places where you can and can't see them. Remembering a photograph, I asked Father Justin the whereabouts of Wisdom (Sophia) and her three martyred daughters, Faith, Hope and Charity. He said they were there all right but in years he had never found them. The general impression left by the Calendar is of a theatre of cruelty: St Sergius is shod with iron shoes by his executioner, St Carpus and St Papilus are each tied to the tails of two galloping horses – a story more pagan than Christian, which goes back to the *Iliad* and surfaces again in a Serbian epic poem, *The Wedding of King Vukašin*. Dečani was painted at a time of war and rebellion and plague. Even the posthumous miracles attributed to its founder Stephen are bloodthirsty. He caused a lying freebooter's tongue to rot and fall out, and a wicked Pasha to die of spontaneous combustion. It is a solace to know that the kind of painting used in the narthex petered out of its own accord.

On the eastern wall is the family tree of the Nemanjid dynasty, as at Gračanica.

The nave is full of Biblical subjects – cycle by cycle – if you can sort them out. The parables and miracles and Passion of Christ are there: the congregation are to be shown his wisdom, power and endurance. Every picture tells its story, some freely, some by use of earlier painters' formulae. The Acts of the Apostles are put in to tell ordinary people how the Church spread and suffered, Genesis for the creation of the world, the Last Judgement for its completion. You find the Great Festivals, Life of the Virgin, saints' lives and founders' portraits as usual: only, the nave in this church becomes a Bible in pictures, and the liturgical elements are half-swamped.

A complicated architecture matches the complicated frescoes. The main part of the church has five aisles; the narthex, three. The easiest way to look at the scattered frescoes is to choose a wall or an aisle at a time – for instance the grand west wall of the nave, where you get a little of everything – parables, princesses, Apostles, a huge Tree of Jesse and in the centre, the Last Judgement above, with the Life and Death of the Virgin below, themes which overflow onto the pilasters on either side. North of this, Constantine and Helena are at the bottom: 'School-children nowadays always think they're husband and wife,' said Father Justin sadly, 'and I have to put them right and *tell* them they're mother and son.' Genesis begins in the last vault at the top and skips into the chapel of St Demetrius in the north aisle, above the capitals, where it mostly is. Noah is on the north side, Cain and Abel on the south. The Genesis scenes are very small-scale: they give a picture of the everyday life of the time. Abel ploughs with two oxen and an iron plough. Cain builds a city that looks like the beginning of Novo Brdo or Maglić – a proper stronghold.

In the southeastern corner of the nave, mostly round the chapel of St Nicholas, are some joyful scenes which illustrate, stanza by stanza, a very long hymn, the Acathist to the Mother of God.[1] 'Someone wrote it in thanksgiving when Byzantium was saved from Slavs who were besieging the place in A.D. 626,' Father Simeon at Studenica had told me, 'and now here we are using it ourselves.' The scene I like best shows the flight into Egypt, when 'the idols fell unable to bear [Christ's] strength'. The idols, little black devils, are falling higgledy-piggledy off the top of a castle while the inhabitants, a noble lady and three men, are welcoming the Mother of God at the door. She is riding an ass and has turned round to stretch out her arms to the Christ-Child. He is being carried on St Joseph's shoulders, but he is trying to reach out to her, and it is very naturalistic. These paintings are a picture-book of praise to the Virgin. 'We see grandiloquent orators voiceless' with wonder at her – kings and noblemen who cannot bring themselves to write anything on their blank scrolls – and elsewhere she stands on a cushion with the infant Christ, and wax candles burn behind her:

> a flaming torch displayed for those who dwell in darkness: for She kindleth the immaterial fire, pointeth everyone to the divine Wisdom, enlighteneth minds by radiance.*

* These three scenes can be found, if you are of a persevering nature, on the south side of the easterly vault; on the south side of the pillar aligned with the southwesterly pillar and south from it; and on the south wall of the church west of the east window, on a wall pilaster above St Theodosius.

Father Justin moved us onto the iconostasis and Stephen's tomb. They open it on Easter Sunday and for big pilgrimages, he said, and the king lies there wearing rings on his hand and a gold bracelet set with pearls on his wrist. While the monk was talking to us, a gipsy woman arrived with a younger girl and some children. She handed a swaddled baby to the girl, and then she and the children crawled several times under the tomb, kissed it and left some money on the pall. The older woman muttered prayers for the younger, who wanted children. 'They *will* do it their way,' said Father Justin. 'We would like to pray over them ourselves – there are fitting words – but they stick to who-knows-what spells of their own.' The gipsies shuffled off and we looked at the fine icons which hang on the iconostasis. Among them is one of Stephen of Dečani, most tragic of the Serbian rulers apart from Prince Lazar. Like Prince Lazar, he is treated as a martyr. Dečani is his shrine. He was partly blinded by his father Milutin and probably strangled by his son Dušan – whose likeness, with thin lips and thoughtful eyes, is painted on the south wall of the nave, where he stands behind Stephen as co-founder of the monastery.

Longinus, the painter of Stephen's icon in the late 16th century, was a monk from Peć, a travelled sickly man of much talent. The icon is his own prayer to the saint to cure him of a terrible skin disease. He must have known Abbot Camblak's biography of Stephen by heart; he pillaged it for incidents which stressed Stephen's own endurance of suffering, the help he gave the sick, and the favour shown him by the heavenly powers. Longinus could paint with force – the central stern-faced figure of Stephen, the clashing cavalry in the battlefield below – and with delicacy. Miniature scenes from Stephen's life frame his portrait: in one of them, Stephen's children sit at the foot of his bed, in another, the tiny white-habited figure of Fra Vito of Kotor balances on a ladder as he supervises the building of Dečani. The colours blaze out red and pink and black on a golden ground.

Because Longinus was poet as well as painter, one is given a little more insight into his mind. His patron saints were St Nicholas and the Biblical St Stephen, and he invoked them both in a hymn to St Stephen:

> Do not forget me, humble and slothful,
> Thy useless servant,
> Consecrate me, let thy glory shine on me, and teach me
> To cry from the depths of my soul

Such words as these:
Hail, joy of those hymning thee,
Hail, balm to those praising thee,
Hail, star of the church,
. . . .
Hail, holy Stephen and great Nicholas,
Sole doers of many wonders.
Hail, for thee, slothful, I strive
To knit together these songs from my love,
Hail, for whose sake I am bold
To sing and to speak.
Hail, Stephen and Nicholas,
For through your divine thoughts
And through your actions
I learnt to limn saints' faces
As far as I was fit to do.
Hail, good and holy ones,
My great defenders,
For your holy images
Many times with my own hand
Have I painted, and your miracles.
Rejoice, apostle and first martyr,
Holy archdeacon Stephen.

Elizabeth had to go back to Belgrade, and late that night I saw her settled into a brand-new sleeping-car. At Peć station, the courtyard was strewn with people half-asleep. In the distance someone was singing a wailing tune, and the sky stretched black, except for a cold sparkle of stars.

It was sad Elizabeth had to leave, because the next day at Dečani the church was empty and Father Justin decided to produce a treat for trusted visitors: we were to look at the treasury. This involved turning several keys until a thick piece of wall swung open as a door, leaving a space about three feet high and broad, two feet above ground level. We half-climbed, half-crawled through that into a room lined with cupboards and piled high with dusty books. Father Justin unlocked a cupboard and drew out two crosses winking with light. One was golden, set with turquoise and malachite, amethyst and topaz, and tiny wood-carvings of the Life of Christ. The second was green enamel and gold, studded with garnets and emeralds. They went back into the cupboard, and out came a silver Gothic censer, a massive golden chalice with its base petalled like a flower, the jewelled pendant made for a

Bishop, and a Gospel book bound in gold and silver. I had seen no riches like these in other monasteries: so much was destroyed under the Turks. The precious things here were fragments of a glory seen in the frescoes. Father Justin turned to a chest full of reliquary boxes and undid the catch of one: a few small bones lay inside. 'These are martyrs' bones,' he said. 'No one embalmed them or did anything like that; they've lain here 600 years and they still smell sweet.' He held the open box up to my nose and I sniffed: it was true, the bones did smell quite nice, of sandalwood and spices – but I wondered about the embalming.

One of the old books was a diptych to use in prayers for the dead: page after page of their names were entered in red letters – a whole volume full. Also lying about was an 18th-century abbot's swordstick, which made me think of the present Abbot's skill with his weapons. I picked up a small filigree cradle. Women brought them in thanksgiving for a safe childbirth, Father Justin said, and never had them made in silver for fear the monks would sell them. When Tito and Jovanka came to visit Dečani, the monks gave her one of these cradles to take home. We locked, climbed and crawled our way back into the church. One day the State plans to reconstruct the old dining-hall in the courtyard to house these treasures. More people will see them then, and they will no longer be hidden in darkness as they have been for so long against thieves and enemies.

9

PRIZREN: THE EMPEROR'S TOWN

Monastery of the Holy Archangels – Bogorodica Ljeviška – an Albanian family at home – tales of the dervishes

The main road goes southeast across the plain to Prizren, past the fringe of Djakovica which looks modern but cannot be altogether as it harbours a sect of dervishes in the back streets. Prizren is Dušan's town. Sometimes it is called his capital, but it was this only in the sense that he held court there for a time. The Serbian kings were conquerors, not builders of cities, and as they took new territory they moved on. They do not seem to have had much urban life, just houses of varnished or painted wood, and Dušan put up any refugee royalty like John Cantacuzene in a luxurious tent. Milutin and Dušan both lived in style, even by the critical standards of Byzantine envoys, and the old poems are near the truth when they describe Dušan drinking wine 'in goodly Prizren' surrounded by his patriarchs and bishops and nobles. His Code of Law makes him sound just and feudal:

> And when a lord dies, his good horse and arms shall be given to the Tsar, and his great robes of pearls and golden girdle, let his son have them and let them not be taken by the Tsar: and if he have no son, but have a daughter then his daughter is free to sell or give it freely.
>
> . . . .
>
> And when a man shall present a son or brother at Court, the Tsar shall ask him: 'Shall I trust him?' And he shall say: 'Trust him as myself.'[1]

When Dušan's thoughts turned towards the conquest of Byzantium, he made his centre at Skopje – a strongly Greek city – and in 1346 was crowned Emperor there.

Dušan left no palace at Prizren, and no one even tells you where he lived. His memorial, as with most of his family, was a monastery, which he put up between 1348 and 1352. It is said that Dušan built thirty churches as an act of penance for killing his father, Stephen of Dečani. For his monastery of the Holy Archangels at Prizren he chose a site two kilometres east of the town. Now a ruin, it remains the proper gateway to medieval Prizren. Military men helped to advise the king on new foundations and it is strategically placed on the road which winds up and over the Šar mountains towards Skopje. Here the Bistrica gorge narrows and Dušan built on the enclosed valley floor, just above the river. A Byzantine castle already stood on the cliff above, and the new fortifications of the monastery were linked to the older fortress uphill.

Elizabeth had managed to come back from Belgrade and I fetched her at Prizren. When we got out to the monastery it was even colder than at Dečani: snow was falling and melting on our chilled faces. An impassive Albanian, who stood on a perpendicular crag between monastery and fortress, watched us and his sheep. Whenever he or one of his flock moved, a shower of stones fell too close for comfort. We looked half-heartedly for Dušan's churches. Then stones and snow stopped coming down, which raised our spirits, and we were able to take stock. In the ruins, some early flowers – grape hyacinths and a low-growing spurge – had come through the turf and softened the harsh landscape. As you go through the main gate, Dušan's tomb-church, after which the monastery is named, is on the left. The ground-plan can be traced clearly: a large church with three apses and a narthex. Massive pillars supported it and their bases are visible. Like Dečani it was made of purple and golden marble, and had carvings outside. Dark red marble was used in the vaults, and it had a mosaic floor encrusted with figures of real and fantastic animals.* Dušan's tomb is marked by a plaque in the nave. We went a little further and right under the cliff is St Nicholas' Church, small but grand: two delicate octagonal pillars remain near the altar, it has facings of dressed stone and signs of an inner and outer narthex. A third building, to the right of the entrance gate, was a dining-hall, built of flat red bricks and stone and several storeys high. The fortress is set into the outer walls, round the curve of the river. It is very substantial, soldiers could have lodged in it: you can sort out a big room and a lot of little rooms and an inner corridor. We went down to the river and looked back at what is left of the outer defences, and suddenly the whole place became a toy model of Byzantium, scaled down to size and seen from the land walls.

If it had been summer we would have picnicked here: as it was, the cold had finished us. Elizabeth was crying out for tea and this time so was I. We hurried back to Prizren. By the entrance to the hotel café an old Moslem woman in red *dimije* rocked rhythmically to and fro,

* Unfortunately one section of this floor has gone to the Museum at Skopje and the rest to the National Museum at Belgrade.

chanting 'Vay-tsay, vay-tsay.' She was the cloakroom attendant, advertising her wares: 'W.C.' Slavicized.

We set off to find the church that Dušan and his Court had used in the town. He did not have to build one: his grandfather Milutin had already done that. The church of Bogorodica Ljeviška is very close to the market: we had to push past loaded carts, piles of hay and groups of gossiping women to get there. It must originally have been something like this: an urban church not a monastery with broad acres, and Prizren, like Novi Pazar and Peć, has always been a trading centre. The market now deals mostly in vegetables and ironmongery, but under medieval Serbian rule fairs were held four times a year, goods were brought from Italy, Greece, Egypt and Hungary and Dušan proclaimed that 'Merchants who trade in scarlet cloth . . . shall travel freely . . . in my dominion.'[2] Prizren continues to be alive with commerce. It is full of shops where we ate sizzling meat in flat Moslem bread beside people going home to their villages; a beggar squatting in the snow with a plastic sack over his head whined and pretended his left hand was missing (it reappeared when no one was looking); and it is the only place west of Istanbul where I have bought *salep* – powdered orchid root – the basis of a milky spiced drink which tastes like Oriental rice-pudding.

At the church we were catapulted out of the crowd into an arcaded porch: a gathering-place for Milutin's Court after the Liturgy, before they went home to their town houses or country estates. Milutin had found a church ready-made at Prizren, a Byzantine building which dated from the 6th century and a Bishop's seat from the 11th. It had been restored in the 13th century, perhaps under St Sava's influence, and was apparently a perfectly good three-aisled, three-apsed church with a wooden roof. Milutin razed it to the ground, as he admits in an inscription on the east front, and used only the old foundations. Then he had it remodelled and painted on a grand scale to fit his Court and the breadth of his kingdom. It is one of the few medieval Serbian churches not built from scratch, so you see what Milutin thought needed altering. Up went a very elaborate building, with five cupolas, a blind dome over the altar and a belfry tower. The brick was worked into all kinds of patterns, some of them round the windows look like cross-stitch. The three aisles became five, and the central nave and inner aisles were made more impressive by a double set of pillars. The three apses stayed. Then he added the open narthex where we stood. Milutin in his own age was a considerable innovator.

The arcaded narthex is battered now, but charms by its subjects. It is painted in a storybook style rather different from the rest of the church. On the west wall, St John Damascene conducts an orchestra of graceful girls just as he says he will in one of his hymns. Plato and Plutarch are up on the wall;* since 2nd-century Alexandria the Eastern Church believed, off and on, that Greek philosophers had foretold Christ, and Plato's scroll says: 'At a certain time the word will come down on earth to live as flesh.' Finally, the painter, Astrapas, and the architect, Nicholas, are named in an inscription, and their rates of pay are given: for satisfactory work they received, monthly, four buckets of flour, two wheaten and two plain, some salt and a pailful of beer.†

There was a slight rumpus over getting into the church. A man wanted to charge us several dinars each. When I protested, he said foreigners always wanted something for nothing. First we argued, then we paid, then he sat sulking in the church jingling the keys and willing us to go. In the end we made friends: Elizabeth and I guessed that the Prizren Town Council had probably voted to charge tourists more, that he had not tried to cheat us, and he saw we were interested and began to point out things.

The church is peopled with large, haunting, impressive figures. All have white flecks where the Turks, adapting church into mosque, keyed the plaster they slapped on the frescoes. Now uncovered again, these figures are revealed as the last monumental art in Serbia, being painted from 1307 to 1309. The first you meet is Stephen Nemanja, over the west door of the inner narthex. Black-hooded and godlike in his monkish dress, he dominates this part of the building. I do not remember another portrait of him that is so huge, and St Sava and Stephen the First-Crowned, on either side of him, are much smaller. A frieze of double-headed eagles runs below. It is as if Milutin wanted to state: our dynasty is absolute, and our founder – a saint and a very great one at that – presides over it.

This makes the church very much of Milutin and Dušan's time: it shows the assurance of royalty in an age of expansion. It is shaped for processions, as it is made long and narrow by the pillars on either side of the nave. We found they acted as blinkers and we could only see, from the west end, the Bishops who bend to fit the curving wall of the apse behind the deserted altar. As we walked eastwards, the church opened out – more Bishops appeared on the flat surfaces north and

* On the west side of the north vault.

† On the west side of the south vault, to the right of a figure of Christ.

south of the altar, and many more frescoes, including the grave Mother of God on the south apse. She is uncomprisingly linear – her nose, her mouth, her hands, the border of her veil are done in the strictest of straight lines, so that the rounding of her nostrils or of her eyebrows seems like an indulgence.

She comes as a wonder, the cupola as pure delight. The Pantocrator is framed in an eight-pointed star that is as filmy as a lawn handkerchief, and in the triangular spaces between fly the angels, their bodies emerging from behind the points of the star. Light floods in on it all from the slit windows of the cupola.

It is worth searching for another magnificent figure of Christ, 'the Guardian of Prizren'. He is all golden and dark sea-green; his right hand twirls into a three-fingered blessing. Not far away is a painting that survives from the earlier church: a stolid Mother of God with a lively Child.* She has a woven basket of the kind made in Serbian and Macedonian mountain districts. Both Christ and his Mother are powerful icons. A small jar of oil with a wick in it was burning on the ledge in front of her. The church, one of the loveliest to survive from medieval Serbia, is supposed to be a museum, but no church in these parts turns thoroughly secular: the saints have been venerated so long, have effected so many cures, that people sneak in to ask their help, and even when the State has taken over, a flicker of life remains.

We had been wandering all day on our own; it was time to go and find Azim, an Albanian schoolmaster – we had been given a note to him. His father being the local blacksmith, they lived close to a market: good for trade, but the house entrance, a blank wall with a small door, was blocked by country carts as their horses queued up to be newly shod. It was very muddy, the horses would not budge to let us through, and we nearly went away again. It was hard to believe that a family could exist normally in the midst of so much shouting and pushing and crowding and with all the squashed cabbage leaves and dung underfoot. We had reckoned without the privacy of Moslem living, for in the end someone pushed a steaming horse aside, and called the schoolmaster's mother. The little door opened and we went through into a quiet, clean courtyard where a tall woman was waiting to welcome us. Slipping off our shoes, we went into her house. Our hostess was perhaps forty, dark and bonily good-looking, entirely at her ease with strangers.

* Christ the Guardian is on the south face of an inner pillar, the most westerly one. The Mother of God with her Child is in the south transept.

We sat on blue-and-white check floor cushions. As she made coffee she talked to us in Serbian which, like ours, was hesitant. She normally spoke Turkish at home, as do most Albanians in Prizren: it is the town-language and Albanian is thought countrified by the older generation; the young like to speak it for cultural reasons.* Azim's mother said her son was down at the school, she would take us there later. Time had become unimportant; now we had found her, everything would happen in due order, and we sat on while the sounds of her husband striking his anvil came through the window. She was illiterate, we had been told. Illiteracy in England sounds and is ugly, because in a developed society it is like a physical handicap that cripples someone for everyday life. But Azim's mother belongs to the last generation of women in Yugoslavia who can carry illiteracy gracefully: it made no difference to her household skills and her dignified manners. This may be because she belongs – just – to a traditional society. When we went to find her son, she asked her husband's permission before leaving the house, tied a close black headdress over her hair, hitched up her *dimije* under a long grey ulster (of the kind that nannies used to wear in England) and became as anonymous as every other Moslem woman who was wearing the same uniform, so much so that the next day we stopped to greet her, only to find a stranger. In the street we met three chattering schoolgirls in miniskirts who were learning languages and hoping to be nurses and secretaries and doctors and liked pop music and the Forsyte Saga on television. The generation gap in Prizren was wide – among women at least. Azim's mother handed us over and the girls bore us off triumphantly to Azim, her son and their teacher. He was the schoolmaster one hopes to find – and so often does not – in strange places: tactful, proud of his own inheritance, a good linguist. He dropped everything and came with us (what can have happened to his classes?). Had we been to the castle? No. Or to the Sinan Pasha Mosque? No, again. We would all go. Coffee, inevitably, and then we did go.

Being with Azim meant that we saw a different Prizren. Like Peć it faces two ways and so far we had been looking at the face that was medieval, Serbian and Orthodox. Now we saw the later, Albanian, Moslem side. Azim took us up a winding path to the castle. As he did, he pointed to a group of old houses huddled together: 'That's the Serbian quarter.' He might have been referring to foreign settlers.

* Albanian is spoken in Djakovica and the villages. In 1970, notices on the Town Hall at Prizren were in Turkish, Albanian and Serbo-Croat.

The Church of the Holy Saviour, built by one of Dušan's lords under the castle walls, he passed without a word. To him the castle was Turkish – though it had earlier belonged in turn to the Prizren Bishop and to Dušan's monastery of the Holy Archangels. From the south-eastern ramparts, where the river flows under the walls, I could see the Byzantine fortress in the distance: the Prizren castle is on an elbow of the river and commands the Skopje road: the two fortresses must have been of considerable importance when they remained in the same hands. Prizren castle had become a Turkish stronghold in the late Middle Ages and had lasted to be a garrison town during the Balkan Wars; it has a ruined mosque in the centre. Azim's grandfather had served there at the time of the great defeat of the Serbs by the Albanians 'when the White Drim ran red with the blood of thousands of Serbs. . . .' The light was beginning to go, and the sky turned yellow behind black mountain peaks and minarets. We started home again; by the time we got down, a half-moon was shining onto the domed Turkish baths and the sweetmeat shops were brightly lit. We went into a mosque. Sinan Pasha was Vizier here and when he died in 1604 the Mosque was built as his memorial. Many of the stones were stripped from the Holy Archangels' church.* It is a handsome place, though the carpets are modern. The Imam was at his prayers, and people came in and out to join him – quite a lot of them. We stayed for a while and then went and sat with Azim in a *kafana*. He was pleased to escort us through the Corso as Elizabeth was wearing a maxicoat and this gave our party a certain air.

I asked him about the dervishes in the neighbourhood. The old sheikh had been a friend of his father's, he said, and had recently died. His son had succeeded him but was over at Rijeka where he kept a shop.† Azim had been to the old man's funeral. He had been much respected as a wise man and two or three thousand members had attended. The dervishes who took part had worn long black robes with red upper garments, and their chanting became hypnotic, so that Azim, who is a non-believer and a Party member, found himself swaying and chanting with them. The Prizren dervishes hold their most important ceremonies on 6 May. I had hoped to see them but nothing happened because of mourning for the old sheikh. Fortunately, a Yugoslav television film was made of their initiation rites. Maces

* Memories are long. In 1919 the local Serbs tried to destroy the mosque in revenge; mercifully they failed.

† Most pastry cooks and jewellers on the northern Yugoslav coast are Albanian.

whirled in the air, and the monotonous chanting that Azim had described continued until men in a state of trance stuck needles into their cheeks. This is of medical interest; the trance may be due to 'over-breathing' or hypnosis, the lack of pain and bleeding to vascular constriction from fright or to the trick of pressing a finger to the cheek when the needle comes out.

It is less sensational, and therefore less known, that dervishes are mystics, and as such, not always approved by other Moslems. Several sects exist in Yugoslavia, the most interesting are the Albanian Bektashi now to be found at Djakovica and formerly at Prizren.* They have never met in mosques, but in their own *tekke.* They believe in the reincarnation of human souls into animals. 'A really devout Bektashi of the old school wears bells upon his shoes, that he may warn the little creatures of the grass to avoid his footsteps.'[3] They preach a universal love of mankind – Christian and Moslem alike. The dervish initiate advances from one 'grade' to another until he enters

> the Choir of the Saints, since all the saints are linked hand in hand, and thus he enters into this company, and into the chain of these Lords, as in a dance.
>
> . . . .
>
> Here must he know himself, for he who knows himself knows what God is.[4]

I was all the more regretful not to have met the old sheikh when I read about his predecessor of sixty years back, Hadji Adem Baba. He was renowned as a holy man who often spoke in parables, and he received both men and women. Brailsford called on him in Prizren:

> Gentle, dignified and courteous, he spends an innocent old age in a retired garden of red roses and old-fashioned stocks. To visit him was to step into an atmosphere of simplicity and peace. An active life lay behind him. He had spent long years wandering over the Moslem world. He had sojourned in India and studied in Bokhara, listening whenever some noted doctor had a thought to give or an influence to bestow. At the end of his pilgrimage, laden with the wisdom of the East, he even made his way to Rome, anxious to prove his tolerance by paying his respects to the Pope. He waited some months for an audience, and came away grieved by the rebuff. . . .[5]

* The Prizren dervishes are Sadi, a sub-order of the Rifai or 'howling dervishes'. The Bektashi probably go back to 14th-century Persia, but became popular through Janissary support and later were very strong in Albania.

We left Azim, that excellent companion and guide. He promised dervishes for the next year, when we could not come to see them.

The next day we set off for Belgrade, in the light that is special to Metohija: misty, with sun striking through clouds. The fields were green and damp. We went up over wooded heights and came out south of Gračanica, to rich earth and poor people. A man, standing upright in his cart like a charioteer, galloped a single horse across the plain.

10

GIPSIES AT GRAČANICA

A Roman city – the church and its guardian – the feast of Velika Gospojina – dancing in the dark

The first time I went with Richard to Gračanica we pitched a small tent in the fields near the church: it was autumn and all night the tall dense stems of maize whispered at us. We lay awake and wrongly named the ghosts in the maize: for we took them to be soldiers from Kossovo, whereas in fact the battlefield was twenty miles or so to the north. If there were ghosts, they were more likely to be Roman ones, for we were lying on the grass-covered stones of a Roman town, Ulpiana. It was more than a fortress – a substantial city which stretched over the plain and which is still being excavated. The next morning, we found the town entrance: for safety's sake they built it narrow, just wide enough for a horse and man to pass between two flanking towers with houses or guardrooms behind them. We saw modern irrigation pipes close beside the Roman water-supply system, the atrium of a house with a mosaic floor, the remains of a big basilica. In the clover fields there are graves, two of them Christian ones and a tombstone to Clementilla, who died at seventeen years old, 'a worthy wife'. These plains, fertile, high and cool, have always been inhabited, as witnessed by the magnificent Neolithic masks – slant-eyed, with triangular noses – in the Priština Museum; and by the henbane, which always grows where men have long cultivated the ground. Despite its local name 'the stinker' (*smrdljak*), it is a lovely flower, white, dark-veined and trumpet-shaped, with rank green thistle leaves.

As we walked about the Roman town, peasants tilled the fields and a small railway engine puffed by, its open wagons heaped with lead and zinc from the mines in the hills above. The Romans had worked these mines for silver and gold, as did the Serbs after them. Half a mile away, we could see the medieval church of Gračanica. It rises delicate and fantastic from a green slab of courtyard, enclosed by lower, later buildings and a stone wall. This church is built for a plain; to counteract the heavy horizontal pull of earth, its five cupolas soar up behind an

19 Old Serbian women walk along a Peć street

20 Gračanica: the prophet Elijah fed by a raven

21 The Ottoman Sultan, Bajazeth I

22 Gračanica: a gipsy woman with her child at the Feast of the Dormition

23 Gračanica: the northern side seen from Bora's yard

arched and pillared porch.* It is not a very big church, but its height makes it seem so. At that distance, although the pinkish stone is hewn into heavy blocks and the tall windows are herringboned with brickwork, the lift of its arches and vaults, the frilled edge of the domes, take it riding into the sky, light as an elaborate bubble which floats above the ground.

Nuns farm the diminished monastery lands at Gračanica, but the custodian of the church was Bora, a young Belgrade painter who had gone there to get peace and a studio. He and his wife, Zvezdana, and later a small baby, Nada, lived in two rooms in the courtyard. He copied frescoes and sculpted heads out of the knotted tufa rock from Novo Brdo. Bora was one of many wandering scholars we met while travelling. I have mentioned already the painters, art historians, botanists and geographers who thronged the Serbian countryside in summer: a few, like Bora, had settled in rather primitive conditions, the others were simply 'in the field' (*na terenu*), which could mean Mount Athos or remote places in their own land. Their stories were like nothing we knew. A woman friend told us: 'To get to the monastery I walked and walked in the heat, and thirsted dreadfully, but there was no water. When I saw a plum-tree, I stretched up and took a ripe plum. It was delicious. . . . Then I remembered nothing more till I came to, lying on the path. The peasant who was our guide stood over me and shook his head, saying: "Fool! Surely you know that you must never eat plums when the blood is heated. No wonder you fainted!" '

Gradually the place began to dominate Bora. Not only had he begun to look like a saint from the frescoes, with his narrow face, black Byzantine eyes and beard, but when he wrote us letters they were headed 'In the autumn of the Lord 1966 in peace – Amen. Sent from the Monastery of the Holy Mother of God at Gračanica,' and his Cyrillic script was deliberately archaic in style. The peasants often took him for a priest when they found him in the church, and asked a blessing, while in the crowded country buses he suffered from much hand-kissing. None of this appeared to displease him – rather the contrary: he had found his roots in the theocratic glories of the Middle Ages.

It was Bora who showed us the church. King Milutin had built it,

* The exo-narthex has now been opened up by the restorers to look as it did when built in the late 14th century. In the 1930s, Rebecca West met an architect who was threatened with excommunication by the monks if he removed this porch. Now, Church and State seem to have accommodated each other.

in 1321 – a man as much married as Henry VIII, and not unlike him in his ruthless exercise of power. In old age, he showed his devotion to the Church by founding all kinds of monasteries and churches – in this, following Byzantine royal custom. A fine new place of worship for his capital, a convent tucked away in the Skopje foothills, a small chapel tossed into the courtyard beside the towering older church at Studenica, a handsome village church – these were Milutin's foundations. Gračanica, last and perhaps finest of all, he had built in his hunting-grounds and made the seat of the local bishop. Wherever he went, he could command the best craftsmen, and the signatures of the famous Michael and Eutychius can be traced on the shield of a warrior saint in the humble church of St Nikita.

Inside, the Gračanica church is very grand – royalty everywhere. On one wall, there is a family tree of the Nemanjid dynasty: tiny figures like the kings and queens who fell out of cigarette packets in the 1930s. The only other paintings we ever saw of that size were in the Greek monastery of the Great Meteora, which a Serbian princeling turned monk had a hand in building.*

But 'all the important personages are together', as Bora commented, and they are painted almost life-size: the Emperor Constantine and his mother Helena; the parents of Milutin, Uroš I and Helen of Anjou who shares a wall with the Christ-child; Milutin himself and his child-wife, the Byzantine princess Simonida – married into a strange land at six years old. Opposite them, on the west wall, as if to remind the churchgoer of eternity, is the strange world of the Last Judgement, with its classical personification of the Sea which comes straight from ancient Rome, although it illustrates the Book of Revelations. This tension between earthly and heavenly glory, between kings in their splendour and souls in torment, is characteristic of Gračanica: Christ and a Queen stand together, the saints who circle the church walls seem to look towards the founder and his wife, the kingly and the saintly portraits are all painted in the same spirit, which is unusual in Byzantine art. Superstition has laid its mark on Simonida's portrait: her eye sockets are damaged, for peasants have scraped away the paint and plaster, in order to powder and swallow them as a cure for weak eyesight. Because of this custom it is as usual to see eyeless saints in Balkan churches, as to see headless or armless ones in Roundhead-sacked English ones. Traces of cobalt, however – a precious paint used only for portraits of the most eminent – still linger in the depths of

* Father Joasaf, born John Uroš Palaeologus and a half-nephew of the Emperor Dušan.

Simonida's eyes. The mutilated portrait of the young Queen is very touching. A Serbian poet, Milan Rakić, wrote some verses on her; he ended:

And now in the church, on the stone pillar,
In your elaborate mosaic of robes,
While you calmly endure your uncouth fate,
I watch you, pale and sorrowful in your pomp.

And just as stars, their fire put out,
Still shed their light on man,
Man sees in you the brightness, form and colour
Of distant stars which already don't exist.

Thus, from the dark wall,
On the soot-laden, ancient surface
Your eyes shine on me now, sad Simonida,
Your eyes, put out so long ago!

Once a Yugoslav tried to explain to us the interior architecture of an Orthodox church. 'Here is open, here is secret,' he said emphatically. This goes for Gračanica, where much is secret, kept in shadow. It is a very dramatic church, built as a cross within a cross, shut off into narrow dark vaults supported by powerful pillars, on one of which is Simonida's portrait. The sense of height echoes the exterior architecture, and the vaults surround a free central space leading up to a vertiginous cupola. As the height increases, so does the light: the onlooker gazes up at a heavenly clarity, in which the scenes from the life of Christ are illumined, while below, all remains in earthly darkness. You can peer into side-chapels and find secrets there: in the south Chapel, Elijah* in his cave, his sandalled feet breaking the jagged circle of cave mouth, and his long face gazing intently at the raven who brings him a neat disc of food marked with a Cross, a symbol of the Eucharist. His hermit's wrap of skins crosses him in a fluffy diagonal, like a woman's stole. This, and his flowing hair and beard, and two feathery trees, counteract the harsh lines of cave, rock and bony hermit. The colours are rich and few: a warm honeyed yellow for his tunic and halo, purplish-brown for skin and cave-depths, dark clear green for the trees, all set against the paleness of rock. Beneath him is an inscription about the founding of the monastery.

* 'Saint Elijah' (*Sveti Ilija*) has many mountain-peaks named after him in the Balkans and in Turkey. For the Slavs, he may have replaced their pagan God, Perun the Thunderer.

In the same chapel lies a Bishop of Lipljan. The rounded niche above his tomb holds a painting of his funeral: monks cense his body, priests in tall conical hats stand by. The portraits are good 15th-century work. Hidden away in the north chapel is the most marvellous sight of all: there, painted on a high curve of wall, is the giant figure of John the Baptist (*Sveti Jovan Krstitelj*), like a man made out of white and grey flames (his hair, the skins he wears) while his eyes, confident, strong and slightly veiled, look down on the faithful below him.

Not everything is hidden at Gračanica. In open glory, an army of saints line the south, east and north walls of the church. They stand two tiers high: horizontal painted bands – a substitute for marble incrustation – anchor them to the walls and frame their portraits. These saints seem to march from east to west and from west to east, old and young alike, Svetozar Radojčić wrote, 'as if in some monumental quadrille'.

There is a remarkable harmony about the frescoes at Gračanica. The anonymous Master of Gračanica uses, in a way typical of his age, an abundance of subject-matter: ten great cycles drawn from the Life of Christ, the Virgin Mary and St Nicholas, besides the Church Calendar and the Last Judgement. Yet although he enriches the narrative painting with details, he never overloads the composition with them. The Master of Gračanica seems to have been one of the greatest painters whom Milutin used – expressive, original and controlled. He could not, of course, paint all the walls, and in obscure corners, as usual in Orthodox churches, the assistants were put to work. But Elijah, John the Baptist, the Mother of God, the noble first row of warrior saints, seem to be his as well as the Harrowing of Hell, the Dormition of the Virgin and the myrrh-bearing Women in the Garden.

'Come back for *Velika Gospojina*!' Bora shouted at us as we left Gračanica. He had earlier explained to us what *Velika Gospojina* (The Dormition of the Virgin) meant at Gračanica. It was three days' feasting – and for the first night and day Orthodox gipsies came from far and wide and camped in the courtyard. Then they vanished like ghosts and the Serbs would fill church and courtyard in their turn. Like *Sveti Vračevi* at Sopoćani it was a *vašar* – a gathering, a fair, a religious festival all rolled into one. Gračanica is the most curious *vašar* in Serbia, because the Kossovo gipsies have made it their own. The gipsies may have come here from Anatolia as early as the 14th century, and in 1669 Edward Browne, Sir Thomas Browne's son, fled from the plague nearby and took on a gipsy guide who brought him safely through the region. Nowadays the gipsies work as blacksmiths or musicians; music is their chief enjoyment and St George's Day and the Dormition are their favourite festivals.

By 27 August, we were enduring the full heat of summer. I set off this time with Celia Williams and with Melanie Anderson, a young anthropologist from Oxford who hoped to write about Yugoslav gipsies. The journey from Belgrade was a dusty trek over bad roads: it left us dry-mouthed and weary. In the Ibar valley, men in white summer trousers and shirts worked the tawny slopes of Kopaonik. At Kosovska Mitrovica, everything was ugly except the English villas, built for pre-war engineers at the Trepča mines, which sat in trees under the grim fortress-peak of Zvečan.

It was twilight when we reached Gračanica. The warmth of the day still stayed in the air, and every sound carried with the distinctness of summer. From the village street, we could hear the drums beating in the monastery courtyard. I went through the gateway, and found the grassy enclosure starred with fires. Under the arcade of the monastery, tambourines were shaken, and unseen figures played wooden trumpets (*zurle*). Bagpipes, far more raucous here than in Scotland, moaned in strange rhythms. There was a solitary singer. The music had a wailing, repetitive Eastern sound, quite distinct from the Slav melodies with their full-blooded melancholy.

In the church, a choir of women from Skopje, led by a priest, sang the Liturgy and a crowded congregation listened half-attentively to them. The gipsy women held candles, and in that light their round faces looked warm, pearly and moist, as if made of rosy alabaster. Their eyes too were round, popping with wonder, and full lips were parted to show milky teeth. The bunches of thin brown candles, like pencils on fire, were balanced above babies in their arms, babies whose faces were miniatures of their own, framed in pleated white sun-bonnets. The mothers were dressed in ample Turkish trousers. A straight apron bound the trousers in narrowly from waist to knee: below that, they belled out again. The women wore white or coloured blouses, often left open to reveal a full breast at which the baby suckled while the priest intoned and the frescoes glowed dimly in the shadows above. Their head scarves, printed in black on white or yellow as in Bosnia, were edged with their own addition – a fringe of sequins, beads and small tassels, and the ends were wound round behind and tied over the top of the head so that they seemed to be wearing a narrow, beaded garland. The men wore ordinary clothes – and had dark, fine Indian features, a strong contrast to the priest who conducted the service – and who later accompanied us to Novo Brdo – with his broad reddened face and childish blue eyes.

The gipsies had brought their offerings with them. They left fruit, vegetables, live sheep and chickens with the nuns in the monastery: inside the church they had made piles of wheat grain, bread and a little wool. At the entrance to the church, my head hit something soft and taut. Childless women had walked round and round the building to bind it with a long thread of white wool as if it were an enormous parcel. By nightfall, it was like walking into a spider's web. Both men and women, hopeful for children, would kiss the thread and the door of the church. All the gipsies, even the small children, walked backwards out of the church, till they reached the porch. This was a custom they had invented for themselves.

Later, Bora took me out into the courtyard. Near the monastery, men were dancing the *kolo* to the beating of drums. The traveller Aaron Hill wrote sourly about Balkan gipsies in the early 18th century:

> they always choose some *even spot of Ground* . . . where the Men and Women *Sing* and *Dance*, in awkward *Gestures* all day long, *run*, *hop*, and toy away their Hours in various kinds of active entertainments.[1]

He may have been prejudiced as the gipsies had embarrassed a bashful young gentleman in the party by dancing naked and picking his pockets. Everyone has to see things their own way – Bora and I watched gipsies who leapt high in the air. Intent on the dance, they moved with electric energy. The gipsies danced in small circles of twelve or fifteen men; sometimes the group would snake out in a long line into the blackness, and re-form again in a circle a few yards further off – the leader tossing coins to the musician to continue. This perpetual movement, in the obscure light, made them seem elusive and disembodied, mere shadows cast on the summer darkness.

Beyond them, under the arcade of the guest-house (*konak*) straw had been thrown down, and on it lay more solid figures: women asleep in the attitudes of utter exhaustion, their bodies sprawling as if they too were filled with straw, arms flung out like bolsters set awry. Other men and women squatted there and watched the dancing, or crammed food into their mouths, and ragged children clutched themselves to ward off cold dewy airs. We turned left under the archway. At the foot of the stairs, more straw, more sleepers. An old withered woman rocked a baby in a rug turned hammock, slung on ropes between two wooden pillars. We waded up the stairs through a slushy morass of water-melon peel and seeds. Light shone down from the first floor which was nothing but a wooden gallery or landing with benches round: at least sixty or seventy people were encamped there for the night. The pale straw set off the brilliant reds and blues of the women's clothes; some of the gipsies sat and stared at all-comers, some smoked reflectively, a few slept. As under the arcades, their attitudes were abandoned, voluptuous, oriental. Two bicycles were propped up against the stairhead – apart from that, it was like walking into a scene from Delacroix.

Through the windows came a hubbub of people feasting. Outside, the music and singing went on all night; the courtyard fires were stacked with more and more wood and glowed bright and warm. When dawn came, only a quiet bee-like murmur of many voices broke the silence. Not many of the gipsies had had much sleep that night, and by 7 o'clock the field beyond the monastery was full of people cooking breakfast. Clouds of smoke rose from newly-stoked fires. Someone had piled up a great heap of melons: footballs made of malachite. In a corner a makeshift coffee-house had been installed and all the men entering it automatically cursed the drunkard who lay snoring over the table.

In the courtyard, more gipsies sauntered round the church. Two girls walked arm-in-arm. They wore brand-new versions of an old costume. Each had a *jelek* – a sleeveless short waistcoat – and *dimije* that were very wide and caught up in kirtle-like folds at each side. One was in pink satin, one in blue. Their blouses were of rough, faintly-striped, crinkled yellow-and-white silk with trumpet-shaped sleeves, and they had slung yard upon yard of pearl necklace round their necks.

The service inside the church seemed never-ending. A scrum of people pushed their way out; as at Sopoćani, exasperated nuns were trying to control them and to enforce some kind of order, but the crowd, kissing icons, lighting candles, greeting friends, outwitted them. It grew hot from the candle-flames around us. A woman asked: 'Where are you from? Oh, from England. Well, I'm from Brus (about 70 kilometres north across the mountains) but my daughter married into this village so I thought I'd come and see her for the Feast.' Soon we were too warm to stay in the church and came out to find a table near the porch laid with *žito*, bread, water and a bunch of sweet basil. Many women in the church carried bottles of water with them: it would be blessed by the priest, a sprig of sweet basil put inside the bottle, and the whole screwed up tight and only used in case of illness. The water keeps surprisingly well because of the essential oils in the basil.

The service at last ended and the priests led a procession out of the church. With their banners and brocaded vestments, they reminded me of the legendary description of Gračanica in an epic poem, when Prince Lazar summoned 'the Serbian patriarch and twelve great bishops' to the field of Kossovo, where he had built a church 'not from marble, but from pure silk and scarlet cloth'. Three Roman Catholic nuns from Priština, in neat black habits with white Peter Pan collars, walked in the procession, and were kissed warmly by the Orthodox Sisters. The Roman Catholic Church in Priština exists to serve the Albanians there: these nuns worked as nurses in the local hospital. A drifting raggle-taggle of Serbs and gipsies made up the *cortège*. One old woman, who all the morning had been squatting under the church wall, brewing coffee and chatting with her neighbour, now swung magnificently along. Her fine brown wool *dimije* were caught at the base by braided anklets of the same colour, and her waist was swathed in a beautiful red and green Kashmir shawl, folded to make a wide cummerbund – a legacy from Turkish times. Later, we gave her a lift into Priština, and she bewailed the passing of the good old days although she added quickly: 'Of course, there's plenty of *progress* now, one must say that.' Priština, set on hills among hills, looks like a *ville lumière*: all cubes, white or pale blue, with three tall tower blocks to centre it. The skyscrapers and factory-chimneys on the horizon echoed her words.

On the way back to Gračanica, we met a boy who seemed to be wearing a golden many-pointed crown. It was a ripe sunflower head which he had put on as a hat: the dried petals made his royal crown and the domed centre of black seeds exactly matched the colour of his hair.

Near the monastery, the gipsies were coming away; their own day at the feast was over. Before us, crowds of Serb villagers walked towards the monastery; their day was just beginning. In the evening, they swarmed in front of the church in a thick mass, in which a monotonous *kolo* was the only movement, and thumping accordion music the only sound. Bora's mother didn't like our mixing with them: 'Two young men came up and said something to Zvezdana just now, and she had to call for Bora. . . . Stay together, you must please stay together.' So we did, and nothing befell us.

II

FROM NOVO BRDO TO KOSSOVO FIELD

A ruined city – medieval silver miners – Turkish villagers – the battle on the plain

We slept the night soundly on the floor of Bora's house, and the next day set off for Novo Brdo (the New Hill). In the Middle Ages, Greek and French travellers wrote about this place and like all sources of treasure, it attracted popular legend: 'It yields up gold and silver like a well and to him who digs anywhere here it offers gold and silver dust – most plentiful and beautiful and better than India.' The wealth of the medieval Serbian kingdom did partly depend on the mines of Novo Brdo. Kings kept up monasteries, both in Serbia and on Mount Athos, with gifts of its silver. Formerly a flourishing city of miners and merchants, it is now an isolated ruin.

The old priest at Gračanica, who had once had Novo Brdo as his parish, joined us furtively outside the monastery gates. He had told the Abbess that he was going out on parish business. She had believed this, he explained, as he often went about his duties in the scattered upland villages:

'These village feast-days turn me into a slave, nothing but a slave. I go from house to house to bless the *žito* and the cake – I take the bus and then walk across the hills, sometimes all night long. And they *will* each have four feasts a year, and I have to visit every house. It's terrible, terrible. . . .'*

Some shadow from the past lay over the old man's life – we never discovered what it was. He was frightened of the Abbess finding out that he had gone with us, but excited at the journey. The Land-Rover climbed past an artificial lake, built to supply water to Priština. It was set in dry, stony country: what seemed to be forest turned out to be scrub: oak and juniper – it may have been forest once until cut by man

* The feast-day (*slava*) is usually celebrated on the day of a particular saint for each family. But some saints have winter *and* summer festivals. Each church has its own *slava* as well. So does each village. A priest may also be required on other occasions such as St George's Day or at the beginning of Lent. See also Glossary and Chapter 19.

or eaten by goat. In time, we came to pasture, and here and there were little plots of kitchen garden, but the earth was still only a thin covering over stones. Two hoopoes flew out of the pumpkin flowers. They flashed and turned before us: crested and exotic, they looked the royal birds of Egyptian legend, whose wings protected King Solomon from the rays of the sun.

The hills now rose steeper ahead of us: tall deformed trees were a reminder of the bitter wind-racked winters of this region. Beyond the first range rose a summit which even in August was clouded in cold mist. As we approached it, the sky cleared but remained a sombre grey. Outlined against it was a darker mass, a high tumbled heap of stones that menaced and reared, the ruined fortress of Novo Brdo. We left the car and started climbing the hill, eating wild plums as we went, and came to a grassy wide path edged with stones, once the medieval road to the city gates, and an important highway, for the medieval Novo Brdo formed a significant link between Serbia and the West.

The 12th and 13th centuries were a time of prosperity in Western Europe. Men sought silver and gold for their own value and also to provide worthy ornaments for the great cathedrals then being built. The quest for precious metals had a special fascination for medieval man. There was a European Gold Rush. Traders and settlers searched in every direction for new mines: in particular the Germans, who had their own silver town at Freiberg, explored Central Europe and the Slav lands further south. Saxon miners first reached Serbia, apparently, in the mid-13th century. By the early 14th century the mines of Gračanica were well-known and those at Novo Brdo were opened during Milutin's reign. Under his successor, Stephen of Dečani, Novo Brdo became the biggest mining centre in the Balkans, both for lead and for *glama* (silver mixed with gold).* Gradually most of the Saxons went away, leaving the work in Serbian hands. The town prospered, and in the 14th century probably had 40,000 inhabitants, more than Paris had at that time. Though the Saxons had left, other foreigners stayed. Dubrovnik merchants formed a large colony. They traded with the inhabitants and supplied their needs, even their luxuries: wine, saddles and harness, majolica-ware and cloth. The mining community, as elsewhere in Europe, formed a state within a state. They had their own representatives who treated with the King's officials. Their presence is reflected in the Emperor Dušan's Code: the Saxons were allowed to fell timber for their 'business' (i.e. mining) but not to clear

* The mines are still worked for silver and zinc.

the forest and settle there, like the Serbs. Goldsmiths had to stay in the towns: to avoid illegal minting of coins, they were threatened with branding if found in a village.

These laws dealt with all foreigners in Serbia. Although Dubrovnik merchants settled elsewhere, probably the largest concentration of foreigners was at Novo Brdo, the place where Dušan is said to have compiled his Code. The miners were an *élite*, and later developed their own laws based on Saxon and Bohemian mining-law. A fine illuminated MS, 'Despot Stephen Lazarević's Law on Mines' was found by chance after the Second World War in a Vienna saleroom. It was written for Novo Brdo in the early 15th century. The first part is extremely technical, the second part is more general and shows how the miners were given economic protection: if they bought luxury goods, maximum prices were regulated by law. But the miners had to obey the national interest: industrial disputes were proscribed in time of war; they had to be settled later, when peace was restored. On one page of this manuscript are portrait miniatures of the Serbian dignitaries who drew up these statutes.

The miners must have lived well. Their incomes were high: it was easy to smuggle money out of the Mint or silver from the workings. A Dubrovnik merchant's book of the 1430s lists their expenditure, and the names of shopkeepers. By then, the inhabitants were mostly Serbs from every corner of the land, from Vranje to Smederevo, but they also included an Albanian, a Bulgar, a Vlach, a Macedonian and a Saxon innkeeper.

It was the last real moment of prosperity for Novo Brdo: sixty years after the battle of the Marica, nearly forty years after Kossovo, most of Serbia had fallen. Soon the inhabitants of this remote and independent city, Ragusan and Serb alike, were to defend its walls against Turkish assault. In 1427 Murad II besieged the city for a year and failed to take it. In 1434, with the revival of the Serbian Despotate, George Branković held Novo Brdo – and, thought the French traveller Bertrandon de la Broquière, would have lost his lands without its riches to help him. But in 1455, after a bombardment of forty days, the city surrendered to Mohammed II. Over the next few years, most of its churches, Orthodox and Roman Catholic, were pillaged or turned into mosques. Leading citizens were killed: others were transported to Constantinople. The children became janissaries, the women, slaves.

None the less, though the town and its revenues dwindled, life at Novo Brdo seems to have had a curious continuity about it. The city had always been a little apart, by virtue of its specialized community and remote situation, from conditions in the rest of Serbia, and this seems to have been true – at first – even under the Turkish occupation. Suleiman the Magnificent treated with them and sent them new mining-laws. One of the Roman Catholic churches, 'Sancta Maria in Novomonte de Dogni Targ' was still in use in 1497. Strangest of all, in the 16th century, someone at Novo Brdo translated the *Olympian Odes* of Pindar and Aeschylus' *Seven against Thebes* into Serbian.

In the end, the Turks did stifle the life of Novo Brdo. What in 1499 had been an entirely Christian town of nearly 900 houses, with tailor, butcher, tanner, goldsmith and blacksmith, gradually became Moslemized and fell into decay. In the 17th and 18th centuries, little is known of it. Miss Irby and Miss Muir Mackenzie, who travelled through Serbia in the 1860s, heard of Novo Brdo from an account given by Major Zach, the Austrian Consul. When he reached it in 1858, he found only sixteen houses – one Christian, fifteen Moslem: the latter being descended from Asiatic colonists. There were tales, too, of the last 'hereditary governor', an Albanian chieftain, who, as elsewhere, had been allowed to pillage Serbs under Turkish rule.

Now, Novo Brdo is a wretched Turkish hamlet under the battlements. The houses are mean and dirty, half stable, half human habitation. We could see figures moving beyond an open door, but no one came out to greet us. A few sheep grazed round the houses and strayed under the walls of a broken-down mosque with a stump of minaret. Even the plants were dusty grey in that village: blunted short mulleins, the 'bandit's herb' (*Achillea millefolium*), spiky thistles and wormwood.

You can still see the main shape of the city: but it is easier to recreate its character as an isolated fortress rather than as a bustling town. The Turks live on the sloping eastern face of the hill, where many houses must once have stood, and where the crumbled foundations of St Nicholas' Church, once more magnificent than Gračanica, crown the bluff. The walls are layered in dark red and white stone: the sockets and base of huge pillars, the lower part of the bell-tower, the altar – all are still there, but little more, and plants spring from every crevice.

The upper fortress, hexagonal in shape, right on top of the hill, had a fine stone gate and corner towers, edged with red tufa, a kind of scarlet pumice stone. It faces west. The easternmost tower has a huge tufa cross set into the grey rubble of the main walls. The cross must have been visible to travellers a long way off. The broken grey stone of the ruined fortress now gives it the look of a natural outcrop of rock: only the hewn red stone recalls the hand of man.

Below the upper fortress is an oblong lap of land about fifty yards deep and rather more in width. Then the earth falls away in a steep drop. The lower fortress fans out on this level piece of land: its square towers stand at the bottom edge of the oblong, above a precipice. To the north, the drop is sheer from the inner fortress walls; to the south again there is a gentler curve of land. The fortress dominates the whole region and it is easy to see why the Turks found it hard to take the city.

We went into the upper fortress and climbed over rubble to look at the deep embrasures in the towers. A hare ran out from the stones. We found the powder magazines, but not the wells and cisterns of which there were plenty, the archaeologists say. Novo Brdo is confused, magnificent, tragic: a southern Elsinore destroyed by Turkish fire. The memories of its glory, especially of its fine churches, still linger in the peasants' talk. There are ruined churches everywhere. One spot is called Markove Crkve ('Marko's Churches'), another Sabornica ('the gathering-place'), a third, Jovanća (a diminutive of Jovan, or John) – but who Jovanća was, donor or priest, there is no knowing. The church which became a mosque, St Nicholas, is nicknamed Sveti Petka ('Saint Friday') like others at which the Turks worshipped.

When we came away down the hill again, the old priest met a parishioner who recognized him. 'Well, yes, I was in Novo Brdo for five years, but I didn't come much to this end of the parish: they're mostly Moslems here.' He told us about their burial customs: the *hodža* or *hodžinica* (according to the sex of the dead person) has to wash the body and to tie up the mouth and seal the other orifices so that the soul shall not escape. Then the body is put in a white linen sack and slung on carrying poles (as as the Novi Pazar mosque) and taken to the graveyard. There everyone stamps on the earth above the corpse to make sure he's dead. 'They throw down coins and cry: "St Peter, here's your money, now take his soul to heaven!" and then run away, and that's that.'

We drove north past Priština, till we reached the field of Kossovo. Like an inland sea – which, in the tertiary age, it once was – it rolls and heaves itself into waves of tawny stubble and rich black plough: good earth for farmers at peace; a natural battlefield in time of war. In 1953 the Republic of Serbia put up a memorial to the famous battle of 1389:

a tower that is stonily bleak and appropriate. When we climbed to the top of it, we could see the shining rivers, Lab and Sitnica, between which the Turkish and Serbian armies had encamped. A hundred yards from us, on a little knoll, stood the white tomb of a Turkish standard-bearer, like a child's top thrown on the golden land. We had once visited it in the spring, just after St George's Day, and had found the ground littered with chickens' heads which the gipsies had sacrificed. St George probably took over the Roman Shepherd Festival and in common with other sites in the Balkans the place is both holy and pagan. We looked further off, where the sun caught and blinked on the many-windowed house by Sultan Murad's sepulchre, bowered in feathery trees, and further still, to the cradle of distant mountains in which Kossovo lies. To the south, the high grey peak of Ljuboten heralded Macedonia; to the north, smaller mountains dipped into the valley through which the Serbs had fled after the fight.

By the end of the 14th century, the Ottoman Turks, led by Sultan Murad I, were advancing with irresistible force into the Balkans. They were already well established in Macedonia and Bulgaria. At Kossovo they faced the remains of the Serbian Empire, which had dwindled to a princedom led by Prince Lazar, and which barred their way northward to Central Europe.

Murad's army had made a long march to reach Kossovo. They had started from Plovdiv (now in Bulgaria) where the Sultan had wintered his troops, and on the way a Serbian envoy had met them with a letter from Prince Lazar; Murad had sent him packing. Then the army moved steadily on to the Southern Morava, to the point where the river forks south. There they halted. Banners were unfurled, trumpets played, drums beat, and the troops set off again in full battle-order. By midday they had covered the thirteen miles to Novo Brdo; they hardly paused except to take captive two 'unbelievers', probably Serbian reconnaissance troops, who strayed across their path. Then they encamped under the walls of the silver-mining city; it was so well fortified that they did not attempt to take it. The next day they reached Kossovo Field, a crossroads for the Balkan trade-routes, and set up camp on high land there.

The Serbs, who according to popular tradition had set out from Kruševac, Lazar's capital, were already encamped to the north of the Turks. Murad and his commanders were much dismayed by the Serbian numbers – about 25,000 men – and decided to rest their soldiers overnight before launching an attack. In fact the Turks greatly outnumbered the Serbs and their forces have been estimated at nearly 40,000. The Serbs' own alarm survives in one of their epic poems, where a knight describes his reconnaissance of the enemy lines:

From Zvečan Fortress, brother, to Čečan,
From Čečan to the mountains' summit –
Everywhere the Turkish soldiers pressed:
Horse upon horse, hero on hero,
Their battle-lances like black mountain-peaks,
Their banners like the clouds
And their tents like winter snows;
If heavy rain had dropped from the sky,
Nowhere would it have fallen on the earth,
But on goodly horses and heroes.

On the next morning, 15 June (old style), St Vitus' Day, both sides had drawn up their troops for battle, straddling the road from Priština to Belgrade. The Serbian lines faced southeast. The centre was commanded by Prince Lazar himself, who had royally feasted his commanders the previous night. Now his son-in-law, Vuk Branković, was at the head of the right wing, and the left wing was headed by another Serbian leader – traditionally, Miloš Obilić – and his men; with him were the Bosnian troops sent by King Tvrtko.

The Serbs had no standing army: Lazar depended mainly on troops raised by feudal lords from their lands and by his allies, and on foreign mercenaries. Archers from the feudal levies were placed in the front rank, and behind them were ranged the cavalry, who bristled with weapons. Each horseman wore a belt slung diagonally over his shoulder: on the left side hung his terrible two-edged sword, on the right, long and short knives were stuck into the belt, ready to hand. Some carried halberds and knobbed maces. They had fantastically-shaped helmets, some horned or shaped like an eagle, and heavy armour. Their stout shields, made of wood faced with leather and iron, were brilliant with heraldic devices. Behind them was the rabble of untrained foot-soldiers.

Opposite them, the Turks were massed in formidable order. The greatest difference between the Turkish and Serbian forces was that the Turks had a standing army: firstly, foot-soldiers paid by the State and secondly, the Corps of Janissaries founded by Murad himself; men taken as children from Christian territories, converted to Islam and turned into an admirable fighting force. The larger part of the army was still made up of feudal troops, apart from some vassal contingents, as both Turks and Serbs had inherited from Byzantium the system of military fief-holders.

Turkish archers formed the front line; behind them was a terrible obstacle, a deep ditch studded with sharp stakes and covered up with loose earth. It protected the centre and right-wing infantry only; the left wing had free if dangerous passage towards the enemy. Then came the cavalry: Sultan Murad faced Prince Lazar in the centre. Round him was a cluster of flags: four marked the place where he stood; another, his personal banner, had been lettered in gold. Military hierarchy was strictly observed: the Begler Beg of Rumelia (Turkey-in-Europe), Murad's elder son Bajazeth, led the right wing; the Begler Beg of Turkey, Jakub Čelebija, the left, with troops from Asia Minor. (Had they been fighting in Asia, the positions would have been reversed.) The Turks' helmets were pointed and often covered with coins. The plates of their armour were inscribed with texts from the Koran and with the name of the Sultan, but they preferred to wear chain-mail if they could because it was more comfortable. They had lit fires and brought up camels to frighten the enemy horses when they charged. Their commissariat carts were drawn up as a barrier behind the soldiers.

The battle seems to have begun at sunrise (4 a.m.) and to have ended about four hours later: a long time for a medieval conflict. There have been many contradictory accounts of the action. What seems clear is that it fell into four phases: a Turkish attack, met by a Serbian offensive (apparently successful), a Turkish counter-attack, and the final flight of the Serbs. The Serbs probably opened hostilities with a volley of arrows, which gave the cue for the Turks to launch their first charge. Bajazeth's right wing was engaged with the Serbian left, who, with the river Lab behind them, defended their positions fiercely. The Serbian right wing must have stayed at their vantage-point near the top of a slope during the opening phase of the battle. Now they charged, and this onslaught of heavily-armoured cavalry forced the Turks back. The janissaries and other foot-soldiers fought desperately, the bowmen inflicting heavy losses on the Serbs. The battlefield, strewn with heads and with turbans of many colours, reminded one Turkish chronicler of a huge bed of tulips. It is likely that at this stage of the action Sultan Murad was stabbed to death by the Serbian commander Miloš Obilić, who is said to have penetrated to the Sultan's tent by posing as an informer. Victory seemed near for the Serbs, but the stake-strewn trenches proved a deadly barrier and their casualties there stopped them from following up their advance.

Bajazeth assumed his father's command and began to counter-attack. First he ordered out the *bukaći-bozundžije*: men paid by the State to alarm the enemy. They shouted: 'The unbeliever has been routed. He has fled.' Bajazeth saw the danger to the Turkish left wing and centre from the Serbian right's attack. He tried to divert the battle westwards towards the river Sitnica by attacking the Serbian centre. It wavered, and the surviving janissaries and cavalry from the centre seem to have joined him as well as the retreating Turkish soldiers who surged back to help their comrades.

The last phase of the battle was an overwhelming advance by the Turks. With their superior numbers they were able to drive back one section of the Serbian right wing led by Vuk Branković,* the rest started to retreat northwards and the whole Serbian line broke. Prince Lazar was captured along with many of his nobles and taken before Bajazeth who had already ordered the assassination of his brother and rival Jakub. According to Constantine the Janissary, a 15th-century Serb who had been in Turkish service:

> Then said Sultan Bajazeth to Prince Lazar: 'Now thou seest my father and brothers laid on biers, how hast thou dared to try and oppose my father?' Prince Lazar was silent, but Duke Krajmir began to speak: 'Gentle prince, answer the Sultan thus: the head is not a willow-tree, that it grow again a second time.' And Prince Lazar said to the Sultan: 'A greater marvel is this: that thy father dared to attack the Serbian kingdom.' Then he continued: 'Had I known what I now see with my own eyes, thou wouldst have lain on a fourth bier, but the Lord God did not will it so, because of the magnitude of our sins. May God's will be done this day!' Then the Sultan ordered that his head be cut off, but Krajmir prevailed on the Sultan by his entreaties, to hold a dish beneath the head of Prince Lazar, that it might not fall to the ground; then Duke Krajmir bent down his head and said to Prince Lazar: 'I have sworn today to the Lord God that where the head of Prince Lazar shall be, there shall be mine,' and both heads fell to the ground. About the same time, a janissary brought in the head of Miloš Obilić and threw it before the Sultan's feet, saying: 'Here, O Sultan, are the heads of your two fiercest enemies.'

Although the Serbs had lost the battle, their rulers and many of their leaders, for a time the Turks seem to have been so dazed by the death of their own Sultan and his son that they hardly claimed the victory.

* Vuk Branković's treachery, mentioned in the Serbian epic poems, has no historical foundation. On the contrary, he held out against the Turks until 1392, when he finally accepted vassalage. He may well have become a scapegoat because he survived the battle alive while Lazar died for his people.

Confused rumours of the outcome spread round Europe. In the West, Kossovo was at first celebrated as a victory of the Serbs over the infidel: there was great rejoicing in Florence, and a Te Deum of commemoration was sung in Paris at Notre-Dame. Probably this mistake arose from the letter sent by the powerful Bosnian king Tvrtko to impress Trogir and to other cities in Dalmatia and Italy: in it he announced that he had defeated the Turks at Kossovo. He may genuinely have believed, from his commanders' reports, that with such heavy casualties the Turks could not have won a clear victory.

Soon a cloud of Christian and Moslem propaganda partly obscured the record of the battle. The Serbian monks, who wove eulogies of Prince Lazar into their services, gave the dead ruler a martyr's crown; the Turks in their documents did the same for Murad, alleging that his assassin had 'caused the illustrious Sultan to drink the sherbet of martyrdom'.

For both sides Kossovo was a heroic story. Murad was the first Ottoman Sultan to be killed in battle: his tomb became a shrine and still is. The Turks had conquered the unbeliever, but Kossovo, the most costly battle in their advance through strange lands, is often described in their poems and chronicles as a tragic triumph. For the Serbs under Turkish domination the memory of Kossovo was at once their defeat and their glory, to be recalled in magnificent epic verse.

Kossovo was not, as is often made out, the strategic turning-point of the Ottoman advance through the Balkans. But in other ways it can be considered as one of the most important battles of the Middle Ages. It was a major confrontation between Christian and Moslem forces at a time when Europe was forced to think of keeping the infidel at bay. It was also a vast pitched battle fought on the open field when siege warfare, though in decline, was still the usual means of making war.

The tower, the tombs, the clumps of Kossovo paeonies with their sticky petals of purest red – these are all that are left, physically, to remind the traveller of the fearful bloodshed that even in England, 200 years later, caused Richard Knolles to write in his *Generall Historie of the Turkes*: 'It is thought, greater armies than these two had sildome before met in EUROPE.'[1]

12

MORAVA: PRINCE LAZAR AND PRINCESS MILICA

The nuns of Ravanica – a country wedding – Kruševac: a prince's capital – commemoration of the dead – Jefimija's lament – Abbess Barbara of Ljubostinja

After the battle, Lazar's body was carried to Ravanica in a solemn procession; his daughter and her husband, Lazar's co-ruler, Vuk Branković, came with their nobles to meet him and to see him placed in the church which he had had built to hold his tomb.

Ravanica is a small monastery only a few miles east of the Morava valley and off the main road which has always carried travellers between Greek and Turkish lands and the West, but it might be at the end of the world. You reach it by going through a pretty village, Senje, where houses and barns jostle each other haphazardly among vines and apples and flowers on either side of the track, and then by driving along a ravine. The road appears to stop just short of the monastery, which lies below hills furred over with trees. A husk of ruined fortress breaks open and inside is a tall church of red brick and white stone: its five high cupolas are capped with flattened frilly roofs. The calm of the place is rent by thin screams, for the nuns keep some spectacular peacocks. At least, they are spectacular most of the year, but when their moulting season and a feast-day coincide, their tail-feathers are plucked out and given to the faithful as a charm against the evil eye, though peacocks officially live on church lands because they are a symbol of the Resurrection.*

The nuns arrived here in 1946. Since the monastery was founded, its inhabitants have come and gone. At the end of the 17th century the Turks sacked it and the monks with their pupils and their holy relics – including Lazar's body – fled north to settle at 'New Ravanica' in the Fruška Gora hills beyond Belgrade. They were able to return and to rebuild the monastery in the 18th century, but in the Second World War their successors had to abandon it. The older nuns in the present

* For this reason, you find them on early Byzantine tombs and iconostases.

community once lived in the Vojvodina, where in wartime they were driven from one monastery by the Hungarians only to be hunted down by Croat terrorists at another. Now they live at peace, grumbling at the archaeologists who will tear down useful outbuildings in their search for medieval foundations.

The nuns are ruled over by a remarkable woman. To find her, I had to play the game of Hunt the Abbess. This consists, like chess, of certain set moves followed by long pauses. The visitor asks the nun guarding the church whether the Abbess is at home. The nun says No. The visitor then begins making notes on frescoes, and after a while goes outside to rest in the churchyard. The nun smilingly brings her a cup of coffee. The visitor then continues to make notes on frescoes. A second nun appears: the Abbess would like to see the foreign guest. These moves may be prolonged over several days; at Ravanica they were concluded within a few hours. A nun took me to a room where an excellent lunch of monastery produce had been laid, and the Abbess Gabriel, a tall, dour-faced woman, came in, seated herself and ordered me to set to. I had been warned about her extreme austerity. Life, she believes, should consist entirely of manual work and divine worship, and that goes for life inside or outside a monastery. She praised one of her workmen who laboured from dawn till dusk and then went home to sleep:

'Work is good; it keeps people from being influenced by television or books.'

'Are such things *bad* for people, then?' I asked.

'No, not necessarily bad, but they are distractions, they keep people away from work, and work is what we are made for.'

She came back to this again when we were talking about her community. She directs sixty-five nuns and nearly half live, for a year at a time, in another monastery, St Petka near Paraćin, where they run a State Home for mentally retarded children. Then they return to her. At Ravanica they take in only the mothers of nuns and not, as in some communities, other elderly people who need nursing. She is resolved that life at the mother-house should be contemplative: 'We aren't here for social work, we're here for worship.' Once, I knew, she had been asked to pray, along with her community, for a convent of English nuns by name: the list had boomeranged back to the sender, with her note attached: 'We have no need of this; we already pray for the whole world.' The nuns live hard. They rise at 3.30 a.m., spend two hours in church and then work until Vespers at 6 p.m. Their only holidays are on Sundays or on Church feast-days. The room we sat in was small, but it had seven beds in it. 'We want to build another house, but we can't afford it, and anyway suffering is our lot – that's what the religious life is about.' In the West, Ravanica would be called an enclosed convent: the nuns did not travel or visit their families, they did not even go into the village, except the Abbess on monastery business – though their church with its three priests serves the whole parish. The Abbess was held in loving respect in the village, where they called her the 'heavenly soul' (*rajska duša*).

Ravanica was unique among the monasteries I visited; each to some extent varied in character according to the personality of the abbess or abbot and the same may have been true in the Middle Ages, as the chronicles stress the achievements of individual abbots. This is quite unlike the West, where membership of a particular religious order largely determines the kind of life led in each monastery.

Abbess Gabriel, like some other fanatics, has great personal charm. Of this, no one had warned me. She shows the relaxed self-confidence of someone who long ago decided on a particular path and has stuck to it ever since. Her way of seeing things is narrow and all of a piece, and she defends her views with friendly certainty. Unwillingly, I succumbed: out of a rigid framework she had created her own world.

The pattern of spiritual life at Ravanica may well be influenced by the memory of St Romil, to whom Lazar gave refuge in 1375 while he was still building the monastery. At that time the Balkans were alive with refugees from Mount Athos, Bulgaria and Byzantium who were fleeing westwards from the Ottoman advance. They included many monks: some were painters, some, like St Romil, were mystics.* He set up as a hermit in a cave nearby; when he died a year or two later, his bones, buried in the church, were reported to cause miracles of healing. He turned Ravanica into a sacred place before Lazar himself came to lie there; they became the twin saints of the place, and when Sir Thomas Browne's son, Edward, rode by in 1669, he saw 'a noted church, wherein is kept the body of Kenez Lazarus, and the body of St Romanus'.[1] St Romil came to mind now when I talked to the Abbess Gabriel and watched her nuns taking a loaf from the oven or trundling a wheelbarrow full of stones to repair a house. In St Romil's own autobiography he described the ideal monk who should do physical work, like himself in youth, and be able to hew stone, use a lime-kiln

* St Romil and his companions were followers of the Hesychast movement led by St Gregory Palamas. They emphasized mystical prayer within the normal life of the Church.

or help out a baker. What comes through most of all is the saint's resigned and submissive spirit.

If St Romil is a source of the nuns' day-to-day life at Ravanica, then Lazar gives the place its measure of history and poetry. The prince, and his son Despot Stephen after him, were among the last rulers of medieval Serbia; they went on to establish monasteries as their predecessors had done. The Serbian Empire had split up and their lands were northerly, between the Turks and the Hungarians. They chose churchless districts remote from earlier centres of power: in the forests south of Belgrade and in the side-valleys of the Morava. Even in decay, Serbia possessed great wealth from its mines, and Lazar could endow his foundations richly from his own feudal estates at Novo Brdo.

Lazar finished building the church in 1371–2 but it took him at least ten years more to decorate it with frescoes and to add monastic cells, a hospital in the Byzantine tradition for sick monks and travellers, and to fortify it. In Lazar's day, peasants assured a 19th-century traveller, a lantern was lit on the highest tower at the beginning of Vespers, and priests far away in the capital city, Kruševac, watched for it so that the Prince could go to service there at the same hour. Mileage and mountains make this a tall story and in fact the monastery can barely have been finished before Lazar's own death at Kossovo.

The Serbian Church was prompt to canonize the dead prince, and the monks at Ravanica were among the first to compose hymns and services of intercession in his name. Lazar is glorified in verse: he had attacked the Turks 'like a lion in action' or like a 'new David' rising up against Goliath. The monks saw Lazar as a soldier of Christ, welcomed in heaven because he had fought to the death to protect his people: it is for this that he receives his martyr's crown – he is a warrior saint like those painted on the walls of Ravanica.* The cult of Lazar grew, and popular bards chanted poems about his exploits in war and peace. One of these, *The Building of Ravanica*, is filled with a sense of triumph over inevitable doom, characteristic of the defeated Serbs. The poem builds up a picture of courtly splendour seen through peasant eyes: the knight Miloš Obilić with a silver feather in his sable cap, the glittering ritual figure of Lazar's wife, Milica, the prince's plan to make a church at Ravanica with silver walls and golden roof, studded with pearls and precious stones. Then all this magnificence is thrown aside as Miloš speaks his sombre prophecy:

* The idea that he passively accepted defeat in order to gain a heavenly Kingdom must be a later interpolation. See Appendix II.

Take, O prince, the ancient books,
look thou what the books tell us:
the last days have come,
the Turks will take the Empire,
the Turks will soon be the rulers;
they will wreck our chantries,
they will wreck our monasteries,
they will wreck the church of Ravanica,
the foundations of lead will be ripped out
and melted for cannon-balls,
our castles will be destroyed.
. . . .
they will unthread pearls from the church
to thread on their ladies' necklaces,
take out the precious jewels
to decorate sabres and sword-hilts.
. . . .
But hearken to me, glorious prince Lazar!
Let us quarry the marble rock,
let us build a church of stone,
and the Turks shall take the Empire
and our churches shall praise the Lord
through the ages till Judgement Day.

In the poem, Lazar does as Miloš advises, and the 'church of stone' still stands. Ravanica is evocative in its faded beauty of the end of an Empire. The Morava valley churches share this elegiac quality, and especially in autumn it is possible to read into the architecture and painting of Ravanica a melancholy which may not always have been there. The church when it was first built was of splendid appearance: the older chronicles stress the seven high towers built all round: any monastery designed then had to be well-prepared against attack by thieves and enemies and the Turks were several times repulsed at Ravanica soon after it was built. Parts of the defensive walls are still being excavated.

The church by contrast is very delicate. It once had an arcaded porch, now gone. The real pleasure of the exterior lies in the way brick and stone have been used to make flat and raised patterns in colour, as if an architect had chosen to embroider and quilt the whole surface of the church. Milutin had started this fashion in his church of Bogorodica Ljeviška at Prizren, but at Ravanica it becomes virtuoso work. On the walls the patterns are abstract – checks and stripes and diamonds; round the windows oriental beasts and birds are carved in stone. Inside the long narrow building, the three apses are shaped like a clover leaf and the nave makes a thick stalk.* The frescoes fit closely into this architecture. In the conch of the south apse the Entry into Jerusalem uses the curve of the wall. Christ rides a horse; no donkey ever looked so well-groomed or stepped so high. Christ is treated as an Emperor and it is a courtly painting. On the far side of him is a medieval city with people leaning over the parapets and a crowd of burghers outside its walls to welcome him. A woman with two children at her feet centres the picture and holds up a branch of palm. The details are lively and contemporary, joyfulness being the keynote.† It is sad that so many of the frescoes at Ravanica have faded away. The Turks cannot altogether be blamed: the plaster was badly prepared and the colour went very quickly.

In the apse, another painter worked, and what survives of the Communion of the Apostles is very fine. So is the Mother of God. They are painted with strong tranquillity and a sense of the eternal. A third painter went up into the cupola and did not do it justice: he painted some poor little prophets, clockwork figures who simper and look dull.

It is difficult to imagine the Ravanica frescoes as a whole but once the paintings showed the Miracles of Christ, arranged as they appear in the liturgical book which runs from Easter through Pentecost. In the second zone, below the Entry into Jerusalem, is the healing of the blind man as described in the service for the 'Sunday of the Blind Man':

> With eyes spiritually blinded I come to thee, O Christ, as did he who was blind from birth, and penitently cry unto thee; thou art the shining light of them that are in darkness.[2]

The treatment has a certain realism: the face of the blind man, with his hand outstretched towards the gentle Christ, expresses suffering and deprivation. The red and blue of the robes, the column of marble and gold in the building behind the blind man, are dark and rich-looking. To the left of this scene is another miracle: the paralysed man sits up in his bed, and again, the details come from the liturgical and not the Biblical version. Below are warrior saints who might be knights from Lazar's army, so soon to be defeated, and more of them stand opposite, to the north.

* The trefoil church was an ancient Byzantine model revived.

† The painting can be compared with those on the same subject in the churches of the Peribleptos and of the Pantanassa at Mistra.

So faint are the traces of other miracles and parables that one must take on trust Gadarene swine, loaves and fishes from the scholars who have deciphered their fragments. North of the iconostasis are two ghostly portraits of the founders, Lazar and Milica, with their sons – bare lumpy faces with gold-banded foreheads – underneath. Lazar's tomb, now in the Cathedral Church in Belgrade, lay here; it was among them, wrote one monk,

> like a purple rose,
> a sweet-smelling apple,
> a lily of the field.

* * *

Kruševac is far away, and before I drove there I had to find a night's lodging. The first householder I asked in the village of Senje took me straight home to his wife, and they gave me the bed in their kitchen – their winter kitchen, that is, for outside the house, in a shed, was the summer kitchen where Mrs Popović and her friend were putting piles of green peppers and apples ready for cooking: jars of plums and peaches were already on the shelves. This second kitchen is very necessary in the country because every smallholder grows, and his wife preserves, so much against the winter. I have even seen, in a small town, a newly-built garage appropriated by the women of the household and filled with barrels of newly-salted cabbage and vats of steaming jam; the car stood in the street. The Popovićs' house was comfortable, one-storeyed, with three rooms, an electric cooker and a coal stove for heating. Water was kept in an earthenware pitcher. The Popovićs accepted me quite easily. They had a nephew-by-marriage who was an Englishman: out came the photographs. A good boy, they said. But we must go outside, not sit indoors, there was a wedding on. The day before, the bridegroom's family had been to fetch the bride from her village; now, on the second afternoon, after the civil wedding and the church blessing, it was time for eating and dancing. The *kolo* moved up and down the main street, older people in one circle, younger people in another. The Popovićs were in mourning for a relative so did not dance, and found this a hardship: to peasants of their age whom the television and the cinema have not quite reached, each wedding or feast-day is a happy relaxation. After several hours, the dancers stopped for a meal. A neighbour had prepared the banquet for 116 people: 'We were two chief cooks, with several assistants: we gave them soup and cabbage rolls and stuffed paprikas and roast sucking-pig and pastries and cakes.' About 7 p.m. the dancing began again. The bride did not come out until quite late in the evening. A strong girl in a dark coat and skirt and a plastic tiara, she danced untiringly beside her good-looking husband with his white buttonhole. The musicians were Serbs: they had violins, accordions and a double-bass to keep the rhythm. When, later on, I went to bed, it sounded more like a drum – half Eastern again. At 5 in the morning I heard the buses revving up to take everyone home. The wedding was a mixture of old and new customs. In Macedonia things are more traditional with the bridegroom's gifts displayed by horsemen, old men singing bawdy songs and rifles fired for *feu de joie*, but in both regions, gaiety and lavishness rule the day.

In the morning, I sat drinking coffee with Mrs Popović and her friend as they worked in the summer kitchen. The friend asked:

'Why does your husband let you travel around like this?'

'He has confidence in me, I suppose.'

'That's all very well, but a young woman like you. . . .'

'I'm forty-three, and if that isn't a safe enough age, what is?' They both disbelieved me. It is difficult to explain one's age to women who work so hard in and out of doors and are old at thirty. Mrs Popović gave me some plum jam and kissed me good-bye.

I went to see Kruševac, for Lazar's church there stands on a hillock surrounded by the dusty ruins of his capital: two palaces, the citadel, the merchants' quarter below. Here he lived and worshipped and defended his kingdom. Not far away are the crumbling castles of his and his sons' nobles. Stalać, placed where the main road north of the town crosses the Morava, belonged to a commander who, according to one poem, threw himself into the river as did his wife, rather than be taken by the Turks. The most impressive fortress is Koznik, far up in the juniper hills to the southwest.*

The first thing I saw in Kruševac was a falcon in a cage on a house-wall, a poor relation of the grey falcon of the poems, who foretold what was to come at Kossovo. Kruševac is the centre of legends about the eve and aftermath of the battle. There Lazar feasted his knights, there his wife pleaded with her brother to stay with her while others fought, but he went:

* Koznik can be reached by driving through Aleksandrovac to the village of Milentije Polje; from there it is two hours' walk. The best view of it is from the road that cuts across the mountains to the Ibar valley, via Aleksandrovac and Jošanička Banja.

to shed my blood for the honourable Cross
and to die with my brethren as I pledged my word.

There a wounded squire finally came to her and told her how Miloš had killed the Sultan:

he leaves a memory to the Serbian race
to tell and tell again in story
as long as men and Kossovo shall be.

Lazar's capital church is built in a style similar to Ravanica, about 1370. It has the same high walls, this time with rose windows let into the top band of decoration and repeating the curve of the arcading above. So far, so good: the main walls are well-proportioned, their brickwork admirable. Then it becomes over-elaborate: the rose-windows appear again on the towers beneath the cupola and over the narthex, and the roofs seem piled up on one another for no particular reason. The windows are of every possible shape. The craftsmanship is remarkable, but where Ravanica is a disciplined fantasy, the Lazarica has got out of hand. The decadent effect is the same inside the church. The perfect marriage between outer walls and inner surfaces has been dissolved: the walls have thickened and small niches have been hacked out of them; the trefoil shape has lost its purity. The frescoes have vanished, though a haunting 18th-century portrait of Lazar, with piercing eyes, does survive and may be seen in the National Museum at Belgrade.

I stood inside the church rather at a loss, then noticed an 18th-century Russian Bible, bound in silver, on a lectern. It may have been a gift from a Tsar or a monastery. I had looked at the title and was beginning to turn over the pages when I received a tingling slap on the hand. It was the old woman who had charge of the church: 'The Bible's for kissing, not for reading,' she croaked angrily, and hustled me out.*

After a night in the Kruševac hotel, I drove to Ljubostinja in the early morning without hurrying: along the Western Morava valley, past villages with names that recalled the Turkish occupation of Serbia: Čitluk and Bivolje.† Then, crossing the bridge at Trstenik to the

* Before leaving Kruševac, it is worth seeing the *Slobodište*, a Partisan war memorial: winged stone shapes are set irregularly in a field, so that their composition, always satisfying, changes as you walk through them.

† *Čitluk*: a village where the Turkish owner enforced Serbian serfdom – a system wide-spread during the 18th century. *Bivolje*: Buffalos.'

north bank of the river, I found the signpost marking the way to the monastery. A smart Opel car with two nuns in it shot out from the lane and paused before turning into the main road. I leant out of the window and asked for Abbess Barbara.

'That's me,' said a nun wearing sun-glasses who occupied the passenger-seat, 'I'm going to the hospital. Back at 4 o'clock. Come and see us then.' Her driver let in the clutch and they were off.

If this had happened at the beginning of my travels, I should have felt frustrated in a Western way: a whole day wasted, another Abbess gone. . . . By now I knew that if one thing did not materialize, with luck another would.

Some while before, I had been reading the memoirs of an English nurse who had worked in this district during the First World War. She had described walking across the fields from Vrnjačka Banja, where the improvised hospitals were, to an old and pretty graveyard. Cemeteries, being placed on hillsides, are easy to spot, and soon I was talking to two cheerful grave-diggers, their hands gloved in white mortar dust. I'd come to the wrong graveyard, they said, the new one: the Partisans lay here and a local celebrity who had died earlier, a fine headstone, wasn't it? They pointed out the way to me. The nurse had been right: the old graveyard looked over the fruitful landscape of the river valley. I wandered among stone Maltese crosses, turned a corner and came on a crowd of thirty people gathered round a newly-made grave. They were all chattering. Then came silence, a wall of it and I didn't know if it were hostile. I had to go forward and explain myself. The older men knew about the foreign doctors and nurses who'd been at the Banja. A young man said: 'Please make yourself welcome and eat with us. We are celebrating my father's *parastos*. He died twenty days ago.' Everyone watched me. I awkwardly took a candle and lit it for the dead man, and stuck it in the ground beside a lot of others. Rather too late, I saw that I should have put some coins in a box to pay for the candle. At the head of the grave a scarlet apple and a branch of green privet were tied to the makeshift wooden cross. A tablecloth had been spread right over the hump of the grave, and on it were endless dishes of food: fish, chicken, cake and prunes. First I was given the ritual food for the dead, *žito*, grains of wheat cooked and mixed with sugar and nuts. They handed me cold brandy and hot brandy. I did my best to eat and drink heartily as to do otherwise would have shown a gross lack of respect. A thoughtful old man handed me a handkerchief for my sticky fingers. The dead man's son made a very dignified host: his sister, blotchy-faced with tears and alcohol, drank continually from a bottle of beer in her hand. A smart Alec cracked jokes to make sure I took notice of him. I was asked about English burial customs: they were all shocked that we visit our dead so little after the funeral. For them there are set intervals, up to a year, and the cult of death is very strong. The host said this was only a small *parastos*; forty days after the death, the priest would come, that would be a bigger occasion altogether. His father had been seventy, and paralysed for two years before: it was a merciful death.

I took three women back to the main road with me. They talked about the keening there had been at the graveside earlier that day. I had heard this elsewhere: an unearthly broken wailing which rose to a crescendo; then one woman cried out her praises of the dead man. An old woman said:

'I couldn't keen, I couldn't weep when I heard that the Germans had shot my husband. I just knew that all was finished. It still is.'

A younger woman half-whispered to me:

'I know you're a foreigner, but between ourselves, I wept and keened when my husband died, and I go on doing it. Mother tried to stop me coming today, she didn't want me to join in the keening.'

The dead man's daughter was by now beyond speech; and beer slopped from her bottle as the car jolted over a track of corrugated earth.

In the afternoon I went back to Ljubostinja. It is built, like Ravanica, at the end of a wooded valley and in the same trefoil style, only it has no fortifications and no fantasy. The architect, Rade Borović, carved his name on the sill of the inner door – he need not have bothered: he is immortalized as 'Rade the Builder' in the poems. He made the church classical, sober and simple, and when I went there, it was mostly whitewashed, which accentuated its plainness. Once it was pale red brick and whitish stone, criss-crossed in places with red-painted lines. By now the restorers may have completely altered its appearance, overpainting it red on pale pink and making the tracery on the rose-windows dark-red. Ljubostinja is a place where time has emphasized its original purpose: it was intended as a place of retirement by two widowed princesses. The church needs to remain faded and a little melancholy in its dark woods.

Princess Milica founded this monastery in 1395, not long after her husband Lazar was killed, and became a nun here. Her relative, Princess Helena, widow of a Despot killed in the earlier battle of the Marica, came to join her here and took the religious name of Jefimija. They were both educated women, and from Ljubostinja they journeyed to Sultan Bajazeth's Court together, to visit the Sultan's wife, Milica's daughter, and to negotiate the future of the Serbian State. But most of their later life was spent here, and they are both buried in the church. Milica died in her monastery in 1405, about the time it was completed. Jefimija was a writer who embroidered her own lament for Prince Lazar on a piece of silk which is now in the Patriarchate Museum at Belgrade: it is beautiful to look at or listen to:

> From thy youth thou wast brought up amongst the great of this world, O new martyr, O prince Lazar, and the mighty hand of the Lord singled thee out as strong and glorious among his rulers on earth . . . thou hast fulfilled two desires: to slay the dragon and to receive from God a martyr's crown.
>
> And now forget not thy beloved children, whom thou hast left desolate by thy departure . . . if God gives us help, to thee shall we give praise and thanksgiving. Gather together thy companions, the holy martyrs . . . inform George, stir up Demetrius, convince Theodore. . . . Come to our help, wherever thou art.
>
> Look on my small offering and count it to be much, for I bring praise to thee not according to thy merit, but according to the power of my weak reason. Therefore I await little reward. . . . And now my prayers to thee are twofold: sustain me and calm the raging tempest of my soul and body. Jefimija with all her heart offers this to thee, O holy one.

Inside the narthex of the church, Milica's tomb is on the left, Jefimija's, carved with acanthus leaves, on the right. The portraits of Milica and Lazar near her tomb have been over-painted and look clumsy; their two sons, Vuk and Stephen, left of the main door, are fainter and finer. A small door half-way up the north wall marks the traditional hiding-place for Milica's jewels; it also served to shelter a rebel leader in the 18th century. Over the inner door is carved the name Macarius; a monk-painter of this name worked near Skopje in St Andrew's Church at Treska – he had come there from the Meteora, then under Serbian patronage. From the style, which is vigorous, emphatic and rhythmical, it looks as if he was at Ljubostinja – but only a few frescoes survive in the church itself: the prophets in the cupola, and two miracles of Christ, the healing of the blind man in the north apse, the healing of the lame man in the south. Ljubostinja and the hermitages round it were a refuge for painters. Another monk, Radoslav, whose illuminated Gospel is now in Leningrad, once lived in these parts. Forced to flee, he had many adventures, living among brigands in Hungary, besieged in a Danube castle, hiding in the woods. Finally, knowing that death might be close at hand, he finished his manuscript in 1429 in a small monastery in Eastern Serbia. He left a warning to anyone who should find his precious work: 'Don't dirty it, or let the candle drip on it, or spill lamp oil over it.'

Sadness and danger mark the past at Ljubostinja; the present life there is quite different. In the office, I found Abbess Barbara back from hospital, where she had been paying her bills. A small woman, she wears her veil pulled well back on her shining dark hair. She is extremely communicative. I asked after her health. 'Oh, they gave me some good German capsules, the very latest treatment for gall-stones.' Her energy and enterprise are remarkable. Ljubostinja was always a good wine-growing area; she has completely re-planted the neglected vineyards with Black Hamburg and Hercegovina vines, and now produces 10,000 kilograms of wine a year. Under the old guesthouse on one side of the courtyard, with its black beams and brown-tiled roof, stood a large pile of crates labelled EXPORT. She also supplies one of the best hotels in Belgrade with her wine. She has created a small industry of wicker-work chairs and embroidery: most of this, too, goes to the capital. She fattens calves for the local Co-operative; they were shown at the biggest Agricultural Fair in Yugoslavia, in Novi Sad, while the Co-operative Director told the newspapers: 'A calf reared by Mother Barbara is as good as a calf from the best stock-breeder in Serbia.'

She is a delightful person to meet and she undoubtedly has a flair for publicity: when she visited the same Fair, she was interviewed on television. The church needed repairing, so she wrote direct to Tito and his wife – and the work got done. Hers was the first monastery to boast tractor, cultivator and car. She is well-known beyond Church circles as a kind of tycoon among abbesses and abbots. To me she murmured discreetly that the Church must move with the times.

She works in a traditional framework, though, and is more like the Ravanica abbess than one might think. Both have strong personalities, both have been abbess for over twenty years and have set a mark on their community. They impose a strict discipline on the nuns. Both believe in work, but one is practical, one is contemplative, one likes innovation, one is conservative.

Ljubostinja, like Žiča, resembles a great estate with the abbess as its

24 Novo Brdo: the castle on the summit, with the cathedral walls below

25 Manasija: a 15th-century monastery fortified against Turkish invaders

26 A hermitage built into the crags of Gornjak

27 A Vlach house under the Roman walls of Gamzigrad

head; the labour-force consists of the fifty-two sisters under her care. The best description I heard of her was from the local Director of Monuments: 'She's the old-fashioned great lady – she doesn't do any manual work herself, but she knows where everyone is, and what they're doing, at any given moment during the day.'

13

THE COURT OF DESPOT STEPHEN AT MANASIJA

The church in the woods: Kalenić – Vespers at Manasija – company from France – Stephen's church and court – the end of an era

The road from Ljubostinja to Kalenić, the next monastery, was so bad that I turned back – disappointedly, as it ran up through delectable wooded country – and spent another night at Kruševac. From there the road up through Jasika was bumpy but negotiable. It crossed a patchwork of field and forest. Every village was alive with people: a market in one place, a gipsy wedding, complete with dancing bear, in the next. Further up in the hills, I passed a handsome white villa with a pergola of roses, fit for a retired opera-singer. I slowed down to read the brass nameplate: it belonged to the local midwife.

Kalenić has the same kind of wooded setting as Ravanica and Ljubostinja, but higher and more remote, and the forests were once a hideout for brigands. Round the small monastery, trees have been cleared, and I reached the buildings by walking through an orchard, past geese with ruffled feathers, black piglets eating up windfall apples and sheep like rugs munching the grass. A squirrel watched everything from an apple-tree, and the omnipresent pied wagtail whom we used to call 'the monastery bird' flew from one roof to another. On that autumn day, the nuns were too busy picking up and shelling walnuts as a man knocked them down from the branches, to attend much to a tourist; they also had plum jam on the boil and a heap of peppers in the yard: they were scurrying to provide for the winter before them. Their Abbess was invisible, laid up with varicose veins, they said. A middle-aged woman, whose mother and sister were nuns, found the key of the church and showed me round.

The monastery was begun in 1407 and finished in 1413. After 1402, when the Ottomans were defeated by the Mongols, Byzantium and the Balkans enjoyed a respite from hostilities, and during this prosperous lull Lazar's son Stephen was created Despot of Serbia by the Byzantines. He and his Court commissioned new churches, and it was one of his officials, the Protonotary Bogdan, who endowed Kalenić.

At first sight the church looks as if it had been scribbled over. The east end is covered with Church Slavonic inscriptions in brick in a band round the middle of the building. They tell you that Stephen the First-Crowned's body lay there in 1818, and that later Prince Miloš Obrenović gave a new iconostasis to the church. Then the architects have scribbled round the windows the same kind of figures and arabesques as in the other Morava churches, but with greater delicacy. Each window is different in detail but they all have the same slightly pointed arch with a flat pilaster dividing the window into two, except for one, to the southwest, with a twisted pillar instead. The carvings in each window-head delight by their energetic individualism. In the southeast two griffons lick each other, in the east a man wrenches open a lion's jaws, and the lion has a kink in his tail. In the north the centaur Chiron plays his lute, in the northwest a dog with jaws like a pair of scissors is trying to save his master from an attack by bears. Some of the carvings are serene: the two birds drinking from a cup of pure water, in the southwest; the monumental Mother of God with her child over the south narthex. Not only the detail of Kalenić is fine, but the whole church. It is conceived very much on the same plan as the Lazarica, but the architect has avoided an overcrowded roofline: he has made a shallow dome over the narthex and a gently-curved roof over the east end, so that the high cupola of the inner church keeps its importance. Kalenić has one weakness in common with the Lazarica: the exterior and interior do not match each other. They have similar thickened walls with niches in them. There the likeness ends, for by great good fortune many of the frescoes at Kalenić have survived.

The painters made a careful plan which is still visible on the walls. As in the other Morava churches, they added the miracles and parables of Christ to the older scheme, but they also gave great prominence to the Life of the Virgin, and have painted scenes which compare with those in the King's Church, Studenica, and with the mosaics at Kariye Camii at Constantinople, both designed a century earlier. At Kalenić the Life of the Virgin is mostly in the narthex, where the middle and upper zones are covered with a very detailed series of scenes. Only two scenes, the Presentation of Mary in the Temple (to which the church is dedicated) and the Birth of the Virgin, are further in, at the west end on the north wall of the nave. Among the paintings in the narthex is the Flight into Egypt, similar in composition to that at Dečani, on the north wall, and on the south wall, level with it, a rare and beautiful scene, from St Luke's Gospel, of Mary and Joseph in Bethlehem, just before the Birth of Christ, because 'there went out a decree from Caesar Augustus, that all the world should be taxed' and that is what they have come to do. The subject appears in mosaic at Karije Djamii, and perhaps the version at Kalenić is derived from it or both from an earlier model, but the fresco has gained in economy and in balance, for a soldier who was crammed into the middle of the Constantinople scene has been moved far over to the left, and the buildings in the background have been unified by a canopy draped right across them. The painted figures of the Virgin, the ruler Cyrenius and St Joseph are more lyrical at Kalenić, more dramatic at Constantinople. Below the story of the Virgin are hermits on the west wall and donors on the north: Bogdan and his wife Milica in the centre, Bogdan's brother Peter on the left, Despot Stephen on the right. Milica is dressed in pale green and gold, Bogdan's robe is brocaded with carnations and leaves in rich browns and reds. The Despot looks melancholy, and his robe is less fine than Bogdan's: he is probably there with them because he exercised such tight control over church-building and he is to be found in other churches which were not, strictly speaking, his own foundations.

Within the church, two frescoes are particularly impressive: one is the half-length figure of the dead Christ, to the north, above the side altar. The idea of the altar as the grave of Christ belongs to late Byzantine theology, but this is a painting one might expect to find in an Italian church. As in the great Crucifixion at Studenica, in the Virgin's Church, the face of Christ expresses weariness, but the features are quite different, almost a portrait of someone known. The body is formalized into the semicircular curves made by chest and stomach, and into the pitifully straight lines of the strained muscular arms. The Wedding at Cana, to the left above the window in the south apse, has by contrast a joyful tranquillity. The painter, as in the Taxation of Mary and Joseph, has uncluttered the scene and again given it a single canopy. Only a few figures have been left: the central group of the bride and groom and servant with a wine-cup shows subtlety and refinement. The 'ruler of the feast', as St John calls him, sits at his ease beside them, and the Mother of God implores her son to give them wine. Christ, on the far left, in shining blue robe, is balanced by the wedding-guest, in drab mortal brown, on the right. The whole scene is a ravishing example of late Byzantine painting.

The frescoes in general have a dark ground, and a lot of gold and grey on the figures. Everyone has grown quite mild: the prophets are no longer rugged, and St Michael's sword rests on his shoulder. The holy warriors lean nonchalantly on their spears. They are marvellously decorative, with curved bows, zig-zag leggings, thonged waistcoats and elegant haloes. The pictorial style of each Morava monastery varies greatly: the warriors at Kalenić are ethereal, those at Manasija are vigorous, ready for battle. The painters came to Serbia as refugees; some had great talent, some little, some chose to paint in a monumental style, some were merely naïve. No longer could the Serbian rulers send to Salonica or Byzantium for master-painters. If they were lucky, these painters drifted their way. They were still patrons and, in the case of Despot Stephen, extremely discerning, but the grand age of church-building had passed. Something haphazard has crept into the planning for these later foundations: it is a game of chance rather than a statement of certainties. They reflect the uncertain times in which they were built, and because they were the last of their kind, they sometimes possess, as does Kalenić, their own perfection. Each church mirrors the age in its own way: one sees this very clearly at Kalenić and at Manasija, where most has survived and where great masters worked. At Kalenić the horror and bloodshed of the Ottoman threat have been put aside and forgotten. Several painters worked there in harmony: in their creation the saints live in an ideal world. It is a world without power in the earthly sense, though it has all the intensity of a dream which vanishes on waking and yet lingers in the mind as a lasting vision of beauty.

* * *

A year before Bogdan started to build Kalenić, his master Despot Stephen began work on Resava monastery, later known as Manasija, and it took from 1406 until 1418 to complete the church intended for his own mausoleum.

I had to reach it by a rather tortuous route from Kalenić, by going north to Svetozarevo, doubling back along the main Morava road towards Belgrade, and then turning east through Svilajnac.* I arrived in mid-afternoon. It was very quiet, and I was weary from so much dusty driving, and longing for sleep. Manasija is the largest and most imposing of the Morava monasteries. Eleven towers, including the

* It would be easier for any traveller starting from Belgrade. Like Ravanica, from which it is not far, Manasija is reasonably close to the main road (25 km).

great donjon called the Despot's Tower, stand up above the Resava river. It is placed in a valley, but as Deroko points out, the strength of its fortifications makes up for its vulnerable position. When the heavy gates are closed at night, you are conscious of being secure within the moated fortress.

The Abbess was in. We sat on a bench inside the fortress and talked of the friend who had sent me, and she told me how she was soon going to France to stay at a Russian convent near Paris. There she would find her aged 'spiritual mother', the nun Theodora, who had long ago, after the 1917 Revolution, come to live at Hopovo in the Vojvodina. Meanwhile, would I like to stay with them for a few days? I said with regret that I had only two nights, knowing that this hardly counts as a visit. But she nodded, and sent for a nun to show me the guest-house. As I went, she added, 'Please be at Vespers at 5; my sisters are at work in the fields, and we have only a small congregation.' I lay down on a bed and set the alarm-clock: it roused me a bare hour later. I found some cold water in a jug, splashed it over my face and came to.

I crossed through the roofless medieval dining-hall, now a grassy space where the nuns have planted flowers against the walls, and reached the west door of the church which stands inside the castle. The scale is striking. The architect was told by the Despot 'to make the church so high that nothing will surpass it'. He obeyed his orders: Ravanica and Kalenić seem like toy models for Manasija, and to add to its majesty, the church is built of smooth blocks of stone. The church is characteristic of the Morava valley in its height, in the shallow pilasters which run up to the roof, and the soaring central cupola flanked by four smaller ones. But the exterior exuberance of decoration has gone, and only a single line of blind arcading under the roof saves it from complete austerity. The narthex has been rebuilt, an extra cupola added and a rose-window lost, but a fine floor remains. It is a ruler's church, the outside so plain that one remembers how Stephen Lazarević loved the company of hermits, the interior so rich that one remembers how he kept his Court here.

The service had begun. The Abbess had been right to co-opt me into the congregation: with her was one elderly sister, presumably unfit for field work, and a youngish priest with his long hair bundled up into an untidy bun. He chanted and swung the censer and it left trails of smoke behind him, ghostly puffs and swirls which grew smaller as the incense burnt low. The central cupola at Manasija is supported by four tall pillars painted with full-length figures of the saints down below, and medallions of others, in torso, above. Even in daylight the saints seem to recede from one's gaze into the eternal spaces above, and I saw by candle-light that in some places on the pillars, a saint was missing, and with shadows everywhere against the white plaster of these blank spaces, the priest's silhouette made a saint for a moment on a pillar where none had been. Then the great fresco of the infant Christ appearing to St Peter of Alexandria, on the northeast pillar, on its south side, was illuminated in all its richness of colour. A vase of flowers, the curve of the pillar itself, another nun who had come in, all made firm shapes on the white walls in turn as the censing light blew about in the air. Outside, a train rattled up the valley to the mines above.

The singing swelled as more nuns came in. The service was Mattins and Vespers rolled into one, because the sisters go out to work so early in the summer. The nun who read parts of the service wore a black cowl, edged with red and with a red cross on the front, like Stephen Nemanja in the frescoes. I had lost all count of time by now, but I saw that the choirstalls had gradually filled with nuns, about twenty of them. They came out and formed into a line across the church, sang a hymn and then in procession, two by two, they kissed the icon on the lectern in the centre of the church, as did the young priest – his bun by now had come uncoiled and his hair flowed down over his shoulders – and an old priest who shuffled out of the shadows. Then the nuns re-formed, with extreme precision, along one side of the church, from east to west. They sang once more. One of them, in her cylinder hat and long overcoat, alone broke the symmetrical line of hooded, caped, black bodies. It was the end of the service. They changed into individuals, putting out candles, seeing where I had got to, closing service-books. But the memory of their movement during the service, suggested that a drama had been enacted in the church. Now it was finished and the stage-hands, who were also the actors, were clearing up. 'The church is a theatre for angels and men'; and I never saw this aspect of an Orthodox service – the solemn drama – more strongly displayed than at Manasija.

While this was going on, I had vaguely heard the door of the church open and shut, and voices whispering in the background. At the entrance of the church I found a young French couple. They had been searching without success for a lodging, and had arrived at the monastery after dark to find the huge wooden doors of the entrance-tower closed against them. The Abbess had taken pity on them, as on me, and had offered them a room for the night. We had supper together off a table in their bedroom, and a young French-speaking nun served us. She had studied theology and languages at the Faculty in Belgrade, something unthinkable at Ravanica. Now she coaxed us to drink hot milk. When she was not there, we talked freely. The Frenchman was rather frustrated:

'I lit a cigarette here earlier, and the nun told me to put it out; I was blaspheming the holy icon, but how was I to know *that* counted as one?'

He pointed to a garish oleograph of the Virgin Mary. I sympathized. There is a lot of tolerance in monasteries, and a lot of Do's and Don't's. Some I have never got clear: for instance, why it is unseemly to wear gloves during a service? Even in the coldest weather, busy peasant women will sometimes pull them off your hands with a scolding.

The Frenchman's wife, like me, had been impressed by the scene in the church.

'To arrive, in the dark like that, and to see them, so disciplined, in such a magnificent place – it was extraordinary. I asked myself if I could have found something like it if I'd gone into a Benedictine abbey, say, at home, but no, I don't think so . . .'

They were good travellers, uncomplaining about minor hardships, delighted with what they had found. I suddenly realized how grateful I was for their company: for about ten days I had been unable to discuss frankly what I'd seen. One has to praise and be praised for everything in Serbia. To quote one acquaintance, 'Under the Turks we learnt to cringe and smile and say we were pleased, when we weren't, and we still do this. We lost our self-respect (*lična kultura*) that way.' He overstated, but there is something in it.

Eventually we went to bed. The other bed in my room was occupied by an old lady who snored. Wandering in these parts is an ordeal by noise, and after all-night weddings in villages and all-day transistor music in towns, I had hoped for monastic peace. In the morning she turned out to be a widow from Belgrade and a regular visitor to Manasija; she had come for the feast-day just past. I promised to drive her home with me: she stipulated that it mustn't be too early in the day, it would be safer to go when the sun was up, less likelihood of catching cold. . . . (Even so, she wedged a handkerchief in the car window to keep off draughts, and I found it there several days later.)

The French left. She gave a nun her bead necklace to use as a rosary, and received a peacock feather in return. The Abbess went into town.

The local policeman came up to make a list of the foreigners whom he knew to be sleeping at the monastery, found everything in order and went away again.

I stayed in the empty church with an old toothless nun for company. She knew the saints in the frescoes, but not much more. Despot Stephen intended Manasija to be the most splendid church in the Morava region. He took many details from his father's church at Ravanica: the medallions of the saints, the colouring of azure and gold, the sumptuous background of painted ornament like silversmith's work. But he seems to have been a very different man from Prince Lazar, and he built Manasija in quite different circumstances. As far as one can judge from the accretions of chronicles and legends, Prince Lazar was a warrior prince of diplomatic ability; he held his dominions together as long as he possibly could, knowing that an Ottoman attack was inevitable, and then was killed resisting it.

His son, for at least part of his reign, was able to enjoy a short period of peace. While he must have been well aware it could not last for ever, he had enough confidence to resettle the lands round Manasija with Serbs who had been made homeless by earlier Ottoman attacks. He was a military leader who rebuilt the fortress at Belgrade, but he was also a gifted writer who sought the company of others. He kept Kruševac as his capital, but he made Manasija a cultural centre, lived there in his tower and attracted scholars to his Court. From Bulgaria, for instance, came Constantine the Philosopher, later to write Stephen's biography. Others produced historical and didactic works. The *scriptorium* (writing-school) at Manasija was famous and must have been inspired by the Despot himself. This is part of his 'Letter of Love':

> Summer and spring the Lord created, as the psalmist says, and in them are many beauties: the birds have their swiftness and their flight, which is full of gaiety, the mountains their tops, the forests their vastness and the meadows their wide spaces. Who can worthily bear witness to the filling of the light air with wonderful sounds, and the gifts of the earth which are flowers of a goodly scent and greenness? Even man's nature is renewed and rejoices. . . .'

Not, as one might expect, a love-poem, but addressed to his brother who threatened civil war.

The refinement and grace of Stephen's Court is praised by his contemporaries, and it is difficult to find a parallel among the Nemanjid rulers, who lived sometimes in simplicity and sometimes in splendour, but without the note of personal taste that appears at Manasija in the early 15th century. It is not decadence; rather a last flare-up of vigour before the Serbian kingdom finally disappeared under the Ottomans.

All this directly affected the painting in the church. Stephen was fortunate in finding a master-painter who may have come from Salonica or Mount Athos. He seems to have employed few assistants and the frescoes, complex in their subject-matter, have great unity. As at Kalenić, an imaginary world has been created, with its own inner order, though in quite another style. The painting is monumental; in some ways it looks back to Sopoćani though the dynamic quality is diminished. The Court of the Despot is transposed into painting: particularly in the north apse in the Parables of the Wedding Guest and of the Rich Man and Poor Lazarus. The guests at the wedding are dressed as Byzantine noblemen, they eat the finest food out of elegant dishes and their decanter with its twists and twirls could be Venetian glass. As for the rich man with poor Lazarus, the setting and clothes are just as luxurious, and the dogs which lick the beggar's sores and nudge him are pedigree hunting hounds.

Under these scenes are the warrior saints: Arethas, Nestor, Nicetas, Mercurius, Theodore of Tyron and Theodore Stratilates, who reflect Stephen's Court in another way, for they are aristocratic knights in armour, ready to fight for the preservation of all that they enjoy and honour. Across the church, to the south, are their brother saints, George, Demetrius, Procopius, Artemius and Jacob the Persian and above them, Christ among the Doctors, the Parables of the Publican and the Pharisee and of the Prodigal Son.

The last two are different in their treatment: the Publican small and modest in his movements and attire, follows the Pharisee timidly up the steps to the Temple, where the Pharisee addresses himself to God with exuberant gestures of his arm from under his fine cloak. But then you see the Publican with a halo, going down 'to his house justified' because 'he that humbleth himself shall be exalted'. The Prodigal Son is in two episodes: on the left, Christ as father, a stern and magnificent figure, divides his goods between the two sons, and on the right, the Prodigal Son is welcomed back into Christ's arms. The faces are damaged, but the stance of Christ, the movement of his embrace, contrasts with the detachment of the first scene; in the second, 'his father saw him, and had compassion, and ran, and fell on his neck, and kissed him'.

These two scenes, so closely based on the New Testament, can best be understood by looking at the other side of Stephen's life. On the west wall, on the north side, is the founder's portrait. Stephen's robes are splendid, embroidered with a double-headed eagle all over. He holds a model of the original church, and from it hangs a scroll which records that 'Despot Stephen gives to sweet Jesus Christ this church' and ends by describing the donor as the greatest of all sinners and the slave of Christ who has come to save him. The three winged figures of the Holy Trinity, to whom the church is dedicated, hover on his right, and beyond them are hermits, in unusually close proximity to the founder. Stephen was austere as well as cultivated. He liked to talk to the anchorites who had settled round Manasija. He lived in comfort but looked to a precarious future. Like the monk from Ljubostinja, he knew that death might come soon, and the whole tone of Manasija is based on this contrast between present earthly pleasure and thoughts of eternal life. Above the west door of the inner church, on the flat surface of the arch, is a mighty long-fingered hand holding a crowd of minute swaddled figures, the whole framed in a seven-pointed star and a circle, symbols of eternity: 'The souls of the righteous are in the hand of God, and there shall no torment touch them,' says *The Wisdom of Solomon* and Solomon himself, with David, is painted on either side of the souls in divine safe-keeping. It is a reassurance for the founder and his followers, as is the painting in the tympanum below – another rare subject in Byzantine art – of Christ as a Child asleep with open eyes, accompanied by the Mother of God and by angels holding instruments of his Passion, so that they foretell what is to come. This composition, 'The Ever-Watchful Eye', has a curious symbolism. In some medieval Bestiaries the lion is said never to sleep except with his eyes open – so Christ here is like a small lion, all-seeing, and a strength to the faithful who are in need of his protection.

Below the marvellous prophets in the cupola, the young bearded Moses, the aged Ezekiel with his mane of hair, the gentle pensive Habakkuk among the rest – and between the fine Evangelists on the pendentives with their angels encouraging them to write like so many Muses, are painted other subjects which repeatedly manifest the miraculous power of Christ. These are the so-called Holy Tile between the northwest and southwest pendentive and the Holy Kerchief, between the northeast and southeast pendentive. They represent the story of the Emperor, who, during Christ's life, sent a painter to make a portrait of him. The task proved impossible, and finally Christ came to him, took the canvas and put it on his own face: it received the imprint of his features. The painter set off back to his Emperor, but attacked by brigands on the way, hid the canvas between two tiles, and when the brigands were driven off, he opened the tiles and found the imprint on one.*

The scheme in the altar space repeatedly declares the Sacrifice of Christ at the Eucharist, for below the Double Communion is not simply a procession of Holy Fathers, but the Consecration of the Host, which they attend. These figures – among them are St Sava and St Sylvester, Pope of Rome† – are a statuesque and slow-moving procession. Above them the rhythm changes, for the Apostles in the Double Communion are moving so fast that their draperies swing about, while angels with tapers and fans encourage them on their way.

The purpose of the church decoration is to demonstrate the sureness of faith in Christ and the painters had the ability to fulfil the founder's intention, and to leave behind them a poignant memorial to the age of Despot Stephen. It is the last great religious foundation of the Serbian Middle Ages. The only monument which followed it was military: the fortress, with a palace and chapel within it, that Despot George Branković and his wife were to build at Smederevo.

That evening I walked round the empty church in darkness. I could only glimpse it through dense globes of trees from which the leaves had not yet fallen. The autumn night was bitterly cold, and the cupolas were framed in stars. Life goes on quietly at Manasija, the Liturgy is sung and the fields are tilled, but the glory departed when Stephen had to leave it to the Turks, for whom it was a fortress to be held like any other, and the writers, the hermits and the painters were scattered from their home, which while it lasted had proved so brilliant and so fruitful.

* The West has the legend of St Veronica, who is said to have wiped Christ's face with a cloth on his way to Calvary.

† St Sava is second from the left, St Sylvester is second from the right. Another Pope, St Martin of Tours, is painted in a medallion.

14
DOWN THE DANUBE

The fortresses of Smederevo and Golubac – the people of Lepenski Vir – the Iron Gates – Romans on the river – Gamzigrad – a legend and a witch – Negotin Fair

From the fortress at Belgrade to the next fortress east at Smederevo, the south bank of the Danube is a land of plenty. I went one September just before the grape-harvest. The river remains wide and sullen at all seasons; the sloping orchards puff up with flowers in spring and later on provide magnificent apples and peaches for every market in the capital. Vuk Karadžić recalled this countryside to Serbian emigrants homesick like himself in Vienna:

> The white wine of Smederevo, if people knew how to set about making it, would be better than any Hungarian wine, except Tokay. (Didn't George Branković, when Tokay was his, bring vines from there, and plant them round Smederevo?) Watermelons and canteloupes grow beneath a clear sky; in the vineyards, in some places, there are even figs. . . .

Since not even patriotism could stop him telling the truth, he notes that the figs 'aren't as sweet as those from the sea-coast'.

Smederevo had been a medieval trading-centre; in the early 15th century, George Branković, who succeeded Stephen Lazarević as Despot of Serbia, made it his capital. By then the Turks held the south and Belgrade was a Hungarian stronghold. The Despot built his palace by the waterside and walled it in with one of the most massive castles in Europe, designed by his Byzantine brother-in-law, George Cantacuzene. In stories and epic poems the Despot's wife, 'Accursed Jerena' (Irene Cantacuzene), is linked with the building of the fortress. She is said to have turned the peasants into slave-labourers and to have made them give up their gold, all to get the work done in two years. Probably the Small Fortress was hurriedly built against the Turks and her brother used forced levies as the Byzantines often did. Legend prefers a wicked princess.

Like Byzantium, Smederevo is built on a triangular site and uses an inlet as one of its defensive boundaries. There the likeness ends. At

Smederevo you will find the original palace and donjon at the apex of the triangle, where the river Jezava flows into the Danube. The Small Fortress, as it is called, is self-contained with a moat on the landward side; from there you can see one tower inscribed in brick with a cross and the words:

> In Christ our God, the pious Despot George, Lord of the Serbs and of the Zeta coast commanded this fortress to be built, 1430.

The fortress was extended inland along the banks of both rivers during the whole of Despot George's reign (1427–56) to make a large enclosure, the Great Fortress, which housed the Royal Mint as well as soldiers' barracks. The high walls are punctuated by square towers which march grandly along the river banks and across the land. 'Every tower is as tall as a minaret' noted the 17th-century Turkish traveller Evliya Chelebi. They can be best seen from the Danube; though extensive damage done by high explosives in the Second World War has weakened their powerful precision.

In the outer enclosure, I found the Smederevo Autumn Show: tents full of vegetables and fruit, and on the dried-up grass stood nineteen brown leather chaises-longues placed in a circle; among them were eight wooden hatstands and, on a pedestal, the plaster bust of a lady with a plaster rose in her ringlets. An attendant said that they were trying to recreate the atmosphere of the Despot George's Court: 'We were a bit short of furniture, so the film studio at Belgrade lent us some.'

The crumbled ruins of the inner fortress, close to the Danube, contained only a few traces of the Despot's life. His palace had had a large hall on the first floor, facing the river. The outline of its delicate ogee windows, more Gothic than Byzantine, remains. In 1435, Venetian envoys came to sign a treaty with the Serbian ruler there, in 'the great audience-chamber at the Court or, you might say, the palace where he lives at Smederevo'. But the Despot's church of the Annunciation was smashed up by the Turks in 1480 and its fragments used to make their cannon-tower at the mouth of the Jezava; another church of his survives, and is well worth looking at, in the town cemetery.

The Burgundian traveller Bertrandon de la Broquière, in company with the Milanese Ambassador to the Porte, visited the Despot in 1433:

> I came to a town, or rather a country house, called Nicodem. It is here

> the despot has fixed his residence because the soil is good, and there are woods and rivers abounding with everything needful for the pleasures of the chase and hawking, of which he is very fond. He was out hawking by the riverside, attended by fifty horse, three of his children, and a Turk. . . .
>
> The prince of Servia is a tall, handsome man, from fifty-eight to sixty years old; he has five children, three boys and two girls. Of the boys, one is twenty years, another sixteen and the third fourteen; and all three, like their father, have very agreeable countenances. In respect to the girls, one is married to the Sultan [Murad II], another to the Count de Seil [Ulrich of Celje]; but as I have not seen them I cannot describe them. When we met him hawking, the ambassador and myself took him by the hand, which I kissed, for such is the custom. On the morrow, we went to pay him our respects. He had a tolerably numerous Court, composed of very handsome men, who wore the beard and hair long, as they are of the Greek Church.'[1]

At this time the Despot could still move freely out of his capital and the Serbian villages looked prosperous. But soon, in 1439, the Turks were to lay waste the country and capture Smederevo. Later, they returned it to the Despot, but finally re-took it in 1459, after his death. The Danube was by then the Turks' own frontier. They enlarged the fortress, and on a marble plaque, they asked Allah to 'bless this place which illuminates the land of Islam with the Sultan's power. . . .'

Once, the Austrians took it from them, and once Karageorge, but otherwise it remained in their hands until 1867, the very end of the Ottoman power in Serbia. A neglected tomb in the garden of Smederevo Museum belonged to the soldier Ibrahim Effendi from Trebizond who had died in the last year of occupation.

It was Dušanka who read the inscription for me on the Turkish gravestone. She managed to arrive from Belgrade a few hours after I did. She is a historian who specializes in the Ottoman occupation of the Balkans, and an ex-Partisan who has worked at the Military Museum. In the fortress, a young lieutenant sprang to attention at the sight of her. Part of the Yugoslav army, in the summer of 1970, had turned archaeologist and was carrying out an emergency operation on the banks of the Danube. With the building of the great dam lower down the river, it was the last chance to excavate medieval and Roman and prehistoric monuments before the water-level rose. Smederevo itself should be safe. The lieutenant was a young Albanian from Macedonia, and very keen on the digging. His men were uncovering Turkish guns along the moat guarding the Small Fortress; no one knew what they would turn up next. We wanted to get onto the next castle downstream, Golubac. The lieutenant directed us inland, through Požarevac.

We met a funeral procession. 'Forbidden by law,' said Dušanka, 'because of hygiene, but everyone goes on doing it.' Mourning women came first, carrying tawdry wreaths of paper flowers. Then four more women holding the coffin lid shiny with varnish. After them, men displayed religious banners and the priest walked with his umbrella horizontal like a black bayonet. The dead man lay in an open coffin on a trestle covered by a white cloth. He had a squarish wrinkled face with a growth of stubble and looked a heavy burden for the men who carried him along. Behind him, women had linked arms four or five abreast. They wore blue or green towels as armbands. The whole procession was very grand, but I am not sure I could bear it if it were for someone I knew well.

We turned north towards the Danube over an undulating country of maize-fields. 'Now it's fertile,' said Dušanka, 'but once it was an empty quarter.' In the later Middle Ages, she explained, it had become a no-man's-land between Hungarians, Serbians and Turks, constantly fought over until in the 15th century the Turks had colonized it with Serbs from Kossovo.

We came on Golubac suddenly. Its towers dramatically enclose a steep rock-face, and the donjon is out on spiky heights to the east. The whole castle is a splendid sight, and visibly guards a whole stretch of river. It overlooks the Danube north and east and west, and to the south its precipitous perch discourages any attack overland. It can hardly be called a Serbian castle, for the Serbs only held it momentarily after Kossovo. It had been built by medieval Hungarians over a Roman settlement, and was then taken over by the Turks, who abandoned it in the 18th century when their frontiers altered.

We stayed the night in a seedy hotel in the village and locked the bedroom door. 'You don't take any chances in this sort of place,' said Dušanka. In the morning, we set off east for the part of our journey we were looking forward to most.

In 1965–68, during a general exploration of prehistoric sites in this area, Professor Dragan Srejović uncovered on the shores of the Danube a buried settlement of very great importance, which dated from 5000 B.C. or even earlier. This was at Lepenski Vir ('the whirlpool of Lepen') and everything he found there pointed to a revolutionary conclusion: that Neolithic culture came from within Europe and that it was not imported from the Near East as had previously been thought.

In 1970, we reached the site by turning off the main road and down a side-valley. It was steep and narrow, rocky and densely wooded, the

28 Vlach girls wearing their dowry necklaces of gold ducats at Negotin Fair

29 At the fair: the owner of a covered wagon with her oxen

30 Viktorina with her sheep at the summer pastures

31 Whitsunday at Duboka: procession with offerings for the dead

reason why the original inhabitants of Lepenski Vir had faced the river rather than the difficult hinterland behind them.

At the mouth of the valley were orange and blue bell-tents and beyond them, the Danube. The place was full of students working on the final excavations before the river rose thirty metres at the completion of the dam. They led us to a house where Professor Srejović and his staff were living. We sat and talked over brandy while a cat and a puppy played games among the glasses on the table. The team have found other sites near Lepenski Vir, the Professor said, houses of the same shape and date, about fifteen kilometres upstream, and also some sculptured heads downstream, placed on either side of a sacrificial victim, not far from Trajan's plaque. We walked along the shore to see the main settlement. I found it moving because it was so small, 170 metres long, 56 metres wide at the most: a sandy spit of land, sheltered and sunny, hemmed in by wooded bluffs above and by the whirlpool. Further off, on the Rumanian side of the narrow Danube, rises a high limestone cliff which seems to 'centre' the site at Lepenski Vir. Professor Srejović suggested there might be some connection, conscious or unconscious, between the cliff's trapezoid shape and the design of the houses, all of the same form, under our feet. 'It's only an idea,' he said apologetically. We looked at the groundplan of the houses, and it was as if someone began to read the runes for us and we saw, not just a place where there had once been a few settlers hunting and fishing their lives out, but a people with their own civilization, thoughtful in their art, their religion, their communal life.

Lepenski Vir does not quite fit into the accepted categories of Paleolithic or Neolithic life. It was a culture that developed quickly, beginning about 5600 B.C., and petered out slowly into decadence about 900 years later. At its height, it was like a city in embryo. They may have had a town plan, with central buildings, a 'market place' and roads leading towards it, and the houses were spread out in a fan towards the Danube. The architecture of the houses was remarkable; they were strictly proportioned, and the mathematical ratio of side to front and back walls can be exactly calculated. Their hearths, the holiest part of the house, were set on the widest wall, at the eastern entrance on the river side. By these hearths the most remarkable finds were made: the fantastic sculptured stone heads and statues, among the most ancient in the world. Some hearths had navel-stones; others, a human skull buried within them. There seemed to be skeletons everywhere, though we were told their numbers were small considering the size and duration of the settlement. In one case the manner of burial is curious: a man is buried in the same shape as the house foundations, to fit into a trapezoidal grave, legs folded back, head bent over forwards.

'We came across five more babies yesterday,' Srejović said. 'Everyone's been complaining that there weren't any babies at Lepenski Vir, but now that we're lifting up the house foundations to place them above the Danube, we've found some.'

As he spoke, workmen and students were dragging stones up a steep earth ramp to a higher level of ground, where they would be reassembled into an open-air museum.

'Did the babies die naturally? Were they sacrificed?'

'We can't say, but they're a month or two old. They may have died naturally, or they may have been killed for economic reasons, the land could only support so many. . . .'

Birth and death were the main religious themes at Lepenski Vir. One small sculpture shows the *vulva* at the moment of birth, and may have been a magic amulet to help women in labour. The worship of dead ancestors is implied by the buried skulls, the 'Guardians of the Hearth'.

We could see the whirlpools now. They were very risky, the archaeologists said; earlier in the season, a student went swimming and had been carried several kilometres downstream; he was seen and saved just in time. But beyond the whirlpools the fishing was plentiful and easy, with rapids and shallows where the original inhabitants could have set dams and traps for sturgeon and smaller fish. 'Yes,' said Dušanka, 'the stretch of river just above is like that, too. Prince Lazar gave it to Ravanica monastery because it was such good fishing.'

The earliest settlers at Lepenski Vir had been hunters. Without going far, they could catch game in the forests and the bones of wild boar, goat and deer have been found. Nuts, berries and wild fruit could also be harvested and still grow there. These people had stone tools, and pottery appears only in the very last phase at a time when new routes opened up and the climate changed for the better. Millstones and mortars date from this period, so the settlers may have grown millet to grind in them.

Then life at Lepenski Vir was suddenly cut short. The reason is unknown; it was not burnt or destroyed. Sheltered, isolated, it stayed a hallowed place for occasional burials, until the Roman Emperor

Tiberius built his Danube road over it about A.D. 30 and a watchtower was set up and garrisoned until the early 6th century.

It remains a strange and marvellous site, inhabited for nearly a thousand years, then deserted for another five thousand, again in use, again abandoned, now drowned but with a permanent memorial. I was glad to have seen it alive with the students singing in the dusk and the pilot of a Russian coal-boat near the Rumanian shore shouting commands which carried across the water.

'Stay to dinner,' said Srejović. We would have liked to, as his expeditions are said to be the best-provisioned in Yugoslavia, but it was growing dark and I was frightened of the drive to Donji Milanovac where we were to sleep. The roads in the afternoon had been all boulders and ruts, and it seemed safer to go in convoy with Nikola, the camp driver, who was fetching some students back. Nikola took us to the solitary hotel. 'What if it's full up?' I asked. 'Donji Milanovac is ours,' he replied with the air of a conqueror, and so it was, and we found better beds than at Golubac. Dušanka, like me, called it a good day.

* * *

Dušanka had only half a day left and with the first light we were off down river to see the Emperor Trajan's marble plaque in the cliffs. The Danube narrows began, fifteen miles of fast and dangerous water which the dam will tame. Some hills to the south are gashed apart by forested ravines, some are rounded plateaux covered with soft Alpine pasture. It is like this near Trajan's memorial. The modern road is built high above the river and we walked down a grassy path past flocks of silky white goats. Serbian folk tales have the Emperor Trajan with goats' ears instead of a donkey-eared Midas. With his luxurious palace and powers over life and death, Trajan may also be mixed up with the goat-eared water-devil who lives under the Danube in a crystal palace and drowns men to make them his slaves. We reached the river; here the Romans had constructed their military road to avoid the narrows. About A.D. 30, Tiberius' legions had hewn a shelf six foot wide in the rock or else fixed planks that jutted out as a platform from vertical cliffs. Trajan completed this task and built a bridge over the Danube for his successful campaign against the Dacians at the turn of the century. The marble plaques were virtually signposts: several Emperors put them up, but only Trajan's survived, listing his titles and boasting of his technical achievement.[2]

Our luck was out. We failed to find the plaque, and thirsty, muddy and blistered, we climbed back to the car. On our way to Negotin we came to the new dam. Then, it was cluttered with cranes and derricks; now, completed, it must look as simple as a gigantic child's toy. The scale is awesome: a 1000-ft difference between the top and bottom locks, and ships must wait an hour and a half for the level to change. Already the lock on the Rumanian side was open; it had to be, as the Danube Convention insists on free flow of traffic at all times. Although the dam, in effect, will drown the Roman road, it does not seem to contradict its purpose. The Romans, like contemporary Yugoslavs and Rumanians, saw the river as a means of communication and Trajan's bridge was at Kostol, five miles to the east. Amber, leeches, armed men came up and down the Danube. Now it is used for caviar and coal and tourists. A fine Roman bronze of Neptune, with a dolphin under his arm, was found near the dam.* He seems a suitable patron for it.

After the next town, Kladovo, the Danube broadens and takes a great sweep southwards through flatter country. The road is lined with poplars; it is like Northern France. At Negotin I put Dušanka safely on her bus for Belgrade and found myself a lodging for the night. The landlord promised to keep a room for me, as I wanted to see the annual fair which started in two days' time. Meanwhile I was free to go south to the biggest Roman fortress in the area: Gamzigrad, near Zaječar.

Gamzigrad was built close to a crossroads between different fortresses in the province of Dacia Ripensis, and lies secure in the hills just to the south of the Black River (*Crna Reka*). A rise of land conceals it from the main valley. No medieval records of it survive; its ruins were rediscovered by two 19th-century travellers, the Austrian Kanitz and the Serb Milićević. Romans and Byzantines had made use of it, yet its Roman name was lost, and this is all the stranger because it was a very grand castle, strongly fortified with exceptionally rich mosaics and stonework. Some scholars think that the administrator of this mining region set himself up in luxury, others, that it may have some connection with the Emperor Galerius, who campaigned here in the early 4th century A.D. The interior has some likenesses to Diocletian's palace at Split – and Galerius had been Caesar of the West to Diocletian. Roman Gamzigrad was partly destroyed. The Byzantines rebuilt it in Justinian's time.

Romans and Byzantines entered by the western gate, and everyone

* Now in the Museum at Negotin.

still does. The polygonal towers once had pointed roofs, and over the entrance, the open arcading included elaborate twisted pillars with acanthus-leaf capitals. The Roman street runs straight ahead. The most important buildings are in the northwest corner, where Romans and Byzantines each made a basilica; the Byzantines adding a clover-leaf baptistery to theirs. The Romans had had an atrium to the north. When they built their dining-hall, to the south, they lined the walls with marble, gave it underfloor heating and decorated it with scenes of hunting and feasting in mosaic. A dog survives, and a leaping leopard with a spear thrust through him. In a group of two huntsmen, the taller has a red-and-white embroidered shirt and a gauntlet on his left hand. Best of all is Bacchus, found at the entrance. His throne is a living leopard who treads on shadowy grass and round the god's head shines a blue aureole. He has a brown and muscular body, the lower part swathed in folds of richly-coloured cloth glinting purple and red. He holds a golden goblet and green leaves grow on his ribboned staff. The young vines which border the scene at each side follow the curve of the leopard's head and the upright line of Bacchus' staff. This god and his attendant beast magnificently celebrate the pleasures of earth.*

In 1970 this mosaic, found the year before, was propped under the eaves of Pera's shed while being restored. Pera is the guardian of Gamzigrad, a Vlach from the village near the castle. In Eastern Serbia, Vlachs are Rumanian by language and – more or less – by ancestry.† Pera told me that last summer they had danced the death dances for a young man, and he called a small boy to show me the cemetery where the gravestones, old and new, had sun symbols carved on them.

Christianity never attracted the Vlachs. One legend about Gamzigrad tells of Gamza the Grey, whom Stephen Nemanja hated and drove from his Court. Gamza settled in the fortress, revived the worship of old warrior gods and brought his son up in this faith. Gamza grew old and died. His son, hunting far away from home, looked over a dark cliff and saw below him a paradise garden where a girl of angelic beauty walked – Nemanja's daughter. They pledged their love, but met again only after the young knight, nameless and heroic, had fought at Nemanja's side and vanquished 'the Emperor of Greece' who asked for tribute. When Nemanja discovered the unknown knight to be

* Some treasures from Gamzigrad were or are kept in the Zaječar Museum.

† They should not be confused with the Kutzovlachs in Epirus, whose settlements are longer established. See A. J. B. Wace and M. S. Thompson, *Nomads of the Balkans* (London, 1914).

Gamza's son, he threw him into a dungeon, but promised his captive marriage with his own daughter if the young man would become a Christian. He refused. The princess came to her imprisoned lover with a cup of poison, saying that she wanted to go to his gods. They drank and died together. This story, with its pagan death-embrace, is utterly foreign to the medieval Serbian world and its saints and miracles.

Later that afternoon, on the return journey, I brushed against the old ways. A woman by the roadside waved me down for a lift. She was big, elderly and dark-faced. When settled down comfortably, she said: 'I'm going to give you something.' Fumbling in the dip between her rag-draped breasts, she drew out what appeared to be a lock of hair. 'It's the magic herb,'* she went on; 'it will keep your husband faithful to you and save your life.' I had only read about the magic herb (*raskovnik*). Many claims are made for its power. One countryman told me: 'It opens all doors, and with it, you will find hidden treasure.'

Mileva was the local witch. Her mother and grandmother knew many things and had passed them on to her: 'Ask anyone round here if you want me again, they all know me.' She went on: 'They give me a thousand dinars for this grass, but I see you're a good sort of woman, so I'll let you have it for less.' She accepted a much reduced fee, and gave me the quince she was carrying: 'It'll last. Make some jam with it.' She heaved herself out.

This is the countryside where the wood-mother still walks by night. She can look young and beautiful enough to seduce any man. Or she can change into an ugly old woman, like Papagena in reverse, and she controls her own magic herb.

Clouds of mauve larkspur lay over the cut maize-fields, and I drove on alone towards Negotin, wondering.

The autumn fair at Negotin starts on 21 September because everyone is free then; the maize has been harvested and the grapes are not yet ripe. Peasants, mostly Vlachs, come from far and wide to enjoy themselves, to marry off their daughters and to buy everything they need for the year, including livestock; and for three days they live encamped in covered wagons.

The town was already full of people; it was the first day of the fair. I settled into my room, drank brandy with the friendly family – the husband turned out to be a driver for the big chemicals factory in the next town, went out to a Turkish house crammed with Victoriana,

* *Siler trilobum.*

once the home of the 19th-century composer Mokranjac, drank coffee there with some Belgrade ethnographers, and slept.

I woke up to loudspeakers: the music of Mokranjac was blaring through the streets. Two festivals coexist at Negotin in the autumn: the old country fair and the new celebrations in honour of the composer. The town prides itself on its culture. When the Turks left, it acquired schools* and hospitals, a new cathedral church built in 1872, where the pews are inscribed with the names of prosperous merchants, and a Choral Society whose members, when photographed, included ladies in wide feathered hats and wasp-waisted dresses. It still has the character of a provincial town; I never met so many brown-haired elderly gentlemen, courteous, communicative and a little self-important, as in the *kafanas* of Negotin. I set off to the fair, but I reached it before I got there, for it is approached by a long street lined with one-storey shops selling necessities and frivolities, enticingly displayed in street or window. The shoemaker sold black-and-white woven sandals with turned-up toes, the coppersmith had got out his largest cooking-pots, the furrier his hats and waistcoats. The sweetshop offered heart-shaped iced biscuits with sentimental verses set in them, and I bought one for Richard. There were even biscuit rosaries with a cross attached. People stopped to buy these fairings or to turn over clothes and kitchenware. I followed the slowly-moving crowd. National dress has slipped a bit, most materials being factory-made, but peasant women still favour dark skirts, white blouses, sleeveless waistcoats and patterned headscarves.

The street opened out into a large field which shone with colour. Covered wagons stood everywhere: about 3000 people packed into them every night. They came from the Danube and Timok villages. The wagons had hooped roofs with woollen coverings, broadly striped, massively flowered, checked like a Scotch plaid. Red and black predominated, and the back was walled in by more homespun hangings. You could tell which villages the people hailed from, by the weaving patterns and by the style of their wagons. If the roof was covered with rush matting, or if the body of the wagon was made of plaited reeds instead of planks, that placed them. So did an open cart painted red and decorated in panels. Carts and wagons were piled high with rugs and brightly-dressed children, and blue seemed to be the favourite colour for water-buckets. The crowded, noisy fair was divided into well-defined sections. Along one edge was the stock-market, where cattle

* i.e., Serbian schools. Under the Turks, in 1817, Negotin possessed a Greek school.

and horses could wait in the shade of uncut maize stalks in the next field. One hungry cow chewed a dried maize stalk at least six feet long, starting at the tip as if she were a sword-swallower. Men walked into the forest of maize to relieve themselves; it was the only private place.

The fair has a central street, and here sideshows with crudely-painted hoardings advertised the 'Living Girl-serpent' and the 'Mini-Orient Circus'. Down this street walked the family processions arm-in-arm; marriageable girls wearing as many as fifty gold ducats round their necks to show off as dowry,* chaperoned by burly brothers. It is a society where women have strong rights, they may be land-owners, the son-in-law often moves in with his wife's family, and used even to take her surname. The girls' faces were powdered dead white; in the local folksongs, it is a sign of beauty to have 'a face like a sheet of paper'.

In the side-streets you can buy anything from a cradle to the headstone for a family grave. The stonemason – from a village with its own quarry – is waiting with his chisel by the blank headstone, to carve your relation's name and date of death on it, so you can take the whole thing home in your cart. Should you need a cooking-stove, it is there, in black iron with a long flue; or you could carry away a glazed jar for pickled peppers, three feet high. Shopping is hungry work, so the cooks have moved in to grill sizzling meat balls or to drop into boiling fat blobs of soft dough for the narrow doughnuts sold only at fair-time.

If I shut my eyes, I could walk my way into Negotin Fair by the smells: the oily scent of sheepskin at the furriers, disinfectant coming out of the chemist's, fresh food that was sweet or savoury, and the sour stench of circus animals.

In the evening Bora from the Tourist Bureau took me to drink beer in one of the marquees. We became part of the cheerful, relaxed crowd who were enjoying three days of rest, the cessation of everyday work, a treat to last the year. One table near us harboured some drunks who smashed bottles and hugged their girls; otherwise everyone was in family parties. Men stood talking quietly together. Bora was born in Negotin and had always gone to the Fair as a small boy; he tried a rifle-range for old time's sake, and won a prize.

Among the sideshows, we picked at random 'The Spider-woman

* In 1851 an Austrian observer calculated that in Serbia at least 300,000 women had necklaces or head-ornaments of gold and silver coins, each dowry being worth at least 10 thalers, so 'there is an emergency savings fund of six million florins, in this land without aristocracy or proletariat'; quoted in *Contrasts in Emerging Societies*, ed. D. Warriner (Indiana, 1965), p. 306. Hoarded away, buried underground during war, much of this money survives, always unspent and handed down from mother to daughter.

of the Twentieth Century', and paid for entry. Inside the wooden shack a girl's head hung suspended in the air, with a woolly spider's body and wire legs all round it. Five or six men stared up at her in silence; the showman stood by. We could see her from the front only. She must have been lashed to a T-shaped roof beam: crucified horizontally behind a piece of flowered cretonne. Lighting did the rest. She had beautiful features and long dark hair, but her sweaty face was dull with pain.

One peasant asked: 'Can she talk?'

'Oh, yes,' said the showman, 'ask her something.'

'Are you married?'

She licked her dry lips and spoke faintly: 'No, I'm not married.'

Then some curtains were drawn; presumably she could stand no more. Bora and I got out, sickened by what we'd seen. He guessed her to be a gipsy. Poverty could have driven her into the showman's shack and kept her there. We had no heart for the other sideshows and went home.

On the last day, I went round with the ethnographers. They saw a merry-go-round and threw themselves on it in a rush, and I, who get giddy, stayed on the ground to guard the women's handbags. Round and round they went in the air, the most melancholy looking carefree, the most cheerful singing with joy as their shadows chased each other on the grass. When the machine slowed down and they came back, they looked quite different. For five minutes they had been children caught up in the pleasure of swinging high away from earth. The Fair had worked for them. It was a place of extremes and its pleasures could be innocent or cruel at will.

15

AMONG THE VLACHS

Their origins – a priest and his house – the widow Zora – gipsies on St George's Day – the Vlachs of Homolje – Radul and Viktorina – the shepherds' bačija *– soothsayers at Whitsuntide*

Negotin gave me a taste of Eastern Serbia but at the Fair I had only seen people in a crowd. I was particularly intrigued by the Rumanian-speaking Vlachs and in the spring and early summer of 1971 I had a chance of going up into a Vlach stronghold, the wooded hills round Kučevo further up the Danube from Negotin.

When the Vlachs arrived is uncertain. People of Rumanian blood have come into this countryside at different times and from different directions giving it continuity: Dacians in Roman times; Rumanians, whom the Turks imported as privileged frontier guards in the 15th century, poor peasants who crossed the frozen river in the 18th and in the early 19th centuries to escape from worse conditions in their homeland. The 7th-century Slavs, who were later to become the Serbs, had driven out the original Illyrians, but under the Turks many of them left; it was the Vlachs who stayed on.

Moreover, the Vlachs kept their language in dialect or in a purer form, along the Danube where Latin had first been widely used by Roman legions. What they have also kept is an abundant mythology: they are a rich quarry for the ancient Slav beliefs which they absorbed, and they retain further beliefs of their own. Anywhere in the Balkans, Christianity, however strong, may be linked with pagan custom, but among the Vlachs in Eastern Serbia, it merely lends the Church calendar to give order to nature-daemons and Fates and human beings, dead or alive, with supernatural powers. Dragons turn to fire-birds who are rain-bringers, the birth of a baby is hedged with careful ceremony to propitiate 'the Kindly Ones'. It is vampire-country. Witches are two a penny. At Whitsuntide in one valley, Duboka, certain women fall into a trance and while in this state, they may prophesy, or enter into communication with the dead.

I went on a voyage of reconnaissance, choosing to arrive just before

St George's Day. I had a letter from the bishop, himself a Vlach, for one of his parish priests. I tracked him to a gipsy village, Brodica, where he was hurriedly blessing houses for the feast-day. Even after reading the bishop's letter his face remained stony with suspicion. He told me to come to his house that evening, but seemed unlikely to help.

I could get a room in the hotel for one night only, and whiled away some hours with the proprietor. He turned out to be the brother of a Minister recently removed from power. The family came from a neighbouring village. He talked about Duboka. Girls in other villages who inherit the gift of 'falling', move into that particular valley, he said. An eighteen-year-old had just done so. He himself had seen a baby 'white as a sheet' and quite rigid, and it wasn't epilepsy either.

It was time to go the the priest's house by the church. He had bicycled home and was in his shirt-sleeves, washing face and hands in a basin while his wife stood by him with a towel. He dried his beard:

'That's better. Some coffee. Now we can talk. Ough, such a day.'

The kitchen where we sat was well scrubbed. Two children did their homework, the smallest watched television in the next room. The priest was younger than I had thought; he had slanting blue eyes, not unfriendly. He questioned me: when had I seen the Bishop, what was my own faith, had I a husband, children? As he began to place me, everything grew easier. Would I like to stay in their house? It was simple, of course, and I might have to share a bed, but a roomy marriage-bed, with two young ladies from the next town, relatives of his wife. I accepted gratefully for the following day.

The priest was a peasant's son from the Golubac district. He had worked in the mines as a young man while his parents helped him to save up the seminary fees. He had completed his religious education in Belgrade to the secondary level. By then he was married and couldn't afford the Faculty course in theology, so he came home to work among the people. He had been five years with the Vlachs, had learnt their dialect, and was growing fond of them. He thought, more or less: 'When they are good, they are very very good, and when they are bad, they are horrid.' The Vlachs were not of course very Christian, but he went on trying. They had their own ways. He would show me what he could. He knew one of the 'falling women' quite well. And tomorrow, on St George's Day, his wife would take me to Duboka to see what went on there and then I could go back to the gipsies with him. After that, we would see. . . . The two of them told me more about 'Theodore's Days' in the first week of Lent when women stop knitting and sewing because of the evil spirits abroad; of Thursday in Holy Week when the Vlachs make little boats with lighted candles in them for the dead and launch them downstream. The Vlachs do not send for a priest often and then only after they have conducted their own rites.

I walked back to the hotel, thinking of the Austrian traveller who, near here in 1725, watched a vampire's grave being opened in the priest's presence and a stake driven through the dead man's heart, of the 19th-century bishop at Negotin, writing to his diocese: 'If anyone asks permission to dig up a dead body, he who asks is to be vanquished with a stern reply and even with punishment.' But old women continued to practise anti-vampire precautions on a corpse before they would open the door to the priest. 'The Vlachs have their own ways.'

On St George's Day, the priest's wife and I drove up the winding valley to Duboka. We forded a stream and walked uphill to a farm where the widow Zora lived. Zora, young and pretty, had buried her husband by the front gate, made a garden of flowers round him, bought him a fine tombstone. When we arrived, she was kneading dough. Once the loaf was in the oven, she wove an odd, charming wreath: quince blossom, wallflowers, young garlic, mint, japonica and striped grass. She tied it up with red wool on top of her milking pail, placed the newly-baked ring of bread over the garland, and threw in grass, coins and water. She milked her ewes after crossing herself, murmuring 'O God, give' and a phrase from the Orthodox liturgy. She added some magical incantations, threw water over the sheep and broke bread under them. She fed bread to the sheep, who ate it, and to the cows in her stable, who did not. Meanwhile, the old man who worked for her fixed some newly picked branches, elm and ash, on the fence.

The widow Zora's life was over at thirty-five. Her children had gone away to marriage or to school. She loved her farm in the gentle valley and would stay on there, honouring her dead in church and by the river, year by year invoking every supernatural power, Christian and pagan, to make her orchards, fields and flocks more fertile.

On the way to the gipsies with the priest, we passed several villages and he said: 'Not a church in sight, you see. The only one is in the town. The Vlachs never bothered to build any for themselves.'

We overtook men carrying sacrificial lambs on their backs, the lambs' feet slung over each shoulder and steadied in their hands, like an archaic Greek statue.

The gipsies at Brodica are Rumanian-speaking and came there in the early 18th century to escape from Phanariot persecution. Their ancestors in Rumania were nomadic 'kings' and 'queens'; they keep to their old occupation and work in wood. They make spoons and bowls and troughs for dough (Zora had one). Sometimes they trade in horses as well. You can tell they are landless people. Their houses have no gardens or vegetable plots, just a few tethered goats. The houses are dumped by a muddy stream or scattered up the hillside. One man had bought land outside the village and had prospered, but most of the gipsies were rich because they worked in Austria or France or Germany as woodcutters or factory-hands. Many had come home specially for the feast-day.

The priest explained his work. He would bless about sixty houses altogether, each of which gave him about 15p. in return. He had no regular income and was dependent on their goodwill. We visited some twenty houses and my mind became blurred by repetition. Outside each house was a column of smoke and a roasting lamb. Inside, the ceremony was perfunctory. The women stood by, and a few kissed the priest's hand. They lit their own incense made from dried bark. He intoned a blessing on each member of the family by name. I collected the fees and soon ran out of change. 'Who is she?' they asked the priest, 'your wife?' 'No, a relation.' It was the only possible answer. In one house a man asked to confess, he had struck his son with his own hand. The priest gave him absolution. More typical was the house where two young men, lithe as tigers, lay on beds and listened to a transistor. They did not move or switch off the music, but their large eyes watched carelessly all that went on. After the stocky Serbs, the gipsies are smooth-skinned and graceful. I watched two young girls. One was stringing pearl beads she had laid out on a table, the other had garlanded a cake with daisies. But the gipsies' taste vanishes when they prosper. Then they fill their houses with shiny rayon quilts and varnished cupboards; the cushions have a galloping horseman picked out in bright machine-sewn thread.

The blessings took a long time and we were given a great deal to eat. Back at the priest's house, the two young ladies had arrived. They were talkative. Despite my misgivings, the wide bed held us all comfortably, but the girls had other difficulties. Their hair had been piled up high and lacquered stiff as sculpture, so they slept nose to pillow. In the morning they anxiously examined each other – not a scrap of damage.

I set out to find the cousin of a Belgrade acquaintance, not knowing she had two namesakes in the town. Fortunately I was misdirected to one of them, a retired Serbian schoolmistress, who had a small-holding among Vlachs at Gložana in the Homolje foothills. A group of her neighbours were leaving for the summer pastures in a day or two, and one friendly couple, Radul and Viktorina, offered to take me with them. Radul was dark and could have passed for a Serb; Viktorina, fair, long-faced and aquiline, would have looked at home in England. I left the priest's house at three in the morning and drove over half a dozen bridges so rickety I could only hope the magic herb had not lost its power. I found Viktorina in the half-dark loading food, bedding and milk-cans onto a cart. Radul had gone ahead with the sheep. Viktorina, her daughter Savica and I packed ourselves in, the horse moved forward, and wooden wheels jolted over the stones. Savica was twelve, very bright-eyed; she acted as interpreter – her mother spoke only Rumanian. A cold dawn came up. Ribbons of cloud trailed across the valley between two lines of pointed hills covered with the green domes of weeping beech-trees. Horse chestnuts remind me of candelabras, but these trees are like lustres with pendants of oval leaves. The landscape was as regular as if someone had drawn one hill and one tree and then reprinted the pattern. Savica jumped out of the cart and picked wild lilac: 'We have to have it for the feast, you see.' Paths led up hill through the trees: 'There's a little house at the top. Soon some old granny'll go and live in it for the summer; anyone old can look after just a few sheep.' We passed a deserted mill and Viktorina said something. Savica was off again: 'Once the valley had more people in it, the mill worked, and there was even a shop.' The road we were following forded and re-forded the river. It went only as far as the pastures and after twelve miles or so we forked left up a grassy side-valley. We heard voices, turned a corner and found six or seven men, including Radul, standing by a small wooden hut, the summer sleeping-place, and a sheepfold roofed with bracken. Pigs, dogs, cows and horses were visible but no sheep. The carcases of six freshly-killed and skinned lambs – one for each family present – dangled from a tree. The day had an ordered ritual. Everyone knew their part. The men had their own corner, down by the river, where they built fires to roast the sheep. The women prepared the rest of the feast inside the hut and the men knocked before they entered. This sense of hierarchy contrasted strongly with their primitive surroundings.

The *koliba** was a lean-to shed, the gaps in the planks stuffed with

* *Koliba*, *bačija*, *bačilo*, *katun* are all used in Yugoslavia for shepherds' huts. In this district, *bačija* seemed to mean the occasion of going up to the mountain pastures in spring.

paper. It had no chimney, only a rudimentary fireplace dented like a large thumb-print into the stones of the back wall against the hillside. A gap was left for smoke to escape below a roof of tiles placed on halved logs. The furniture consisted of a three-legged stool, all knots and bumps, and two low tables. A six-foot wide shelf fixed halfway up the wall served as bed. A weakly lamb, looking more like a panda with its white coat and black-ringed eyes, was penned under it. The lamb bleated, the women shouted as they stirred soup in pots hung over wood embers. I could distinguish a few Latinized words: *perdut* (lost), *car* (cart), *bun* (good), *alor* (their).

Radul offered to show me the pastures. We climbed up a wooded mountain called Glogin and passed small abandoned gold mines covered with brambles. The map showed another mine, three miles north, close by the 'Golden River'. An old road led out from these hills to Majdanpek, where Radul had worked in the copper mines for two years, and had come on Roman pickaxes. Then he had returned home. 'There's plenty to do on the land.' He owned two horses and thirty sheep. He was building his third house as one of his grown-up sons was already married and one was going to be in the autumn: 'Can you come from England for the wedding? It'll last for three days, and we leave the village and walk and dance in the hills.' It sounded a holiday occasion, like the Negotin Fair. Radul was thirty-five, a young patriarch. He loved to hunt: 'We're up at two, back late at night. There's nothing like being up here in the snow and listening to the noise of the dogs – only you can't keep a good hunting-dog: they all get stolen and sold again.' Hunting is forbidden except for two or three days in the year, 'but who's to know – the forester can't get up here to find us. We shoot wild boar and deer and wild goats.' The wolves have gone, killed by systematic poisoning in the 1950s when the forests were felled.

The young wood had grown up again. Radul slashed back branches with an axe to clear the path. A sudden thunderstorm soaked us through; in places the muddy ground had been trampled by animals. 'The sheep take time to settle in,' Radul said; 'they won't stop to graze until they get used to a new place.' At last we heard bells and found the shaggy-fleeced flock guarded by three shepherd girls in the woods. Mystified, I asked where the pasture was? Here, they said. The sheep were nibbling young beech-leaves and making do with what little grass grew under the trees. It is State-owned forest, and the farmers pay a very small sum yearly for grazing rights.

We went down again to the hut. Viktorina worked non-stop, herding pigs, cooking maize porridge, improving the soup with garlic, paprika and fat bacon. She made a very good breakfast for Savica and me: bread dipped in sheep's milk, fried lamb's liver with more bread.

The ewes could not be milked till midday as they must give their maximum yield. At eleven, the lamb-roasting was completed and men gathered outside the hut to make arrangements for the communal measuring of milk. This involved the most complex business of the day. The six families present would each give a certain number of work-days during the summer, so that the 150 sheep they possessed between them would always be under the care of several people sleeping in the hut. How many days each family contributed was determined by the number of sheep each owned and by the total yield of each group of ewes. This calculation also affected the share paid out for the sale of cheese at the end of the summer. The men took two wooden measuring-bowls, large and small. They filled a pail of water to see how many measures it held. It was plain they did not trust each other. They checked and rechecked, argued, cut some tally-sticks and began all over again. Radul, by no means the oldest, acted as arbitrator. He also wrote down how much each pail held. He used Cyrillic script, for the dialect here is no longer a written language. I thought in terms of hours, and grew impatient, the Vlachs, measuring time from dawn till dusk, did not seem conscious of the delay. I walked restlessly down the side-valley and back again. The girls had brought their sheep down the hill and were holding them back offstage.

At midday came their grand entrance. Radul consulted my watch, but could plainly have managed without it. They sent a messenger for the sheep. The men took a bottle of beer in either hand, marched into the sheepfold and sat down in a row, in front of the empty buckets. The women drove the sheep into the fenced sheepfold, somehow sorted them out, and sent them in one by one to be milked. A man notched up a tally of work-days on sticks. It took a full two hours to milk all the ewes; no one hurried. At the end, everyone washed their hands and boots thoroughly in the river. While Radul kept count, milk was measured and strained into a great cauldron. This was carried into the hut and strong rennet added. The cheese fermented quickly and later was drained and placed in a barrel standing in the cool stream.

Work was over; the feasting began. The women had placed an oblong of logs on the grass – big enough for twenty people to sit round – and had heaped young beech-branches within it. On the leaves they had arranged food in set order: the roast lambs in straight lines down each side, with wine beside them, and in the centre round loaves marked with a cross, and cakes on top. Outside the log frame, each family laid two tables for their own dead: more food and wine, lilac flowers and a candle. As we sat down, I blundered by putting my legs outside the frame. 'Please put your legs *inside*,' someone said, 'it means we shall have longer life.' Possibly the structure is meant for a house, a symbol of plenty. A woman stood at the end of the frame, lighted a candle and waved a smoking piece of incense back and forth. She crossed herself and called out confidently: 'For Maria, for Stanko, for Jovan, we send this bread, we send this wine, we send this brandy, we send it to them before God.' Then the food for the dead* was placed within the frame, and we all ate. They gave me the guest's portion, a lamb's foot: 'It's the sweetest meat.' No. The company were polite to a stranger but after a while the language barrier bored them and they talked dialect to each other. A stout freshfaced young man objected angrily to the number of work-days he had been allotted. Radul calmed him. 'They often have discussions like this,' said Savica sagely. The feast ended without gaiety, jokes or kisses. A furtive, secret people, one minute the Vlachs were there, the next they were gone into the woods.

On the way home, Radul coaxed his bony grey mare into a canter. It rained torrents, we shook about like bones in a bag, and I clutched what I had been given, a saucepan full of sheeps' intestines. Radul and Viktorina caressed Savica gently. When I reached the priest's house, I crept into bed beside two motionless figures. The lacquer had held; perhaps it had not rained so hard in the town.

The priest, as he had promised, took me back to Duboka to see one of the women there. While someone went to find her we talked to her brother-in-law, an old sick man as white as a potato: 'Young people have the television now; they don't need the festivals for entertainment any more. I move with the times, too. Look.' He drew out a pair of galoshes from under the bench. They had turned-up Turkish toes, and were fashioned from motor-tyres: 'They've lasted ten years already.' I told him of the death of an Englishwoman, Catherine Brown, who had lived some time in this village. He was unmoved: 'She was old, and the old die.' He stowed his shoes away again. 'She made us sing our songs, and wrote them down and then, you won't

* Some of this was eaten, some laid aside to be put on their graves.

believe it, she sang them back to us, and got them right, too.' He smiled at the memory. A buxom woman came swaggering out of the house: 'I'm the woman who has trances.' This was Mileva; the priest asked about her experiences.

'I know when it's coming. It starts a few days before Whitsun. I feel a great sadness and I weep. Perhaps I think of my dead father and mother, I'm not sure. I only know I can't stop it. And then on Sunday, when they play the music, and the women dance round me, something takes hold of me and I know no more. I only wake when they stop dancing, and I ache all over. Last time I fell, two years ago, my arms and legs gave me such pain, I can't describe it. It means suffering such as I can hardly bear again.'

She told us about the television men who'd been to make a film of Duboka:

'I fell, as they said they wanted me to.'

'Was it real?'

She laughed: 'No, of course not, I just play-acted for them.' We went away. Mileva is known as a hard drinker, and has a red, slightly swollen face; she might have been fifty. These trances, if they happen at all, take place secretly in houses now, not openly in the village. Still, I thought I would return on Whitsunday.

Two assumptions lie behind the Whitsun rites at Duboka: a pious commemoration of the dead, and communication with their spirits in another world.

The feast-day is known there as *rusalija*, from *rosalia*; the Roman feast of roses. This was held in early summer, and people garlanded the graves of the dead to invite them to it. The legions had their own version; on the day before the Kalends of June they decked out their standards with roses. Perhaps it was they who brought the custom to the Danube?

As for communication with the dead, one source of spirit possession is the New Testament. Duboka is the only village in the region which celebrates its yearly feast on Whitsunday (Pentecost), the day on which the Apostles 'were all filled with the Holy Spirit' and 'the Spirit gave them power of utterance'. Among later Christian mystics, a painful trance could be a means of union with God. For Mileva and her like, it was a means to enter the world of the dead. Spirit possession which links the living with the dead is known in many parts of the world and can include soothsaying. In Duboka, women in trance have prophesied the death of a neighbour or the end of a war. But while at the first

Pentecost, 'speaking with tongues' was God-given, in this village it may be considered the work of a demon. Parallels for this are widespread. In Rumania 'the spirit of convulsion', an evil force, attacks women and girls. Mileva called herself a *rusaljka*, meaning a woman who has trances at Whitsun; in parts of Russia the same word is associated with this festival – and it can also signify an accursed person.

At Duboka on Whitsunday, I found the whole day was dominated by belief in the world of the dead. One family celebrated an indoor version of the shepherds' spring feast, and when the mother invoked the dead by name, everyone held on to the edge of the table to make contact with the other world. At another house, women keened and wept their way through the family cemetery on a hill dark with fruit-trees planted at the head of each grave. In the afternoon, tables, like altars loaded with cakes and candles, were set up by the roadside, people collected a shoulderbag full of food for each dead member of the family, kissed it reverently and then joined in a small procession with music which moved three times up and down the main street.

One local legend, which exists in several versions, may be a form of auto-suggestion. A good mile beyond the village is a cave. They say that long ago, at Whitsuntide, two queens were killed in front of it, and one, as she fell, cursed the Duboka women for ever: 'God willing, may everyone from this place on this day fall as I have fallen here.'* I walked up the hill and found a cathedral-like limestone cavern high above a ravine; the river gushed out of a cliff beside it. Below the cave, at the edge of the ravine, is a flat-topped knoll of land where people dance in the spring; by June wild strawberries, bell-flowers and daisies were growing in grass as long and soft as hair. The land drops clear away, and you can see for many miles to the south. It could well have been a holy place, and keeps a numinous magnificence. In a countryside where the Fates rule, the queen's curse must be strong in women's minds. What is preordained, cannot be evaded.

What is preordained can also be encouraged to happen. On Whitsunday, bagpipe music was once played all morning through the village. Now it is relegated to the *kafanas*, where I heard it, and its hypnotic power is plain: it starts with a repetitive drum-beat and then gets faster and louder until it rises to a frenzy. The effect of this on women who have felt for four or five days 'a great sadness', whose minds are already fixed on the dead, is not hard to imagine. When the feast

* The Serbs have a procession of girls called 'queens' who visit houses at Whitsun, and two of them sometimes perform a mock duel to *ward off* misfortune and illness.

started, dancing and words, both ritualized, put further pressure on the women, and a long curved silver knife, 'the queen's sword', was held over them as they fell. The dancers circling round a *rusaljka* used set words to rouse her from her trance:

Away you go, pale one, O!
Get up quick! Try again!
That's the way, pale one, so!
Come along, you hear us, eh!
Away you go, pale one, O!

Then the music used to stop. Mileva had explained to me what usually happened then.

In the 1890s doctors first went up to Duboka. Now they are going again, though it is probably too late. Medically the women were in deep trance and did not react to pain; they sometimes thrashed their limbs about uncontrollably, but no other epileptic symptoms were present. Hysteria is doubtfully diagnosed: during the German occupation a woman was tightly bound and showered with water, to stop her prophesying, but she went on just the same.

The *rusaljke* at Duboka are fewer than they were, and may disappear altogether. Many outside influences affect them – television, work in towns, temporary emigration to Western Europe or to America. But while they believe in the dead at the season of the dead, while they fear the ancient curse, it needs only a crowd and the customary ritual to start them off. Sometimes it does not need even that.

All the same, Whitsunday in 1971 was disappointing. Mileva was nowhere to be found. She did not fall that year, and if others did, they were in hidden places. The Belgrade psychiatrists were out on each street-corner; they talked about Freud and the collective unconscious. At the end of the day, five priest's wives climbed into the car and we drove through thunder and lightning of unbelievable violence, the only supernatural manifestation of the day.

In the town the priest was waiting for us: 'You should have gone to Ševice. There's a woman there, Roksanda. I know her well. She's been having trances for years. You should have gone to Ševice.'

Tired out with failure, I saw this as a consolation prize and asked if we could go to Ševice the following day. He agreed.

On Whit Monday we went to see Roksanda. Ševice lies in the valley west of Duboka and she comes from the village above Duboka and moved when she married. The rain had washed the sky clear blue and clouds sailed quickly about. In a landscape of meadows and neat villages and ripening wheat, the priest began the tale of Roksanda:

'She came to me and asked me to cure her. She's – well, when you see her you'll understand – she's unclean. She has a devil in her, and I must cast it out. Of course, I'm not the Apostle Paul, but I do what I can . . . you'll find she trembles a bit when she sees me. In the village, she's the chief witch. But last year before Whitsun she asked me to pray over her in the church, to make her suffering easier in the trance. I said a prayer for her health – though it wasn't what she meant, exactly. She fell on the church floor and went quite rigid for fifteen minutes. I failed to take a cross out of her hand, which went as hard as wood. It takes four men to lift her when she's like that.'

Roksanda lived in a two-roomed house with beehives in the garden. She is very stocky, with arms and legs like rounded pillars; and fair-haired, as are many Vlachs. But there is something odd about her: her pallid face shows signs of strain, and her blind right eye is turned inwards. Her married daughter has the same build, but she is rosy and open-faced with curly dark hair. Part of the time she interpreted for her mother, who burst into dialect when she got excited.

Roksanda undid most of the generalizations I had heard about the *rusaljke*. She did not fall only in Whitsun week, nor did she need music to send her into a trance. She had not been born with the gift. Aged twenty-five, she had been ill for three months, and this left her partly paralysed: she could only walk on all fours, dragging herself along on her hands and knees. She went from church to church for a cure, as far as Belgrade. At one monastery, a lazy monk failed to come and bless her at midnight as he had promised, but as she waited, the church doors flew open before her. She was often turned away as an evil woman. In the end, she recovered. Then, six years earlier, aged about forty, she had begun to fall into trances. Like Mileva, she suffered fearfully. She had trances in Whitsun week, and on St John the Baptist's Day (7 July) when someone burnt the magic herb under her nose and it eased her pain. The last time she fell was during Theodore's Days. She senses what is coming and calls for a companion, her friend or her daughter. The village women all run to her room to listen to her soothsaying. She had foretold the death of a boy who was drowned and his body found caught up in a tree. His parents mourned: 'Such sorrow, I've never seen such sorrow.'

She is like a woman who carries a great burden, as if she shares some of the grief that she foresees. Some outside power grips her, which she is trying to shake off. When in deep trance, she has broken tiles under her, and cut her hands until they streamed with blood: 'Great is my torment.' Between her and the priest a mutual confidence existed: she talked to him as to a good doctor. He had given her holy water and said a special prayer for her the Saturday before Whitsun, and so far, nothing had happened: 'I feel better. Of course, I don't know if it'll last. But those other priests, they just said I had a devil and shouted at me.'

Probably this priest will cure her, not least because like her, he believes firmly in the Devil who once came and sat heavily on his shoulders at the funeral of a sinful parishioner. I do not pretend to know what ailed Roksanda, but I hope by now she is free of the trances.

At least Roksanda knows easier ways of being a wisewoman. She is skilled in the use of herbs and spells and all kinds of white magic, and they must be quite profitable because she was the only witch I met who owned a refrigerator.*

* In 1946, Denis Wright, then on the staff of the British Embassy in Belgrade, found the chief witch of Duboka in a dark room complete with cauldron, 'her own coffin (discreetly covered) at the end of her bed, broom sticks . . . a shelf of small empty bottles (for filling with love filtres and the like), a row of seven cheap padlocks (for locking up – metaphorically and spiritually – faithless husbands and wives, a common complaint she is called upon to remedy), a ball of red wool (good for casting out Evil), . . . a huge pair of scissors . . . an immense dried sunflower . . . .' Using some of this equipment, she was in the middle of casting spells for two other old women. She could also tell fortunes with maize-grains.

PART TWO

The New Serbia

HISTORICAL BACKGROUND

The monasteries had given me a picture of medieval Serbia and of its Byzantine inheritance. I had still to discover what the Ottomans and Habsburgs, among others, had brought to Serbia since then.

With the coming of the Turks, Serbian life altered completely. By the mid-15th century, many nobles had been killed in battle and some had fled to Hungary. Without its leaders, the feudal state collapsed and the institutions which survived, the extended family (*zadruga*) and village groupings, were small-scale. The Ottoman Porte took over the central administration, which stayed in its hands until the late 18th century. Turks came to live in the towns and ventured into the country only to collect taxes from the Serbs. The Christian peasants (*rayah*) who came into the ramshackle towns were forbidden to ride their horses through the streets. The Serbs were second-class citizens in their own land, though in the villages they kept a measure of independence.

The Turkish rule of subject races was sterile. Their nomadic ancestry showed in their inability to develop their newly-acquired territories: they abandoned the Serbian mines, and taxed but did not cultivate the land. They were soldiers, always ready to move on. They bivouacked in wooden houses not meant to last, and bivouacked comfortably, as they had an eye for pleasant places. In Serbia, they had fortresses but no cities. Their finest monument there was practical: the bridge across the Drina at Višegrad.* It was built in the 16th century by a Slav Vizier, Mehmed Pasha Sokolović, and he had verses carved into the stone: 'It looks as if it were a single pearl upon the water, with the firmament as its shell.'

The Ottomans were warriors of the faith who fought for Islam. They mulcted the conquered countries of money and of talent, since they educated only the forced levies of Christian boys whom they took back to Istanbul, and who were absorbed as Moslems into the Ottoman army as janissaries, or into the civil administration, like Sokolović. In Serbia, the Turks did not set up any schools for they had no interest in imposing their own culture on Christian subjects; they made certain demands on them and if these were not fulfilled, cruel punishment followed, including death by impalement. On

* *The Bridge on the Drina* of Ivo Andrić's novel, translated by Lovett Edwards (1962).

the whole, however, they regarded Christians as the *millet*, a political and religious entity set apart from themselves.*

The Turkish conquest is still remembered in the Balkans as an overwhelming catastrophe in which several countries were snuffed out for centuries. But a strong force of preservation was at work in the Orthodox Church. Without it, the revival of Balkan nationalism in the 19th century would hardly have been possible. In Serbia, it was part of the rural patriarchal society which links the medieval kingdom of the Nemanjids with the peasant fight for independence 500 years later. There are some visible memorials to the activity of the Serbian Church under Turkish rule: the building of churches near the Morava valley in the 15th century, or the artistic Renaissance at Peć a hundred years later. These were momentary. The true continuity lay in the ordinary church activities: the attempts of monks to teach the three *R*'s to peasants with no opportunities of schooling, the church services and monastery feasts which were the gathering-place of a people in bondage.

The Great Migration

Finally, the initiative of the Church led to the formation of a new Serbia outside the old. In 1690, the Austrians had penetrated into Turkish territory as far south as Prizren and Peć. Many Serbs supported them but the Austrian General Piccolomini died of fever and his troops were forced to retreat. With them went about 40,000 Serbian families who were to settle in Habsburg territory north of the Danube and the Sava, in what is now Yugoslav Vojvodina and part of Hungary. Their leader was the Patriarch Arsenius III, and they were well-to-do merchants, craftsmen and farmers; they took with them all that they could.

A simple pattern of migration northwards had been established before this. Monks, themselves seasoned travellers, would give advice on the best places to settle, and sometimes the group would stop half-way for a year or two, then move on. In 1690, the urgency of flight from the Turks and the very large numbers of people involved, demanded more detailed arrangements. The Patriarch, a gentle, determined and skilful man, halted at Belgrade, where he called a meeting: the new emigrants consulted with the older settlers, Abbots from the south with Abbots from the north, *kapetani* (district leaders) with a *birov* (mayor of a town). Together they sketched out a plan. They wanted Serbian autonomy, national and religious, in their new home, and they sent a bishop to petition Leopold I at Vienna for these 'Privileges',

* A settled Islamic society existed where Slav Christians had become Moslems, as in Bosnia, with its capital at Sarajevo.

which were granted though not always honoured. The 'Privileges', along with the creation of a Military Frontier in 1701–2 and Joseph II's Patent of Toleration of 1781, were to be the cornerstones of Serbian development under the Habsburgs. They provided the emigrants with an opportunity to build up a reserve of wealth and talent.*

Difficulties abounded. The Serbian Orthodox Church, with its centre at Sremski Karlovci, proved a unifying force, but it took on a very different character under the Turks and under the Habsburgs. In both Empires it fostered the struggle for future Serbian independence, but the very quality which strengthened it under the Turks – its tenacious adherence to medieval tradition – weakened it under the Habsburgs. The Turks had a closed society, the Habsburgs, by comparison, more or less open. The Vojvodina Serbs belonged to a Church which, after its flowering in the Middle Ages, had lost interest in learning and in other countries. Any Serb who, like Dositej Obradović, saw the urgent need to introduce his people to Western culture, had to break away from the Church to achieve his aims.

Still more serious were the political problems posed by the complexity of Austro-Hungarian relations within the Habsburg Empire. The Serbs negotiated with Vienna, where a Serbian colony flourished, but otherwise they lived mainly on Hungarian territory, and Pešt was a centre of Serbian intellectual life. At times the Hungarians co-operated with them, as in the late 18th century when Serbs were admitted to the Hungarian Diet and achieved high office there. At times they were deadly enemies. The independent status of the Serbs in Hungary was less well-defined than that of the Croats, and constant tension reigned, as the Hungarians, struggling for more power within the Empire, oppressed the Serbs.

The First and Second Serbian Uprisings (1804/1815)

Meanwhile, for the Serbs who remained in Serbia, Turkish rule improved slightly in the 18th century. The later Ottoman administration divided the country into four *pashaluks* and several outlying districts. Within these, Turks from the towns collected the taxes; under them was a Serbian official for each group of villages, who in turn supervised the head of each village, chosen by the Council of Elders. This situation deteriorated rapidly after 1799, when the janissaries were readmitted to the Belgrade *pashaluk* by direct order of the Sultan. With the decadence of the Ottoman Empire, they had turned into lawless freebooters, who lived off the villagers and humiliated the inhabitants. At the least sign of resistance they would use fire and sword; whole families would disappear, never to be heard of again.

* For a fuller description, see pp. 200 and 202.

The Serbs were by no means doomed to remain helpless victims of the janissaries. Many of them were practised in guerrilla warfare from their experience as *hajduci*, brigands with a Robin-Hood reputation, who preyed on the rich and spared the poor. Some were fugitives from the Turks, some simply preferred a free life. The *hajduci* had an open and a close season: they went up into the hills and worked from St George's Day (6 May) to St Demetrius' Day (8 November) and then dug themselves in comfortably for the winter with their protectors in the villages and towns, where they might take a job, though the poems about them suggest they whiled away their time in wine, women and song. The *hajduci* had a romantic appeal, with their handsome clothes and weapons, but the reality of their life was harsh. They killed anyone who betrayed them, and if the Turks caught them, they were impaled alive.

Moreover, at least 10,000 Serbs had benefited from the military training they received during their service in the Austrian *Freikorps* in 1789–90, when the Austrians held Belgrade and other Serbian territory. Karageorge, whom the Serbs were to choose as their leader, was a former *hajduk* and had been a sergeant in the *Freikorps*; he had also served, with many other Serbs, in the Ottoman army which defeated the janissary Pazvan Oglu at Vidin in 1797. He proved a brilliant commander.

When, in 1804, new excesses of the janissaries caused the Serbs to rise in successful rebellion, they embarked on a struggle which was to become an epic.* 'The greatest leader and the humblest peasant alike were heroes.' The Vojvodina Serbs, including the Metropolitan Stefan Stratimirović and Serbian merchants at Zemun, now backed the rebels very strongly by sending them money and ammunition. Some volunteered as soldiers, and so gave the Uprising leaders who were educated for peace as well as for war. This was important, as under the Ottomans, Serbs had been isolated from learning of any kind, though a few achieved material prosperity.

The Serbian Uprisings encouraged other oppressed nations, notably the Greeks, with whom they maintained strong links, through the Society Philike Hetaireia. (It was the Greeks who, in their turn, sent Karageorge on his ill-fated expedition of 1817.)† The Serbs now appeared in a different light to the established powers. For Austria-Hungary, as for Russia, they had ceased to be a subject nation and had become a threat to the *status quo* with Turkey. Both these countries were, in time, tempted by the prospect of increasing their influence in the Balkans during the decline of the Ottoman Empire. Napoleon, too, showed interest in the area, and the Serbs found themselves the object of attentions from all quarters.

* See Chapter 18.

† See p. 221.

Self-interest, as usual, triumphed. In 1812 the Russians helped the Serbs towards autonomy at the Treaty of Bucharest, but the next year, threatened by Napoleon, they withdrew their troops from Serbia, leaving the country open to a disastrous Turkish invasion. Although in 1815 the Serbs under a new leader, Miloš Obrenović, won their Second Uprising, the Congress of Vienna was unsympathetic to the growth of small states and sent the Serbian envoys packing.

Only when Russia had regained her strength after the fall of Napoleon did she put pressure on the Turks in the Balkans, and by 1830 they acknowledged Serbia as an autonomous State within the Ottoman Empire, with Miloš as its hereditary ruler.

The New Serbian State

Although the Uprisings gave Serbia a place, however small, in Europe, her history for the next hundred years or so after 1830 had one strongly domestic aspect: her search for a stable form of government.

For the second time, the Serbs had a state of their own. But the memory of their feudal Empire could give no help to these soldier-peasants, of whom Temperley wrote that they fought for freedom to live as a free people, not freedom to live as a free state, while contemporary Western institutions held little attraction for men like Hajduk Veljko: he 'prayed that Serbia might be engaged in war as long as he lived, but that after his death she might enjoy peace'.

Though the Serbs were and are democratic individually, in the early 19th century they had had no experience of democratic government. For the next seventy years, until the accession of Peter Karadjordjević in 1903, their internal politics were bedevilled by tension between constitutionalists and would-be absolute monarchs, a conflict of far more importance to the nation than the much-publicized rivalry between the Obrenović and Karadjordjević dynasties.

Yugoslavia

Even when after the First World War Serbia became part of the 'Kingdom of the Serbs, Croats and Slovenes' that formed the first Yugoslavia, these difficulties were revived. The parliamentary government of the 1920s gave way to the autocratic rule of King Alexander, and his assassination by a Croat extremist in 1934 left the Regent Paul to juggle with this problem. Within the Kingdom it was further compounded by the clash between centralism and federalism, the first a Serbian, the second a Croat concept, and Serbia's present identity is that of one Republic among six in a federal, Communist Yugoslavia.

Serbia's foreign policy took shape under her one outstanding ruler of the later 19th century, Prince Mihailo Obrenović. Together with his able Foreign Minister Garašanin, he developed his country's role as leader of the other Balkan nations – which she was to keep until 1918. Garašanin, who in the 1840s had written a memoir, *Načertanije* ('The Plan'), on Serbia's aims, contributed an unusual element of continuity to Balkan politics.

Much of Serbia's history in the first half of the 20th century turns again on the themes of war and endurance. The Austrian *Drang nach Osten* and the final convulsions of the Ottoman Empire both endangered her. She had already embarked on the Balkan Wars against Turkey when in 1914 the Archduke Franz Ferdinand, himself a moderate who favoured peace in the Balkans, was assassinated by a young Bosnian patriot in Sarajevo. This time the whole of Europe was involved in war.

The heroic tradition of Serbia has been put to the test on a far larger scale in our own century than ever before. In the First World War an epidemic of typhus ravaged the country in 1915 like a plague, the Austrian invaders treated the civilian population with savage inhumanity, and drove its soldiers – with their schoolboy recruits – into a terrible winter retreat over the mountains of Montenegro and Albania to Corfu, a retreat in which thousands died of exposure and starvation.

In the Second World War, the Germans and their supporters, particularly in their puppet state of Croatia, played on traditional anti-Orthodox feeling among Roman Catholics and themselves committed atrocities unparalleled in Balkan history. National resistance, which began in Serbia and spread right through Yugoslavia, was tragically divided. During 1943 the Communist-led Partisans, by virtue of their iron discipline, unity of purpose and Tito's outstanding leadership, had become the most powerful resistance force, and the Royalist Četniks, under Mihailović, a regular Army officer, had lost their hold. Lasting co-operation between Četniks and Partisans had proved impossible, not least because the Četniks often temporized with the Germans, ostensibly – and sometimes genuinely – to spare the civilian population from reprisals, while the Partisans, both men and women, fought all out against the enemy. Mihailović possessed personal courage, as he was later to show at his trial, but he had imperfect control over the widely-scattered groups under his command. The year 1943 proved to be a turning-point in the history of Yugoslavia. Several British Missions had been sent in during the previous two years, but it was on the basis of the information given by the

Mission to Tito of May 1943 that Churchill was convinced the Allies should transfer their support from Mihailović to Tito.

In November of that year a Committee set up at Jajce in Bosnia appointed Tito Marshal and Acting Premier – and formed the basis of the post-war Communist Government. The Partisans still had to withstand two major offensives launched against them by the Germans. They fought with the spirit but without the resources of a regular army. They were guerrillas, as Karageorge's Serbs had been. If they retreated, it was not to Corfu, but to their own mountains and islands. They suffered heavy casualties in a prolonged ordeal against the Germans on very harsh terrain.

In 1918 the Serbian Army, with the Allies, had fought their way back into Belgrade. In 1944 the Yugoslav Partisans, with Russian assistance, did the same. By then, the whole population of Yugoslavia had been involved in total war; probably one person in ten was killed.

After the war Mihailović was tried on a charge of treason and executed, and Tito became Prime Minister and the effective ruler of Yugoslavia. Serbia became the largest of six Republics within a Federation.

Once more, Serbia had taken part in a triumphant and costly struggle. Since then thirty years have gone by, and the scars of war have healed in so far as prosperity can heal them over the devastation of the past.

16

THE FRANKISH HILLS AND THE HUNGARIAN PLAIN

Road to Novi Sad – Slovak village – a night in the city – some monasteries of the Fruška Gora: Krušedol, Hopovo and Velika Remeta – Bodjani: a Bishop's summer residence – the Abbot of Kovilj

The road from Belgrade to Novi Sad, the capital of Vojvodina, runs pencil straight between poplars over the plain towards Hungary. In early summer the wild flowers make a ribbon of garden along the verges. I was going to look at life among the *prečani*, the Serbs 'on the other side', whose ancestors fled north across the Danube from the Ottoman domination.

The road divided a man-made landscape of vast fields planted with maize and sunflowers. Red-aproned gipsy women were hoeing between the maize plants. The plain gave an overwhelming sense of cultivation since time immemorial, yet only 300 years ago it was a marshy wilderness fought over by the Turks. The Serbs, who formed the largest number of inhabitants, at first did little to improve it; they lived in wretched dugouts and mud huts on the drier land and scattered seed haphazard to grow patches of maize alongside their wheat and oats and melons. The poorer immigrants stayed here; the more well-to-do went on further to Buda and Szentendre and became prosperous merchants and corn-dealers. In the 18th century the Habsburg policy was to colonize this region, and the Serbs were quick to learn new techniques of farming from German, Hungarian, Czech and Slovak settlers. In this way the land took its present shape. It has the same fascination as the black earth of the Ukraine, worked over under wide peaceful skies.

About half-way to Novi Sad I came to Stara Pazova, with its air of privacy characteristic of Vojvodina villages. The houses were close together and faced the main street end on with a single 'gossiping' window (*Kibitzenfenster*). The Habsburg government ordered this arrangement. They wanted no doors on the street where people could

32 The dramatic profile of Golubac castle on the Danube

33 The Iron Gates of the Danube at Djerdap

34 Sremski Karlovci: the chapel which commemorates the Peace of Carlowitz

35 Sunflowers: the great Pannonian plain

gather to plot mischief, but they could hardly stop neighbours calling out of the window to each other. Between each house a high closed gateway led to the garden and the main part of the house.

Because it was Sunday the women were dressed in their best clothes. They were the Slovaks I had seen on Belgrade station when I first arrived. Sixteen petticoats held out their pleated woollen skirts, and they had white embroidered blouses, dark embroidered shawls crossed over and tied behind, embroidered stockings, embroidered headscarves. Even small girls of three or four were turned into bright moving bundles. The bottom drawer of a bride from Stara Pazova must be a splendid sight.

There was more than embroidery to be seen in the village that afternoon. I was stopped by a procession surging down the main road back into the centre. The day before, a wedding had taken place and now relatives and friends were returning from a visit to the young couple. They took no notice of any stranded cars; they were far too absorbed in their own horseplay. Two 'funny men' had bulky sheepskin capes and pointed floppy straw hats, and one wore a white dress like a girl. I slowed down, and on the other side of the road an old woman, shaking with laughter, called out to me as I went by: 'Aren't they marvellous! Simply marvellous! D'you have anything like that in your country?'*

Not far north of Pazova the road passed a slimy duckpond and took a twist uphill. I was going over the Frankish hills (*Fruška Gora*), traditionally the place where Charlemagne halted his progress southwards. These hills provide the second landscape of the Vojvodina. The plain is open, the hills are hidden country, wooded and deeply indented with small valleys which shelter Serbian monasteries.

That day I could not stop to explore them. I had to go straight to Novi Sad and find a lodging. I crossed the Danube close by the massive fortress of Petrovaradin, and came to a city of skyscrapers, wide boulevards, immaculate parks and baroque churches. A widow took me in, a kindly woman for whom the clock had stopped when her daughter had been killed in an accident ten years earlier. She lived like a shadow; but she seemed to enjoy my own doings vicariously. Much concerned with the niceties of respectable behaviour, she warned me I was not to have followers. However, Professors were willingly admitted, and any evening outing of mine became a 'distinguished visit' (*otmeni poset*). Rank counts in Novi Sad. The Serbs are democratic in Belgrade,

* Another Slovak village is Kovačica, where Martin Jonaš and other primitive painters live.

but here the Habsburgs left their mark. In the last century, a grocer's wife would flounce if not addressed as *gnädige Frau* and the village priest's daughter was *Frajla* (Fräulein) *Jula* to the world.

The first evening, I went to a concert of chamber music in a modern hall, with an audience that was old-fashioned. Elderly ladies had their hands kissed by even more elderly gentlemen. Were they *hochgeborene* (colonels and councillors) or *hochgebildete* (writers), I wondered ?* The orchestra was excellent. Novi Sad has a tradition of good violinists. The names of the musicians were nearly all Hungarian or German. They played Telemann and Bach and finally Mozart, *Eine Kleine Nachtmusik*. On the way home, the streets smelt of acacia flowers and popcorn.

In the morning, I found Dinko Davidov, who is a Curator at the Gallery of Matica Srpska,† and we went off to the Fruška Gora monasteries in the hills I had passed the day before. These communities puzzled the Habsburgs; an Austrian official, F. W. von Taube, travelled here in the 18th century:

> . . . the most noteworthy thing is that the Greek [Orthodox] monasteries are not in towns and villages like the Catholics, but always in the woods and wildernesses, in the fashion of the first monasteries of the Christian Church.[1]

It was Dinko, precise and energetic, who explained how these monasteries came into being. In the late 15th and 16th centuries, he said, Serbian families who crossed the Danube were welcomed by the Hungarian feudal lords as troops who could and did defend their southern frontier against the Turks. In return, the Hungarians granted the Serbs the privilege of building monasteries, where their monks settled and enshrined the Nemanjid relics they had brought with them – Prince Lazar's bones were hidden for centuries at Vrdnik ('New Ravanica'). The Fruška Gora monasteries mirror the continuity of medieval Serbian life in exile, in contrast to their later life under the Habsburgs, which was to bring with it so many changes. Dinko drove me into the heart of the hills and I saw a belfry among the trees. An old monk whose robes had faded to a blackish-green shuffled out to meet us and greeted Dinko warmly. We had reached Krušedol, founded as a

* These German titles were widely used in 19th-century Novi Sad, as were their Serbian equivalents *visoko rodni* and *visoko učeni*.

† A good collection of icons and portraits, engravings of the monasteries and copies of their frescoes.

men's community by a member of the Branković family in the early 16th century: born the Despot George,* he chose the religious life and died as Archbishop Maxim. His mother, Angelina, founded a women's community there; she got help from the Russian Grand Duke Basil, to whom she sent four cartloads of sable skins, and her church in a meadow is small and charming.

Maxim's church has frescoes, but many of them were overpainted in the 18th century, in Venetian Baroque style. Maxim and Angelina are buried at Krušedol, as are the two Patriarchs who led the Great Migrations, the *vojvoda* chosen in 1848, and King Milan Obrenović. The small museum at the monastery is full of mementoes of the Obrenović family; it also contains a good collection of English books on the Balkans, a bequest from a Serb *émigré*.

Hopovo, where Dinko took me next, looks Byzantine. 'You can read all about it in my book,' said Dinko, handing me a copy with a flourish and a grin, and he began to talk to the three nuns who welcomed us. Then he relented and told me about the painters from Mount Athos who had come to Hopovo in 1608 and carried out their frescoes, red and gold and dark grey on pale green, which reached up into the high cupola adapted from the Morava monasteries and perched on a tower. Hopovo contains some fine scenes: the Massacre of the Innocents, the Transfiguration, the Raising of Lazarus and the Entry into Jerusalem.† Hopovo lies in a valley as pretty as when the monk Dositej described it in the 18th century, with a stream and walnut tree and vineyards,[2] but not as tranquil: 'You should see it on Labour Day,' said one of the nuns, 'so many tents of every colour, why, it's like the field of Kossovo.'

The Fruška Gora monasteries, especially in spring, can still be a delight. Jazak is remote, with a graceful church housing some Nemanjid bones. Vrdnik shelters the statue of a poetess, 'Milica Srpkinja', in its orchard. Beočin is set in a steep flowery valley near the Danube and has a secret garden with box hedges where a family once built a memorial chapel. But their real life has gone for ever. Many of them were blown up by pro-Nazi terrorists in the Second World War, like Velika Remeta, where Dinko showed me the shell of a fine brick church with decorated windows. Somehow purple irises and a silver birch had come through the holocaust.

* A grandson of the builder of Smederevo. His lands lay close to Krušedol.

† On the east wall of the cupola curve, high on the west wall of the nave, and on the vault by the west wall respectively. Dinko Davidov's *Hopovo* (Belgrade, 1964) is translated into English.

'We can restore the church,' said Dinko, 'but what we can't restore anywhere are the books and manuscripts that were burnt.' He looked angry and hurt. 'It was done by men of education, as often as not.'

I remembered then that Krušedol, which we had just come from, had been used as a concentration camp; one Patriarch's tomb prised open and a pile of bodies thrown into it. Afterwards a scrap of brown paper was found hidden in the hair of a dead peasant woman; it read

> Jelica, my love, my strength, forgive Mother, I am separated from you, Mother gives you three thousand kisses on your little chin, God go with you, my child, dear living sweet heart, Mother is waiting for them to shoot her.

Dinko had taken me on one more journey into the Serbian past in these hills with their record of tenacity, destruction and suffering. From then on, I was to have a very different impression of Vojvodina life.

On my second day in Novi Sad, Slobodan Jovanović, a young architect from the Institute for Protection of Monuments, offered to take me to Bodjani monastery in the Danube marshes. Slobodan is fair, slight, well-mannered and irrepressible. We drove westwards along the river to his running commentary:

'This suburb's called Futog, it used to have tremendous fairs; now we're at Bačka Palanka and that's a good fish restaurant, pity it's too early for lunch. Look across the river and you'll see Ilok in Croatia and that Gothic church right on top of the cliff is full of noble tombs; all those baby mountains are still the Fruška Gora, they go on and on. Now we turn north, how flat it is, that field's planted with hemp. What a lot of beehives, I think you can trust a man who's a fisherman or a bee-keeper, don't you?'

'My husband's a fisherman.'

'Good, you see what I mean, then. Now we come to Bač, the fortress is Hungarian, it's in a shabby state, we may tidy it up soon. That big church is a Franciscan monastery. Here we are at Bodjani, but what on earth are those two doing? Stop! Stop!'

He jumped out of the car and ran towards a couple of monks who embraced him. Abbot Maksimilijan and Father Lukijan were going to drive into town, but Father Lukijan decided to stay with us. I could hardly believe he was a monk, since he wore a white shirt with a gold monogram embroidered on the pocket, black trousers, and carried a braided frogged black jacket over his arm. I was reminded of the list of priests' clothing that an 18th-century Vojvodina bishop had issued to his diocese to get them out of Turkish costume: shoes, boots, linen shirts, two pairs of white gloves for winter and summer, one comb for beard and hair which *must* be carried in the pocket. . . . Lukijan was tall and broad-shouldered, in his early thirties, and the Abbot, a bit older, looked healthy too; I noticed the robust physique of the *prečani* compared with the slighter Serbs who live in the south. 'It's all that bacon,' explained a Vojvodina friend afterwards. We certainly lunched off the fat of the land at Bodjani.

The monks' living standards were as high as anything I had seen in Yugoslavia. They had a magnificent kitchen with built-in units, an extremely well-stocked larder, new bathrooms and a linen cupboard stacked high with clean sheets and thick bath towels. In the corridor, a rifle hung beside the priests' black chimney hats; the marshes nearby produce plenty of wildfowl for the pot. Lukijan dealt in old oil lamps and silver candlesticks.

Anything further from the austere piety of the southern monasteries would be difficult to imagine. Bodjani was once the local bishop's seat and is now his summer residence. It is comfortable, welcoming and materialistic and I am sorry for the Abbot who has now been moved to the beautiful barren wilderness of Morača in Montenegro.

We went into the church. Bodjani has been perpetually rebuilt since its foundation in 1478, when, the story has it, a Dalmatian merchant made a vow that if its spring-water cured his eye disease, he would found a monastery. The present church, given by a wealthy citizen of Szeged in 1722, is as pretty as a picture, a white toy building with grey corners outlined in red paint, and an onion-domed belfry. It is framed on three sides by white buildings which end in curving gables, and the fourth side of the square is an orchard. The whole monastery is cottage baroque, small and harmonious.

Inside, the church is covered with decadent Byzantine frescoes. Hristofor Žefarović worked there. Born in Macedonia, he ranged the Balkans, made a pilgrimage to Jerusalem and died in Moscow. He painted whatever was asked of him, a Byzantine fresco or an equestrian portrait and peddled his own icons, engraved books and embroidered church vestments. At Bodjani, the lumpy saints and women with coarse faces mark a sad farewell to past nobility, but the miniature scenes from Genesis:* Adam and Eve, the creation of the world, and

* On the vault leading up into the cupola.

Noah's ark, partly based on the Athos 'Painter's Manual', have an odd originality and I liked them very much.

We started for home, and were stopped by police on the road; the President was returning from Novi Sad Agricultural Fair to his hunting-lodge nearby. The Fair is a magnificent display of pedigree horses and pigs and cattle and sheep and of farming equipment – a worthy successor to the old Fairs at Futog. We got out of the car and stood under an acacia tree. A Slovak woman beside us picked a branch and buried her face in it. Tito and his wife, two relaxed, bronzed dignitaries, went by with a minimum of fuss, and we were allowed to drive on. A brisk kind of day. 'We'll do some more travelling together,' Slobodan said.

The next expedition was not with him, however, but with the Bishop's Secretary. Father Veselin greeted me at his home in a brand-new block of flats. He wore a very good suit and drove his own Mercedes to Kovilj, another monastery along the Danube, but eastwards this time. Kovilj lies in a shady green place beside a quiet backwater. The monastery was probably once a dependency of Privina Glava in the Fruška Gora and built over the ruins of a Franciscan church. Certainly the foundations of a medieval church can be seen by the *konak*. Kovilj is linked by legend with St Sava: they say he met the Hungarian king here one summer to negotiate peace and the king promised agreement only if the Danube froze. St Sava duly performed the miracle.

The present 19th-century church has an iconostasis containing bad copies of Leonardo's Last Supper and a Raphael Madonna; they made me wish the Serbs had never seen Italian painting. Outside, the church is pleasant and set on a lawn of 'English' grass, neatly mown by the cows who nibble at it. Paeonies flourish round the *konak*, which is grandiose. I walked through a long series of drawing-rooms, 'the red salon', 'the blue salon' and others, filled with gilded furniture and shuttered against mosquitoes. Rajić, the late 18th-century historian, was once Abbot here, and left them his library of Latin and Hungarian books. The present Abbot, who studied music, has added some opera scores, including *Madame Butterfly*. Abbot Leontije is a massive genial figure, who farms Kovilj with one other monk, Miron. At first I thought Kovilj as worldly as Bodjani. The talk was all of promotion: why hadn't one Bishop been raised to Metropolitan yet? Both the Abbot and Miron held the rank of *iguman*, Veselin told me, it was just that Leontije was the 'elder' (*starešina*). In the south, I was more used to monastics giving up their titles – there, one Abbess had refused to be called *igumanija*, out of humility.

We went outside to look at the farm. A Yorkshire sow answered when Leontije called her by name: 'Come here, Milka, there's a good pig.' She had had eleven piglets the day before, and her breed fetch a high price at market.

We walked on to see St Peter's Chapel, where sick people come for a cure. A large dead oak grew out of the east wall and an unknown hand had planted a sapling elm beside it. 'Is it a pagan place?' I asked Leontije.

'Certainly not.' He grew formidable. 'I'll tell you something. A branch of that oak was pressing down on the chapel, and a man climbed up to saw it off. He sawed away, it was as hard as iron, and at last it came off, but he died a few months later, in fearful torments. This is a very powerful place.'

'Christian?'

He glared at me:

'Yes, very Christian. There was a well across the road,' he pointed to a dent in the ground, 'and after the war, two men murdered a woman and threw her in. The Bishop said I was to reconsecrate the well, but it dried up of its own accord.'

I became a trifle uneasy at having photographed the scene and sure enough, the print, when developed, was to reveal a ghostly woman entering the chapel. Father Veselin was looking displeased. He wanted to show me how modern the Church was, and here we were listening to old wives' tales. He manoeuvred me away from Leontije towards the village priest's house. A room was set aside for the forty children who came to catechism on Sundays. Like Bodjani, the house had a magnificent bathroom and kitchen. The pigs lived in concrete sties, a garage waited for the new car, and a plump tortoiseshell cat sat among thriving vegetables.

The priest and his wife were quite young and great travellers: Italy last year, Greece this. The priest asked Father Veselin for permission to go to Jerusalem. 'Yes, of course, and why don't you look in at Mount Athos, too?' It was all very matter-of-fact; south of the Danube, a pilgrimage to Jerusalem or to the Holy Mountain (*Sveta Gora*) – never 'Athos' – would have been a great event.

We went home via Kač. Again a handsome house for the priest, an old one restored, with parquet floors and a grand piano; and a hundred children came to catechism on Sundays.

As we drove on, Father Veselin explained to me his five-year plan. He exacted a kind of tithe on churchgoers: white-collar workers paid 1 per cent of their income, farmers a percentage of wheat on their acreage. He had already built or restored twenty houses for priests and hoped to do as many again the next year (1971 and 1972). I was reminded of Stevan Sremac's novel about two Vojvodina priests, where one of them advises a young ex-seminarist not to await too patiently the will of God, but to watch out for a 'good, fat parish' (*jednu dobru*, *masnu parohiju*) like his own. Prosperity is in the air. 'You don't ask a Vojvodina man what ideals he has,' someone said to me, 'you ask him what he earns.'

17

SOLDIERS, PATRIARCHS AND TRADERS

Vojvodina landscape – 'a wall against the Turks' – the adventures of Simeon Piščević – Sremski Karlovci: a cathedral town – Petrovaradin – Dositej and the West – the golden age of Novi Sad – Čelarevo: a country house

When the priest at Kač had shown me his church, he had pointed out the paving-stones broken by horses that Kossuth's Hungarians had stabled there in 1849. Two dates cropped up in everyone's conversation: 1690, the year of the Great Migration (*Velika Seoba*) from the south, and 1849, the Rebellion (*Buna*) against the Hungarians.

I had come from Belgrade, where the two dates talked about most are 1389, the battle of Kossovo, traditionally the beginning of Turkish domination over the Serbs, and 1804, the first Serbian Uprising against the Turks. 1389 and 1804, 1690 and 1849 — both pairs of dates underlined the heroic quality of life prized by Serbs.

The Vojvodina Serbs had a very different existence under the Habsburgs from their southern brothers under the Ottomans, and up till now their history is more fully documented, especially in the 18th century.

The landscape is a document in itself, and I could not have read it without Father Veselin's help. As we drove along between Kač and Novi Sad, the grey waters of the Danube, never far away from us, seemed to dominate the land. He pointed out the *šajkaški* villages close to the river. In 1696–97, Prince Eugen of Savoy had organized the Serbs into gunboat (*šajke*) patrols along the Danube. They were armed with rifles and bayonets, flew red-and-white flags and in time acquired a uniform of silver-buttoned blue frieze with wide Hungarian trousers they were apt to trip over. Prince Eugen later ordered new boats for them from an English boatbuilder. They controlled a large area including Kovilj. All along the main road, Veselin named for me the old Serbian settlements. It was in this area that in 1701–2 the famous Military Frontier was created. Ordinary soldiers from the national minorities, Serb, Croat, Rumanian and Albanian, received a plot of land there in exchange for military service under Austria.* The Serbs were loyal troops, cheap to maintain and excellent guerrilla fighters (a talent they have not lost). They liked martial music and were provided with drums. Taube was to call them 'a living wall against the Turks', and I could trace the pattern of their life: big villages, the houses tightly grouped together for defence, with strips of cultivated land some way off. In the mid-18th century Maria Theresa had moved some Serbs away from the main road and replaced them with Hungarians and Germans, to avoid a possible uprising. Near Kovilj and Kač, in flat country, I could see the approach roads which still twist and turn, because the Serbs took this precaution to give them time to prepare to repel marauders. When we reached home I was sorry to leave Father Veselin – he had made me see the past so vividly.

Maria Theresa feared discontent because harsh discipline in the army and rural poverty had already led to several rebellions before her accession in 1740. As one song put it,

> Come along, lad, and join us soldiers,
> Put aside that plough and spade.
> Now, for the Emperor, on parade!
> A hundred forints' pay each year;
> Each month a hundred clouts on the ear!

Gradually, due to the Military Frontier, and the opportunities it gave them to become officers, later generations of Vojvodina Serbs were to turn from unsettled refugees into respected, well-educated citizens. 'Take my ancestors,' said one friend from the Frontier; 'from sergeant to general in three generations. And we stayed military. As for me, I was born into an Austro-Hungarian suitcase and ended up a General in Tito's army. . . .' I begged him to go on, but he said his sister was the family historian, and that was all he knew. I was rescued from frustration only when someone else told me I should read Simeon Piščević's autobiography, as it was about 18th-century Serbs on the Frontier. This proved excellent advice.

The son of a 'captain commander', Piščević was born in 1731 at Šid in the Fruška Gora. He had his schooling in German, part of it in Vienna, and most likely spoke German at home, as did many Army families among the Serbs well into our own century. Throughout Piščević's memoirs, it is clear he came from a military *élite*, with

* From the mid-18th to the mid-19th century, they were formed into regiments as the *Freikorps*.

connections everywhere in the Austrian army. He first went into action at the age of thirteen, when he accompanied his father to fight the French in the War of the Austrian Succession, and they crossed the Rhine in a night attack, answering the French challenge with a shout of 'Maria Theresa!' He saw for the first time the dead and the dying and his own father was wounded. As the boy wept, his father wrily comforted him: 'You see what the soldier's daily bread is, and how honour and glory are come by.'

By his own account, the young Piščević was tall, fair-complexioned, his hair long and thick and 'dark as coal' and he could dress up and pass for a girl if he wanted to. Fortune favoured him: an Archbishop gave him a horse, and when his father was wrongfully imprisoned, the Field-Marshal's wife, moved by Simeon's *beaux yeux* as she sat over her embroidery, successfully interceded for him. This done, the boy, still only fourteen, stayed with a noble Bavarian family, dancing and masquerading all winter long. On returning home as A.D.C. to a General, he married the Patriarch's niece.

His story is told with all the picaresque optimism of his age, but he is candid, too, about his difficulties. He disliked peacetime, when he had only half-pay and a gift of land, which, he says, he was too young to know how to cultivate. He returned to his regiment but it was soon disbanded, owing to the Hungarians' pressure on Maria Theresa to use their own troops. The Empress Elizabeth was encouraging Serbs to settle in Russia. Disillusioned, Piščević decided to join them. His General told him to 'get that bug out of your head', and he was sent to the infantry instead of the Hussars, though he arranged himself a transfer back again. Still determined to emigrate, he secretly visited the Russian Embassy in Vienna, only to be taken for an *agent provocateur* because of his perfect German. He persevered, and on his second visit made an eloquent speech to the Secretary there about Serb sheep looking for a Russian shepherd. On his third visit – for which he had been to the barber and put on his Hussar uniform – he saw the Ambassador, who promised to talk to the Austrian Chancellor on his behalf. As a result, Piščević received Maria Theresa's permission to go to Russia and 'I felt as if I were born again'.

With his wife, children and servants, he set off on the long, rough journey, crossing the Russian border south of Kiev.* He was to become

* Elizabeth settled the Serbs in two areas, *Nova Srbija* northeast of Odessa, and *Slaveno-Srbija*, east of Kiev, where the Serbian battalion had its HQ. Piščević was given land in *Nova Srbija*.

a General in the Russian army and lived out thirty years in the land of his adoption.

Piščević tells his readers what it felt like to be a Serbian officer in the Habsburg army. He was privileged, a young gentleman at ease in the world of hunting and libraries. Nationality meant both little and much to him: he could talk freely to his Albanian colonel or to a German princess, yet in the end he came up against the hard fact that he belonged to a subject nation. He experienced humiliation, as the victim of Hungarian military demands in Vojvodina; and real fear in Vienna, where it was dangerous for him, as a Serb, to attempt emigration to Russia.

I thought of Piščević when I went to Sremski Karlovci, for it was there that he met his future wife. The Serbian Patriarchs and Metropolitans had made this town their seat, and the Austrians had sent a delegate to their Church Councils (*Sabori*), which voiced the needs of Serbs on the Frontier. Sremski Karlovci lies close to the Fruška Gora monasteries and the Danube, and I found myself in a small cathedral town quite different from Peć. The main square was planted with large trees which shielded several churches and some imposing buildings, and a crocodile of boys and young men were coming out of one church. They were followed by a priest in immaculate black soutane and purple cummerbund; he turned out to be the Rector of the Seminary. The new Seminary – once the Metropolitan's Finance Ministry – hides the old Seminary, which in turn conceals the old Grammar School of 1791. At the top of the square the new Grammar School, a brightly tiled building, shines in the sun; I looked inside and it was full of children and their paintings were pinned to every wall.

The school was a long time coming. The more fortunate Serbs, like Piščević, were sent away to Vienna or Szeged. Others went to indifferent schools run by Serbian monks, or to Protestant establishments. They avoided Roman Catholic institutions, for fear of being proselytized. In the early 18th century a teacher, Maxim Suvorov, came from Russia, but he met with difficulties and 'wrote to his Metropolitan that, while he had once had his doubts about purgatory, he now believed in it and moreover knew exactly where it was'.[1] In the end, he left for Belgrade.

The grand new Patriarchate, again, overshadows the modest old one in its courtyard – where I was given red and white wine from giant barrels in the Episcopal cellar before getting any further. Upstairs, an apartment is kept ready for the Patriarch:* French white and gold furniture is set off by soft red or green walls. The Council Room is hung with portraits of former Patriarchs. This would have been the house where Piščević had danced with his future wife:

> The Patriarch, even in extreme old age, lived luxuriously. In his house everything was just so. He had a lot of servants; not only was the head servant a German but most of the others, too. As that day was his birthday, all the servants were in sumptuous livery. During lunch, music was played.
>
> After lunch we went into another room which was next to the bedroom. Dessert awaited us there, and coffee was served to us. . . . Yet more guests arrived. . . . From Petrovaradin the director of the Postal Service . . . with his wife, son and two daughters, and a couple of officers, Serbs . . . to congratulate the Patriarch on his birthday. So quite a large company assembled, and their mood was extremely cheerful.
>
> The Patriarch wanted us to dance and asked for the ball to begin. The colonel's son took first place in the dance and I followed immediately after him. I had already plucked up courage and invited my partner to dance. Thus happily occupied, we went on far into the night. The old patriarch was in very good spirits, he liked company so we danced and danced. That's how we passed the day. . . .

No wonder this Patriarch, Arsenius IV Šakabend, could afford to live in style, for he squeezed clergy and monasteries dry, and was never known to refuse a bribe. Perhaps one should not grudge him a comfortable old age, as in 1737, as Patriarch of Peć, he had led out a second large migration from Serbia and one of his followers kept a diary of their hardships. At Novi Pazar the Serbs' cavalry escort and the captain in charge of them had deserted,

> and there was a rumour that the Turks were fast approaching! Then needless terror drove us on to flee, whoever could run the better, each competing with each other, and often looking back lest the Moslems should cut us to pieces!

They hurried fearfully from monastery to monastery, and at Studenica got horses again and crossed the mountains to the river Morava, then on to the north.

Up the street at Sremski Karlovci are old houses. The house of Metropolitan Rajačić's family has a fine stone gateway with a coat-of-arms above. Another town house had balconies which overlooked shaggy box-hedges; it was the quarter where local dignitaries, civil and ecclesiastical, set themselves up in style.

* The Serbian Patriarchate, abolished in 1766, was restored in 1921 and moved to Belgrade in 1932.

The 18th-century Patriarchs and Metropolitans constantly reminded their people of their national identity. They dominated a military theocracy. Army families were closely knit into the Church hierarchy: the Patriarch's niece whom Piščević married was the daughter of the former 'Captain of Stari Vlach' turned Austrian colonel, and in 1849, the young Stratimirović who acted as *Vojvoda*, was a relation of the Patriarch Stefan.

The complement to Sremski Karlovci was its neighbour: the town of Petrovaradin (Peterwardein) on the Danube. The next day I walked from Novi Sad to visit Slobodan at his office there. Petrovaradin is one of the great fortresses of Europe. As I crossed the bridge to the south bank of the river, it rose up in the foreground, tier upon tier of mighty walls reinforcing a strong natural position with cliffs to the west. The Romans probably knew it as Cusum, the Byzantines as Petricon; the medieval Hungarians gave it to some Roman Catholic monks, the Serbs snatched it back from them soon after, only to be ousted by Suleiman the Magnificent in 1526. In the late 17th century the Turks abandoned it to the Austrians; it was rebuilt on Vauban's model and Prince Eugen led his troops to victory outside its walls. They gained a rich booty from the retreating Ottoman army: carpets and jewelled harness, splendid horses and camels. The Prince kept for himself the Grand Vizier's tent, a sumptuous arrangement of silken-hung rooms which required 500 men to pitch it.

Belgrade, placed further south, then took the place of Petrovaradin strategically, but the rebuilding went on. Below the fortress a small town grew up: administrative buildings, officers' quarters and a hospital. It was somewhere down here that one day I went to find Slobodan. Being early, I went up to the very top of the fortress. There, after climbing many steps and peering into dungeons and galleries so claustrophobic that I could not face walking through them – they go on for miles – I found a second town of elegant 18th-century terraces with a clock-tower. A wide *piazza* overlooked the Danube. Some officers' quarters have been turned into a restaurant, but the upstairs rooms have kept their original mouldings on walls and ceiling. Barracks have become artists' studios and a small museum. The ensemble has been carefully preserved and it is not difficult to imagine the Austrian garrison life that went on here, with the *piazza* used as a parade-ground or frequented by strolling officers in uniform. Petrovaradin has grimmer memories, too; in the 19th century chained prisoners emerged from their incarceration underground to act as water-carriers for the soldiers,* and from here the Hungarians mercilessly shelled Novi Sad.

I went into the small museum, full of plans and swords, and one of the staff there told me to look at the Franciscan church in the lower town, where an English officer had been buried. At the bottom of the hill, Slobodan and his colleagues were installed in the old engineer's house under the ramparts, shaded by a great horse-chestnut tree. Slobodan knew nothing of such a tomb, and the church was just along the street. The crypt was unlocked for us by a sandalled nun, who lit two candles and held them close to a red marble slab on the wall. The burning tallow smelt strong in the dank air as Slobodan read out slowly:

ILLUSTRISS. DOMINUS COMES
JOSEPH DE STUART
HIBERNUS GENERAL VIGILIARUM PRAEFECTUS
COELEBS ANNORUM 44
OBIIT 5.9. BRIS 1788.

He was probably a member of an Irish Jacobite family, who had fought as a soldier of fortune for the Habsburgs and died far away from home. We blew out the candles and went out into the street. 'Well,' said Slobodan, 'always something new, and on one's own doorstep.'

I was always intrigued by the rumour of possible connections with England – there were not all that many. A more substantial link than the Irish General Stuart was provided by Dositej Obradović. 'Try his impressions of London,' said Jelena Šaulić, who has studied his life; 'I don't think you'll be bored.' I was not and found that he promised far more. The Vojvodina Serbs, living in a Habsburg society, were exposed to the age of enlightenment, and Dositej became the first Westernizer in modern Serbian history.

Dositej was born about 1743, younger than Piščević. Like him, he wrote his memoirs. He came from the developing *zanatlija* (craftsmen and traders) who had settled in the 'royal free boroughs' which included Novi Sad and Dositej's birthplace, Temišvar (Timişoara, now in Rumania). Vojvodina exported honey and wax to Venice, skins and grain and caviar all over Austria, Germany and Italy. Temišvar was full of painted signboards to attract illiterate peasants coming into town – an inn-cum-shop showed 'The Flight into Egypt' while

* One of the last political prisoners in Petrovaradin was the youthful Tito, accused of preaching pacifism to his fellow-soldiers in the Austrian army in 1914.

apothecaries chose even holier names: 'The Saviour' or 'The Holy Trinity'. Dositej's father was a furrier and Dositej was apprenticed to a quiltmaker, though as a child the pattern of his life was already set. He wanted three things: to be a monk, after reading the Lives of the Serbian Saints, to travel (to Petrovaradin and Budapest) and to learn languages. He had been beaten by his Serbian schoolmaster because he played truant to join the Greek children at their school – he liked the sound of their speech.

Dositej's autobiography reads like an English novel of the period; he certainly knew Richardson and Defoe, both of whom he translated. The author ricochets from one adventure to another, always falling on his feet. At Hopovo monastery, surrounded by ignorant monks, he dreamt of the Russian Empress Elizabeth, 'clothed in the sun from head to foot, seated on her throne, she gave me with her own hand an open book written in many languages and said to me "Study!" '[2] So he ran away in search of learning, and found it first in Vienna. Then Zorić, a Serbian general in Russian service and yet another favourite of Catherine the Great, became his patron and took him to live on his estate in Russia.

A second patron was a rich merchant living in Trieste. Meanwhile, Dositej travelled. He got his Greek schooling in Smyrna, and on the way there listened to the Greek sailors on his ship: 'the words came pouring from their lips like grains of millet'. He also had part of his education in Halle and Leipzig. He knew Rumanian from his boyhood at Temišvar. Latin he had learnt in Zagreb, Albanian on a passing visit to that country. He picked up Italian and French in Vienna, and had a happy stay in England, though when he tried to learn English pronunciation, 'shivers ran down my back and the hair rose on my head'. Patrons abounded there, too; when he left, he found in his ship's cabin a packet of money and this letter:

> I do assure you, my dear Sir, it has been matter of some consideration with me, in what way (the least to hurt your delicacy) I should contribute my mite towards alleviating those pecuniary wants, which have deprived us of you and which you ought not to know. Do not scruple, I beg of you, to accept of the enclosed small sum, and be persuaded it is offered by a man who esteems and loves you. Farewell. Consider me as one of the friends you have made in England, who holds you dear in his remembrance and to whom nothing will be more welcome than accounts of your prosperity and happiness.
>
> London, 27 May 1785. Henry Turnbull.[3]

36 The graceful 17th-century church of New Hopovo

37 In the Fruška Gora: the sloping vineyards of Velika Remeta

38 Stana's brothers roasting lambs for the *slava*

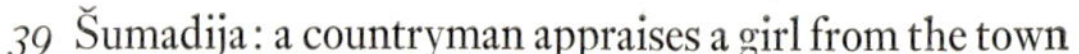

39 Šumadija: a countryman appraises a girl from the town

Dositej was cheerful, resilient, generous and serious. His first aim was didactic. His earliest translation was *Good Manners* (it was a version made by a Greek monk of a tract from Erasmus) and his earliest book is called *Counsels of Sound Reason*, written 'for the benefit of my nation . . . in pure Serbian . . . that all Serbian sons and daughters may understand it, from Montenegro to Smederevo and the Banat'.[4]

Dositej wanted his people to acquire decorum and literacy. He also wanted to introduce them to western civilization, especially its literature. His own translations included Bacon, Swift, Dr Johnson, Lord Chesterfield, Pope, Addison and Lessing. Politically he was a loyal subject of the Habsburgs, subscribed to the Serbian cult of Joseph II and wrote poems in his honour. He was a strong supporter of his own nation's independence; in 1804 he gave half his fortune to help Karageorge's rebellion, and later went to live in Serbia to tutor Karageorge's son and to be a member of his Council. He took over the High School in Belgrade.

Dositej was a townsman, and the new expansion in Vojvodina, from the mid-18th century onwards, was in the town of Novi Sad. Sremski Karlovci remained the seat of Church government, but Novi Sad, which had started as a tiny trading-post for Austrian troops, grew into a commercial and cultural centre. It benefited from Joseph II's dictum:

> I am prepared to employ anyone, let anyone practise agriculture or a trade, or establish himself in a city, who has the required qualifications and would bring advantage or industry into my states.[5]

Novi Sad had already become a 'royal free borough' in 1747, so that it had its own Law Court presided over by its own citizens and the right to send two Senators to the Hungarian Diet. By the early 19th century it had a Grammar School, where the celebrated Slavist, Šafarik, a Slovak, taught, wearing a green coat, white cashmere trousers and a stovepipe hat. He spent his spare time looking at the private libraries of Novi Sad:

> . . . the nest of the Serbian nation is here and many of the townsfolk possess a copy of every ancient book. I've made a catalogue of Serbian books, with a great effort, by going from house to house and turning everything upside-down.

In the bookshops you could buy, in English and German, the works of Richardson, Fielding, Rousseau and Cervantes.

For a long time, though, Novi Sad preserved an oriental air. Its traders included Greeks in caftans, bearded Jews and swarthy Armenians, as well as southern Serbs in Turkish dress. In the early 19th century its citizens more or less westernized their daily life: they bought horsehair mattresses for their beds, filled their cupboards with glass, and some households had clavichords, though if you went into the kitchens you would still find the old cooking-pots, suspended on chains over an open fire.

Foreign visitors were amazed at the showy dress of the women; it was easy, wrote the Austrian apothecary at Petrovaradin, to mistake a craftsman's wife for a general's. Novi Sad, with its bands and cafés and promenades, was the pride of the whole region. A popular poem of the period describes it:

> There's the city's royal palace, dear one,
> There on every side are towers of gold,
> From the water's edge, a straight moat to the town;
> The glorious town, it lies by hill and valley,
> The bridge divides the Danube, boats float down.
>
> O dear one, whatever can you yearn for
> That you'll not find to delight you here?
> Where you can walk dry-shod on real stone, dear one,
> By night chase, in friends' company, fine ladies,
> And with them dance, hear music, take the air?

Trade flourished. Serbian craftsmen worked as tailors, bootmakers, furriers, soapmakers and capmakers. The richer merchants moved out as they bought property and acquired patents of nobility. Slobodan took me to see one of their country houses when he inspected it for repairs.

It was at Čib, renamed Čelarevo after a Partisan hero. At the gateway one stone lion sat firmly on its pillar; the other had gone for good. We picked up the woman caretaker from the lodge, and saw a tangled garden, and a country house, a classical pavilion with pediment and pillars and bronze dogs either side of the main doorway. It was built in 1830, and inside, we stepped back a century or more. The house had kept its heavy draped curtains and its wallpapers, including some oriental scenes on panels, and a shining white ornamented porcelain stove, and good parquet floors. The furniture had been mostly made in Vojvodina from the 18th century onwards and a fine secretaire had come from Maria Tereziopolje (now Subotica) in 1827, with scenes of the town inlaid in coloured woods on the drawers, and a secret hiding-place in its dome. The square piano was German and the grand piano Viennese; the cups were Meissen. In the bookcases were copies of Chekhov in French, *Vanity Fair* in English and Baedeker's *Switzerland* in German. The caretaker said: 'This was Master Ivan's room . . . Miss Catherine liked this view . . . the tutor has retired to Novi Sad.' Through the window the uncut lawn was thick with daisies and in the park grew magnificent trees, sweet chestnut and walnut, oak and grey Serbian spruce, feathery *gleditschia* and a tulip tree. In the distance, men were scything hay. The whole place was reminiscent of a Russian play: the set was there, the family memories, the air of melancholy. In fact, its associations were Hungarian; it was one of many small manor houses built all over Hungary by the minor nobility. Then a Serbian family named Dundjerski had lived there some eighty years. One lady of the house had been a beauty who kept a salon for the Novi Sad intelligentsia, and the poet Laza Kostić had written for her *Santa Maria della Salute*, which is in every anthology:

With us, all's as with wife and husband,
Only no worries and work distract us,
All's turned to gentleness, no burning torments,
Our passion's calmed by heavenly coolness . . .

The family left; Tito used the house for a while as his hunting-lodge. Now it is a museum. Slobodan said there were other country houses in Vojvodina and he specially wanted me to see Kulpin, which had belonged to the Stratimirović family.*

We abandoned the house at Čib to its 19th-century dream, and went back to the town.

The golden age of Novi Sad ended in 1848, the 'year of revolutions' in Europe. Under a weak Emperor, Ferdinand, the Habsburg Empire lost all semblance of unity. There was violent unrest in Vienna, and in Hungary, Kossuth became President Regent of an independent State, with its Parliament in Budapest. The Croatian Diet was abolished. The Serbs, in a series of Councils, petitioned for their national rights under the Habsburgs and under the Hungarian Crown. Kossuth refused them any organization on a national basis, and said: 'The sword shall decide between us.' In Vojvodina, excitement rose high. In May, at Sremski Karlovci, a Patriarch and a *Vojvoda* were elected: church bells rang, hats flew upward; there was weeping and shouting

* He also mentioned houses at Melenci, Novo Kneževac, Temerin, Beodra (at Novi Miloševa), Aleksa Santić, Futog, Bajša and Horgos.

and kissing and singing, and pistols were fired in the air for joy. Several risings, in collusion with the Croats, brought the province into a state of civil war with Hungary. In 1849, the garrison at Petrovaradin, officially under Austrian command, went over to Kossuth and the rebel Hungarian government. When Croat troops took refuge in Novi Sad, it was bombarded from across the river, and the cannon of Petrovaradin reduced the town to a burning ruin. Two-thirds of its buildings were destroyed, and thousands of citizens died or fled. In 1850, a German traveller, looking at the roofless houses, tumbledown walls and blackened rafters, lamented 'the magnitude of the disaster which has befallen the most advanced and well-to-do town in Bačka'.

Under Franz Joseph, ten years of Austrian absolutism followed, but in 1861 the Vojvodina Serbs accepted reunification with Inner Hungary: they had their own territory and *Vojvoda* and seats in the Hungarian Diet. Novi Sad was rebuilt but it was twenty years before the Grammar School was in full working order, and only one factory, the silk weavers', came back. For a while, the town was a cultural and political focus for Serbs. In 1864 the famous institute of *Matica Srpska* moved downriver from Budapest to Novi Sad; Svetozar Miletić, a leading Serbian reformer, became Mayor. In the 1870s the importance of Novi Sad diminished as Belgrade gained in influence. Today the visitor to Novi Sad is aware that it is a long-established city: it has kept a style of its own, as I had noticed at the concert on my first evening there. I visited often, and always by formal invitation, one family: an elderly architect, George Tabaković, who has since died, his wife and married daughter, and I remember with pleasure the times I spent there. My host spoke an old-fashioned and perfect English, and Viennese black coffee with whipped cream was served. Both the formality and the coffee were different from Belgrade. Tabaković had been Dinko's and Slobodan's Professor; they cherished him, and like me, thought him an ornament to their native town.

Dinko Davidov had promised, when I got back from Sremski Karlovci, to take me round. Between the skyscrapers and the palatial new post office, we found the old Novi Sad. It charms not so much by individual buildings as by rows of house-fronts which make a pleasing group, and by the onion-domed churches seen suddenly round corners. We walked down Dunavska Ulica (Danube Street), a narrow winding road where each house opens onto a big balconied courtyard. Here stood the inn called 'The English King'; traders had and have their shops all the way along. Then we passed the Cathedral Church where in

1848 a crowd of Serbian peasants from the Almaška quarter had gathered to shout their anti-Hungarian slogan: 'I won't have my son called Jonas when he was christened Jovan.' We went on to the Almaška quarter itself, where the Serbs first settled in Novi Sad, and as we turned a street corner, there was a fine neo-classical church which I would not have been surprised to find in the City of London.

An unknown architect, German or Austrian, built the Almaška Church between 1780 and 1790, and it is beautifully proportioned though now sadly dilapidated. We found the priest and his key, and went in through a grand doorway decorated with stone garlands and urns, flanked by pilasters with elegant Ionic capitals. Inside, the church was painted blue and white and gold and nobly vaulted. Every detail had been lovingly carried out: the iconostasis of gilded wood, the western pulpit high on the north wall, with a secret staircase leading to it, the chandeliers, the cupboards for treasure in the sanctuary, even the ironwork at the west end, with Austrian eagles by the lock. While I exclaimed with delight, Dinko displayed a more business-like enthusiasm.

'It's time we restored this,' he said to the priest, 'I'll come down here on a feast-day and bring someone from the institute, and we'll speak to the congregation and try to raise some funds.'

'We're not rich,' said the priest, looking at a hole in the roof.

'Never mind, we'll do what we can.'

Outside, on the wall of the church, were the tombstones of two Greek merchants who had lived at *Νεο Φυτομ* (Novi Sad means 'New Plantation') and died at the end of the 18th century. They would have been at home in this church where the Gospel had been read in Greek and Slavonic, by priests trained at Kiev in the Byzantine tradition.

We went back to the priest's house, which was countrified, one storey high, with a big vegetable garden behind, and I felt more as if I were in a village than a town. This is a kind of village, the priest told us, where people leave their houses by horse and cart on Sundays and go out of town a few miles to work their land. It was difficult to get many to come to church on Sundays, he went on, but he could understand, the farming wouldn't wait. He was a modest, devoted man who liked his work and I doubt if a 'good fat parish' would have meant more to him than this one. We said good-bye and opposite the church Dinko pointed to a house, end-on to the street, with a 'gossiping window': 'That's where I lived as a schoolboy.'

It was not far to *Matica Srpska*, where the librarian unlocked a cupboard full of treasures. Dinko showed me the first play written in Serbian, done at the Russian school were Maxim Suvorov had taught, and the first book printed in Serbian, the precious *Oktoikh* (prayer book) from the Cetinje Press in Montenegro (1493–94); some 13th- and 14th-century manuscripts and five versions of Dušan's *Code* (the oldest is in Russia), including one 18th-century copy which had been copied in a beautiful Cyrillic script, and finely illuminated.

It was moving to see what came out of the cupboard, for in a way it was the history of a whole people and their culture. I thought of the Turks sacking monasteries, of the Studenica monk in his cave burning manuscripts rather than let the infidel have them, of the other manuscripts and books in the Belgrade National Library, totally destroyed by bombing in the Second World War. It was a small cupboard, and its contents were slight compared with the great libraries of the West, but in a land where so many records of the past have gone up in flames, it held a priceless inheritance.

These impressions of the Serbs in Vojvodina only brush the surface of its life and history. The Slovaks, Hungarians, Czechs and Rumanians all have their own richness of tradition, and the Rumanians are linked closely with their neighbours across the Danube in Eastern Serbia. There are Albanians and gipsies, Ruthenes, Ukrainians and two mysterious groups of Slavs called Šokci and Bunjevci up near Sombor. Some pieces of this mosaic of races are lost in the past: the Spaniards died of cold at 'New Barcelona' 200 years ago, some Frenchmen from Alsace-Lorraine survive only in a surname or two, the Germans left in this century. Once Novi Sad had churches for seventeen different denominations. The region must contain more nationalities than any other comparable area in Europe, living in peace and prosperity in a fertile land.

18

ŠUMADIJA: THE WOODED LAND

Settlers and farmers – Karageorge at Topola – the First Uprising in 1804 – portrait of Karageorge – his memorial at Pokajnica – Miloš Obrenović and the Second Uprising – Takovo – Mother Anna at Vračevšnica

Unlike Vojvodina, which you must seek out across the plain, Šumadija ('the wooded land') edges its way into Belgrade itself, and it soon became a familiar place for us. From the southern suburbs of the capital we looked out on forested hills; and if we walked only a little way, we found ourselves in parks and woods which quickly turned to open countryside where maize and pumpkins had been planted, with tower blocks rising in the distance. The trees were small to English eyes: spindly acacias and puny oaks, their brown paper leaves rustling in winter; bird cherry and wild plum. In cold weather, hares started up in the fields; in the spring, the salamander, like a black and yellow dragon, confronted us on its bed of damp leaves. Belgrade is an outpost, Šumadija the heartland of Serbia. We often walked there at weekends, and were surprised to find villages in which you could easily spot a feast being celebrated, by the wreaths and flags hung on gateways, and the young men, brandy flask in hand, hurrying down the street to summon the guests. Village people were generous towards us; we gave a woman a lift and she asked us to her *slava*. When we could not go, she came instead to our house on market day, kissed us both and made us a present of some homemade cheese. Everyone was Serbian, apart from a few gipsies, and these are easily recognizable if you see, as we did, two girls squatting by the roadside, one with her hand held out while the other read her palm.

In the late Middle Ages Šumadija was thoroughly settled by people driven north after the battle of Kossovo. In 1555 Busbecq, the Imperial Ambassador to the Porte, travelled through this region and saw, as I had done so much later, the elaborate funeral rites and laments practised by the Serbs; and in 1620 an English merchant, Peter Mundy, watched a *kolo*:

> Then would they gather together younge Weomen and Children, and holding hand in hand in a round, they would daunce and sing very merrily, although with no great melodie.[1]

As the Turks tightened their hold on Serbia, the inhabitants moved off gradually to Hungary or Bosnia, and the Great Migration of the 1690s left Šumadija almost deserted. Lady Mary Wortley Montagu described it in 1717:

> We cross'd the Desarts of Servia allmost quite overgrown with Wood, tho a country naturally fertile and the Inhabitants industrious, but the Oppression of the peasants is so great they are forc'd to abandonn their Houses and neglect their Tillage, all they have being a prey to the Janizarys whenever they please to seize upon it. We had a guard of 500 of 'em, and I was allmost in tears every day to see their insolencies in the poor villages through which we pass'd.[2]

Šumadija was resettled only at the very end of the 18th century, during the lull that followed the Peace of Sistova in 1791, when some of the less prosperous Vojvodina Serbs moved back and made farmsteads in forest clearings. Many Montenegrins joined them. All lived in *zadruge*; usually the family group did not exceed thirty people. The pattern of their settlement is there to be seen: while the larger villages have muddy streets and houses near the *kafana*, most of the farms are scattered independently over the hills. At first glance, Šumadija made us think of the English countryside. At second glance, it is fresher, sweeter, wilder, and suggests the dangerous place it once was. It has been settled, but not tamed. Unlike Southern England, it has not been worked over and perfected, just carved out of woodland, and has stayed close to its natural state; it looks as if it might easily slip back again, as it did once before, into wilderness. Fields melt untidily into woods, willows are dotted about meadows; very little is enclosed. Only in 1930 with the registration of property, was Šumadija divided up into private ownership. Up till then, every *zadruga* had taken what it needed, and the rest remained pasture and common wood. We found Šumadija what it has always been, a land of smallholders. Vojvodina developed a middle class from its military *élite*, *zanatlija* and Church hierarchy. Šumadija, with a different history, remained a place where all men were equal. Their traditional democracy is strong. This region was the centre of the First and Second Uprisings against the Turks in 1804 and 1815, of Radical demonstrations against the Turks in 1876, and of the formation of guerrilla bands in the Second World War. They endured 'submission with set teeth', in Stojan Pribićević's phrase, and when the moment for rebellion was ripe, they rose in force.

One spring, I decided to travel through this countryside looking for memorials of the two Uprisings that had brought the Serbs their freedom, trying to find out what I could about their leaders, and seeing how people lived then and the way they live now.

The village of the first leader, Karageorge, seemed the place to begin. He was born in 1768 near Topola, and most of his working and fighting life was based on Topola, where his fortified house and church survive. Richard and I drove, as we had often done before, south into the hills of Šumadija. To the east rose Avala, an extinct volcano topped by a Post Office tower and Meštrović's temple to the unknown soldier; wolves stroll across its sheltered roads in a hard winter. Further south, to the west, came Kosmaj, higher and more massive than Avala's thin peak, an excursion spot for people from Belgrade who need cool air in summer and sledging and skiing for their children in the snow. Time has telescoped distances; in the early 19th century it took a whole day to get half-way from Belgrade to Kosmaj, and even then you had to cut your way through the forest.

Topola lies under Oplenac, the church-crowned hill above the village. Most visitors drive straight up to the top and spend their time there, in the grand mausoleum, covered with mosaics inside, built by Karageorge's descendant, King Peter I, in 1910–12. It is a straightforward attempt to prove the Karageorges as good as the Nemanjids: a mausoleum church to which Karageorge's own bones were moved and placed in a tomb directly under mosaics of the medieval kings. The founder's portrait is on the south wall, near the entrance – King Peter I, moustachioed, crowned, caped in ermine and velvet over a military uniform, is led by St George to the Mother of God and presents her with his church of Oplenac. The other mosaics are based on frescoes from the Nemanjid churches. The craftsmanship is splendid; the effect totally dull and dead. Below, in the crypt, many 19th-century royal babies are buried and if they survived, it was to die in their twenties. One was called Cleopatra. Forty tombs were built and more than half stand empty. Oplenac is a sad monument to *folie de grandeur*.

The further downhill we went, the better things became. The royal villas at Oplenac are the prettiest country houses in Serbia. In May we could smell wistaria, iris, hawthorn all over the slopes. There are vineyards in the distance. We found a small hotel with an aura of

Edwardian comfort: cretonne curtains, a grand piano in the reading-room, a private dining-room and mahogany panels in the hall; we would have liked to stay there. Finally, at the bottom of the hill, we saw Karageorge's own house. The church at Oplenac had been a false start; now we had reached Karageorge's headquarters during the First Uprising. In 1803 he built himself a wooden house on this site and gave it gun-emplacements as he was already a marked man to the ruling janissaries. What we were looking at was the more elaborate fortress he constructed as his home in 1811–13, with four corner-towers. Its eastern wall was made up of Karageorge's own *konak* with seven rooms and a dining-hall, linked by a vaulted corridor to a small church, with an entrance through the northeastern tower. The church is shut into another walled enclosure. The vaulted corridor is now a piece of ruined wall; here Karageorge had a secret door which gave on to the forest beyond and made a quick get-away easy. The *konak*, a plain-arcaded house, has been made into a modest museum. This place was unique in Serbia in its time, the richest house, the most solid stronghold. Today it remains very evocative of its owner and when we went into the church, the parish priest came along and talked about Karageorge. We were looking at his first tombstone,* erected by Miloš Obrenović's wife, Princess Ljubica, with a gay, naïve copy of Karageorge's portrait painted on the wall beside it, and an inscription saying that Karageorge had had his head cut off by the Turkish government.

'Not true at all,' said the priest, 'of course it was Miloš' men, but she *had* to say that.' He might have been speaking of a friend's quarrel. 'You see, when Karageorge came back over the Danube, he was recognized by the ferryman and then he went to stay with his *kum* thinking he'd be all right there; but he was wrong, his *kum* was a traitor and sent messages to Miloš, and so Karageorge met his death.'

Richard walked over to the wooden iconostasis: 'It reminds me of the two brothers from Debar,' he said.

'It *was* the two brothers from Debar' – the priest sounded confident – 'and there they are.' We peered among the lumpy flowers and tiny Biblical scenes and birds and ears of wheat and saw the brothers had carved themselves sitting at a table in the corner. Their work – or that of other craftsmen from Debar – is scattered all over Macedonia, and here they were again, further north than usual; travelling journeymen in the Balkans, like Žefarović at Bodjani, went far and wide.

* In the narthex, at the end of the south wall on the right-hand side.

Karageorge's neighbour, Petar Jokić, lies buried beside the church. He served as a commander in the First Uprising, and as an old man dictated his memories of how the rebellion began. He was illiterate, as was Karageorge himself, and his successor Miloš. Like many Serbs, Jokić was an excellent story-teller. Other writers have catalogued atrocities; he recreates the insecurity and the petty humiliations of Serbian life under the Turks. A certain Turk, Ibrahim, was the innkeeper (*handžija*) at Topola. In 1801 the janissaries had murdered the Turkish Pasha in Belgrade, Mustapha, because he was a moderate man, nicknamed 'the Mother of the Serbs'. The four chief janissaries assumed power, and the Sultan threatened to send an army of Serbian peasants against them; whereupon the janissaries quickly butchered ten Serbian officials and several famous priests. In their further attempts to deprive the Serbs of their natural leaders, the janissaries dispatched men to kill Karageorge at his home. It was the innkeeper Ibrahim who helped Karageorge's mother to conceal his whereabouts and so saved his life. The same Ibrahim, when he was supervising forced labour for the janissaries, taunted a Serb at the plough. 'Not like that, bear! Do it properly, bear! That's no good, bear!' They came to blows, and Ibrahim took out his pistol. The other men refused to go on working: 'You called him a bear, and he's no bear but a man, our brother, and it's hard on him.' Jokić was loyal to Karageorge, but he intervened to stop peasants burning down the *han* and killing Ibrahim. In the villages Turks and Serbs had to live with each other as best they could, though by then it was autumn 1803 and the janissaries' actions had driven the Serbs near breaking-point.

A few days after Karageorge's own escape, Jokić accompanied him to a wedding-feast at Orašac where an uprising was formally planned. They took part in the eating and drinking, and then slipped away with other leading Serbs to listen to a local priest urging them to rebel against the janissaries, but to wait until the following March, when they could hide their women and children in the woods. He held up a cross and they kissed it and cried 'Amen'. Then he pronounced a curse on all traitors:

> He who betrays us, let his body betray him; should he wish to walk, let him be powerless; let neither old nor young be seen in his house! May everything his hand touches turn to stone; may no sheep bleat in his sheepfold, and no cows low in his pasture. May God grant that he's turned into hard rock, so that no other men may look on him. Let him not be happy nor long-lived, nor ever see God's countenance.

Again they cried 'Amen'. Karageorge went over to Austria to fetch gunpowder, an activity that was to be celebrated in heroic verse, where the janissary Mehmed Aga rages:

> Till I put to death proud Kara-Djordje
> From the haughty village of Topola,
> Who does business with Vienna's emperor,
> Who can buy great stores of shot and powder,
> Purchase them at Varadin the white-walled,
> And buy all the arms that may be needful,
> Who can easily make war upon us,
> He is emperor, I am but subasha . . .[3]

To escape the Turks, Karageorge had to keep constantly on the move. One hideout was in his sheepfold at Krćevac, just north of Topola. On his return from Austria, his wife asked Jokić to go with her to the sheepfold. She slung a sackful of bread over her shoulder and carried a flask of *rakija* in her hand; Jokić took his rifle. The story is the universal story of armed resistance anywhere: the wife secretly carrying provisions to her husband, his companions' suspicions of her escort. They held Jokić at gun-point: 'Get back! Who are you? Get back!' until Karageorge vouched for him. In January 1804, the janissaries increased their attack on Serbian leaders. Among their victims were two leaders in Western Serbia, with whom the Šumadijans kept in close touch. These were Ilija Birčanin and Aleksa Nenadović, whose son, Mateja, an admirable character, was to become a priest, military commander, diplomatic envoy and chronicler of the Uprisings. It was Mehmed Pasha (the janissary of the poem) who treacherously killed them. The Šumadijans held a second meeting at Orašac, this time in a small ravine, well-suited, like so much of their countryside, to the secrecy of guerrilla warfare. Vuk Karadžić reported: 'The local commanders had already said to each other: "Who will be our head? Not a single house can exist without a head, still less so many people. We must know whom we consult and whom we serve!" ' According to Jokić, who was there, the crowd wanted Karageorge to lead them, but he answered: 'I'll go everywhere with you, but I'll not go at your head.' Then they cried out: 'Thou at our head, and we are with thee – through fire, through fire; through water, through water! Only be thou our leader!' Uncertain of himself, his temper, his comrades, Karageorge swore he would put any traitor to the most fearful torture. The gathering, by a show of hands, agreed. He yielded, and was acclaimed as leader.

The rebellion had begun in February, a month earlier than planned, at Sibnica, on the slopes of Kosmaj. The Serbs set fire to the *han* and stole arms from it. What happened at Sibnica was repeated in other villages: *handžije* were killed and in a few days the whole of Šumadija was in open revolt which spread throughout Serbia. Mateja Nenadović describes how, as a member of his uncle Jakov's forces from Western Serbia, he joined up with Karageorge's troops near Belgrade:

> The soldiers sang and were very joyful; but as soon as Gospodar George came to the parade of the whole army and greeted them with: . . . 'Welcome, my brothers, Serbian falcons!' then, believe me, children, there was no soldier there who did not burst into song and many of the older men shed tears of joy at being so greeted. And throughout all Doboko one might have said that not only did the soldiers sing but that every tree and every leaf on every tree acquired a human voice and sang; and so singing, we went to our quarters for the night. . . .
>
> [The next day, they marched forward:]
>
> . . . we heard rifle-fire and a young man ran up to Black George and shouted: 'The Turks are attacking in force and our men are fighting, but they are greatly afraid.' Gospodar George shouted: 'Bring up the cavalry and let the infantry come as quickly as they can!' and put spurs to his horse and went. The whole army was running and I too ran; but Mata, the German, our gunner, shouted: 'For God's sake, Prota, the cannon remains alone. Whatever shall I do with the cannon?' . . . I did not dare to drag the gun onto the bridge after the army for I did not know the lie of the land, but turned into a large field and into the trees. I rushed ahead on horseback, but saw from the hill that we were about to fall right into the midst of the Turks. . . . We pulled the gun to the side and the Turkish cavalrymen were densely packed into the whole field below the pasha's house, and everywhere on the field was cut wheat. . . . We loaded the gun, I helping the gunner. But what could we do then? The gun was sighted directly at our army; here was a misfortune! . . . But misfortune quickens the mind! We ran hither and thither and found two fairly large stones and put them under the wheels; the gun-barrel rose until it pointed full at the Turkish cavalry. The gunner fired and by great good fortune hit his mark, though it was easy enough to do so for the Turkish horsemen were as thick as trees in a forest. As the shot roared out, the soldiers turned back, shouting from below: 'That is our gun! That is our gun!' and once more began to advance and the Turkish cavalrymen scattered. Meanwhile we had again charged the gun and the balls fell right among the foot-soldiers who had surrounded the house, who all fled behind the hill and our men after them (on the hillside the wheat was already cut into stooks). . . . Thenceforward Pljakić called me his blood-brother. That was on the summer feast of St Nikola, 1804.'[4]

The Serbs won victory after victory against the janissaries. At first they considered themselves loyal servants of the Sultan, and hoped he would restore centralized Turkish rule. When in 1805 they learnt he had abandoned them, they set out to free the whole of Serbia from Ottoman power, and a year later fought their way into Belgrade. Their heroic campaigns were marred by ruthless personal intrigue – such as the killing of Hajduk Ćurčija witnessed by Vuk Karadžić – and by national revenge: Suleiman Pasha and 200 followers were ambushed and massacred after leaving Belgrade.

Karageorge had, for the time being, freed his people from the Turks. When we were visiting his house, we wondered what he had been like. He became a folk-hero, so it is hard to disentangle truth from legend. He started as commander of Šumadija and became 'Supreme Leader' of the rebellion. In appearance, he seems to have been tall, powerfully-built but scrawny. His round face was dark-complexioned, his forehead high, his eyes small and fiery. His long nose made him recognizable from a distance. His contemporaries remembered his light womanish voice, which became strident in anger; his way of saying 'One way or another' ('*kojekude*') and of swearing 'Choke him!' ('*po duši ga*!'); his habit of gnawing his fingernails as he sat thinking. In war he fought mainly on foot, carrying a pistol and an Albanian carbine, though he loved his bay mare. He was not a noble savage, as has sometimes been suggested. Two portraits of him hang in the Topčider Museum at Belgrade, the pigtailed brigand – he later ordered his men to cut off their pigtails so that the Turks could not grab them – and the broad-chested uniformed leader. They reflect the contradiction in his character. He was a cool, resolute commander who inspired the utmost devotion in his followers, but he had a terrible temper. He stormed at the faithful Mateja Nenadović, calling him traitor, until the priest went away and wept bitterly under a plum-tree; and on one occasion Karageorge tried unsuccessfully to shoot his scribe, Steva, in anger. He could also show a ruthless justice in cold blood, as when he had his own brother hanged for rape, to maintain discipline. To a foreign observer such as the Russian Marshal Diebitsch in 1810, Karageorge was a great man, rough-hewn, who could adapt himself to changing circumstances.

From 1805 to 1813, Serbia was partly at peace, partly at war. In peacetime, Karageorge wore peasant clothes, worked in the fields with his men at Topola, liked to drink and dance and had a weakness for pretty women. He tried to establish law and order. In 1804 the Russians had recommended the Serbs to form a governing Council for negotiation with other countries; they did so, but Karageorge at times resented its powers which covered internal affairs as well, and kept as much personal control as he could. He improved education by starting schools during his period of leadership.

In 1813, when the Turks reinvaded Serbia, Karageorge rallied his forces but they were hopelessly outnumbered. Negotin fell first, under the heroic Hajduk Veljko, who fought to the last. The Austrians allowed Serbian refugees to cross into their territory, but Karageorge seems to have envisaged a second Great Migration and started negotiations which would allow 'the Serbian people' to settle in Russia. For this he failed to obtain an Austrian safe-conduct or a Turkish armistice, and eventually crossed into Vojvodina with the Russian representative and the Belgrade Metropolitan. Mateja Nenadović saw him at the monastery of Fenek and tried to persuade him to go straight to the Emperor Alexander I at Brussels. Karageorge, weeping, bewailed his lack of a safe-conduct. Temporarily, he had suffered an emotional collapse. It did not last. He found refuge in Bessarabia and recruited volunteers for service in Serbia.

His place was taken by Miloš Obrenović, one of his former commanders, who in 1815 successfully led the Second Uprising, and later that year, made peace with the Sultan. In 1817, eager to start a third rebellion, Karageorge crossed the Danube into Eastern Serbia, made his way over the mountains, and as the Topola priest had told us, went to stay with his *kum*, Vuica Vuličević. His *kum* broke the sacred laws of kinship and betrayed him to Miloš, who wanted the country kept quiet in order to exert maximum pressure on the Turks. The unsuspecting Karageorge was killed by an underling, with Turkish connivance. His head was taken to Miloš, whose wife, Miloš' French physician Cunibert wrote, wept over it. Then the skin was stuffed with straw and sent to the Sultan, who had it displayed on the walls of Istanbul, with the inscription 'Head of Karageorge, the Serbian rebel'.

Treachery and barbarism were followed by two pious observances. Karageorge's body and skull were first buried, as we had been told, in his own small church at Topola. The *kum* who broke faith, and the ruler who killed his rival, together built a wooden church, known as Pokajnica (the Penitent), within walking distance of the shepherd's hut where Karageorge died.

To reach Pokajnica I turned off the Belgrade–Niš motorway for Velika Plana, and went south to Staro Selo. The church lies on a rise of land which looks over fields and hills, and morello cherry trees with shining red fruit grow close to it. It seems an idyllic monument to commemorate dark doings. From the west end, the church looks circular, an optical illusion, as it is a long building curved at both ends. Its wooden tiles have weathered grey; they lie in steep rows like the roof of a Bosnian mountain cottage. The open west porch makes a useful shelter. Inside the church, under the women's gallery, are painted dragon fish, yellow on red, with cheerful eye and fearful jaws busy gulping down smaller fish. The iconostasis is topped by more dragons at work, this time carved in wood and gilded: they hold icons of the saints propped between their teeth. Pokajnica is all of a piece. It has village icons – St Nicholas of Bari is a present from 'Sophia the Shoemaker' – and a countrified Pantocrator in a cap, painted on a wooden disc hung from the roof; wreaths of dried flowers lie around. Churches in Serbia can be grand or homely.

Outside, I noticed the belfry. When Pokajnica was built, in 1818, it was a silent church; the belfry came later, in 1830, when the Turks let the Serbs ring their church-bells again.

Miloš Obrenović (Karageorge's successor) had come to power almost by chance. Born in 1780, he worked for his elder brother Milan, a merchant and one of Karageorge's leading commanders. When Milan went as Serbian envoy to Bucharest in 1810, Miloš, already a seasoned soldier in the First Uprising, took his place temporarily. Milan died, and Miloš retained his brother's command over three districts. This sturdy man, with his deep voice and quick decisive speech, was a complete contrast to Karageorge. He was primarily a negotiator who considered that the end justified the means. He would manipulate money and men as he pleased and break his oath to gain what he wanted. He fought the Turks with their own weapons, patience and cruelty, whereas Karageorge fought them as a Serb with all the force of his warlike tradition.

Miloš showed his qualities in 1813, when the Turks invaded. Vuk Karadžić records him as saying:

> 'What, me run away to Austria to save my skin and let the Turks enslave and sell my own mother and wife and children for the sake of keeping me alive! God preserve us! I'd rather go to my own district, and where some people remain, there I'll be too; enough people have been killed alongside me; there'll be no injustice done if I die and fall with the people.'

40 Novi Sad: the porch of the Almaška Church

42 Serbian soldiers in the First World War take cover behind a haystack

41 The Stanišić family of Belgrade: mother and daughter wear mid-19th century city costume

He went home, sent his wife and children to a monastery, and held the town of Užice for the winter. An amnesty had already been declared, so he went out to meet the Turks, who saw in him their agent; Suleiman Pasha appointed him *oberknez*. In return, Miloš hoped to gain good conditions for his people because of the Ottoman desire for peace in Serbia. He had reckoned without Suleiman Pasha's hatred of the Serbs, soon displayed in a wave of atrocities. By spring 1815 Miloš, who had advocated restraint, realized that the only hope lay in a new rebellion, and gathered the Serbian leaders at Takovo, near his own village.

Takovo is only thirty kilometres southwest of Orašac where Karageorge had raised the First Uprising, and I found it an easy journey from Pokajnica. The scale of Šumadija is small, but the lie of the land has always counted against the enemy. The Turks could not stamp out rebellion in this countryside of forests and miniature mountains, where rebels met easily at weddings and church feasts, and even the priests were warriors. On the way to Takovo, I left some luggage at Vračevšnica monastery where I was to stay the night. Vračevšnica lies up a wooded valley; to me, it looked like the end of the road, but the nuns told me it was the beginning of paths which led from village to village. No wonder that guerrillas have often lain up in it: Karageorge received the Russian envoy here, Miloš held a Council, Tito's partisans made it their lodging. Three nuns decided to come to Takovo; it was no distance, but like me, they had never seen it. In 1815, the Abbot of Vračevšnica had accompanied Miloš to Takovo by the same route, for Miloš and his men had been hiding above Vračevšnica in a village, Gornja Crnuča, where they planted plum-trees by day and went round the neighbourhood plotting rebellion by night.

Takovo cannot have changed much since Miloš was there on Palm Sunday, 1815, the same time of year as I saw it. The graveyard church stands in a flowery meadow below the hills. It is a tiny church, even simpler than Pokajnica, and very well-built. The nuns and I fingered the dovetailed joints admiringly. On that Sunday morning in 1815, people crowded into it for the service and streamed out into the field below. The ceremonies of Orašac were repeated. Miloš called them to rise, in God's name, against their oppressors. Peasants swore loyalty to him under the famous Takovo oak (*Takovski grm*) and kissed the Abbot's cross. Back at Gornja Crnuča, Miloš paraded at his front door in commander's uniform, and handed his personal banner to a neighbour, saying: 'Here I am; there you are; war to the Turks!' The Second

Uprising was a war of attrition. Miloš beat the Turks and spent the next fifteen years outwitting them.

I photographed the church at Takovo and the nuns ran helter-skelter down the field. Serbian nuns are often made angry, or as at Takovo timid, by the sight of a camera. We drove back to Vračevšnica on good terms again.

As we drew up in the monastery courtyard the Abbess, Mother Anna, came towards us, stooped over her stick: 'God and St George have sent you,' she said. Some nuns needed to go to Belgrade for their varicose veins the next day, and England's patron saint had directed me to his monastery, complete with car. In the evening sun, Vračevšnica seemed even more enchanting than during the day. It has a stone 15th-century church looped round with blind arcading and garlanded in vines. It was founded in 1431 by one of Stefan Lazarević's nobles, Radić Postupović; legend says as a thank-offering for his safe return from Kossovo. In the 18th century, it was restored by the Patriarch Arsenius IV, before he escaped to live so well in Vojvodina.* On either side of the church are white houses with wooden balconies. The more elaborate one, with a central bay, was originally put up by Miloš, and in front of it is a monument to his mother. Vračevšnica is peaceful after a turbulent history, and when I was there it had a presiding genius in Mother Anna who was then well over seventy. She ordered me to sit down beside her on a garden bench, and told me how she had been born into an educated Belgrade family. The Balkan Wars stopped her going to school in Switzerland and she went instead to Rumania, where she met some nuns and decided on the religious life. She studied theology at Belgrade and then became a would-be nun with nowhere to go. During the 1930s she worked as a lay sister in a children's home in Macedonia; an Orthodox bishop had founded it: 'He told me the Moslem children were to go to the mosque on Friday, just as our children went to church on Sunday.' In the 1940s she went to another children's home in Serbia. Finally she was accepted as a nun at Sretenje; it was from there that she had come to Vračevšnica. She obviously delighted in children's company. A small boy ran up to her in the garden. One of the girls from the children's home had come to stay, and this was her son. 'He's the monastery's grandchild,' said Mother Anna, putting an arm round him. 'He lives in Belgrade, and last night he heard the frogs croaking; he'd never heard that before.'

A sister came to take me to my room. 'I'm talking,' said the Abbess,

* See p. 203.

'and I don't wish to break off.' The sister waited, the conversation went on, and at length she was allowed to take me upstairs. My room, on the first floor of the older *konak*, had an arcaded balcony. I could hear running water, as the house was built over the millstream; their mill was below, said the nun, by their vineyards. Radić Postupović, the founder, had had vineyards too, but further up the valley, near his country house. I was taken to the dining-hall for supper. Nuns came in and sang to me, songs about the saints, in rather nasal voices, with much gaiety and chattering in between. I had barely finished eating when a summons came from the Abbess. This time she was in her room. A window-sill crowded with pots of scented pinks framed a view of precipitous forests.

'Take out your notebook,' said Mother Anna; 'I am going to tell you a great many things I have seen and known.' I obeyed, like the scribe I had become. 'I am an old woman now, and have had a long life . . .' I wrote as fast as I could . . . 'Stop! I will tell you when to write and when not to. Put down your pen.' I did so. 'Now I will begin . . .'

What she had to tell me was the answer to something that had puzzled me on several journeys – why Serbia has so many nuns. The story was rambling; the essentials were these.

In 1915, the Austrians had put Serbian soldiers – and others – into camps where many died. They held Bible readings and prayed for strength in their hardship. When peace came, the survivors returned home and founded brotherhoods (*bratstva*), each with its patron saint. The Serbian Orthodox Church, after some doubts as to whether they were heretics, recognized them. 'They kept a fiery faith,' said Mother Anna. The light had faded; she lit an oil-lamp and I wrote on as best I could. It was their daughters who led the return to a monastic life. Already a group of Russian nuns, escaping soon after the Revolution, had arrived at Hopovo in 1921. Their leader was the Abbess Katerina: 'She was of royal blood, and as a young girl she ran away from a Court Ball in short sleeves to a monastery; first they turned her back, then they took her in.' She received Serbian girls at Hopovo and started a sister-foundation at Kuveždin in the same neighbourhood. Then a seamstress from Montenegro had started a monastic revival after a vision, and she had been helped by Kasijan, one of the hermits I'd met at Studenica.

I tried to sort out Mother Anna's total recall. Probably the *bratstva* daughters had been the most important numerically in the late 1930s, but the Russian nuns must have provided a base for them. I remembered the Manasija Abbess, off to visit Mother Theodora, one of the original Hopovo nuns, in Paris. The seamstress must have given the movement its countrified, peasant roots. The story explained Mother Anna's own difficulties in the '20s and early '30s.

'I'm tired,' Mother Anna said; 'put down your pen. I would like you to stay longer. I have much to tell the world before I die.' She nodded in her wicker chair; I went out and a nun came in to attend to her.

The noise of the millstream was like a lullaby; I soon dropped off to sleep. When I woke in the morning and looked down into the courtyard, the younger nuns were heaving kegs of white cheese into an ox-drawn cart to take to market. Mother Anna asked for me again; my last chance of walking up into the hills to Miloš' hideout had gone. We had to set off for Belgrade. Two nuns were sadly carsick, and the third sang loudly all the way.

19

SLAVA AT CIKOTE

Stana – her village in Šumadija – the family feast: old customs, new prosperity

For a long time, our casual encounters on Sunday walks were all we knew of village life in Šumadija, this heartland where 'people loved freedom above all'.[1] Then Stana came to work in our house, a merry divorcée with three daughters to bring up. Stana had left her home in Šumadija shortly before, and she talked about it: how she had spent days looking after the flocks as a child; how her father liked his children to read the old ballads to him (here she stopped dusting the drawing-room to show me his favourite poem in the book that lay on our table); how the waltz was first seen in the village, shocking everyone who was used to the traditional dances. Her mother had died of an infection ('it wouldn't happen nowadays'); her husband had made her mourn his relations by taking food to the graveyard on Saturdays ('a terrible expense, some families got into debt over it, you had to make a show'). Her ex-husband was a garage mechanic and a champion *gusle* performer: '*gusle govore bez reči*' ('his *gusle* speaks without words'), as the saying was. Later on he had taken a common-law wife into the house (this is unusual), so she left with her daughters and found shelter with her schoolmaster brother in the town, and soon set off to earn her living in the capital and pay for her children's board. Stana looked rather as Miloš' wife Princess Ljubica must have done: strong, stocky and comely. She walked along our suburban street as if she were setting off cross-country, and when I drove through Šumadija I often thought I saw her, because so many women, seen back view, walked the same way as she did. She had a voice like a corncrake and was shy of no one. 'You've got the wrong number, brother,' she would say on the telephone, 'they're foreigners here. No, brother, you can't be wanting them.' Only a swift intervention would save a friendship from being lost for ever. In time she adopted us as part of her *zadruga*. Again on the telephone, to a neighbour: '*Naši* (our family) have just got back from seeing the old lady (my mother-in-law).' Her daughters came to live with us in turns, one trained as a secretary, two as student nurses. Coffee was constantly being served to brothers and 'relatives' – an umbrella word which covered all male visitors – up from the country.

In return, she took us to her village on any possible feast-day, and especially to her family *slava*, which took place on 25 May (St Mark's Day). Stana lived in the southeast corner of Šumadija, near the town of Kragujevac which had been Miloš Obrenović's capital. We went up the Dulenska valley, a plain hidden between hills, where paprikas grew protected by little battlements of earth to keep the moisture in. Maize, wheat and potatoes had been planted in neat plots, like a wide market garden. It was surprisingly rich flat land to find in the middle of hill country. Tečić, where Stana's ex-husband lived, was a street of white-arcaded houses, each in its own enclosure. Stana's two younger daughters ran out and climbed into the car; the eldest had come with us from Belgrade. We went on through woods and orchards, to her own village, Cikote, which lay on higher ground. This part of Šumadija has long been a fruit-growing district; Milićević lists the kinds of apple that were planted there: Peters, Elijahs, Ox's, sweet, sour, green, rose, reddish; and the pears – juicy, winter, hard, sheeps', dark, Arabian . . . Nowadays, there is wheat as well. Stana's house was surrounded by a high wall with a roofed gateway and inside was a village green where roses grew and ducklings waddled. Several houses lay within the walls: the old family house where the feast was held, the new *zidana kuća* (brick-built house) to which every family aspires, ugly, two-storeyed and stuccoed green all over, a small cottage where an old aunt lived. We were given *slatko* in each house, met Stana's elder brother, the farmer, 'not a single house can exist without a head . . .'; her younger brother the schoolmaster; a little niece who was born lame, but getting better after two operations in Belgrade; and Stana's stepmother, a tall old woman with calm features framed in a dark scarf, who could have been a model for the Mother of God at Peć. We were seeing the remnants of a *zadruga*.

The feast was nearly ready. In the open space between the barn and a golden stook of last year's maize, vine branches had burnt down to embers. Through a cloud of hot smoke we could see three men crouched on the ground and turning wooden spits which transfixed piglets and lambs.

We crowded into the old house. It had an earth floor, a living-room and a sleeping-room and a cellar beneath for storage. In the living-room a large table had been set with food. It was easy to see what animals and crops they had from what appeared on the table. Every possible use was made of the sheep: its caul was stuffed with rice and chopped liver, and cooked in a sauce with dried red pepper; the ewes' milk had been made into rich yoghourt; the pastries were filled with white cheese or apples or spinach. For vegetables we had pickled green peppers and cucumbers. There was no question of eating as yet, the *slava* ritual came first. We were caught up into the same ordered world of ceremonial and enjoyment that I had seen at the Vlach shepherds' gathering. This time we were safeguarding the house and its inhabitants and the land, and invoking a blessing on them for the next year; and again it was pagan, with Christian touches here and there. The family made welcome their neighbours, who would summon them to their *slava* in turn, unless they happened to share the same saint's day. The farmers work together, hoeing and harvesting and winnowing – though more mechanization is changing this – and they celebrate together.

We were told to stand. The farmer, as *domaćin* (householder), took a round loaf of bread. On it he placed a round cake, and on the cake a candle, incense and flowers. He covered the whole edifice with a white cloth and set it at the head of the table. A second man removed the cloth and gave it back to the farmer. He was the *kolačar*, the man who cuts the cake, and the householder has to choose him carefully, for, as with the first-footer at a Serbian Christmas, the luck of the house for the next twelve months depends on him. He had better be healthy, of good character, and well-versed in his duties. Next the farmer took up a small incense-burner, like a brown pottery mushroom with a pierced cap and a bite taken out of it. He lit it, made the sign of the cross over the cake, kissed it and turned to the guests: 'Forgive and bless! Let us light the candle to God and to what is holy!' The guests roared back: 'God and Christ!'

He lit the candle at the incense-burner and stuck it in the cake. The men took off their caps, he censed the cake and the guests, meanwhile praying to God and to St Mark, the family's patron saint, to give everyone present help and happiness. Then he held up his glass of wine to the guests, and they shouted back. He had much more to recite, the key words being '. . . where the *slava* is celebrated, harvest and prosperity, life and health, peace and justice are forwarded and glorified . . .' Then everyone clinked glasses, the children got very excited, and we drank a toast. The farmer poured wine over the cake, the *kolačar* asked the farmer what he wanted? Back came the answer:

'A barrel of wine and a roast pig.' The *kolačar* cut a cross on the surface of the cake, and sprinkled wine on it in four places, saying: 'In the name of the Father, Amen, and the Son, Amen, and the Holy Spirit, Amen.'

The guests crowded round the cake, which the farmer had taken back. As many as could fit in, put a hand under it, and they twirled it round, shouting 'Lord have mercy!' Then they raised the cake high in the air: 'Glory be to God, the house and the householder!' At last the cake could be cut and distributed to the guests, amid crossings and kissings and cries of 'Christ in our hearts!' The farmer's wife was given her piece by her husband on a sieve 'so that it may be a plenteous year', and he threw a few coins on it as well.

The toasts continued, host to guest, guest to *kolačar* and so on. The host ordered the guests to bow to God and they crossed themselves and sat down, though he remained standing throughout the feast.

Up till now prayers or silence had been the order of the day. The time for talking had come, and although the women brought in the roast meat, and Richard and I looked on hungrily, it grew tepid on the table while the men started their discussion. The farmer mentioned the sale of his wine and *rakija*, which brought him more profits than anything else. One of the big firms in Slovenia was buying wine from these villages to blend with its own output. He himself had tried private enterprise by going to Bosnia with some samples and had said to the manager of a new hotel: 'If you want to taste good *rakija*, try that.' But the hotel bought only from co-operatives and he was sent away. 'You had more luck with your peppers, though,' prompted Stana, who was filling up everyone's glasses. One year, her brother said, he had a bumper crop of green peppers; there was a local glut and Kragujevac market was overflowing. So he borrowed a lorry, drove his peppers to Belgrade, and sold them very well there. Šumadija is not as prosperous as Vojvodina; the farms have always been small, five hectares being average, ten the permitted maximum. The soil is variable but farmers make a decent living from their land. Land counts most. Stana was scornful of the Dalmatian coast when we took her there: 'Tourists and boatbuilding and quarrying – what sort of a life is that? They've no earth to till – it's all rock.' The richest houses are now 'mixed'. In Karageorge's day this meant they contained a livestock dealer, but now it means that one or more members belong to the town *zanatlija* or have become professional men. Stana's family was like this, and her eldest daughter married a local doctor. The Šumadijans like comfort; they are quite canny but not very ambitious and I rather doubt the man who said to another foreigner, Joel Halpern, 'Give us twenty years without war, and we will make of Šumadija a little America.'

At last we ate. 'Our men are served first,' Stana whispered in a stage-direction; 'your customs are different.' The food, though half-cold, was very good and carefully cooked. The two of us soon ate our fill, and as usual had to eat more out of politeness. The worst hazard of travel in Yugoslavia is overeating, though *rakija* helps everything down.

The food was left on the table and people helped themselves as they talked. The schoolmaster hectored us about life, economics and education. Stana must have received a lot of noisy advice while sheltering in his house, though he had been a good brother to her. An old man was discussing Balkan politics with Richard: 'Say what you like, the British will never give up Cyprus . . .' The wine went round again; someone struck up a song and then another. This district is famous for its drinking-songs:

Very high a falcon flew,
Spread its wings out broadly,
Searching for a grape-vine,
Searching for cool water.
Called a maiden to the bird:
'Come down here, O falcon,
Here a noble grape-vine grows,
Here you'll find cool water,
Cool it is as if 'twere ice
And sweet as any honey.'
Drink, brother, drink!
We're all of us merry!

The evening was on us, Belgrade was two hours off, and Richard had to work the next day. We tried to leave. A chorus of voices begged us to sleep at least one night in the house: 'It's a big bed! You'll be comfortable! You're welcome!' But we had to go, though Stana stayed on. Everyone came through the gateway and Richard took a photograph. They were all laughing until he held up the camera; then they went Sunday-faced. Afterwards, they crowded round and kissed us. Twenty of them, two of us, and both cheeks: that makes eighty kisses given and taken. We drove away, and at first the figures, waving and smiling, were distinct: the fine old stepmother; Stana and her farmer brother, as stocky as each other; her three pretty daughters; the little lame niece on crutches. Then came a bump in the earth road, and a cloud of dust with it, and they vanished behind it, family and house and *slava*, into memory.

20

THE CHANGING FORTUNES OF BELGRADE

Our house – strolling round Belgrade – the fortress of Kalemegdan – the medieval and Turkish city – a visit to the Imam – Lady Mary Wortley Montagu and the Pasha

Our house, up a hill, faced north, and when I stood on the balcony I breathed the fumes of brown coal which floated up from the city. Between the balcony and the horizon, where the Sava flowed into the Danube, was Belgrade, full of tiled stoves like our own, bringing warmth, comfort, fog and bronchitis. In the evening, I could watch the sun set over the Fruška Gora. At the back of the house, the slope went up into the suburb and blocked any view towards the bulwark of hills that rolled south higher and higher through Šumadija, dropping down into the Western Morava, jutting up again above the Ibar valley, falling a little to Kossovo's high plain, and in Macedonia building a wall of mountains which came down into the oakwoods of Northern Greece.

The suburb, Senjak, looked as if it had been put up at the turn of the century, but little in Belgrade is as old as it looks, and until the 1930s the king's soldiers had kept their hay (*seno*) there. Then came the French pavilions, Japanese houses, Swiss chalets and neo-classical mansions set in lawns and flower beds. They never quite ousted the wooden cottages and vegetable patches where we walked in the summer evenings along winding paths overgrown with clematis. People sat talking at wooden tables by each front door, while chickens scratched around, and one such place we called the 'Tolstoy gardens'. Our own house was built by a General for his mistress and had three balconies where Stana and I grew geraniums or sunbathed. Opposite us was a high wall covered with Virginia creeper, a waterfall of delicate green leaves, and the street was lined with judas trees, magnolias and catalpas. A neighbour's daughter, Vera, bicycled along precariously, calling in when her tyres grew flat to borrow our pump, and her mother would have me in to coffee, and tell me about Vera and her sister wanting to adopt a Skopje baby after the 1963 earthquake, or we would borrow English novels and Yugoslav poems from each other. Sometimes I would walk our dog past Vera's house through small parks and thickets to the next hill, Dedinje, a much grander place where Tito and his Ministers lived along a pleasant avenue. On Dedinje, too, I found country paths and cobbled lanes. I went out every day, in fine weather when a lizard came out in the rock garden, in thick mud when a frog sat in the puddle at our gate, in the much-hated spring wind, the Košava, and on slippery ice when Tito's guards stamped up and down with the cold and the plain-clothes men turned up their coat-collars.

The Belgrade we knew was a shabby *belle laide* among the capitals of Europe, but I walked in the outskirts and in the centre, for the same reason I had once walked in London and in Rome – to see what was round the next corner. At the door of a fashionable shoemaker a countryman was asking to have his wife's shoes mended, and being rebuffed and not noticing it, and talking on about the harvest. The military cadets, proud of their uniform, strolled stiffly in one park; in another, on Sunday afternoon, soldiers and peasants started dancing a *kolo* to gipsy music.

On early summer mornings, before the sun grew too hot, I would drive down to Kalemegdan, the fortress which for thousands of years *was* Belgrade, or Weissenburg or Castelbianco, and before that, to the Romans, Singidunum. Kalemegdan stands on a great bluff overlooking the junction of the Danube and the Sava; a crag with a plateau on top. Like Petrovaradin, it is a fortress which starts to tell its own history as you look at it; a dramatic place, especially if seen from the West bank of the Sava.*

On the west side are inaccessible cliffs, now terraced with 18th-century Austrian fortifications. The northwest side, too, is very steep; only to the northeast does the ground slope down more gently to the Danube, and inland, to the southwest, the ground is flat. Kalemegdan was for centuries divided into the Lower Fortress, facing northwest across the Danube, and the Upper Fortress which had access inland. The Lower Fortress housed the artisans and merchants necessary to support military life; they were protected by ramparts and walls but under attack could retreat into the greater safety of the Upper Fortress.

The part where I went most often was probably the first Roman

* A riverside walk runs beside the restaurant Ušće Sava, near the excellent Museum of Modern Art.

castrum, a square greensward inside the Upper Fortress, in the north-west corner, near Meštrović's statue on the point, a warrior who was swivelled round on his pedestal to face the two rivers, as his frontal nudity offended some citizens. I reached the Danube ramparts via the inner Stamboul Gate and a moat and an Austrian clock-tower and a Moslem shrine, and once, at seven in the morning, I found a Minister's car drawn up there; the occupant sat contemplating the wide river before starting his official day. It was the Turks who named Kalemegdan the 'hill of reflection'. They also called Belgrade 'the house that makes war for the faith' and it was this for Christians and Moslems and others before them, for the Illyrians, Celts, Romans, Huns, Ostrogoths, Avars, Byzantines, Hungarians and Serbs who occupied it.

If it poured with rain, I would go inside the Military Museum, which sets out most admirably the history of the South Slav lands at war, which means most of their history. If the rain stopped, I went out past tanks and cannon to look at the *krajputaši*, upright tombstones from the roadsides of Šumadija and Western Serbia. One was a soldier with medals on his stone uniform. Sometimes women are portrayed with a Singer sewing-machine. *Krajputaši* may have terse rhymes carved on them,

> Here I lie;
> and thou lookest on me.
> I would thou lay,
> while I looked on thee.[1]

The other walk on Kalemegdan which I often took, began at the old medieval entrance by the Zoo with a pungent smell of lion, and took me through Leopold II's gate and a second set of walls pierced by Zindan Gate with its two massive round towers. Then I turned right, past the restaurant called *Kalemegdanska Terasa*, down some steps in the wall of the Upper Fortress, and emerged, still on a slope, into the Lower Fortress, by Ružica, now a church and once a Turkish powder-magazine. Further down the path was a smaller church, Sv. Petka, built over a healing spring where people crowded to draw water. Sv. Petka had a cool courtyard with a white mulberry tree to sit under. Below was a dusty plain – all that is left of the Lower Fortress, its houses and churches and mosques. *Nebojša*, an octagonal tower, stands there; it was used by Turks and Serbs as a prison, and the ancestor of one friend, whose family had been pro-Obrenović, spent some unpleasant years in its dungeons during Prince Alexander Karadjordjević's reign. At least he came out alive. The Serbs held there by the

Turks in 1813 ended up displayed on Stamboul Gate. An Austrian baroque gateway, some Turkish baths, the vestiges of outer walls and the Danube quay – that was all that was left. Lorry-drivers thundered by on the road which encircled the lower wall, and yelled dubious endearments, tramps lay snoring among the bushes, and an underworld of pedigree dog-fanciers and racing touts used the place for their meetings. I climbed back to the *Terasa*, and had coffee in the shade, and thought of Evliya Chelebi, that indefatigable 17th-century traveller, who used to sit in a Turkish kiosk somewhere up here and look across the river. The small house behind Ružica Church, with its garden of walnut and apricot trees, was sunk into a canyon of earth between the criss-cross walls, and looked inviting. Perhaps the priest lived there; I never found out.

The Romans had made their *castrum* on this high point in the 1st century A.D. When they were fighting the Dacians, Singidunum became the permanent headquarters for a legion and may have held 6000 troops.

The pattern of the fortress' settlement was now firm; only the occupants and the buildings were to change with time. The Huns drove out the Romans in the 5th century, the Byzantines won it back precariously for a hundred years, until the Avars descended when they were working in the fields, and took the castle. Barbarian darkness descended and only lifts in A.D. 885, when *βελαγράδων* is mentioned, a Christian city with a bishop under the rule of the Bulgarian Khan. The Byzantines were back by the late 10th century.

When I stood on the high point of Kalemegdan and looked over the cliff at the two rivers, it was easy to imagine how in the Middle Ages the owners of Belgrade controlled trade and traffic over a very wide area. They needed a fortress because of the constant danger of pillage, Crusaders being a special menace. The Byzantines created a citadel and donjon. After Manuel Comnenus' death, the Hungarians marched in, but they let the Serbs have Belgrade back when the Nemanjid king Dragutin married one of their princesses. King Milutin lost it to the Hungarians; in 1403, Despot Stephen Lazarević, as a Hungarian vassal, gained possession, and, in the words of his charter, 'restored it and dedicated it to the Mother of God'. In his day Belgrade must have looked very splendid though perhaps his Court writer, Constantine the Philosopher, was earning his keep when he likened it to Jerusalem. As at Manasija, Stephen aimed at strength and refinement. He built double ramparts, towers, moats and drawbridges and made a 'small fortress' within the Upper Fortress. This contained a luxurious palace and treasury, and probably a library and chapel as well. Excavation goes on, and in 1971, I was shown a stone lion's head that had just been found.

After Stephen's death, the Hungarians held Belgrade under great pressure from the Turks, who wanted a base so that they could press further north into Europe. The Turks had to besiege Belgrade three times – in 1440 when the declaration of a Crusade helped to save it, in 1456 and finally, in 1521, when Suleiman the Magnificent took the fortress by using boats, ladders and mines. Busbecq, passing by in 1555, reflected:

> These events ought to be a lesson to the princes of Christendom and make them realize that . . . they cannot be too careful in securing their . . . strongholds against the enemy. The Turkish armies are like mighty rivers swollen with rain, which, if they trickle through at any point, in the banks which restrain them, spread through the breach and cause infinite destruction. Even so, and with still more terrible results, the Turks, when once they have burst the barriers which restrain them, spread far and wide and cause a devastation which passes belief.[2]

The Turks built a pontoon bridge across the Sava and sent their troops northwards. They expanded the civilian town, building mosques and *medresi* (seminaries), baths and *hans*. The list of inhabitants included civil servants and gardeners. The Turkish dignitaries had their own palaces, and Evliya Chelebi went sightseeing in the commander's house and found the walls decorated with weapons 'such as you might see . . . only in Baghdad'. In 1621, the French Ambassador to the Porte, the Sieur des-Hayes, called on the Pasha at Belgrade. He was led into a large room, where the floor was concealed by a Persian carpet, and on top of that, red velvet had been laid for the guests to walk on. The walls, decorated with marble, were hung with squares of red velvet embroidered in gold, so that anyone who leant against them was prevented from coming in contact with the cold stone. When the Pasha appeared, he wore a caftan woven in silver thread; his outer garment was of cloth of gold lined with sable. His turban was so high that if he had laid it on the ground beside him, it would have reached to his waist. He received the letter sent him by Louis XIII with expressions of humility and gratitude.[3]

Trade flourished in 17th-century Belgrade; Edward Brown stayed comfortably at an Armenian merchant's house, and John Bunbury with a Greek, who brought out his best wines, got cheerfully drunk, and beat a drum. Both Brown and Chelebi mention the noble caravanserai put up by the Grand Vizier Sokolović. It was as strong as any castle, and an inscription on the gate read: 'All who have stayed in this caravanserai have gone out of it again.'

I could find small trace of this Moslem Belgrade. The mosque was locked; the shrines, one by Studentski Trg, decaying. The Turkish pastrycook on Knez Mihailova Street was crowded with Serbian students drinking *boza*, a drink made out of maize meal. Then Dušanka telephoned; she had been to see the Imam with her students and had promised to go back. Would I come?

The mosque stands in Jevremova Street, in the old Turkish quarter of Dorćol. It is a good building except for its graceless minaret; the Austrians shortened it when they turned the mosque into a Franciscan church in 1690. It dates from the mid-16th century, probably from Suleiman the Magnificent's time. Its name, the Flag-Mosque (*Bajrakli-Džamija*) goes back to the days when its banner showed all other mosques in the city the hour of prayer.

In the courtyard we found the Imam playing football with his two small boys, Mustapha and Mohammed. He was thirty-five, a Bosnian Slav with an Egyptian wife he had met during his University studies in Cairo. He took us into the mosque. Nasser had sent some carpets, King Hassan of Morocco a Koran, and the Indonesian Embassy had promised a chandelier. The fine *minber* (the high, roofed-in pulpit from which the sermon is recited) was made in Konjic, a village in Hercegovina we had often passed through without realizing it contains a family of traditional wood-carvers. A Belgrade scholar had painted prayers in a beautiful Arabic script on boards that now hung round the walls. The congregation built the women's gallery. 'We don't discriminate against women,' said the Imam, 'but the separation makes it easier to concentrate on prayer.'

He took us into his house behind the mosque. It looked as Turkish houses must have looked in Belgrade 200 years ago. The corner cupboard was heavily carved in dark wood, and its niches were filled with books and *džezve* and brass jugs; we sat on a *minderluk*, the curtains were carpets, a metal lamp hung from the ceiling. The Imam's wife brought us strawberry cordial and sweetmeats. The Imam showed us one of his treasures: an illuminated manuscript with an inscription dating from Alexander Obrenović's time (before 1903): 'Good Lord,

43 Portrait of Karageorge, leader of the 1st Serbian Uprising

44 Belgrade in 1849

45 Autumn in Šumadija : Ostrvica hill

the mosque has been restored and the Christians have done it themselves.' He told Dušanka he had given up all idea of studying for a doctorate; he had too much work. He needed a larger mosque here, and his 'parish' included Vojvodina, with its Bosnian and Albanian immigrants who had half-forgotten their Islamic inheritance. He showed us an *Ilmihal* (catechism) published in Serbo-Croat and Albanian for them. They lacked education, religious and secular. He was anxious they should go to school and to University. He had just buried a student at Novi Sad:

'I told them not to wash him but to treat him as a warrior, a warrior who had fought not on the battlefield but for learning.'

I had to ask Dušanka, *sotto voce*, what this meant, and she explained that in Islamic practice, soldiers who have been killed in action do not undergo the ritual washing at death.

The Imam also described his first appointment, in Bosnia:

'I arrived at the mosque in shirtsleeves and sandals – it was very hot. They took me for a tourist and told me: "We're waiting for our new Imam." They were very uneasy when I disclosed myself. I was bareheaded, you see. Then I spoke to the elders, promising I would serve them faithfully if they chose me, but I said that when I was free I must be free, to take out a girl (it was before my marriage) or to study. They shook their heads: "An Imam who studies . . ." But they accepted me.'

An older man, solid and cautious, in a worn suit, joined us. The two of them told us about the *hadj*, the great pilgrimage. They had been twice: twenty-three days by bus, or five hours by aeroplane to Jiddah, no distance from Mecca:

'There, king and workman are equal; all wear white cloths and go barefoot and walk from one sacred place to another. An atheist came with us, just to see, but when he had walked and chanted with us, he wept and believed.'

Then they discussed mysticism. The old man disapproved of dervishes. The Imam felt he could not; he had had a mystical experience, something like theirs, while meditating on the name of Allah. Just then 'Cuckoo, cuckoo' rang out, and gave me a start, and I turned round and saw the wooden bird come out on the clock on the wall. Outside, the voice of the *muezzin* was calling the faithful to midday prayer. The Imam put on his fez and hurried into the mosque; Dušanka and I walked home.

*

As a Turkish city, Belgrade's fortunes were linked with the rest of Europe. In 1683, the Ottoman army laid siege to Vienna and was turned back by Prince Eugen of Savoy, who in 1688 captured Belgrade. From then on Austrians and Turks competed for the fortress. In 1690 the Turks got it back and employed an Italian architect who constructed admirable fortifications on far too small a scale. The Habsburgs never held it long enough to leave a marked influence on town life as at Novi Sad.* It remained an oriental town, but less safe than before. In 1717, Lady Mary Wortley Montagu wrote a long letter to Alexander Pope, and another to the Abbé Conti, which make a vivid commentary on the time and place where she found herself. On the way, at Carlowitz (Sremski Karlovci) she had seen the dead bodies of men killed at Prince Eugen's last great victory (Petrovaradin, the previous year) and had reflected on 'the Injustice of War, that makes murther seem not only necessary but meritorious'. The warlike janissaries in Belgrade had mutinied and killed their peace-loving Pasha – as they were to do a century later. 'You may imagine I cannot be very easy in a Town which is really under the Government of an Insolent Soldiery.' The English party were heavily guarded, and she spent her time indoors. The icy weather made her think herself in Greenland, and she sat by a large stove, talking to her host, a charming Effendi who read Arabian poetry to her every evening and explained to her that educated Mohammedans were deists. 'He has wit and is more polite than many Christian men of Quality.'[4]

The uncertainties, political and military, which she notes, were borne out the next year. Prince Eugen retook Belgrade in one of his most celebrated campaigns. He only just gained the victory by a night-attack on the fortress from inland, where a Turkish army had surrounded him from the south. The Austrians held Belgrade and most of Serbia for twenty years. They enclosed the fortress and the town in bastions. The town bastions, each section with a saint's name, including one Slav, St Alexander Nevski, have been destroyed, but some of the star-shaped bastions in Vauban's style can be seen in the fortress. The Turks seized Belgrade back in 1739, and it was to change hands once more in 1789, when General Laudon took it:

* Austrian architecture in Belgrade is mainly 19th century, and the German words commonly used for tradesmen, domestic objects and food probably derive from German merchants and Vojvodina Serbs, e.g. *šnajder* for tailor, *šnejšlag* for egg-whisk, *koh* for pudding.

An Austrian army awfully array'd,
Boldly by battery besieg'd Belgrade;
Cossack commanders cannonading come,
Dealing destruction's devastating doom.[5]

A year later, the Turks were back, and stayed there until 1806 when Karageorge captured Belgrade for Serbia in the First Uprising. The town developed very little because Karageorge was constantly at war. In 1813 the Turks drove Karageorge's forces out and the Pasha even threatened the Austrians at Zemun with a further advance towards Vienna. The Turks ended their domination of the town – they were to remain in the fortress – with threats and horrors. That year, 1813, they decorated the outer Stamboul Gate, which once stood between the existing equestrian statue of Prince Mihailo and the National Theatre, with the heads and impaled bodies of captured Serbs.

Nowadays students arrange to meet each other *kod konja* (by the horse) and a *kafana* puts its tables out in that corner of the square in summer – where a great many people eat their ice-creams, as I did, in happy ignorance of what they might have seen on the same spot in the past.

21

LIFE IN THE SERBIAN CAPITAL

Cathedral, Patriarchate and Palace – the market at Zeleni Venac – the growth of Miloš' city – the Turks move out – Belgrade in our own times

The beginning of Serbian Belgrade, as it stands today, came with Miloš' rule. However autocratic, he did try to lead his nation out of the 15th into the 19th century. Town life hardly existed. Miloš used Kragujevac as his capital until 1841, when he transferred it to Belgrade, and he began to renovate the civilian part of Belgrade in the 1820s. The control of the town remained partly in Turkish, partly in Serbian hands, with a Pasha in the fortress, a Serbian prince in the town, and separate law-courts and police for both nations. Slowly, it changed from a Turkish into a Serbian town, and the population grew.

The Turks had built their houses east of Kalemegdan, facing the Danube, in Dorćol, where the mosque stands. They lived comfortably and had large gardens, above the old market, a double row of booths in what is now Dubrovačka Street. Under Miloš' orders, the Sava side of the town was developed. I could walk here and find among skyscrapers and apartment blocks the shape of an older Belgrade.

The quarter called Varoš-Kapija after the 'Town Gate' on Brankova Street had long been inhabited by Christians. Here, between the present Hotel Palas and the Cathedral Church, Serb, Greek and Cincar* merchants had their shops. Miloš now decided to site houses for himself and his family there. His own palace has been destroyed and the present-day Patriarchate stands on its site, but next to it his wife's house survives. A Macedonian built it for Princess Ljubica in 1830. It has two storeys – this in itself was a sign of grandeur – with a gabled *doksat* (women's balcony). Its tiled roof has clusters of domed chimneys. In June, the garden was overgrown with climbing roses, and the hay had just been cut. Its countrified, Eastern appearance must have been heightened by the massive gateway and walls seen in

* Kutzovlachs, originally shepherds from Northern Greece.

old photographs. It would look at home in Novi Pazar. The wooden front door, diamond-patterned, leads into a pillared hall which divides off the bow-windowed room at the back with its intricate carved ceilings, and this is really on the first floor, for the ground drops away at the back of the house and the back room is supported on pillars from below. On the south side is a Turkish bathroom with a pierced and vaulted ceiling, once heated by the hall stove; the steam under the stone floor made it warm. Upstairs is a delightful landing, with an octagonal roof lantern that has a small balcony for strolling. Turkish houses must have been good to live in. When I was there, a Moslem builder from Prizren was carefully restoring it.

Next to it is the Cathedral Church of 1837. Miloš was thought to be taking risks when he ordered its construction. The old said: 'We're still Turkish tenants, and they're building themselves towers.' It looks slightly Austrian, but inside it has the tomb of Prince Lazar, which people file up to kiss at the service on 28 June, the anniversary of the battle. Stana, standing beside Richard and myself, tried to be detached about it: 'It is our people's custom.' She was attracted to the queue despite herself and came back glowing. At Christmas we went again, and prayed for the Patriarchs of Antioch and Rumania and for 'Lord German, Patriarch of Serbia', and as we left, Stana said: 'I always dream of my father at the great festivals – I dreamt of him last night.' We walked on straw for the manger, at the entrance, and outside, on snow. This church was always full, with gipsies and beggars doing well at the door.

Opposite was the Patriarchate, where we went to call on the Patriarch on his name-day and sat in a circle of elderly Belgrade ladies, while nuns served *rakija* and blackcurrant juice. A side entrance led to the Patriarchate Museum, a small place full of treasures: icons and Jefimija's embroidered lament which had been used as a cover for Prince Lazar's bones, and the robe of faded Lucca brocade, patterned with dragons which he is said to have worn at Kossovo (the single button left bears Lazar's emblem, a horned helmet). Like Jefimija's silken cover, it travelled everywhere with his relics.

On the other side of the church, in 7 Jula Street, is a comfortable *kafana*. One owner in the 1890s named it 'At the Cathedral', the priests objected, the name was painted out overnight and replaced with a question-mark, which remains. A bookseller's used to stand alongside it, the first in Belgrade, which became a reading-room for Vuk Karadžić and his friends. Vuk, grammarian, lexicographer, editor, folklorist and historian, dominated Serbian intellectual life here as in Vienna.

It is easy to walk from here to Kosančićev Venac, with its cobbles and lime-trees, and old houses at the top end, and half-way down, a place to sit, with a view back over the church or downhill to the railway and the Sava below and a Russian hydrofoil for tourists going down the Danube. A hundred years ago, I should have seen, at the bottom of the steps leading down from Kosančićev Venac, the Sava quay, or *Liman*, busy with its Customs house and Turkish shops. In early summer, Bosnian *beys* landed fresh fruit, honey and besoms for sale, and then sat on cushions round a charcoal brazier in the *kafana*. It was to this quay that camels loaded with cotton came in from the East, and donkeys brought panniers of salt from Rumania. Nowadays donkey and horse-drawn traffic is forbidden by a city bye-law, and a Frenchwoman with a donkey who, in 1965, came on pilgrimage to Jerusalem in fulfilment of a vow made during her daughter's illness, was unable to cross the Sava. Then her Consul sent a lorry on which the donkey rode triumphantly through Belgrade, and she went on foot behind.

From my perch in Kosančićev Venac I could also see south, in the direction of the railway station. This part of the town was Sava Mala. In 1834 Miloš decided to build his Ministries there, and his soldiers drove out the old inhabitants by force from their small houses with courtyards where geese lived and women did their washing at a fountain. They all went to Palilula, on the Danube side. Sava Mala changed; Miloš' son Mihailo built the Church of the Ascension on the corner of Kneza Miloša Street, and Milan Obrenović, the railway station in 1884. The lower part of the district, round Sarajevska and Nemanjina, has kept its furriers and metal workers.

Kosančićev Venac, with its slight curve, followed the line of the old city boundary. The Austrian bastions had been replaced by a dirty moat full of refuse and a wooden palisade whose stakes were stolen as more peaceful times prevailed. It had led round, via the outer Stamboul Gate, down to the Danube.

Not far from here was Zeleni Venac (the Green Wreath) a market where Stana and I went by Land-Rover to do most of our shopping. Princess Ljubica had gone there by ox-cart in spring, for it used to be an excursion-spot, with a lake and boats for hire, and the inn sold good beer from Zemun. In 1840 the site was drained, and the market dates back to 1847. Its name came from a boarding house kept by a Saxon woman, on the corner of Brankova Street.

Zeleni Venac must have been a swampy pleasure-garden and makes a vigorous market, especially in summer, with all the fruit and vegetables. Baskets and trolleys hung from us as we forced our way through the crowds. 'Let me ask the prices,' said Stana, 'they'll be lower; it's your foreign accent that does it'. So I left her to bargain with the butcher, and looked round. I was bumped and jostled and held on tight to my bag as she told me.

The setting was theatrical. Many booths stood in the main arcade, pierced by three arches. Two had miniature houses over them and all the steep roofs shone with coloured tiles and had undulating eaves. It was like the backdrop for a Russian opera; the foreground was the crowd scene. More open stalls, and peasant women: Serbs, Albanians, Slovaks and gipsies. The crowd from the station had moved on to their destination. A woman held out a sliver of smoked sausage: 'Taste it, it's the best in the market.' Her neighbour joined in: 'No, mine is.' Stana and I tasted, decided. We passed a sign which offered us the queen bee's elixir and instant rejuvenation. We bought powdered red pepper for seasoning, peaches and plums for preserving, a new shopping basket, lilies, sweet williams and carnations. I talked to the herb-woman, who offered me her latest mixture, homemade Friar's Balsam. We stopped at the fish-stall to see if there had been a fresh catch. Carp swam in a freshwater tank and were always eaten at Michaelmas. In 1621 the Sieur des-Hayes was given a carp three foot long, and that was nothing out of the ordinary. His companion found the fish at Belgrade the best in Europe 'et à si bon prix que cela n'est pas croyable'.[1]

The market never failed in its variety, and was a reminder how Belgrade drew in the countryside. Even the supermarkets, described in my first letter home as 'full of cream cheese and plastic and sweet liqueurs', sometimes had vegetable or flower-stalls alongside them.

The market was not the only place to be put in order. Terazije, now the main street, had been a marsh where wildfowling was popular. Miloš drained this land and moved in unwilling new inhabitants, this time blacksmiths and wheelwrights. Miloš and his successors shared the task of changing Belgrade's appearance, of turning it from a Turkish *palanka* (small town) into a European city. Otto Pirch, a German who visited Belgrade in 1829, saw many well-to-do houses like Princess Ljubica's, but observed that often one room was furnished in European fashion, and in it hung the owner's European clothes, which he wore when calling on his friends across the river at Zemun.

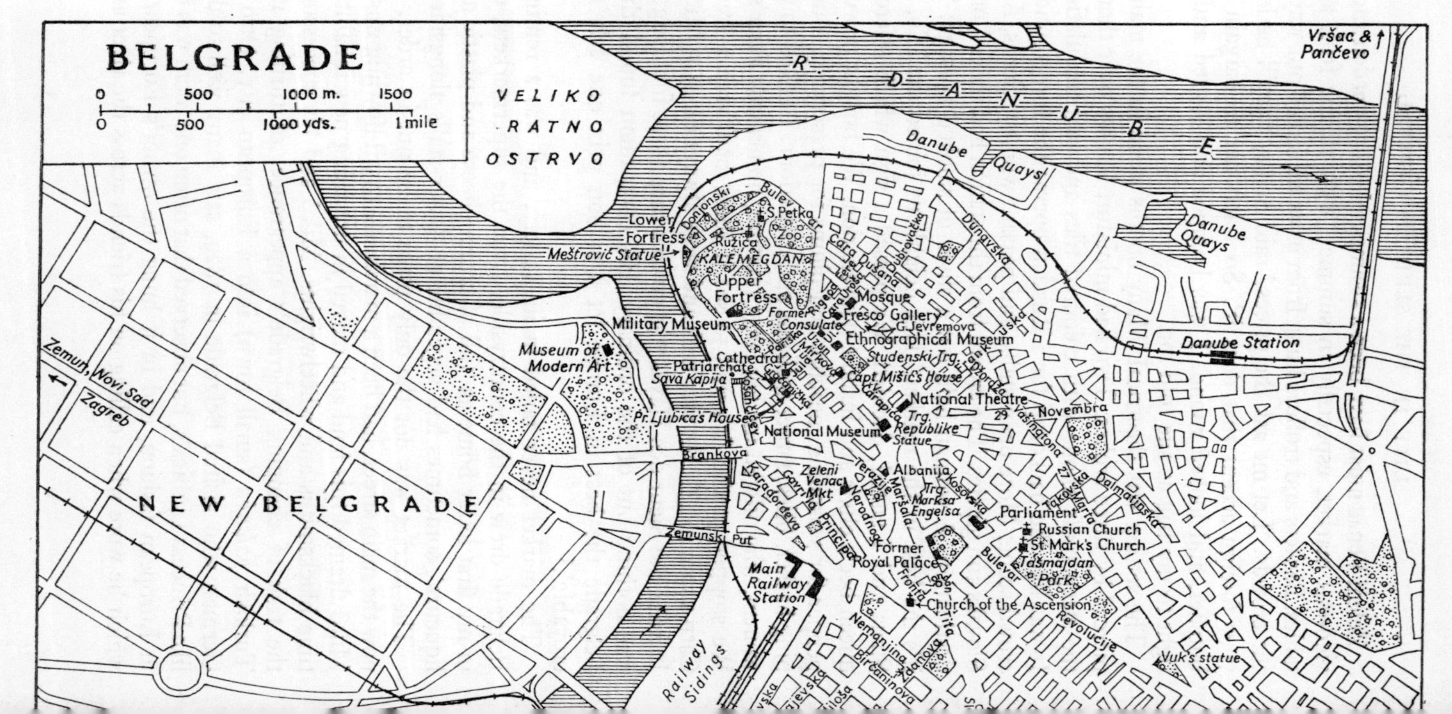
BELGRADE
0 500 1000 m. 1500
0 500 1000 yds. 1 mile
VELIKO RATNO OSTRVO
R. DANUBE
Vršac & Pančevo
Danube Quays
Danube Quays
Danube Station
Dunavska
Lower Fortress
Meštrović Statue
KALEMEGDAN
Upper Fortress
S. Petka
Ružica
Zoo
Donjonski
Cara Dušana
Dubrovačka
Mosque
Former Consulate
Fresco Gallery
G. Jevremova
Military Museum
Ethnographical Museum
Studenski Trg.
Museum of Modern Art
Cathedral
Patriarchate
Sava Kapija
Capt. Mišić's House
National Theatre
Pr. Ljubica's House
National Museum
Trg. Republike
Statue
29 Novembra
Vašingtona
Brankova
Albanija
Zeleni Venac
Gavrila Mkt.
Terazije
Karađorđeva
Trg. Marksa Engelsa
Kosovska
Parliament
Takovska
Dalmatinska
Russian Church
St. Mark's Church
Tašmajdan Park
Zemunski Put
Main Railway Station
Former Royal Palace
Principa
Narodnog Fronta
Bulevar Revolucije
Church of the Ascension
Tita
Nemanjina
Birčaninova
Ždanova
Railway Sidings
Vuk's statue
Zemun, Novi Sad
Zagreb
NEW BELGRADE

R. SAVA
ADA CIGANLIJA
Radnička
Obrenovački Put
Racecourse
Bulevar Vojvode Mišića
Koste Glavinića
Glišića
Simićeva
Laze Simića
Sanje Živanovića
Kovačevića
Andre Nikolića
Vase Pelagića
SENJAK
Vojvode Mišića
Topčider R.
Bulevar Vojvode Putnika
Bulevar Oktobarske Revolucije
Humsko
Stadium
Užička
Tolstojeva
Puškinova
Šekspirova
Church
Teodora Drajzera
Prince Miloš' palace (Topčider Museum)
DEDINJE
Bulevar Franše Deperea
Bulevar Jugoslavenske Narodne Armije
Ustanička
Stevana Prvovenčanog
Smederevo & Niš by motorway
Bulevar Vojvode Stepe
Kragujevac
BANOVO BRDO
Požeška
Radnička
Camping Site
Topčiderska
KOŠUTNJAK HILL
Mihailo's grave
Rakovački Put
Rakovica only
TOPČIDER PARK
ŽARKOVO
Ibarsko magistrala
Čačak & Ibar valley

Miloš preferred Turkish dress or military uniform (to be seen at the Topčider Museum) but forbade the fez to be worn in churches. English travellers in the 1840s remarked on the oriental appearance of the Court, though a few notables, like the Foreign Minister Garašanin, wore European clothes. The women were slower to change their dress; they wore flat jewelled caps with their hair braided round, long silk dresses and embroidered over-waistcoats, until nearly the turn of the century. Their children often went to be schooled in Vienna, Budapest or Leipzig and, as in Vojvodina, brought back Western ways and furniture. In Laza Lazarević's story, *The School Icon*, an old peasant describes how he stood in a Belgrade Professor's house and was afraid of making himself ridiculous, there were so many things one didn't know what to do with, and then, one couldn't spit on the floor, but had to use a spittoon . . . .

It was not enough that children should go away to school. This brought Miloš to his second task: the setting-up of educational institutions which would create a civilized life. Capricious, coarse and brutal, Miloš did achieve, in terms of bricks and mortar, the beginnings of a capital. On the other hand, when he founded schools at Kragujevac and Belgrade to carry on the work started by Dositej under Karageorge, he changed his mind unpredictably. He sent his sons to school, and had them tutored in French and German, but he abandoned his own efforts to read and write under pressure from his courtiers. He alienated his most valuable ally, Vuk Karadžić, who served as a magistrate and an organizer of schools and who left Belgrade in 1832. Serving Miloš was precarious; he murdered some of his associates and had his daughter's suitor hacked to pieces. Vuk, safely at Zemun, wrote a famous letter to Miloš which pinpoints the faults of his regime. As Vuk said, Miloš feared education, feared the making of a proper constitution or of a Code of Laws and was far too busy feathering his own nest (by buying up villages in Wallachia). Schools were built, however, under Miloš and later, and an educated class grew up.

Belgrade now has several student quarters, but the oldest is a short way from Kalemegdan. The house where Dositej set up his High School in Jevremova Street is now the Vuk and Dositej Museum and close by is Studentski Trg (Student's Square) dominated by Captain Miša's Foundation – an elaborate 'Venetian-Byzantine' palace, given by a businessman-politician in 1863. It was the start of Belgrade University, and is still in use. A Chair of Medicine followed, and the first hospital. A seminary and a military academy already flourished; commercial and agricultural schools faded away. The Girls' High School had a ladylike syllabus: Christian knowledge, domestic science and dancing. Languages, drawing and piano lessons were extras. A library had developed out of the original bookseller's shop, and in the 1860s it had the great good fortune to have Janko Šafarik, son of the famous Slavist who had taught at Novi Sad, as librarian, and then the scholarly Stojan Novaković. The 'Learned Society' founded about this time met with difficulties. The Minister of Education was fearful that it would promote revolution, as it acquired the works of Garibaldi and Herzen, and Prince Mihailo brought it under Government control. Not until 1886 did the Serbian Royal Academy achieve independent status. The second half of the 19th century yielded some talented poets, prose-writers and the portrait-painters whose work can be seen in the National Museum. Many writers and painters, though not all, came under strong foreign influences. The most original writers of this age and of the early 20th century were its scholars: the historian Stojan Novaković, the geographer Jovan Cvijić, the gazetteer Milan Milićević, the naturalist Josip Pančić, the ethnographer Tihomir Djordjević. They built up a corpus of knowledge about their own land as earlier Vuk Karadžić had done (Novaković was a pupil of a pupil of Vuk's). They wrote with style and enthusiasm, and they nourished the creative writers who came later.

This intellectual activity existed against a background of thriving commercial life. Miloš had found merchants and craftsmen and markets; he encouraged the livestock trade and pigs and horses were exported. So were wool and butter. Very little was imported: sugar from Trieste, wheaten flour from Vojvodina, some dress materials, pistols and powder. In Miloš' time, industry was undeveloped. Belgrade had two mills, a brewery, a soap and candle factory, and like Novi Sad, a silk factory. English companies became interested: one set up a slaughterhouse and produced bacon; another bought timber. Palmerston thought Serbia might be a useful new market for Birmingham and Manchester goods; moreover he was anxious to counteract any Russian political influence over Miloš. In 1838 Colonel Hodges was appointed British Consul in Belgrade. The colonel had the lowest possible opinion of the Serbian ruler. He bribed Miloš' doctor Cunibert, and entertained the Serbian Prince and his wife lavishly. It was the first time women had sat down together with Miloš at table. Two Queen's Messengers lodged at Aleksinac and brought the mail to and from Istanbul; one dressed in hunting pink and they fed their English guests on plum pudding.

The Russians quickly sent a Consul, so did the French. Serbia continued to attract foreign capital after Miloš' death. In the 1880s a French company built a bridge across the Sava; and the first railway (Niš–Belgrade) made a transport link with the Austrian frontier at Zemun; soon after Austrian works at the Iron Gates made the Danube navigable for larger ships.

Belgrade increased her links with Western Europe in other ways. Western travellers were often passing through, some for pleasure, on the way to the East, some observing the plight of their Christian brothers under the Turks, some interested in the new princedom. Along with Serbian contemporary records, they act as a barometer of change. Kinglake, in *Eothen* (1844), treats Belgrade as half-way East:

> the still air that you breathe is loaded with the scent of citron and pomegranate rinds scorched by the sun, or . . . with the dry dead perfume of strange spices.[2]

He uses this setting to write an entertaining and imaginary interview between an Englishman and a Turkish Pasha, and makes off towards Lady Hester Stanhope in the Lebanon. Ami Boué (1840) considers the city as the last outpost of civilization: he advises the purchase of a piece of waxed linen to keep off bedbugs. Rifles should be handed out to the servants.[3] *Murray's Guide* (1854), returning, agrees: 'At Belgrade the traveller discharges his tatar, and enters Christian Europe.'[4] Archibald Paton noted the progress made in Belgrade by 1843–44. The new cathedral was finished, shops fronted and glazed, and he saw 'German' houses two or three storeys high. He describes a ball at the palace: 'the parquet was inlaid and polished. . . . The roof admirably painted in subdued colours, in the best Vienna style.'

The meal was German, and with the dessert, 'the prince rose with a creaming glass of champagne in his hand, and proposed the health of the Sultan, acknowledged by the Pasha.'[5]

Over the hill from our house was Topčider, where Miloš had built a country residence, the most charming house in Belgrade, designed by the same architect as Princess Ljubica's palace. A huge plane-tree almost touches the windows of the *doksat*, where paintings line the top of the walls: naïve scenes of eagles preening themselves, a coach with horses, a Turk on a bridge, one man with a scythe, another with a pipe. Lions, fruits and vines make a frieze below. The house is now a

Museum of the Two Uprisings, so it has kept its memories of Miloš and added some of Karageorge. The 19th-century travellers must have seen, as we did, the fine park laid out by a Frenchman with stone statues, and Miloš' church, built by an Italian, across the way. The Reverend William Denton visited Miloš' son, Mihailo, here in 1862. Behind the house he observed the Košutnjak hills which were – and are – 'the favourite lounge for the citizens of Belgrade on all holidays'. Denton was most interested in Mihailo's model farm and glasshouses, which survive in a nursery garden on the slope across the road. Denton found the Prince 'of gentlemanly bearing' and admired how simply he lived, walking or driving almost every afternoon at the same hour, with the princess, towards Topčider, sometimes without a servant.[6] This was not so happy an augury as the writer thought.

Denton also describes the last outburst of Turkish violence in Belgrade. The transition from an oriental to a western city was difficult not least because Serbian and Turkish institutions continued to co-exist. Inside Kalemegdan, morale was low. By 1850, it was held by raw boys from Kurdistan serving under Turkish officers, and Denton noted that it housed hundreds of Druse prisoners, who died there under appalling conditions. Formalities were preserved; the Serbian commander called on the Turkish Pasha each Friday, the Pasha on the Commander each Sunday, but the situation was tense. In 1862 a Turkish apprentice, drawing water from a street-fountain, triggered off a brawl in which two Turkish policemen were killed. The Turkish garrison shelled the Serbian quarter of the town, causing serious damage to property and some casualties. The English Consul, Longworth, left his house (now the Pedagogical Museum on the corner of Uzun Mirkova) near Kalemegdan, and at considerable personal risk tried to negotiate for peace. The Serbs declared a state of martial law. Then the Serbs were given complete jurisdiction over the town, and five years later the Turks at last marched out of Kalemegdan. That day was one of great rejoicing and of personal triumph for Prince Mihailo.

He had previously travelled to Istanbul to receive, from the hands of the Sultan himself, the *firman* which decreed that Kalemegdan and the remaining Turkish fortresses should be handed over to the Serbs. The Sultan awarded Mihailo an order glittering with diamonds and five pure-bred Arabian horses. On his return, the *firman* was read out in the presence of Prince, Pasha, Metropolitan and Consuls. Serbian and Turkish troops played military music. Two salutes of twenty-one guns were fired as the flags of the two nations were run up, and Prince

Mihailo gave a dinner at which the menu included *Punch Impérial* and *Charlotte à la Russe*.

Prince Mihailo achieved much. The simplicity which Denton had admired led to his tragic end in 1868:

> The stability of the Serbian institutions has lately undergone a severe trial. As the reigning prince, Michael Obrenovitch, was taking his evening walk with two ladies in the grounds of his suburban villa, six men drew up on either side of the narrowest and most secluded part of the path, and saluted him with their left hands, keeping their right hands on their revolvers. The prince became deadly pale, but returned the salute, and was immediately fired into from behind. In her endeavour to protect him, the elder lady flew upon his assassins, and was found, after death, with her hands full of hair. The prince was killed with fearful mutilation. The younger lady ran for her life, which she owed either to the mercy of her pursuer or to his belief that she was already dead, for she did not escape without two wounds. This was the work of a rival faction, but public opinion pronounced at once against the assassins and their instigators, and the hold of the reigning family upon the affections of the people had been confirmed. The ghastly details were told us on the spot by the British Consul-General, who happened to be driving in the neighbourhood on the evening of the massacre, and was the first to give assistance.[7]

A Regency was proclaimed; the Obrenović dynasty continued. A Russian painter and Slavophile, M. O. Mikeshin, designed a chapel-grotto with palm-trees and fountains, surmounted by a gigantic statue of the reclining prince to be erected on the spot where he was killed. It was never built, probably because the Serbs wanted Austrian support. Instead, a dank corner of Košutnjak is chained off for Mihailo's memorial.

Belgrade expanded. In 1886, a Scotsman, Mackenzie, applied to the City Council for permission to develop 'a convenient and pleasant site' near the present Hotel Slavija. Mackenzie had been converted to Methodism in a severe thunderstorm. He built a chapel on the Square, and houses in a street named after him, Makenzijova. A clause in the lease of each house forbade alcohol to be served on the premises. (By our time, the houses had mostly been pulled down; and the chapel was transformed into a cinema with a flourishing bar.) Belgrade was now a town where everything looked more Western. A picturesque Jewish quarter remained, which held winter carnival in the streets at the feast of Purim. Serbian, not Greek and Turkish, was heard on the streets. Milićević grumbles that too many foreign words have crept into his native language. A glance at the newspaper advertisements in 1903 shows that a bookshop had in stock Renan's *Leben Jesu*, Shakespeare's Works and Herbert Spencer's *Principles of Sociology*, all in 'elegant bindings'. At this period the theatre was putting on plays by Shakespeare, Molière, Goethe, Schiller, Victor Hugo, Ibsen and Gogol, as well as by Serbian writers. Concerts, tennis, rowing and fencing were all popular. The young men found Liberalism slow-moving, and turned to Socialism.

After the First World War, Andrić wrote, this modest social world was swamped. He notes a new, formless community who found themselves together because of 'a great political and social upheaval, and one of the greatest military victories in the annals of the country'. People had lost their roots; no one knew where they were. 'There never was a better time for humbug and self-delusion!'[8]

The Belgrade we knew did not go back so far, but occasionally we had glimpses of what it had been like in the 1930s. Once we went to a musical evening given by elderly people. A young pianist played, who was going to study under Février in Paris. A silver-haired man, a cousin of the family, leant over the piano. 'A voice like an angel,' said one lady, pointing to him, 'like an angel. . . .' We ate Crème Arabe off a table covered with a fine lace-edged cloth, and the cupboards were crowded with porcelain, and on the sideboard stood a samovar from Tula, where all the best samovars come from.

Another time we took an elderly Hungarian Radical, long resident in England, to visit a Serbian poet of his own generation, also of the Left, and half-French by culture. The two had never met before. A book was lying open on the table and the Hungarian turned the pages idly and came to a photograph. He looked at the Serb: 'The Countess Julia Karolyi – you remember how beautiful she was?' They both sighed, and began to reminisce in French about pre-war Hungarian politics. We caught a hint of the Central European intelligentsia to which they had both belonged, and went away without their noticing.

In another house, a portrait on one wall reminded me of what the 1930s had led to. A politician who served Yugoslavia faithfully before and after the war had two sons, both killed in action. With the first, Yugoslavia lost a potential leader; the second was a gifted painter. Just before the war, he completed a double portrait of himself and of the girl he was engaged to. Their faces, serious, large-eyed and slightly elongated, gaze at the world; she holds a guitar. They are so young that they can look only at the future, a future which held for him a premature and violent death, and for her, grief, imprisonment, torture and ultimately, work, marriage, children and grandchildren.

In Belgrade there was another reminder of the dance of death from the Book of Hours. We stumbled on the wartime execution ground at Jajinci, in its well-kept suburban park. It could have been a deserted fairground, with decaying wooden booths, until, on one booth, we deciphered a scrawl: 'Here the Germans shot my brother dead.'

I saw again how in the Balkans people disburden themselves of a close and painful past by living only for the present moment; as we were sitting with friends in a *kafana*, two men at a neighbouring table started to sing the old town songs from Vojvodina, and the whole place joined in, word-perfect and joyful.

It was the same when finally we left for England, and Stana, tense and weeping, embraced me; I knew that in a few days our departure would no longer be her tragedy, though for that particular moment it was.

Stana stood at the gateway and we drove away from our house, down through the city and across the Sava bridge. I looked back at the gilded spire of the Cathedral Church which had once seemed so alien and which, over three years, had turned into a welcoming landmark after each journey away from Belgrade. I was leaving, as I had arrived, a stranger, but a stranger at home.

APPENDICES

APPENDIX I

FURTHER PLACES TO VISIT

For a comprehensive survey, use the guide-books. I have noted churches of interest, some of which are not widely known. Any traveller who looks for them will need patience. A village child is usually the best guide to the whereabouts of the church and its guardian. The churches vary in quality. Some roads are very poor and impassable in winter.

Chapters 1–3, pp. 18–47

Within 8 km of Studenica, and accessible by Land-Rover, are:

DOLAC. 12th or 13th c., two-storeyed church with crypt, in strict Byzantine style.

PALEŽ. 14th-c. small roofless church of rough stone. Good faded frescoes of St Nicholas, Baptism of Christ, Constantine and Helena, and St Sunday, martyr (*Sveta Nedelja*).

VRH. Mountain village church, 1619. Built partly underground because of Turkish regulations. Rustic iconostasis and frescoes, which include St George with Princess.

Closer to the main Kraljevo–Raška road are:

GRADAC. South of Ušće, up Brvenica valley to West. Impressive late-13th-c. church, built by Helen of Anjou and wholly Gothic in appearance. Frescoes.

NOVA PAVLICA. Close to Gradac, on opposite side of Ibar. 14th-c. trefoil-shaped church with 18th-c. tower. Donors were Musić brothers, nephews of Prince Lazar, and church contains their portraits.
(STARA PAVLICA nearby is a 12th-c. ruin, dynamited to make room for the old railway which runs below. It is now being restored.)

TRNAVA. 10 km west of Raška, on side road. 16th-c. village church given by local dignitary or rich peasant, so frescoes are of village saints, e.g. St Friday (*Sveta Petka* or *Paraskeva*) believed to be more gentle and powerful even than the Mother of God, Sts Cosmas and Damian, the Wonder-workers, and St Elijah (*Ilija*), who rides by in his chariot when it thunders.

BANJSKA. Just off the main road, north of Kosovska Mitrovica. This monastery was one of Milutin's richest foundations, and he built the church

(1313–15) as a mausoleum for himself and his queen Theodora. It was once as magnificent as Studenica and is now a finely proportioned ruin.

Chapters 4–5, pp. 48–70

TUTIN. 1650 church just outside the town, behind lime-kilns. Greek painters did the graceful frescoes of angels within, and the fearsome Last Judgement on the outer west wall of the narthex: souls in torment include those who lie late in bed on Sundays instead of going to Church.

CRNA REKA. 2 km by Land-Rover from the village of Ribariće, where the main road from Novi Pazar to Ivangrad crosses the Upper Ibar. Cave-church, late 16th c., inside a hermitage. Hermit in residence, 1971. Frescoes are rather fine, and so is the setting in a mountain gorge.

Chapter 6, pp. 71–81

ARILJE. Monastery founded by King Dragutin, 1295. In the 15th c., a bishop's seat. Frescoes of historical interest: portraits of Nemanjid dynasty and of bishops.

OVČAR-KABLAR gorge. On far bank:

BLAGOVEŠTENJE. Turn off from road at OVČAR BANJA. 12th–13th-c. foundation. Present church 1602. Frescoes 1632. Fine Transfiguration on north wall, Pantocrator and Heavenly Liturgy in cupola. South of the nave door, the Three Kings are greeted by an angel on horseback. Its dependency, ILINJE, is 4-hr walk and has a big feast-day on 2 August.

NIKOLJE. Some way off by road and bridge. Most easily accessible by water, from Čačak-Ovčar Banja road. Shout 'Sestro' (sister) and a very old man will be sent to punt you across, murmuring, as he does so, 'England, a great Empire – India and the Ionian Islands'. Frescoes in narthex date from 1637, probably by same painter as at BLAGOVEŠTENJE. 1697 frescoes in nave include a curious damaged medallion of the Holy Spirit with Seven Spiritual Gifts depicted as angels (north apse).

Also JOVANJE, with very down-to-earth Abbess, Katarina, and USPENIJE.

On near bank, VAVEDENJE and PREOBRAŽENJE by road, VAZNESENJE and SVETA TROJICA uphill. Also:

SRETENJE. Accessible on foot from OVČAR BANJA (1½ hr) or, by car from main road towards ČAČAK (turn off at PAKURAĆ and go up through DUCALOVIĆ and SVIRALJTE) over very precipitous, rough track. Foundation probably 16th-c. Its restorer was Bishop Nikofor who in 1814 made money out of the plague by 'burying the dead and praying to God for the living'. His narthex dates from 1818, church from 1847. Smaller church, 1845. Sretenje has enchanting nuns, and a matchless mountain setting.

Further north, on a minor road leading from Titovo Užice to Kosjerić, is:

THE WHITE CHURCH at KARAN. 14th-c. village church. Frescoes of Nemanjid dynasty and of Peter Brajan, Greek-born ruler of this region under Dušan, with his wife, sister and little daughter. Also of St Marina striking down the Devil with her hammer, a popular subject in Greece though rare in Serbia.

Chapters 8–10, pp. 92–119

DEVIĆ. Can be reached by car (just) by turning off the Kosovska Mitrovica–Peć road at Gornja Klina for Srbica, and then asking the way. Some 16th-c. frescoes. Nuns live there, surrounded by Albanian farmers. It contains a shrine for the mentally sick. Set in a ravine, very pretty in spring.

Chapters 12–13, pp. 130–54

SISOJEVAC. Near Ravanica, off road to Senjski Rudnik. Ruined late-14th-c. church. Frescoes similar to Ravanica, but cruder.
Round Kuršumlija and Prokuplje is a group of churches, some of which date from the Nemanjid period.

CARIČIN GRAD. Near Leskovac, a ruined Byzantine town, with remains of 6th-c. churches. Possibly the birthplace of Justinian.

Chapters 14–15, pp. 155–80

GORNJAK. South of Požarevac in ravine formed by river Mlava. Late-14- and early-15th-c. monastery with 'hermit's' (or hesychast's?) cell. Modest architecture, picturesque surroundings.

DONJA KAMENICA. South of Zaječar, near Knaževac. Church with late-14th-c. frescoes.

Chapters 16–17, pp. 192–212

SREMSKA MITROVICA. As SIRMIUM it was the capital of Lower Pannonia and became a famous Roman city by the 3rd c. A.D. The foundations of a palace, a forum, baths, temples, theatres and shops have been found and excavations continue. In the 4th c. it was a Christian centre, and the birthplace of St Demetrius, though the centre of his cult was to be at Salonica. In A.D. 582 the Avars finally destroyed Sirmium. An inscription, scratched in halting Greek on brick, survives: 'Lord Christ, help the city and smite the Avars and watch over [the Empire] and the writer. Amen.' A Greek monastery of St Demetrius was founded in the 11th-c. and later on handed over to the Benedictine Order.

NOVI SAD. Uspenska Church, with baroque iconostasis (1731–36). Nikolajevska Church (1749).

SREMSKI KARLOVCI. In a suburb called Švabca, near the Danube, is the Peace Chapel, which commemorates the Peace of Carlowitz (Karlovci), 1699, between the Turks and the Austrians. A curious classical rotunda with a pavilion in front, it looks as if it may have been reconstructed from the buildings erected for the delegates to the peace conference, and as if the surviving pavilion was that of the English envoy, Paget.

SUBOTICA. A Habsburg fantasy in 19- and 20-c. Baroque. LAKE PALIĆ is a faded watering-place, full of greenery and goulash.

PANČEVO, VRŠAC and SOMBOR are all pleasant towns to visit in Vojvodina. Over the border in RUMANIA, ARAD and TIMIŞOARA (TEMIŠVAR) have Serbian minorities and monuments. So does SZENTENDRE (SENTANDREJA) in HUNGARY.

Chapter 18, pp. 213–26

BLAGOVEŠTENJE and VOLJAVČA. North of Vraćevšnica; two other small medieval monasteries connected with the Uprisings. They can be reached via the Kragujevac–Belgrade road and Stragari, but are difficult of access.

RAMAĆA. St Nicholas' Church has well-preserved wall-paintings, provincial but good, from the late-14th or early-15th c.

Chapter 21, pp. 242–54

RUSSIAN CHURCH. Very small, and almost hidden behind St Mark's Church in Bulevar Revolucije.

GALLERY OF FRESCOES (No. 20 Cara Uroša Street). Displays excellent full-size copies of frescoes from the different monasteries. The exhibitions are changed from time to time, and it is a good way of becoming familiar with the great churches and their paintings.

(A complete list of Belgrade Museums can be found at any Tourist Office.)

Postscript

Because of frontier changes, many of Serbia's medieval churches and monasteries now lie outside her boundaries. The most important are:

MONTENEGRO

On the main road near Kolašin, the Serbian monastery of MORAČA was founded in 1252 by a grandson of Stephen Nemanja. Its surviving original frescoes are hidden behind the iconostasis, so they are accessible only to men. Women visitors can enjoy two very fine 17-c. icons as well as the later frescoes in the main church and in the chapel of St Nicholas in the courtyard.

Yugoslav Macedonia

North of SKOPJE, off the road to KAČANIK in the Skopska Crna Gora, are three 14th-c. churches: two at KUČEVISTE, and ST NIKITA near BRAZDA. The last was painted for King Milutin by the artists Michael and Eutychius who decorated the porch at Gračanica. They were also responsible for STARO NAGORIČANE off the Belgrade–Skopje road near KUMANOVO. (The church of the PERIBLEPTOS at OHRID – now called ST KLEMENTI – where they worked earlier, was the gift of a Byzantine general.) South of SKOPJE two notable painted churches, ANDREŠ in the Treska gorge and MARKOV MANASTIR (Marko's monastery) near DRAČEVO, are of 14th-c. Serbian origin. So are two churches at OHRID, ST NIKOLA BOLNIČKI and BOGORODICA BOLNIČKA.

(There are also many purely Byzantine foundations, of great magnificence, e.g. NEREZI and ST SOPHIA, OHRID.)

Greece

The monk Joasaf, a founder of the GREAT METEORA, was a nephew of Stephen Dušan.

On Mount Athos, VATOPEDI has associations with Serbia: Stephen Nemanja and St Sava lived there while HILANDAR was being built. HILANDAR (CHILANDARI) remains a Serbian monastery and a treasure-house of architecture, frescoes, manuscripts, icons and traditions.

APPENDIX II

SERBIAN HEROIC POETRY

Serbian heroic poetry, handed down from oral tradition, has aroused sporadic interest in Western Europe. The Abbé Fortis, in his two books of travels published in Venice in 1771 and 1774,* recorded several South Slav songs found in Istria and Dalmatia, and gave an Italian translation of *Hasanaginica*, which, with its appealing theme of a wronged wife, became widely popular. The rich collections of lyrical and heroic verse made in the 19th century by Vuk Karadžić attracted considerable attention from the leaders of the Romantic Movement, including Goethe and Jakob Grimm. Serbian poems were translated into English,† French and German. Goethe himself translated *Hasanaginica*; so did Walter Scott. By 1827, their fame inspired Prosper Merimée to invent a South Slav poet called Hyacinthe Maglanović and to publish his life and works. This hoax deceived even Pushkin, to whom Merimée wrote a letter of confession.

In the First World War, concern for Serbia's fortunes prompted a revival of interest in her heroic literary tradition; R. W. Seton-Watson, Helen Rootham and David Low brought out new translations.‡ In 1932 Dragutin Subotić published *Yugoslav Popular Ballads*, a critical study which is useful apart from its odd conclusion that the poems were written in Dubrovnik. Ten years later came W. A. Morison's translations of the poems on the Serbian Uprisings. More recently, the work published by the late Milman Parry and by A. B. Lord has drawn the attention of scholars to Homeric parallels in composition and imagery.§ To sum up, the literary content of the poems has been examined from time to time, and this process continues.

Far less comment has been made on the common culture which the Serbs have inherited through their heroic poetry. For older people a living myth exists. They may have read these poems at school or seen them in printed collections, but they are 'felt in the blood and felt along the heart', not least

* *Saggio d'Osservazioni sopra l'Isola di Cherso ed Osero*, pp. 162–8 and *Viaggio in Dalmazia*, I, 98–105.

† John Bowring, *Servian Popular Poetry* (London, 1827).

‡ R. W. Seton-Watson, *Serbian Ballads* (Kossovo Day Committee, 1916). H. Rootham, *Kossovo,Heroic Songs of the Serbs* (London, 1920). David H. Low, *The Ballads of Marko Kraljević* (Cambridge, 1922).

§ *Serbo-Croatian Heroic Songs*, ed. and trans. by A. B. Lord (Harvard, 1954). A. B. Lord, *The Singer of Tales* (Harvard, 1960), and various articles. Milman Parry, ed. by Adam Parry, *The Making ofHomeric Verse* (Oxford, 1971).

by those who have survived the Second World War and have needed to rely on the values embodied in these poems.

The poems provide firstly, a moral code, part-Christian and part-pagan,* and secondly, an imaginative resource of great importance to a whole nation.

The origin and development of the heroic poems is far from clear. A few of the so-called *bugarštice* ('sad songs') survive, written in monotonous lines of fifteen or sixteen syllables. They were succeeded by the *deseterci*, in which a ten-syllabled line falls into five trochaic feet. The natural stresses of the Serbian language make this metre very flexible and it was adopted by the oral poets. The *deseterci* include medieval or pre-medieval poems which display a cruel, kingly pagan world, as in *The Wedding of the Emperor Dušan*. Some of the poems are pan-Balkan, for instance, *The Building of Skadar*.†

About seventeen of the finest poems are based on the battle of Kossovo.‡ They are not written as a cycle: but as separate poems which cast oblique glances from different angles at a common centre of history and myth, and this gives them their unity. They display an extraordinarily rich poetic technique, ranging from the ritual solemnity of the *Death of the Mother of the Jugovići* to *Banović Strahinja* which becomes a *novella* in verse.

The remarkable poems which deal with Kraljević (Prince) Marko exist in Serbian and Bulgarian versions. They have not received their full due, perhaps because Marko is a 'mixed' character. He is heroic, with his noble birth, his strength, his magic horse, his massive wine-drinking and his loyalty. Historically, Marko, the son of a Serbian ruler, became a Turkish vassal, and his first duty is to fight for his lord, the Sultan Bajazeth. But in the poems, Marko is also the epitome of survival – a quality which the subjugated Serbs needed as much as the inspiring memory of Kossovo. Marko lives by a combination of brain and brawn; he is cunning enough to outwit the Turks as well as strong enough to kill them in combat. A Christian theme appears when, dying, he gives one purse of golden ducats to ornament churches and another as alms for the crippled and blind.§

Later heroic poems exist about the *hajduci* and about the Serbian Uprisings; they form a vigorous poetic record of courageous deeds and national spirit. During the 20th century, the First and Second World Wars inspired a number of poems, though the style gradually deteriorates, and the lowest

* See Jovan Brkić, *Moral Concepts in Traditional Serbian Epic Poetry* (The Hague, 1961).

† An English translation is given by Duncan Wilson, *op. cit.*, p. 270, and a Greek variant by Philip Sherrard, *The Pursuit of Greece* (London, 1964), pp. 167–8.

‡ For quotations, see pp. 126, 134 and 138 above, and pp. 124–30 for the historical background.

§ See David H. Low, *op. cit.*, 'Marko Kraljević and Mina of Kostur', 'The Death of Marko Kraljević'.

ebb is reached with *Death in Dallas*, a piece of bad journalese about President Kennedy.*

So much for the known history of the poems. Their style is epic, in that they embody the feelings of a nation:

> Whosoever is a Serb and Serbian born,
> Serbian his blood and his lineage,
> Who has come not to fight at Kossovo,
> By his own hand shall he bring forth nothing:
> Neither golden wine nor fine white wheat.
> There shall be no harvest from his lands
> Nor in his house children of his blood.
> While his race lives, they shall waste away.

Sometimes the poems are both individual and collective in tone. In *Stevan Musić*, a young serving-man appears:

> The servant Vaistina takes supper,
> he takes supper, he drinks enough wine,
> he walks out of the palace of his lord,
> he sees the sky pure and clear:
> and the bright moon is sinking down,
> and the day star rising in the east,
> and it is time for them to make their journey
> to Kossovo, the fine, level ground.†

On one plane, this is a universal description of a young soldier before battle, seeing the beauty of the world for perhaps the last time in his life. But read in the context of the whole poem, it is a refrain. The words are first spoken by Vaistina's master, Stevan Musić, as an order: he is to observe the weather and mark the time. And it is formulaic, derived from a cruder, shorter version, *Bušić Stjepane*, in the *bugarštice*.

Like most oral verse, the Serbian tales have been modified by different singers. Vuk Karadžić's collections contain the finest versions, composed during the two Uprisings, a heroic age which harked back to the past. The changes can sometimes be traced. For instance *Banović Strahinja* is the story of a Serbian nobleman's wife, who willingly runs away with a Turk at the time of Kossovo. In the original *bugarštice*, the story was brutal: the faithless wife was recaptured and put to death by her husband and brother for the sake of family honour. The later and best-known version was recited in the 19th century by a singer whose own wife had betrayed him, and who

* Available on a gramophone record, *Smrt u Dalasu*.

† I am deeply grateful to Peter Levi and Anne Pennington for making this translation and the one below.

introduced autobiographical detail in his long, subtle composition.* The scene is viewed through the girl's own eyes:

And the Turk in his tent on the mountain
loved Strahinja's love through the night.
And this Turk had a bad habit,
at earliest morning he liked to sleep,
at earliest morning while the sun warms,
he shut his eyes and passed his time of sleep.
It was no matter how strongly he loved
Strahinja's love, the young slave girl,
his head drooped down in her lap.
Mighty Vlah-Alija is in her hands,
she has opened the doors of the tent
and she looks out on Kossovo meadow.

The poem ends with Strahinja's taking back his wife, herself the sister of other heroes, and forgiving her in his heart.

The poems were sung by Serbs under the Turks and by Serbs in exile in Hungary or Poland. The philosophy which gradually became embodied in them, lies deep in the Serbian consciousness. The concepts are patriarchal: honour and revenge – and Christian: compassion and martyrdom. The poems are cathartic. Their essential themes are love and war. The love (and hate) is between man and woman and, even more strongly, between kindred, whether child and parent, brother and brother, or brother and sister. Stevan Musić's true love tries to prevent his going to Kossovo. The mother of the Jugovići mourns her sons, dead before their time, and then dies of grief herself. The girl walled up as a human sacrifice in the bridge at Skadar pleads for a space to be left so that she may suckle her child. Prince Lazar's knights feast with him on the eve of battle, and talk angrily of faith and treachery.

The Serbs are by nature imaginative storytellers, and their heroic poetry has given them a whole mode of thinking. During the 19th-century Uprisings, Karageorge compared his men with the medieval warriors. In the First World War, a Serbian General roused his troops by speaking of the Emperor Dušan; in the Second, at least one Partisan group took their oath of loyalty in the same words that Karageorge had used for his. In 1968, when Czechoslovakia was invaded, an old peasant in Vojvodina said: 'If we must fight, we shall not fight alone, for *they* are with us, the men of Salonica, the men of Kossovo. . . .'

* Information: Svetozar Koljević, whose important book on the heroic poems, *Naš Junački Ep* (Belgrade, 1974) appeared too late for me to make full use of it.

APPENDIX III

SERBIAN DYNASTIES

THE NEMANJIDS

RULER (Grand Župan of Raška)

c. 1167–96 Stephen Nemanja
Died on Mt Athos, as monk Simeon

KINGS

1196–1228 Stephen the First-Crowned
Died as monk Simeon

1228–1234 Radoslav
Abdicated, and later died as monk John

1234–1243 Vladislav

1243–1276 Uroš I
Died as monk Simeon

1276–1282 Dragutin
Died as monk Teoktist

1282–1321 Uroš II Milutin

1321–1331 Uroš III (Stephen Dečanski)

1331–1355 Stephen Dušan (King and Emperor)

1355–1371 Uroš IV

After Dušan's death, quarrels divided his Empire. King Vukašin ruled in Macedonia: killed at the battle of the Marica in 1371, he was succeeded by his son, Marko Kraljević, who was a Turkish vassal, whatever folklore may say to the contrary. Prince Lazar, who claimed kinship with the Nemanjids, ruled in the north from 1371–89, when he was killed at Kossovo. His son, the Despot Stephen Lazarević (1389–1427), followed him. From 1427–56, the Despot George Branković ruled in Eastern Serbia. His successors quarrelled and when Smederevo fell in 1459 it was virtually the end of medieval Serbia.

KARAGEORGE AND OBRENOVIĆ FAMILIES

LEADER (Vožd)

1804–1813	Karageorge (Djordje Petrović) *Assassinated 1817*

PRINCES

1815–1839	Miloš Obrenović
1839–1842	Mihailo Obrenović
1842–1858	Alexander Karadjordjević
1858–1860	Miloš Obrenović
1860–1868	Mihailo Obrenović *Assassinated*
1868–1882	Milan Obrenović *Crowned King 1882*

KINGS

1882–1889	Milan Obrenović *Abdicated in favour of his son Alexander Obrenović*
1889–1903	Alexander Obrenović *Assassinated*
1903–1914	Peter I Karadjordjević *Abdicated because of illness in favour of his son Alexander*
1914–1921	Alexander I Karadjordjević (Regent)
1921–1934	Alexander I Karadjordjević. *Crowned King 1921. Assassinated. Succeeded by his son, Peter II, a minor*
1934–1941	Paul Karadjordjević (Prince and Regent. Alexander's cousin)
1941–1945	Peter II Karadjordjević

N.B. While Karageorge's death was not easily forgiven, no blood feud existed between the two dynasties. This practice, usual in Montenegro and Albania, was unknown in Serbia. Each assassination of a Serbian ruler had a different and often complicated cause.

NOTES

These refer only to English, French, Latin and German sources and to Yugoslav texts already published in English translation, which have been quoted above. Other passages have been translated from Serbo-Croat.

Chapter 1, pp. 18–32

1. Taken from the 'Book of James'. See M. R. James, *The Apocryphal New Testament* (1924).
2. From *Holy Week as sung in the Orthodox Church* (Bussy-en-Othe, 1969), p. 144.

Chapter 3, pp. 39–48

1. Mother Mary and Archimandrite Kallistos Ware, *The Festal Menaion* (London, 1969), p. 254.

Chapter 4, pp. 48–59

1. *The Alexiad of Anna Comnena*, transl. from the Greek by E. R. A. Sewter (London, Penguin Classics, 1969), p. 104.
2. 'Mr. Harrie Cavendish His Journey to and from Constantinople 1589 by Fox his Servant;' *Camden Miscellany* XVII, (London, 1940). Camden Third Series, LXIV, p. 14.
3. *Manchester Guardian*, 17 October 1881.
4. Gabriel Louis-Jaray, *L'Albanie Inconnue* (Paris, 1913), p. xii.

Chapter 5, pp. 60–70

1. From an unpublished translation of *Deobe*, made by Nada Prodanović.
2. Vasko Popa, *Earth Erect*, transl. by Anne Pennington (London, 1973), p. 17.
3. Gaston Gravier, 'Le Sandzak de Novi Pazar', *Annales de Gèographie* (Paris, 1913), 22, p. 52.

Chapter 8, pp. 92–100

1. Printed in full in *The Orthodox Prayer Book* ('Russian Day' Committee, Pennsylvania, 1959), pp. 400 98.

Chapter 9, pp. 101–09

1. 'The Code of Stephen Dušan,' transl. by Malcolm Burr, in *The Slavonic and East European Review* (1949), XXVIII, 70, 207, 208.
2. *Ibid.*, p. 520.
3. H. N. Brailsford, *Macedonia* (1906), p. 245.
4. F. W. Hasluck, *Christianity and Islam under the Sultans* (London, 1929), II, p. 558. From a pamphlet first published in Albania in 1880–81, which sets out the Bektashi beliefs and hierarchy.

5. H. N. Brailsford, *op. cit.*, p. 247. See also Gabriel Louis-Jaray, *op. cit.*, pp. 81–6.

Chapter 10, pp. 110–19

1. Aaron Hill, *A Full and Just Account of the Present State of the Ottoman Empire . . .* (London, 1709), pp. 199–200.

Chapter 11, pp. 120–129

1. Richard Knolles, *The Generall Historie of the Turkes . . .* (London, 1603), p. 200.

Chapter 12, pp. 130–43

1. Edward Brown, M.D., *A Brief Account of some Travels in divers Parts of Europe . . .* (London, 1685), p. 33.
2. *A Manual of Eastern Orthodox Prayers*, with explanatory notes by N. Zernov (London, 1968), p. 43.

Chapter 14, pp. 155–67

1. 'The Travels of Bertrandon de la Broquière,' in Thomas Wright, *Early Travels in Palestine* (London, 1848), p. 359.
2. See *Documents Illustrating the Principates of Nerva, Trajan and Hadrian*, ed. E. M. Smallwood (Cambridge, 1966), p. 135.
   'Imp. Caesar divi Nervae f. Nerva Traianus Aug. Germ. pontif. maximus trib. pot est IIII pater patriae cos. III. montibus excisis anconibus sublatis viam fecit.' ('The Imperial Caesar, son of the divine Nerva, Nerva Trajan Augustus Germanicus, *pontifex maximus*, in the fourth year of his power as a tribune, the father of his country, in his third year as consul, made a road, after he had cut into the mountains and shored up the supporting stone.')

Chapter 16, pp. 190–98

1. F. W. von Taube, *Allgemeine Beschreibung von Slavonien und Syrmien*, (Leipzig, 1777, 1778), 3 vols. in 1, p. 91.
2. *The Life and Adventures of Dimitrije Obradović who as a monk was given the name Dositej* . . . edited and translated by G. R. Noyes (California, 1953), p. 188.

Chapter 17, pp. 199–212

1. Quoted by Duncan Wilson, *The Life and Times of Vuk Stefanović Karadžić* (Oxford, 1970), p. 48.
2. *The Life and Adventures of Dimitrije Obradović . . .*, p. 205.
3. *Ibid.*, pp. 298–9.
   The English version is from the original text.
4. *Ibid.*, p. 133.
5. Quoted by Ernst Wangermann, *The Austrian Achievement, 1700–1800* (London, 1973), p. 96.

Chapter 18, pp. 213–26

1. *The Travels of Peter Mundy, in Europe and Asia, 1608–1667*, ed. R. C. Temple (Cambridge, 1907), I, 77.

2. *The Complete Letters of Lady Mary Wortley Montagu*, ed. Robert Halsband (London, 1965), I, 310.
3. W. A. Morison, *The Revolt of the Serbs against the Turks (1804–1813)* (Cambridge, 1942), p. 48. (Translations of contemporary Serbian heroic poems.)
4. *The Memoirs of Prota Matija Nenadović*, ed. and transl. by Lovett F. Edwards (Oxford, 1969), pp. 84–6.

Chapter 19, pp. 227–32

1. J. M. Halpern, *A Serbian Village* (London, 1958), p. 220. (A useful study of life and traditions in Orašac.)

Chapter 20, pp. 233–41

1. Leposava Žunic-Baš, *Folk Traditions in Yugoslavia* (Belgrade, n.d.), p. 119.
2. *The Turkish Letters of Ogier Ghiselin de Busbecq, Imperial Ambassador at Constantinople (1554–1562)*, transl. by Edward Seymour Forster (London, 1927, reprinted 1968), p. 15.
3. Anon. *Voiage du Levant* . . . (Paris, 1624), quoted by Radovan Samardžić, *La Ville de Belgrade et la Serbie du XVIe et du XVIIe siècles dans les écrits des contemporains français* (Belgrade, 1961), pp. 409–10.
4. *The Complete Letters of Lady Mary Wortley Montagu* (London, 1965), I, 304–08 and 317–18.
5. *The Trifler* (London, 1817), XX, 233. (Probably written by Alaric A. Watts.)

Chapter 21, pp. 242–54

1. Quoted by R. Samardžić in *La Ville de Belgrade* . . ., p. 408.
2. A. W. Kinglake, *Eothen* (2nd ed., London, 1845), pp. 13 and 20–5.
3. Ami Boué, *La Turquie en Europe* (1840), IV, 453.
4. *A Handbook for Travellers in Turkey* (John Murray, 3rd ed., 1854), p. 134.
5. *Servia, The Youngest Member of the European Family* . . . by Andrew Archibald Paton, Esq: . . . (London, 1845), pp. 62–3.
6. Rev. W. Denton, M.A., *Servia and the Servians* . . . (London, 1862), pp. 233–5.
7. Sir Charles Trevelyan, *From Pesth to Brindisi* (London, 1876), p. 9. (Journey made in 1869.)
8. Ivo Andrić, *Gospodjica*, transl. by Joseph Hitrec as *The Woman from Sarajevo* (1966), pp. 158–9.

FURTHER READING

(Works in Serbo-Croat have been omitted, but I am particularly indebted to scholars such as Aleksandr Deroko, Vojislav Djurić and Svetozar Radojčić for their rediscovery of medieval architecture and painting, and to Dušan Popović for his historical study of Serbs in the Vojvodina.)

GENERAL

Cvijić, J., *La Peninsule Balkanique*. Paris, 1918.

Geographical Handbook Series (Naval Intelligence Division, London), *Jugoslavia*, 3 vols. 1944–45.

'Odysseus' (Sir Charles Eliot), *Turkey-in-Europe*. London, 1908. Reprinted, 1975.

Pribićević, Stojan, *Living Space*. London, 1940.

HISTORY

Clissold, Stephen, ed., *A Short History of Yugoslavia*. Cambridge, 1966.

MEDIEVAL PERIOD

Dvornik, Francis, *The Slavs in European History and Civilisation*. Rutgers, 1962.

Jireček, Konstantin, *Geschichte der Serben*, 2 vols. Gotha, 1911 and 1918.

Miller, William, 'The Medieval Serbian Empire,' in *Essays on the Latin Orient*. London, 1921.

Obolensky, Dimitri, *The Byzantine Commonwealth*. London, 1971.

Ostrogorsky, George, *History of the Byzantine State*, transl. Joan Hussey. Oxford, 1968.

18TH AND 19TH CENTURIES

Djordjević, Dimitrije, *Revolutions Nationales des Peuples Balkaniques*. Institut d'Histoire, Belgrade, 1965.

Picot, A. E., *Les Serbes de la Hongrie*. Prague, 1873.

von Ranke, L., *History of Serbia*, transl. Mrs Alexander Kerr. London, 1847.

Temperley, H. W., *History of Serbia*. London, 1917.

20TH CENTURY

Auty, Phyllis, *Tito*. London, 1970.

Deakin, F. W., *The Embattled Mountain*. Oxford, 1971.

Dedijer, Vladimir, *The Road to Sarajevo*. London, 1967.

Seton-Watson, Hugh, *The East European Revolution*. London, 1952.

—— *Eastern Europe Between the Wars, 1918–41*. Archon Books, London, 1962.

Seton-Watson, R. W., *The Southern Slav Question and the Habsburg Monarchy*. London, 1911.

—— *The Rise of Nationality in the Balkans*. London, 1917.

Stavrianos, L. S., *Balkan Federation. A History of the Movement towards Balkan Unity in Modern Times*. Northampton, Mass., 1944.

TRAVEL

Cuddon, J. A., *The Companion Guide to Yugoslavia*. London, 1974.

Irby, A. P. and Muir Mackenzie, G., *Travels in the Slavonic Provinces of Turkey-in-Europe*, 2 vols., London, 1877.

West, Rebecca, *Black Lamb and Grey Falcon*, 2 vols., London, 1942.

ART AND ARCHITECTURE

Demus, Otto, *Byzantine Mosaic Decoration*. London, 1947.

Grabar, André, *La Peinture Byzantine*. Paris, 1953.

Hamann-Maclean, Richard, *Die Monumental-Malerei in Serbien und Makedonien*. Giessen, 1963.

Mango, Cyril, *The Art of the Byzantine Empire, 312–1453, Sources and Documents*. New Jersey, 1972.

Mathew, Gervase, *Byzantine Aesthetics*. London, 1963.

Millet, G., *L'Ancien Art Serbe, Les Eglises*. Paris, 1919.

Radojčić, S., *Yugoslavia: Medieval Frescoes*. London, 1955.

Srejović, Dragan, *Lepenski Vir*. London, 1972.

Stewart, Cecil, *Serbian Legacy*. London, 1960.

Talbot-Rice, D., *Art of the Byzantine Era*. London, 1963.

—— *Byzantine Painting: The Last Phase*. London, 1968.

INDIVIDUAL MONASTERIES

The work of Yugoslav art historians is gradually becoming available in English translation, e.g. Milan Kašanin and others, *Studenica* (Belgrade, 1968). Pamphlets are usually available in churches.

COUNTRY LIFE

Ćurčija-Prodanović, Nada, *Yugoslav Folk-Tales*. Oxford, 1957.

Lodge, Olive, *Peasant Life in Yugoslavia*. London, 1941.

Trouton, Ruth, *Peasant Renaissance in Yugoslavia, 1900–1950*. London, 1952.

Tomasevich, J., *Peasants, Politics and Economic Change in Yugoslavia*. Stanford, 1955.

RELIGION

Ware, Timothy, *The Orthodox Church*. London, Penguin, 1967.

FICTION

Footman, David John, *Half-way east, short stories*. London, 1935.

—— *Pig and Pepper*. London, 1954.

Johnson, Bernard, ed., *New Writing in Yugoslavia*. London, Penguin, 1970.

Yugoslav Short Stories, transl. Svetozar Koljević. Oxford, 1966.

FLORA

Huxley, Anthony, *Mountain Flowers in Colour*. London, 1973.

Roger-Smith, Hugh, *Plant Hunting in Europe*. Bedford, n.d.

Turrill, W. B., *Plant Life of the Balkan Peninsula*. Oxford, 1929.

It is also worth looking for books in Serbo-Croat on medicinal plants (*Ljekovite Biljke*) which are illustrated and give Latin names.

GLOSSARY

Čika. 'Old man.' This and its feminine equivalent Tetka (literally 'auntie') are used by adults to address elderly people and by children to address anyone they consider to be old – usually the owner of a watch who can tell them the time.

Ćilim. From *kilim* (Turkish, Persian) anglicized into *kelim*. Any rug woven from wool, usually to a traditional oriental design.

Dimije. Cotton or silk trousers, very baggy, worn by Moslem – and sometimes by Orthodox – women in parts of Serbia, Bosnia and Macedonia.

Druže, Drugarice. See Gospodine, Gospodjo.

Duhovi. Whitsun. Literally, 'the spirits'.

Džezva. The beaked copper jug, with a long handle, in which Turkish coffee is made and served.

Firman. An Imperial Order issued by the Ottoman Sultan or by his Grand Vizier.

Gospodine, Gospodjo. Lord, Lady (old style), officially replaced by Druže, Drugarice (Comrade, Comradess).

Guslar. Performer on the *gusle*, a single-stringed wooden instrument played with a bow. It produces a monotonous twanging sound to which the *guslar* would chant a heroic poem composed or adapted by him. The tradition is now weak in Serbia; it survives more strongly in Montenegro.

Hadjuci. See p. 186.

Han. A sleeping-place for travellers, whether a village inn or a large caravanserai.

Hodža (Hodžinica). Popular term for a Moslem priest (correctly an Imam) and his wife. The word originally meant someone who taught the Islamic faith; in Turkey, any university or school teacher may now be called a *hodža*.

Imam. See Hodža.

Kafana. Café, coffee-house.

Kajmak. A soft cheese made like Devonshire cream, then salted.

Koliba. See footnote in Chapter 15, p. 172.

Kolo. A round dance, with regional variations in the steps used.

Koljivo. See Žito.

KONAK. (i) Palace; (ii) overnight lodging or inn; (iii) the guest-house in a monastery.

KUKANJE. Keening for the dead, wordless or in a ritual lament.

KUM, KUMSTVO. There were three different kinds of *kumstvo*. A *kum* was needed: (i) at baptism, as a godparent; (ii) at marriage, as a witness; (iii) at the first cutting of a boy's hair. In the old days, Turks and Christians could be *kum* to each other for this last purpose. Now, the word is used most often in its first meaning, but a *kum* is much more important than a godparent in Western Europe, and retains very close ties with the whole family involved. It is more usual to hear people say: 'He is my *kum*,' than 'He is my cousin.'

MUEZZIN. 'Interior officers of the mosques, who from the minarets call to prayer.' (Murray's *Handbook*, 1854). Today the cry is sometimes relayed over a loudspeaker while the muezzin remains at ground-level.

OBERKNEZ. This German-Slav title was used of Serbian officials who controlled large districts under Ottoman rule in the late 18th and early 19th century, e.g. Miloš Obrenović in 1813.

PARASTOS. Church service held in the graveyard forty days after a death.

PASHA. (i) (two-tail pasha) ruler of a town or district, e.g. Šabac. (ii) (three-tail pasha) vizier or ruler of a *pashaluk*, e.g. Bosnia or Belgrade.

PASHALUK. See PASHA.

PREČANI. Serbs living on Habsburg territory, literally 'on the other side' of the Sava and the Danube rivers.

RAKIJA. Any form of distilled liquor, usually made with plums in Serbia (*šljivovica*), but also from grapes, apricots, etc.

RASKOVNIK. The 'magic herb', often *Siler trilobum*, which is popularly believed to unlock doors and padlocks and to reveal money hidden in the earth.

SABOR. (i) A Church Council or Synod; (ii) any gathering of people, whether for a saint's day, a fair or a mass X-ray.

SANDŽAK. Within the Ottoman Empire, a major administrative district, ruled by a Bey with the right to fly a standard (*sancak*).

SLAVA. This family feast is celebrated on the patron saint's day. It is now performed with varying degrees of sophistication, and in Belgrade could sometimes be mistaken for a long-drawn-out cocktail party. In villages it traditionally lasts three days and is regulated by custom and ritual formulae. For further details, see Chapter 11, p. 120 and Chapter 19.

SUBASHA. Minor Turkish official in the last phase of Ottoman rule, who supervised, often tyrannically, a Serbian village.

SVETA GORA. The Holy Mountain, Mount Athos. An object of great interest to many Serbs because of their own monastery, Hilandar, there.

ŠUMADIJA. 'The wooded land.' The area between the Morava and the Kolubara rivers, south of Belgrade. (See Chapter 18.)

VAŠAR. Fair, market.

VLACH. (i) A Rumanian (Wallachian); (ii) a shepherd.

VOJVODA. Duke, commander.

VOJVODINA. 'The Duchy.' This includes the regions of Banat and Bačka north of the Danube, and Srem, south of the Danube but north of the Sava. A fourth region, Baranja, is now part of Croatia. The Serbs demanded their own VOJVODA in 1690, but the office was filled only in 1848–9 and again in 1861.

ZADRUGA. (i) The ancient Slav institution by which a number of related families lived together and held their possessions and flocks in common under a *starešina* (elder), usually the grandfather or another of the older men, and occasionally a woman. The *starešina* allotted tasks to each man and woman in turn. This made work lighter than in a single family, though discipline was strict. Vuk Karadžić mentions *zadruge* of thirty persons within Serbia, but Serbs in Dalmatia and in the Lika (Croatia) lived in groups of sixty and even ninety. Patriarchal households of any size are now rare, but traces of the system can be found in villages (see Chapter 19, pp. 228–29).

(ii) State co-operatives for agriculture, wine-making, forestry, fruit-growing, etc.

ŽITO. Boiled wheat cooked with sugar and nuts. Used as an offering in remembrance of the dead, and also eaten at a *slava*, possibly with the same significance.

INDEX

Albania, Albanians: dervishes, 108; domestic life of, 82–3, 91, 92, 105–6; foreign influences on, 91; retreat of Serbs through, 82 *n.*, 188; in Vojvodina, 212; in Yugoslavia, 2, 71, 89–91, 92, 106–7, 239, 249
Alexander I, Emperor of Russia, 221
Ali Pasha of Jannina, 71
Anderson, M., 115
Andrić, I., 49, 183 *n.*, 253
Anna Comnena, Princess, 51
Anna Dandolo, Queen, 64
Arad, 260
Arilje church, 72, 258
Armenians, 208
Arsenius I, Archbishop, 83–4, 87
Arsenius III, Patriarch, 68, 184
Arsenius IV Šakabend, Patriarch, 203, 224
Astrapas, 104
Atanasević, J., 72
Athos, Mt, 8, 40, 132, 152, 193, 197, 276; Hilandar monastery, 15–16, 18, 22, 39–40, 42, 261, 276; Vatopedi monastery, 86, 261
Austria, Austrians, 1; invasions by, 157, 184, 186, 188, 225, 240; railway link with Belgrade, 250; Serbs in Army of, 186, 199–201
Avala, 215
Avars, 13, 235, 236, 259

Bač, 194
Bajazeth I, Sultan, 52, 127–8, 141, 263
Balkan wars, 5–6, 107, 188
Balkans: Ottoman conquest of, 125, 144; Russian interest in, 187
Balsom, E., 82–99, 102–9
Banjska, 28, 257
Basil II, Emperor, 13
Bele Vode, 72–5, 80–1
Belgrade, 7, 48, 210, 224, 233–54; British Consulate (former), 251; Capt. Miša's Foundation, 248; Cathedral Church, 136, 242, 243, 250, 254; Church of Ascension, 244; Gallery of Frescoes, 49, 260; High School, 207, 248; Kalemegdan, 234–7, 242, 244, 251; Košutnjak, 251, 252; Military Museum, 157, 235; Mosque, 238; Museum of Modern Art, 234 *n.*; Museum of the Two Uprisings, 250–1; National Library, 212; National Museum, 15, 59 *n.*, 102 *n.*, 138, 249; Patriarchate and Museum, 141, 203 *n.*, 242–3; Princess Ljubica's house, 242–3; Russian Church, 260; Ružica Church, 235–6; Serbian Royal Academy, 249; Stamboul-Gate, 236, 241; Station, 1–21, St Mark's Church, 53; Topčider, 220, 248, 250–2; Vuk and Dositej Museum, 248; Zeleni Venac, 244–5
Beočin monastery, 193
Berenson, B., 65
Berlin, Congress of, 55, 73
Birčanin, I., 218
Black Ahmed, 57 *n.*
Blagoveštenje monastery (Šumadija), 260
Blečić, V., 72–5
Bodjani monastery, 194–6; Church of the Presentation of Mary at the Temple, 195–6
Bogdan, Protonotary, 145–7
Bogomils, 58, 85
Borović, Radc (Rade the Builder), 140
Bosnia, Bosnians, 90, 126, 184 *n.*, 188, 214, 230, 239, 244
Boué, A., 250
Bowring, J., 262
Brailsford, H. N., 90, 108
Branković, Angelina, 193
Branković, George, Despot, 122, 154–7
Branković, George, Despot (Archbishop Maxim), 193
Branković, Vuk, 126, 128, 130
Brazda, 261
Brkić, J., 263
Brodica, 169–71
Broquière, B. de la, 122, 156–7
Brown, C., 175
Brown(e), Edward, 115, 132, 237–8
Broz, Jovanka, 100, 142, 196
Budapest, 185, 190, 206, 209–10, 248
Bulgaria, Bulgarians, 5–6, 13, 20, 45, 83, 125, 132, 236
Bunbury, J., 238
Bunjevci, 212
Busbecq, G. de, 213, 237
Byzantium, Byzantines, 7–9, 13–15, 22, 97, 132, 144; art of, 15, 19, 21, 22–4,

Byzantium—*contd.*
25–9, 49 *n.*, 50–1, 65, 95–7, 261; fortresses of, 162–3, 204, 235–6, 259; trade routes to, 48, 55

Čačak, 48, 54, 76, 258
Čakor pass, 82 *n.*
Camblak, Grigorije, 93, 98
Cantacuzene, George, 155
Cantacuzene, Irene ('accursed Jerena'), 155
Cantacuzene, John, 101
Careva Glava, 73
Caričin Grad, 259
Catalan Company, 39–40
Catherine the Great, 206
Catholics: Albanian, 90, 92, 118; Roman, 14
Cavendish, H., 52
Čelarevo (Čib), 208–9
Čelebija, Jakub, 127–8
Celts, 235
Četniks, 188
Charlemagne, 191
Chelebi, E., 156, 236–8
Christ, frescoes: grave of, 146; Angel at Empty Tomb, 50–1; Ascension, 84; Baptism, 27, 257; Consecration of Host, 154; Crucifixion, 23–4, 27, 66; Deposition, 51; donor's portrait, 153; Double Communion, 26, 154; Entry into Jerusalem, 24, 27, 59 *n.*, 135, 193; Ever-Watchful Eye, 153; In Glory at the Last Judgement, 22, 52, 67, 88, 97, 114, 258; Harrowing of Hell, 27–8, 66, 86, 114; as Infant with St Peter of Alexandria, 149; Last Supper, 22; Miracles, 24, 29, 59, 135–6, 141, 145–6, 153, 193; Nativity, 86; Pantocrator, 29, 84, 95–6, 105, 222, 258; parables, 64, 145, 152; Passion, 84, 96; Pentecost, 59 *n.*, Presentation in the Temple, 152; Transfiguration, 27, 193, 258; other portrayals, 21, 46–7, 62, 65–6, 87, 95, 105, 112–14
Churches, *see under place name*
Churchill, Winston, 30, 189
Cikote, 228–32
Cincars, *see* Kutzovlachs
Constantine I, Emperor, 46, 97, 112, 257
Constantine the Janissary, 128
Constantine the Philosopher, 151, 236
Constantinople (*see also* Byzantium, Istanbul), 44, 46; Kariye Camii (Church of the Chora) in, 145–6
Corfu, 82 *n.*, 188
Ćosić, Dobrica, 64
Crna Reka (Sandžak), 88, 258
Crna Reka (Upper Studenica), 77–79
Crna Reka (Zaječar), 162
Croatia, Croats, 13; German puppet state, 188; in Hungary, 185, 209–10; in Yugoslavia, 187; Serbian *zadruge* in, 277; Ustaše terrorists, 5, 131, 188
Crusaders, 14, 15, 22, 44, 236–7
Cumans, 20, 83
Cunibert, B. S., 221, 249
Cvijić, J., 249
Czechoslovakia, Czechs, 190, 212, 265

Dacians, 161, 168, 236
Dalmatia, 10, 262, 277
Danilo II, Archbp, 26, 39–41, 64, 85–7
Danube, river, 155–67, 184, 190, 192, 194, 199, 233, 234, 244, 250
David, King, 153
Davidov, D., 192–4, 210–12
death customs: Moslem, 57, 124, 239; Serb, 62, 77, 139–40, 158, 213, 276–7; Vlach, 163, 170, 175–8
Debar, 216
Dečani, 15, 91–2; Church of the Ascension, 68, 93–100; Monastery, 92–100
Dedinje, 234
Deliblatska Peščara, 3
Della Francesca, Piero, 51
Demus, O., 29
Denton, Rev. W., 251
Deroko, A., 272
dervishes, 101, 107–9, 239
Dević monastery, 88, 259
Diebitsch, Marshal I., 220
Diocletian, Emperor, 162
Dionysos of Fourna, 49 *n.*
Divčibare, 81
Djakovica, 101, 108
Djordjević, T., 249
Djurdjevi Stupovi monastery, *see* Novi Pazar
Djurić, Vojislav, 272
Dolac church, 257
Domentijan, 67
Donja Kamenica church, 259
Dorćol, 238, 242
Dositej, *see* Obradović, D.
dragon legends, 70, 168
Dragutin, King, 59, 236, 258, 266
Drim, White, river, 207
Duboka, 168–70, 176–81
Dubrovnik (Ragusa), 15, 48, 55, 121–2
Ducas, C., 51
Dulenska valley, 228
Dundjerski family, 209
Durham, Edith, 9, 62 *n.*
Dušan, King and Emperor, 14–16, 53, 93, 98, 101–3, 261, 265; Code of Law (*Zakonik*), 88, 101, 121–2, 212
Dušanka (Lukač), 157–62, 238–9

Elizabeth, Empress of Russia, 201, 206
England, English, 9–10, 81, 206, 249

Eugen of Savoy, Prince, 199, 204, 240
Eutychius, painter, 112, 261
Evans, A., 53
Ezekiel, 153

feast-days, 3–4, 27–8, 120; Ivandan (John the Baptist), 3, 76; Palm Sunday, 88–9; St George's Day, 4, 120 *n.*, 125, 169–171; St Mark's Day, 228–32; St Vitus' Day (anniversary of Kossovo battle, 1389), 126; Sveti Vračevi, 60–4, 114; Velika Gospojina (Dormition), 114–19; Vlach *rusalija* (Whitsun) 176–80;
Fortis, A., 262
Forty Martyrs of Sebaste, the, 47
France, French, 149–50, 171, 201, 212, 250, 251
Franz Ferdinand, Archduke, 188
Franz Joseph, Emperor, 210
Frederick Barbarossa, Emperor, 14
Freikorps, 186, 200 *n.*
Fruška Gora, 130, 191; monasteries of, 192–4, 202
Futog, 194, 196

Galerius, Emperor of Rome, 162
Gamzigrad, 162–4
Garašanin, I, 188, 248
Germany, Germans: in Austrian army, 200; Dositej in, 206; gipsies work in, 171; influences language, 240 *n*; invades Yugoslavia, 40, 42, 66, 94–5, 188–9, 212; in Novo Brdo, 121; in Vojvodina, 190
Giotto, 53, 65, 66
Gipsies, 2, 4, 68, 71, 125, 213, 245; musicians, 62, 64, 115; Orthodox, 7, 98, 114–18, 171; Rumanian-speaking, 170–1; Vojvodina, 212
Goč, 81
Goethe, J. W. von, 262
Golija, 71–81
Golubac, 157–8, 169
Gornja Crnuča, 223
Gornjak monastery, 8, 259
Gračanica, 109, 121, 124; Monastery of, 110–18; Church of Mother of God, 88, 110–14
Gradac monastery, 257
Gravier, G., 56, 68
Greece, Greeks, 8, 15, 70, 77, 186, 211, 242, 261
Grimm, J., 262
Gusle, 34, 227, 275

Habakkuk, 153
Habsburgs, 1, 184–5, 190–1, 192, 199–202
Hajduci, 186
Hajduk Veljko, 187
Halpern, J., 227, 231
Hasluck, F. W., 61 *n.*
Hayes, Sieur des, 237, 245
Helen of Anjou, Queen, 64, 112, 157
Helena, mother of Constantine, 97, 112, 257
Hesychasts, 8, 132 *n.*
Hilandar monastery, *see* Athos, Mt
Hilferding, A., 53
Hill, A., 116
Hisardžik, 53–4
Hodges, Col. D. J., 249
honour, 10, 264–5
Hopovo monastery, 148, 193, 206, 225–6; Church of Purification of the Virgin, 193
hospitality, 9, 62–3, 231
Hungary, Hungarians, 1, 14, 131, 209, 212, 235; in Belgrade, 235–7; Serbian relations with, 185, 199, 209–10; Serbs migrate to, 13 *n.*, 184–5, 190, 192, 214
Huns, 235–6

Ibar valley, 20, 39–41, 55, 115
Illyria, Illyrians, 13, 58, 71, 91, 168, 235
Ilok, 194
Irby, A. P., 55, 81, 123
Istanbul (*and see* Constantinople), 221, 250–1
Italy, Italians, 15, 205
Ivan the Terrible, 52
Ivanjica, 72, 75, 80

Jajinci, 254
Janissaries, 87, 108 *n.*, 126–8, 183, 185–6, 214, 217–18, 219–20, 240
Jankov Kamen, 72–3, 76, 79
Jastrebac, 81
Jazak monastery, 193
Jefimija, 141, 243
Jereningrad, 54
Jerusalem, 45, 49, 53 *n.*, 84, 197
Jews, Jewish, 22, 52, 252
Jiddah, 239
Joasaf, *see* Palaeologus, John Uroš
Jokić, P., 217–18
Jonaš, M., 191
Joseph II, Emperor of Austria, 185, 207
Jovanović, S., 194–6, 204–5, 208, 210
Judas, 22, 84
Justinian I, Emperor, 13, 162, 259

Kač, 197, 199–200
Kalemegdan, *see* Belgrade
Kalenić monastery, 31, 144–7; Church of Presentation of Mary, 145–7
Kanitz, F., 162
Karadžić, V., xvi, 20, 63, 155, 218, 220, 222, 243–4, 248, 249, 262, 277
Karageorge (Djordje Petrović), 157, 186, 207, 215–21, 222, 223, 241, 251, 265, 267
Karageorge dynasty, 267; *see also* Karadjordjević

Karadjordjević, Alexander, Prince, 235, 267
Karadjordjević, Alexander I, King, 187, 267
Karadjordjević, Paul, Prince and Regent, 187, 267
Karadjordjević, Peter I, King, 187, 215, 267
Karadjordjević, Peter II, King, 267
Karan, White Church at, 259
Kariye Camii, 146
Kašanin, M., 45 *n.*, 273
Kiev, 26, 201, 211
Kindersley, R., 1, 18, 32, 48, 54, 56, 60, 76–81, 82, 110, 215–16, 230–2, 243, 253–4
Kinglake, A. W., 250
kinship, 9–10, 33, 71, 227–8, 276, 277
Knolles, R., 129
Koljević, S., 265 *n.*
Konjic, 238
Kopaonik, 55, 115
Kosmaj, 215, 219
Kosovska Mitrovica, 115, 257
Kossovo, xv, 55, 83, 114, 125
Kossovo, battle of (1389), 16, 124–9, 199; in myth and in heroic poetry, 16, 118, 128, 129, 262–5, 266
Kossuth, L., 199, 209–10
Koštampolje, 55, 68–70, 77, 79
Kostić, L., 209
Kostol, 162
Košutnjak, 251, 252
Kovilj monastery, 196–7, 198, 199
Koznik (Golija), 73
Koznik fortress (Morava), 137
Kragujevac, 228, 230, 242, 248
Krajmir, Duke, 128
Kraljevo, 41, 43, 44, 47 *n.*
Krćevac, 218
Krušedol monastery, 192–4; Church of Annunciation, 193
Kruševac, 125, 133, 137, 144; Church of St Stephen (*Lazarica*), 138, 145
Kučeviste, 261
Kučevo, 168
Kulpin, 209
Kumanica, 77
Kuršumlija, 259
Kutzovlachs, 71, 163 *n.*, 242 *n.*
Kuveždin, 225

Lab River, 125, 127
Laudon, Gen. G., 240
Lazar, Prince, 16, 98, 118, 125–30, 132, 133, 141, 151, 160, 243, 266; representations of, 136, 138, 141
Lazarević, Laza, 3, 248
Leopold I, Emperor of Austria, 184–5
Lepenski Vir, 158–61
Leskovac, 259
Lika, 277
Lipljan, 114
Lissac, A., 48–9, 53, 56
Ljubica, Princess, 216, 221, 227, 242, 244, 250
Ljubostinja monastery, 138–43; Church of the Dormition, 140–2
Longinus, painter and poet, 98–9
Longworth, Consul, 251
Lord, A. B., 262
Louis XIII, King of France, 237
Louis-Jaray, G., 55
Low, D. H., 262

Macarius, painter, 141
Macarius, Patriarch, 87–8
Macedonia, 2, 16, 125, 137, 224, 261
Maglić, 39–40
Manasija monastery, 40, 147–54, 226; Church of Holy Trinity, 148–9, 151–4
Manuel Comnenus I, Emperor, 14, 23, 236
Maria Theresa, Empress of Austria, 200–1
Marica, battle of, 16, 122, 266
markets: Belgrade, 82, 230, 244–5; Ljubljana, 82; Peč, 56, 82–3; Priština, 82; Prizren, 56, 103; Sarajevo, 82; Skopje, 58; Zagreb, 82
Marko Kraljević (Prince), 90, 263, 266
Markov monastery, 261
marriage customs, 4, 54–5, 62, 166
Maximian, Emperor, 77, 85
Mecca, 57–8, 239
Mehmed Pasha (19th-cent. janissary), 218
Mehmed Pasha Sokolović, 87, 183
Mérimée, Prosper, 262
Meštrovic, I., 215, 235
Metaphrastes, Simeon, 85
Meteora, monasteries of, 22, 112, 261
Metochites, Theodore, 15
Metohija, 82, 83, 109
Michael and Eutychius, painters, 112, 261
Migration, Great, 68, 184–5, 193, 199, 214
Mihailović, D., 76, 188–9
Mikeshin, M. O., 252
Mileševa monastery, 45, 48–54; Church of the Ascension, 49–53
Miletić, S., 210
Milica, Princess, 133, 136–8, 140–1
'Milica Srpkinja', 193
Milićević, M., 162, 249, 252
Military Frontier, *see* Serbia, Serbians
Milovan, painter, 67–8
Milutin, King, 14, 15, 16, 25–6, 28, 39–40, 47, 86, 98, 101–4, 111–12, 114, 134, 236, 257–8, 261, 266; representations of, 26, 47, 59, 112
millet, 184
Mistra, 135 *n.*
Mohammed II, Sultan, 122
Mokranjac, S., 165

Monasteries, 7–8, 15, 20, 31–2, 41–3, 83–4; *see also under name of monastery*
Montenegro, Montenegrins, 2, 76, 82; Albanians and, 89–90, 267; princedom of Zeta, 13, 13 *n.*; in Serbia, 74, 88, 214; Serbia Army retreats through, 82 *n.*, 188; Serbian monasteries in, 260–1.
Morača monastery, 195, 260–1
Morava, valley of: 20, 55, 74, 203; Morava churches, 130–54; style of, 40, 130, 134, 145, 147, 148; Western Morava, 41, 137, 138
Moravica, 76
Morison, W. A., 262
Moses, 153
Moslems, 2; at Belgrade, 238–9; at Novo Brdo, 123–4; at Prizren, 105–9; in the Sandžak, 49, 52–9, 62, 69–70
Mother of God, frescoes: Acathist to, 97; Annunciation, 51; Birth of, 26, 145; With Christ-Child, 21, 47, 97, 105, 145; in Crucifixion, 24, 27, 66; donor's portrait, 22, 86, 215; Dormition, 24, 28, 46, 66–7, 114; Flight into Egypt, 97, 145; Presentation in the Temple, 26, 145; Taxation of Mary and Joseph, 146; other portrayals, 22, 29, 84, 85, 86–7, 95–7, 105, 114, 135, 153
Muir Mackenzie, G., 55, 81, 123
Mundy, P., 213
Murad I, Sultan, 16, 125–7, 129
Murad II, Sultan, 122, 157
Mustapha Pasha, 'the Mother of the Serbs', 217

Napoleon, 186–7
Negotin, 162, 164–7, 168, 170, 221
Nemanja, Stephen, *see* Stephen Nemanja
Nemanjid dynasty, 14–16, 44–5, 64, 266; genealogical tree, at Peć, 87; Dečani, 96; Gračanica, 112
Nenadović, Aleksa, 218
Nenadović, Mateja, 218–21
Nerezi monastery, 77, 261
Nicaea, 14, 44, 65
Nicholas, architect, 104
Nicholas II, Emperor of Russia, 47 *n.*
Nicodemus, 51
Nicodim, Archbishop, 85–6
Nikofor, Bishop, 258
Niš, 55, 62 *n.*
Nova and Stara Pavlica, 257
Nova Srbija (Russia), 201 *n.*
Novaković, S., 249
Novi Pazar, 55–9; Altum-Alem Mosque, 56; St George's Towers (Djurdjevi Stupovi) monastery, 58–9; King Dragutin's Chapel, 59; St Peter's Church, 58; Turkish *han*, 55–6
Novi Sad, 191–2, 194, 205, 207–12; Agricultural Fair, 142, 196; Almaška Church, 211; Matica Srpska, 192, 210–12; Nikolajevska Church, 260; Uspenska Church, 260
Novo Brdo, 111, 120–4

Obilić, M., 126–8, 133–4, 138
Obradović, Dositej, 30–1, 185, 193, 205–7, 248
Obrenović, Alexander, King, 267
Obrenović dynasty, 267
Obrenović, Mihailo, Prince, 188, 241, 244, 249, 251–2, 267
Obrenović, Milan, King, 193, 222, 244, 267
Obrenović, Miloš, Prince, 145, 187, 216, 221–4, 228, 242–5, 248–51, 267
Ohrid, churches of, 65, 261
Oplenac, 215–16; mausoleum church at, 215
Orašac, 217–18, 223
Orthodox Church, 7–8, 14, 15, 28–32; Calendar, 28 *n.*, 96, 114; Lent, 29–31; Liturgy, 7, 29, 43–4, 47, 115; Prayer Book, 32, 212; Vespers, 148–9; *see also* Feastdays *and* Byzantium, art of
Ostrogoths, 235
Ottoman Empire, Ottoman Turks: in Belgrade, 237, 240–2, 251; their conquest and domination of Serbia, 6, 13 *n.*, 16–17, 19, 52–4, 55, 87–8, 90, 122, 125–9, 138, 183–5, 217; decadence and fall of, 185, 188; retreat from Petrovaradin, 204; Serbian autonomy acknowledged, 187, 251–2; Serbian uprisings against, 186–7, 199, 214, 219–24; treatment of churches, 66, 87, 104, 122, 124
Ovčar-Kablar monasteries, 258–9

'Painter's Manual', 196
Palaeologue renaissance, 65
Palaeologus, John Uroš (Father Joasof), 112 *n.*
Palež church, 257
Palmerston, Lord, 249
Pančevo, 74, 260
Pančić, J., 249
Parry, Milman, 262
Partisans, 138 *n.*, 188–9, 223, 265
Paton, A., 250
Paul, Regent, *see* Karadjordjević, Paul
Pazvan Oglu, 186
Peč, 56, 82–9, 184; Patriarchate: Church of the Holy Apostles, 84–5; Church of St Demetrius, 85–6; Church of the Mother of God, 86–7
Pešter, 68–9
Peter, King, *see* Karadjordjević

Petrovaradin (Peterwardein), 191, 204–5, 210, 240
Philike Hetaireia, 186
Piccolomini, Gen. O., 185
Pirch, O., 245
Pisano, G., 24 *n.*
Piščević, S., 200–4
Plato, 104
Plutarch, 104
Pokajnica church, 221–3
Popa, V., 66
Postupović, R., 224–5
Prijepolje, 55
Priština, 82, 110, 118, 120
Pribićević, S., 215
Prizren, 53, 56, 101–9, 184; Church of Bogorodica Ljeviška, 103–5, 134; Church of Holy Saviour, 107; Monastery of Holy Archangels and St Nicholas' Church, 40, 101–2, 107
Prokuplje, 259
Pushkin, A., 262

Radojčić, S., 52, 85–6, 114, 272
Radoslav, King, 21, 45–7, 266
Radoslav, monk-painter, 142
Ragusa, *see* Dubrovnik
Rajić, J., 196
Rakić, M., 113
Ramaća, St Nicholas' Church, 260
Ras (Pazarište), 20, 58, 60, 73
Raška, *see* Serbia, medieval
Raška valley, 59, 60, 70
Ravanica monastery, 3, 130–6, 160, 259; Church of the Ascension, 130, 133–6, 148, 151
Ravanica, New (Vrdnik), 130, 192–3
Ravenna, 77
Resava monastery, *see* Manasija
Rijeka, 107
Romans, 13, 110, 157–8, 161–3, 259; fortresses, 162–3, 204, 234–6
Romil, St, 132–3
Rootham, H., 262
Rumania, Rumanians, 168, 177, 212, 224, 260
Russia, Russians, 177, 186–7, 189, 201–2, 220–1, 250
Ruthenes, 212

Šafarik, Janko, 249
Šafarik, Josip, 207
St Anne, 26
St Alexander Nevski, 240
St Basil, 85
St Carpus, 96
St Constantine and St Helena, *see* Constantine I *and* Helena
St Cosmas and St Damian, 60, 257
St Cyril of Alexandria, 45
St Cyril and St Methodius, 13, 15
St Demetrius, 85, 141, 152, 259–60
St Elijah, 113–14, 257
St Ephraim the Syrian, 52
St Gabriel, Archangel, 95–6
St George (of Cappadocia), 59, 70, 152, 215, 224, 257
St George the New, 87, 88 *n.*
St Gregory Palamas, 132 *n.*
St Gregory of Sinai, 8
St Gregory the Younger, 8
St Jacob the Persian, 86, 152
St John Baptist, 20, 27, 114
St John Damascene, 104
St John the Evangelist, 22, 24, 27, 66
St Joseph, 97, 146
St Longinus, 24
St Luke, 46, 87, 88 *n.*
St Marina, 259
St Mark, 59
St Martin of Tours, 154 *n.*
St Matthew, 47
St Michael Archangel, 87, 95–6, 147
St Nedelja, 257
St Nicholas, 46, 85, 86, 98–9, 114, 222, 257
St Onofrius, 51
St Papilus, 96
St Paul, 47
St Paul of the Thebaid, 68
St Peter, 46–7, 66, 84
St Peter of Alexandria, 149
St Petka, 124, 131, 257
St Sava, 14–15, 19, 21–2, 24–5, 30, 43–5, 47, 48, 50–3, 84, 261; legends of, 36–7, 53, 196; representations of, 51, 104, 154
St Sergius, 96
St Stephen Martyr, 46, 50, 98–9
St Sylvester, 154
St Thomas, 28, 84
St Veronica, 154 *n.*
St George's Towers, *see* Novi Pazar
St Nikita monastery, 112, 261
Saints, warrior, 141, 152
Salonica, 55–6, 85, 147, 152, 265
Samuel, Emperor of Bulgaria, 13
Sands, F., 81
Sandžak, the, of Novi Pazar, 48, 70, 73, 77, 276
Sarajevo, 49, 55, 82, 188
Šaulić, Jelena, 205
Sava River, 5, 184, 233–4, 237, 244, 250
Saxons, 15, 121–2
Scott, Sir Walter, 262
Senjak, 232–3
Senje, 130, 136–7
Serbia, Serbians: arrival in Balkans of, 13, 168; art: *see* separate monasteries *and* Byzantium, art of; epic poems, 9, 16, 90,

101, 118, 126, 128, 129, 133–4, 138, 262–5; farming, 3–4, 19, 41–2, 124, 142, 155, 160, 170–1, 172–5, 190, 198, 214, 228, 230–1; First and Second Uprisings, 185–7, 199, 214, 215–24; flight from Ottomans, 168, 184, 192, 203, 212, 213, and resettlement, 13 *n.*, 190–212, 214; folklore, 3, 4, 6, 9, 23, 36–7, 53, 54, 61, 70, 71, 77, 81, 118, 164, 177, 227–32, 266; Kingdom of Serbs, Croats and Slovenes, 187–8; as medieval state, 14–16, 44–5, 64, 78; Military Frontier, 199–200; mines, 15, 110, 120–3, 133, 173, 183; 19th century State, 187, 242–52; under Ottoman rule, 16–17, 87–8, 138, 152, 155, 157, 183–7; peoples, 1–2; rebellion against Austrians, 200, and Hungarians, 209–10; relations with Byzantium, 13–15; Serbian Church, 14–15, 20, 30–1, 83, 87–8, 184–5, 225–6; Socialist Republic of, xv, 189
Seton-Watson, R. W., 262
Sherrard, P., 263 *n.*
Siena, 51 *n.*
Simeon Metaphrastes, 85
Simonida, Queen, 15, 26, 112–13
Sinan Pasha, 107
Sirmium, *see* Sremska Mitrovica
Sisojevac, 259
Sitnica River, 125, 128
Sjenica, 55
Skopje, 1, 40, 55, 58, 101, 102 *n.*, 115; Serbian churches near, 261
Slaveno-Srbija (Russia), 201 *n.*
Slavs, 9, 13, 90–1, 97, 113 *n.*, 168, 212
Slovaks, 1, 190–1, 212, 245
Slovenia, 6
Smederevo, 17, 154–7, 266
Šokci, 212
Solomon, King, 153
Sombor, 260
Sopoćani monastery, 15, 55, 60–8, 70; Church of the Holy Trinity, 60–1, 64–8
Spain, Spaniards, 16, 212
Spells, 23, 70, 79, 98, 112, 116, 164, 172, 177–80, 276
Srejović, D., 158–61
Sremac, S., 198
Sremski Karlovci (Carlowitz), 185, 202–4, 207, 209, 240; Patriarchate, 202–3; Peace Chapel, 260
Sretenje monastery, 31, 224, 258–9
Stalać, 137
Stana, 227–32, 243–5, 254
Stara Pazova, 190
Stari Vlach country, 71, 204
Staro Nagoričane, 261
Stephen of Dečani, King, 86, 93, 96, 98, 101, 266
Stephen Dušan, King, *see* Dušan, King
Stephen the First-Crowned, 14, 19, 21–3, 41, 45–6, 61, 64, 145, 266; representations of, 47, 104
Stephen Lazarević, Despot, 16, 122, 133, 141
Stephen Nemanja, 13–15, 19–23, 58–9, 64, 85, 104, 163–4, 261, 266
Stuart, General J. de, 205
Stratimirović, S., Metropolitan, 186, 204
Studenica, monastery, 18–32, 97, 203; Church of Mother of God, 19–25, 47, 88; King's Church, 25–8, 33; St Nicholas' Church, 20 *n.*; hermitages, 33–8
Subotić, D., 262
Subotica, 208, 260
Suleiman the Magnificent, Sultan, 123, 204, 237
Suleiman Pasha, 220, 223
Šumadija, 43, 213–26, 227–32, 277
Suvorov, M., 202, 212
Sveta Gora, *see* Athos, Mt
Szeged, 202
Szentendre, 53, 190, 260

Tabaković, G., 210
Takovo, 223–4
Talbot-Rice, D., 66
Tara (Serbia), 81
Tatić, B., 72, 74–5
Taube, F. W. von, 192, 200
Temišvar (Timişoara), 205–6, 260
Theodore Lascaris, Emperor, 44
Theodore's Days, 169–70, 179
Tiberius, Emperor, 161
Tito, Josip Broz, President, xv, 100, 142, 188–9, 196, 205 *n.*, 209, 223, 234
Topola, 215, 217–18, 221
Trajan, Emperor, 161–2
Trepča, 115
Treska, St Andrew's Church (Andreš) at, 141, 261
Trnava church, 257
Turkey, Turks, *see* Ottoman Empire
Tutin, 60, 258
Tvrtko, King of Bosnia, 54, 126, 129

Ukrainians, 212
Ulpiana, 110
Uroš I, King, 52, 61, 64–5, 112, 266
Ustaše, *see* Croats

vampires, 9, 91, 168; precautions against, 170
Vatopedi monastery, *see* Athos, Mt
Vauban, General, 240
Velika Remeta monastery, 193
Veljko, Hajduk, 187, 221
Venice, Venetians, 14, 52, 54, 156, 205

Vienna, 185, 187, 202, 206, 240–1
Vito, Fra, of Kotor, 93, 98
Vlachs, 14, 163–6, 168–80, 277; at Negotin Fair, 164; pagan customs of, 168, 170, 175, 176–80; Rumanian dialect, 163, 168, 173
Vladislav, King, 50, 52, 61, 266
Vojvodina, xv, 131, 148, 190–212, 249, 277; country houses of, 208–9; migration of Serbs to, 184–6; Military Frontier, 199–200; peoples of, 212, 239; *see also* Hungary, Novi Sad *and* Serbia
Voljavča monastery, 260
Vračar, 53
Vračevšnica monastery, 223–6, 260; Church of St George, 224
Vrdnik, *see* Ravanica, New
Vrh church, 257
Vrnjačka Banja, 43, 139
Vršac, 260
Vukan, King of Zeta, 19, 45
Vukašin, King of Macedonia, 266

Warriner, D., 166 *n.*
West, R., 111 *n.*
Whitsunday (*Duhovi*), Whitsuntide, 4, 70, 168–9, 176–80
Williams, C., 56–7, 61, 63–4, 67, 69, 115, 119
Wilson, D., xv, 202, 263
witches, wisewomen, 164, 168, 179–80
World War I, 139, 188, 253, 265
World War II, 4–5, 40, 42, 94–5, 130–1, 156, 193–4, 212, 253–4
Wortley Montagu, Lady Mary, 214, 240
Wright, D., 180 *n.*

Yugoslavia, xv, 187–9; Communist, xv, 189; kingdom of, 187; races of, 1–2, 13, 212; Resistance movements in, 188–9, 214–15; restoration of ancient buildings in, 45, 59 *n.*

Zach, Major, 123
Zagreb, 10, 82, 206
Žefarović, H., painter, 195–6
Zemun, 186, 241, 244, 245, 248, 250
Žiča: Bishop's Palace, 43–4; Church of St Sava, 47 *n.*; Church of Holy Saviour, 20, 43–7; Monastery, 41–7, 83
Zlatibor, 81
Zorić, General, 206
Zvečan, 115